Horace Hayman Wilson

Works

Horace Hayman Wilson

Works

ISBN/EAN: 9783741182150

Manufactured in Europe, USA, Canada, Australia, Japa

Cover: Foto ©Andreas Hilbeck / pixelio.de

Manufactured and distributed by brebook publishing software (www.brebook.com)

Horace Hayman Wilson

Works

WORKS

BY

THE LATE
HORACE HAYMAN WILSON,
M.A., F.R.S.,

MEMBER OF THE ROYAL ASIATIC SOCIETY, OF THE ASIATIC SOCIETIES OF
CALCUTTA AND PARIS, AND OF THE ORIENTAL SOCIETY OF GERMANY;
FOREIGN MEMBER OF THE NATIONAL INSTITUTE OF FRANCE;
MEMBER OF THE IMPERIAL ACADEMIES OF ST. PETERSBURGH AND VIENNA,
AND OF THE ROYAL ACADEMIES OF MUNICH AND BERLIN;
PH. D. BRESLAU; M. D. MARBURG, ETC.;
AND BODEN PROFESSOR OF SANSKRIT IN THE UNIVERSITY OF OXFORD.

VOL. XI.

LONDON:
TRÜBNER & CO., 60 PATERNOSTER ROW.
1871.

SELECT SPECIMENS

OF THE

THEATRE OF THE HINDUS

TRANSLATED FROM

THE ORIGINAL SANSKRIT.

BY

HORACE HAYMAN WILSON, M.A., F.R.S.,

BODEN PROFESSOR OF SANSKRIT IN THE UNIVERSITY OF OXFORD,
ETC. ETC.

IN TWO VOLUMES.

VOL. I.

Third Edition.

LONDON:
TRÜBNER & CO., 60 PATERNOSTER ROW.
1871.

ERRATA.

VOL. I.

Page xl. line 21, instead of *khungra*, read *khángra*.
- lxx. 13, „ Hanuman- read Hanúman-
- 15, „ Viddhá-Śálábhanjiká, read Viddha-śála-bhanjiká.
- 24, „ Sárada- read Sáradá-
- 15, 33, „ Kánda, read Káńda.
- 27, 18, „ Duhśásna, read Duhśásna.
- 59, 16, „ ríní, read ríní.
- 109, 21, „ its, read it'a.
- 116, 4 infra „ Márkandeya, read Márkańdeya.
- 5 „ „ Chandipáth, read Chańdipáth.
- 193, 3 „ „ Tilloltamá, read Tilottamá.
- 260, 5 „ „ Vedhaka, Rochaka, read Vedhaka, Rechaka.
- 317, 5 „ Vasishtha, read Vasishtha.

VOL. II.

Page 65, line 2, infra. instead of 143 read 148.
- 121, 1, „ „ MÁLATI, read MÁLATÍ.
- 144, 12, „ „ divided it into, read divided into.
- 363, 1, instead of NATAKA, read NÁTAKA.
- 375, 1, „ MURARI- read MURARI-
- 590, 1, „ DUTÁNGADA, read DÚTÁNGADA.
- 593, 1, „ MADHAVA, read MÁDHAVA.
- 395, 1, „ ABHIRAMAMANI, read ADHIRÁMAMANI.

TO

HIS MOST GRACIOUS MAJESTY

GEORGE THE FOURTH,

AS

THE PATRON OF ORIENTAL LITERATURE,

THIS ATTEMPT

TO FAMILIARISE HIS BRITISH SUBJECTS

WITH

THE MANNERS AND FEELINGS

OF THEIR FELLOW-SUBJECTS IN THE EAST,

IS

MOST RESPECTFULLY INSCRIBED

BY

THE TRANSLATOR.

Calcutta, 16th *May* 1827.

ADVERTISEMENT TO THE SECOND EDITION.

Upon the first publication of the Specimens of the Theatre of the Hindus, I stated explicitly the object which I had proposed to myself in the translation, and explained it to be my ambition to secure to the Hindu Theatre a place in English literature. It was not my purpose to furnish the student of Sanskrit with a class-book, and I did not, therefore, attempt to render the text word for word or line for line. At the same time I expressed my belief, that few translations of the same class could pretend to greater fidelity, as nothing had been added, little omitted, and the expressions of the original had been adhered to as closely as the genius of the two languages, and my own command of either, would allow. To this character of accuracy I can now more confidently lay claim, as in preparing the present edition for the press, I have carefully compared the translation with the text, and corrected those mistakes which inadvertence, interruption, and erroneous, or undecipherable manuscripts, had led me, as I formerly stated I anticipated they would lead me, to commit. Since the publication of my translation also, the original Sanskrit plays have been printed and published in Calcutta, under the authority of

ADVERTISEMENT.

the Committee of Public Instruction; the edition was prepared from my manuscripts, collated with others belonging to the Sanskrit College and to different individuals, by Jaya Gopála Tarkálaṅkára, the professor of Sanskrit literature in the college; and although the work may present a few typographical errors and some questionable readings, it is upon the whole a highly creditable specimen of unassuming editorial erudition and care. It is with this printed edition that I have compared my translation, and some alterations have been rendered necessary by following the reading there adopted, when it differed from that of the manuscripts which I originally employed.

Oxford, 15th December 1834.

ADVERTISEMENT TO THE THIRD EDITION.

The third Edition of the "Select Specimens of the Theatre of the Hindus" is a literal reprint, generally page for page, of the second Edition, after a careful correction of typographical and analogous errors which, in the latter, had been overlooked. The orthography for the transliteration of Sanskrit words in Roman characters is, in the present edition, the same as that adopted by Professor Wilson in his later writings, and adhered to, throughout, in the previous volumes of his "Works."

THE PUBLISHERS.

May 15, 1871.

CONTENTS OF VOL. I.

	PAGE
PREFACE, ...	ix
TREATISE ON THE DRAMATIC SYSTEM OF THE HINDUS:	
1. The Authorities of the Hindu Dramatic System, .	xix
2. Different kinds of Dramatic Entertainments, .	xxiii
3. Dramatic Arrangement, ...	xxxiv
4. Conduct of the Plot, ...	xxxvii
5. Characters of the Drama, ...	xli
6. Objects of Dramatic Representation, . . .	xlviii
7. Diction, ...	lvii
8. Scenic Apparatus, ...	lxvi
List of Hindu Plays, ...	lxx

DRAMAS TRANSLATED FROM THE ORIGINAL SANSKRIT.

The Mṛichchhakatí; or, The Toy-Cart, ...	1
Vikrama and Urvaśí; or, The Hero and the Nymph, . .	183
Uttara-Ráma-Charitra; or, Continuation of the History of Ráma,	275

PREFACE.

MANY years have elapsed since the translation of *Sakuntalá*, by Sir William Jones, announced to the literary public of the western world that the Hindus had a national drama, the merits of which, it was inferred from those of the specimen published, might render it worthy of further investigation.

Notwithstanding the expectation thus excited, the subject has received little subsequent illustration. The translation of the *Prabodha-Chandrodaya*, or "Rise of the Moon of Intellect," by the late Dr. Taylor of Bombay, throws more light upon the metaphysics than the drama of the Hindus; and the account given of the *Málatí Mádhava* in the Asiatic Researches, by Mr. Colebrooke, was subordinate to the object of his essay on *Sanskrit* and *Prákrit* prosody, and was unlikely to fall in the way of general readers. These two contributions, therefore, to the elucidation of Hindu dramatic literature, have added but little to the notice secured for it by the publication of *Sakuntalá*.

The objects for which an ancient dialect may be studied are its philology and its literature, or the arts and sciences, the notions and manners, the history and belief of the people by whom it was spoken. Particular branches of composition may be preferably cultivated for the due understanding of each of these subjects, but there is no one species which will be found to embrace so many purposes as the dramatic. The dialogue varies from simple to elaborate, from the conversation of ordinary life to the highest refinements of poetical taste. The illustrations are drawn from every known product of art, as well as every observable phenomenon of nature. The manners and feelings of the people are delineated, living and breathing before us, and history and religion furnish the most important and interesting topics to the bard. Wherever, therefore, there exists a dramatic literature, it must be pre-eminently entitled to the attention of the philosopher as well as the philologist, of the man of general literary taste as well as the professional scholar.

Independent, however, of the claims to notice which the Hindu theatre possesses, upon principles that equally apply to the dramatic literature of every nation, it may advance pretensions to consideration on its own account, connected both with its peculiar merits and with the history of the stage.

Neither of the dramas hitherto published, *Śakuntalá* or the *Prabodha-Chandrodaya*, can be considered to convey an accurate notion of the Hindu theatre. Each is but the species of its own genus. The latter belongs to the metaphysical, the former to the mytho-pastoral class of Sanskrit plays; but these two varieties are far from representing every class and order. Their wide dissimilarity might lead us to anticipate the extensive range of the theatre to which they belong, and to infer that where such striking distinctions were to be found, others less decidedly marked must prevail. The inference would be justified by the fact, and the Hindu theatre affords examples of the drama of domestic, as well as of heroic life; of original invention as well as of legendary tradition.

At the same time, there are many peculiarities belonging to the Hindu theatre which it is necessary that we should know, before we can safely delineate the history, or propose the theory of the drama. Hitherto the views of all writers upon the subject have been circumscribed by the practice which alone was open to their observation, and their speculations have been grounded upon the narrow basis which the dramatic literature of classical antiquity supplied. To this must now be superadded the conclusions that are to be derived from the dramatic compositions of the Hindus.

The theatrical representations of modern Europe, however diversified by national features, are the legitimate offspring of the classical drama. Widely as the mysteries and moralities differed from the plays of Æschylus or Aristophanes, they emanated from the only schools where those writers were read, and the cultivation of the cloister, unembued with the animation of social life, produced no worthier harvest than those crude and absurd compositions. Such as they were, however, they formed the connecting link between the ancient and the modern theatre, and allied the compositions of Shakespeare, Lope de Vega, and Racine, with the songs of Bacchus and the monologues of Thespis.

Whatever may be the merits or defects of the Hindu drama, it may be safely asserted that they do not spring from the same parent, but are unmixedly its own. The science of the Hindus may be indebted to modern discoveries in other regions, and their mythology may have derived legions from Paganism or Christianity, but it is impossible that they should have borrowed their dramatic compositions from the people either of ancient or modern times. The nations of Europe possessed no dramatic literature before the fourteenth or fifteenth century, at which period the Hindu drama had passed into its decline. Mohammedan literature has ever been a stranger to theatrical writings, and the Mussulman conquerors of India could not have communicated what they never possessed. There is no record that theatrical entertainments were ever naturalised amongst the ancient Persians, Arabs, or Egyptians; and the Hindus, if they learned the art from others, can have been obliged alone to the Greeks or to the Chinese. A perusal of the Hindu plays will show how little likely it is that they are indebted to either, as, with the exception of a few features in common which could not fail to occur, they present characteristic varieties of conduct and construction which strongly evidence both original design and national development.

The Hindu theatre belongs to that division of dramatic composition which modern critics have agreed to term romantic, in opposition to what some schools have been pleased to call *classical*. This has not escaped the observation of one of the first dramatic critics of any age, and Schlegel observes, "The drama of *Sakuntalá* presents, through its oriental brilliancy of colouring, so striking a resemblance, upon the whole, to our romantic drama, that it might be suspected the love of Shakespeare had influenced the translator, if other orientalists had not borne testimony to the fidelity of his translation." The present collection will afford ample evidence to the same effect.

Hindu dramatists have little regard for the unities of time and place; and if by unity of action be meant singleness of incident, they exhibit an equal disdain for such a restriction. At the same time, as we shall subsequently see, they are not destitute of systematic and sensible rules, and they are as unfamiliar with the extravagance of the Chinese drama, as with the severe simplicity of Grecian tragedy.

There is one peculiarity in the Hindu theatre which remarkably distinguishes it from that of every other people. Although there is little reason to doubt that the Sanskrit language was once a spoken tongue in some parts of India, yet it does not seem probable that it was ever the vernacular language of the whole country, and it certainly ceased to be a living dialect at a period of which we have no knowledge.

The greater part of every play is written in Sanskrit. None of the dramatic compositions at present known can boast perhaps of a very high antiquity, and several of them are comparatively modern; they must, therefore, have been unintelligible to a considerable portion of their audiences, and never could have been so directly addressed to the bulk of the population, as to have exercised much influence upon their passions or their tastes.

This circumstance, however, is perfectly in harmony with the constitution of Hindu society, by which the highest branches of literature, as well as the highest offices in the state, were reserved for the privileged tribes of Kshattriyas and Brahmans. Even amongst them, however, a small portion could have followed the expressions of the actors so as to have felt their full force; and the plays of the Hindus must therefore have been exceedingly deficient in theatrical effect. In some measure, this deficiency was compensated by peculiar impressions; and the popularity of most of the stories, and the sanctity of the representation, as well as of the Sanskrit language, substituted an adventitious interest for ordinary excitement. Still the appeal to popular feeling must have been immeasurably weakened; and the affectation or reality of scholarship, as at the Latin plays of Ariosto, or the scholastic exhibitions of Westminster, must have been a sorry substitute for universal, instantaneous, and irrepressible delight.

Besides being an entertainment appropriated to the leading or learned members of society, the dramatic entertainments of the Hindus essentially differed from those of modern Europe in the unfrequency of their representation. They seem to have been acted only on solemn or public occasions. In this respect they resembled the dramatic performances of the Athenians, which took place at distant intervals, and especially at the spring and autumnal festivals of Bacchus, the last being usually preferred, as the city was then filled with strangers, its tributaries and allies. According to Hindu authorities, the occasions suitable for dramatic representations are the lunar holidays, a royal coronation, assemblages of people at fairs and religious festivals, marriages, the meeting of friends, taking first possession of a house or a town, and the birth of a son. The most ordinary occasion, however, of a performance was, as will be seen, the season peculiarly sacred to some divinity.

Amongst the Athenians, also, a piece was never performed a second time, at least under the same form; and it is clear that the Hindu plays are written with a view to but one specific representation. At other times, and in other places, probably, successful dramas were repeated both in Greece and India; but this was a distant and accidental, and not, as with us, an immediate and anticipated consequence of success.

As the plays of the Hindus were only occasionally enacted, we can readily comprehend why they should be so much longer than our dramatic writings, and why they should be so few. The Hindu plays do not, like the Chinese, it is true, afford employment for ten days, but they sometimes extend, as we shall see, to ten acts, and those none of the shortest, and they must have occupied at least five or six hours in representation. With respect to their number, Sir William Jones was undoubtedly misinformed, when he was led to suppose that the Indian theatre would fill as many volumes as that of any nation in ancient or modern Europe. Many pieces, no doubt, are lost, and others are scarce; but it may be doubted whether all the plays that are to be found, and those of which mention is made by writers on the drama, amount to many more than sixty. We may form a tolerably accurate estimate of the extent of the Hindu theatre by the fact, that no more than three plays are attributed to each of the great masters of the art, Bhavabhúti and Kálidása; a most beggarly account, when contrasted with the three hundred and sixty-five comedies of Antiphanes, or the two thousand of Lope de Vega.

Although, however, the plays of the Hindus must have been less numerous than those of any of the nations of highest repute in theatrical literature, yet they must have existed in some number, to have offered the multiplied classes into which they have been divided by their critics, and which exhibit at least no want of variety. It may also be observed, that the dramatic pieces which have come down to us are those of the highest order, defended by their intrinsic purity from the corrosion of time. Those of an inferior description, and which existed sometimes apparently in the vernacular dialects, may have been more numerous and popular, and were more, strictly speaking, national. Traces of these are still observable in the dramatised stories of the *Bhanrs* or professional buffoons, in the *Játras* of the Bengalis, and the *Rásas* of the western provinces. The first is the representation of some ludicrous adventure by two or three performers, carried on in extempore dialogue, usually of a very coarse kind, and enlivened by practical jokes not always very decent. The *Játra* is generally the exhibition of some of the incidents in the youthful life of Kŕishńa, maintained also in extempore dialogue, but interspersed with popular songs. The mistress of Kŕishńa, Rádhá, his father, mother, and the Gopís, are the ordinary *dramatis personæ*, and Nárada acts as buffo. The Rása partakes more of the ballet, but it is accompanied also with songs, whilst the adventures of Kŕishńa or Ráma are represented in appropriate costume, by measured gesticulations. The Hindus have a strong relish for these diversions, but the domination under which they so long pined, and which was ever so singularly hostile to public enjoyments of a refined character, rendered theatrical representations infrequent, and induced a neglect of dramatic literature. Plays, however, continued to be written and performed to the latest periods, especially in the west and south of India, where Hindu principalities still subsisted. Performances also seem to have been exhibited at Benares in recent times, and we have one piece which was written, and possibly represented in Bengal, but a very few years ago. All the modern compositions, however, are of a mythological and sectarial character, and are intended to celebrate the power of Kŕishńa or of Śiva. They are also discriminated from older writings by the predominance of narrative, and by wire-drawn common-place descriptions of the periods of the day or the season of the year, of the rising and setting of the sun or moon, of the scorching heats of the summer or the reviving influence of spring. There is no attempt at incident beyond the original story, and many of the subjects for action, which the legend affords, are thrown into dull and tiresome dialogue. These defects are, indeed, to be found occasionally in several of the earlier pieces, but to a limited extent, whilst they form the substance of all later compositions.

When the art of theatrical composition had passed its zenith, and began to exhibit symptoms of decay, the same fate befell it in India which it encountered in other countries, and criticism usurped the authority of creation. Plays gave way to theories, and system-mongers took the place of dramatists and poets. Indian criticism, however, has been always in its infancy. It never learned to connect causes and effects; it never looked to the influence exercised by imagination or passion in poetry; it never, in short, became either poetical or philosophical. Technicalities were the only objects within its comprehension, and it delighted to elicit dogmatical precepts from the practice of established authors. The question of the "unities" is quite within the sphere of the Indian critic, had the poets ever descended to their observance. Some approach, as observed above, has been made to this important theme, but a text was wanted for its due appreciation. In the absence of this, and of loftier discussion, the critics of the Hindu school set themselves to classify plays, persons, and passions, until they wove a complicated web out of very spider-like materials. The distinctions thus multiplied are curious in themselves, and of some value for the record they afford of the compositions whence they are derived, and it has been thought advisable, therefore, to annex a view of the system, assigning to it a distinct section, as it can have little to attract or entertain general readers.

ON THE

DRAMATIC SYSTEM OF THE HINDUS.

1. THE AUTHORITIES OF THE HINDU DRAMATIC SYSTEM.

THE invention of dramatic entertainments is usually ascribed by Hindu writers to a *Muni*, or inspired sage, named *Bharata*; but, according to some authorities, they had a still more elevated origin, and the art having been gathered from the *Vedas* by the god *Brahmá*, was by him communicated to the *Muni*. The dramatic representations first invented consisted of three kinds : *Nátya*, *Nritya*, and *Nritta* ; and these were exhibited before the gods by the *Gandharbas* and *Apsarasas*, the Spirits and Nymphs of *Indra's* heaven, who were trained by Bharata to the exhibition. Siva added to these two other styles of performance, the *Táńdava* and *Lásya*.

Of these different modes of representation, only one, the *Nátya*, is properly the dramatic, being defined to be gesticulation with language. The *Nritya* is gesticulation without language, or pantomime ; and the *Nritta* is simple dancing. The *Táńdava* and *Lásya*, which appear to be grafts upon the original system, are merely styles of dancing ; the former so named from *Tańdu*, one of Siva's attendants, whom the god instructed in it ; whilst the *Lásya*, it is said, was taught by Párvatí to the princess Ushá, who instructed the *Gopís* of Dwáraká, the residence of her husband, in the art ; by them it was communicated to the women of Suráshtra, and from them it passed to the females of various regions.

In these legends, as well as in the radical purport of the three original terms, we observe the intimate connexion between the idea of dancing and dramatic representation, which no doubt subsisted in the classical drama. The dances of the Chorus were no less important than their songs, and the arrangement of the ballet was as much the task of the author as the invention of the plot.

The attribution of dramatic performances to Bharata is no doubt founded upon his having been one of the earliest writers, by whom the art was reduced to a system. His *Sútras*, or aphorisms, are constantly cited by commentators on different plays, and suggest the doctrines which are taught by later authors: but, as far as has been ascertained, the work of Bharata has no existence in an entire shape, and it may be sometimes doubted whether the rules attributed to him are not fabricated for the occasion. This is not of much importance, as there are scarcely any debatable points in the technicalities of the drama, and the aphorisms, whether genuine or not, conform to the principles generally recognised in the standard authorities: a short notice of the principal of which will not perhaps be thought misplaced in this stage of the inquiry.

One of the best and earliest existing treatises on dramatic literature is the *Dasa-Rúpaka*, or description of the ten kinds of theatrical composition, of which the term *Rúpaka*, that which has a form, is the most appropriate designation. This work is exclusively devoted to dramatic criticism. It consists of a Text and a Gloss, with examples. The Text is the composition of Dhananjaya, the son of Vishńu, who styles Munja his patron, and who consequently wrote in the eleventh century, by which time, therefore, the dramatic art of the Hindus was complete, or rather was in its decline. The Gloss might be thought to be by the same hand as the text, the author being Dhanika, the son of Vishńu; agreeing in the patronymic, and differing little in the name. Amongst his illustrations, however, a number of passages are cited from the *Ratnávalí*, a play written in the beginning of the twelfth century, which is rather incompatible with the author of the *Dasa-Rúpaka's* having written in the eleventh. There is also another difficulty in the title of the commentator, who calls himself an officer of a different prince, Maharája Srímad Utpala Rája Mahásádhyapála, the chief usher, or minister of the illustrious Utpala Rája. Whether *Utpala* be the name of a prince or a country is uncertain, but in neither case can it apply to Munja or Bhoja. The date of the Gloss must therefore remain undetermined, although as the work is but rarely met with, it is no doubt of some antiquity. Ranganáth, a commentator on the *Vikrama* and *Urvasí*, cites a comment on the *Daśa-Rúpaka* by a writer named Páńi (Páńi virachita Daśa Rúpaka ṭíkáyám), which, if found, may tend to throw some light upon the history of this work.

The *Saraswati Kaṅṭhábharaṇa* is a work ascribed to Bhoja Rája. It treats generally of poetical or rhetorical composition, in five books, the last of which comprehends many of the details peculiar to dramatic writing. The examples quoted are from a variety of poems and plays, and they offer the same difficulty, as to the accuracy of the attribution, as the *Daśa-Rúpaka*, by including illustrations from the *Ratnávalí*. We might expect the plays of Kálidása and Bhavabhúti to be quoted, and we have no grounds for suspecting any anachronism in the examples derived from the *Mudrá-Rákshasa* and *Vení Sanhára*; but Bhoja must have reigned some years later, or Harsha some years earlier, than has been hitherto believed on scarcely disputable grounds, for a composition of the one to be cited by the other. There is a commentary on this work by Ratneśwara Mahopádhyáya, but he takes no notice of the author.

The *Kávya-Prakáśa* is also a work on rhetorical composition in general, and is an authority of great repute, as well as the preceding. It is divided into ten sections, in different portions of which are scattered such details relating to dramatic writings as are common to them and other poems, illustrated, as in the preceding, by extracts from the most celebrated poems, which, however, are never named, either in this or in many other works of the same class. It is necessary, therefore, to be able to identify the passages from previous reading, to derive from these treatises that information respecting Sanskrit literary history which they are capable of affording. The author of the *Kávya-Prakáśa* is Mammaṭa-Bhaṭṭa, a Cashmirian, and the work is prior to that next described, although subsequent to the *Ratnávalí*, and may be about five centuries old.

The *Sáhitya-Darpaṇa* is also a work of great merit and celebrity, on poetical writing, in ten sections, of which the sixth is mostly appropriated to theatrical technicalities. The quotations from the different plays are specified, and all the principal pieces in the present collection are named, besides several of which copies are not procurable. The date of the work is not known, but it is comparatively modern, and subsequent to the *Kávya-*

Prakása. One manuscript of it exists, which was copied, according to the date, in Saka 1426, or A.D. 1504. It is the work of a Bengali pandit of the medical caste, Viswanátha-Kavirája, the son of Chandra-S'ekhara, and is especially current as an authority in Bengal. According to universally-received tradition, the author lived beyond the Brahmaputra, in the district of Dacca.

The *Sangíta-Ratnákara*, as the name implies, treats more especially of singing and dancing than of dramatic literature. It furnishes, however, some curious notices of theatrical representation and gesture. It is the work of Sárngi-Deva, the son of Sorhala, the son of Bháskara, a Cashmirian pandit, who sought his fortunes in the south. His grandson is patronised by a prince named Sinhala-Deva, but of what time or place he does not inform us. It is clear, however, that he wrote between the twelfth and fifteenth centuries, as he names Bhoja amongst his predecessors in the science; and a comment on his own work was written by Kallinátha, by desire of Praudha, or Pratápa Deva king of Vijayanagar, from A.D. 1456 to 1477.

Amongst the works which treat generally *de Arte Poeticá*, and which are exceedingly numerous, some of the principal are, the *Kávyádarśa* by Dandin, the author of the *Daśa-Kumára*, and supposed to be contemporary with Bhoja; the *Kávyálankára Vritti*, by Vámana-Áchárya; the *Kuvalayánanda*, an enlargement of the *Chandráloka* of Jayadeva, by Apyaya Díkshita, who was patronised by Krishńa Ráya, sovereign of Vijayanagar about 1520; the *Alankára Sarvasva* of Bháma; the *Rasa-Gangádhara* of Jagannátha Pandita Rája, and the *Alankára-Kaustubha* by Kavi Karnapúraka, a Vaishńava Gosain, who illustrates all his rules by verses of his own, relating to the loves of Krishńa and Rádhá, and the pastimes of the deity with the Gopís of Vrindávana.

Besides the general systems, there are several treatises on the passions and emotions which poetry is intended to depicture or excite, as the *Śringára-Tilaka* of Rudra-Bhatta; and the *Rasa Manjarí* and the *Rasa Tarangiñí* of Bhánu-Datta. The latter comprises a number of rules, which are quoted as those of Dharata.

In addition to the information derivable from these sources, as to the system or history of the Hindu drama, the commentaries by which several of the plays are accompanied furnish important accessions to our knowledge of both. With respect also to the latter, we have in the *Bhoja-Prabandha* and *Sárngdhara-Paddhati*, two satisfactory guides for the verification of the writers prior to their respective dates. Of the *Bhoja-Prabandha* I have given an account elsewhere, and have seen no reason to alter the opinion there expressed. The *Sárngdhara-Paddhati* is a similar catalogue of earlier writers written by Sárngdhara, the grandson of Rághava-Deva, the spiritual guide of Hammíra, prince of Sákambharí, in the beginning of the fourteenth century. This work is consequently not later than the end of the fourteenth or the beginning of the fifteenth century, and determines within that limit the existence of the writers it names, several of whom are included amongst the dramatic authors, as we shall have hereafter occasion to notice.

These different authorities, it might be thought, would afford a tolerably distinct and accurate view of the dramatic literature of the Hindus, and will no doubt convey quite sufficient for our purpose. The brevity and obscurity, however, of the technical definitions, the inconceivable inaccuracy of the manuscripts, and the little knowledge of the subject which the pandits generally possess, have rendered the taste of interpreting them laborious and painful, to an extent of which readers accustomed to typographic facilities can form no adequate conception.

2. DIFFERENT KINDS OF DRAMATIC ENTERTAINMENTS.

The general term for all dramatic compositions is *Rúpaka*,—from *rúpa*, form,—it being their chief object to embody characters and feelings, and to exhibit the natural indications of passion. A play is also defined, a Poem that is to be seen, or a Poem that is to be seen and heard.

Dramatic writings are arranged in two classes, the *Rúpakas* properly so termed, and the *Uparúpakas*, the minor or inferior *Rúpakas* "le théâtre du second ordre," although not precisely in the same sense. There are ten species of the former, and eighteen of the latter class.

RÚPAKAS.

1. The *Nátaka*, or the Play *par excellence*, comprises all the elements of a dramatic composition, and its construction, there-

fore, is fully explained in the original systems, before any notice is taken of the inferior varieties. This method is perhaps the most logical, and obviates the necessity of some repetition; but in an inquiry of the present description, the first point to determine appears to be, what the dramatic amusements of the Hindus really were, before we examine their constituent parts.

Specimens of the *Nátaka* are not wanting to illustrate its technical description, and we can therefore follow the original authorities with entire confidence. It is declared to be the most perfect kind of dramatic composition. The subject should always be celebrated and important. According to the *Sáhitya-Darpańa*, the story should be selected from mythological or historical record alone; but the *Daśa-Rúpaka* asserts that it may be also fictitious or mixed, or partly resting on tradition, and partly the creation of the author. The practice of the early writers seems to have sanctioned the latter rule, and although they adopted their plots from sacred poems or *Puráńas*, they considered themselves at liberty to vary the incidents as they pleased. Modern bards have been more scrupulous. The restriction imposed upon the selection of the subject is the same as that to which the French theatre so long submitted, from whose tragic code all newly-invented topics were excluded, in supposed imitation of the Greek theatre, in which however the *Flower of Agathon*, founded altogether upon fiction, was an early and popular production.

Like the Greek tragedy, however, the *Nátaka* is to represent worthy or exalted personages only, and the hero must be a monarch, as Dushyanta; a demigod, as Ráma; or a divinity, as Kŕishńa. The action, or more properly the passion, should be but one, as love or heroism. The plot should be simple, the incidents consistent; the business should spring direct from the story as a plant from its seed, and should be free from episodical and prolix interruptions. The time should not be protracted, and the duration of an act, according to the elder authority, should not exceed one day; but the *Sáhitya-Darpańa* extends it to a few days, or even to one year. When the action cannot be comprised within these limits, the less important events may be thrown into narrative, or may be supposed to pass between the acts; or they may be communicated to the audience by one of the actors, who holds the character of an interpreter, and explains to the persons of the assembly whatever they may require to know, or what is not conveyed to them by the representation; a rather awkward contrivance to supply the deficiencies of the piece, but one that would sometimes be useful to insinuate the plot into the audiences of more polished communities. The diction of a *Nátaka* should be perspicuous and polished. The piece should consist of not fewer than five acts, and not more than ten.

In many of these characteristics, the *Nátaka* presents an obvious analogy to the tragedy of the Greeks, which was, "the imitation of a solemn and perfect action, of adequate importance, told in pleasing language, exhibiting the several elements of dramatic composition in its different parts, represented through the instrumentality of agents, not by narration, and purifying the affections of human nature by the influence of pity and terror." In the expansion of this definition in the "Poetics," there are many points of affinity, and particularly in the selection of persons and subjects; but there are also differences, some of which merit to be noticed.

With regard to the Unities, we have that of action fully recognised, and a simplicity of business is enjoined quite in the spirit of the Greek drama. The unity of place is not noticed, as might have been expected from the probable absence of all scenic embellishment. It was impossible to transport the substantial decorations of the Grecian stage from place to place, and therefore the scene was the same throughout; but where everything was left to the imagination, one site was as easily conceivable as another, and the scene might be fancied, one while a garden, and another while a palace, as well as it could be imagined to be either. The unity of time is curiously modified, conformably to a principle which may satisfy the most fastidious; and "the time required for the fable elapses invariably between the acts." In practice there is generally less latitude than the rule indicates, and the duration of an act is very commonly that of the representation, or at most "one course of the sun," the night elapsing in the interval. In one piece, the *Uttara-Ráma-Charitra*, indeed, we have a more extensive period, and twelve years are supposed to pass between the first and second acts. This was the unavoidable consequence of the subject of the play, and affords an analogy to the licence of the romantic drama.

Another important difference from the classical drama, and from that of most countries, is the total absence of the distinction between Tragedy and Comedy. The Hindu plays confine themselves neither to the "crimes nor to the absurdities of mankind;" neither "to the momentous changes, nor lighter vicissitudes of life;" neither "to the terrors of distress nor the gaieties of prosperity." In this respect they may be classed with much of the Spanish and English drama, to which, as Schlegel observes, "the terms Tragedy and Comedy are wholly inapplicable, in the sense in which they were employed by the ancients." They are invariably of a mingled web, and blend "seriousness and sorrow with levity and laughter." They never offer, however, a calamitous conclusion, which, as Johnson remarks, was enough to constitute a Tragedy in Shakespeare's days; and although they propose to excite all the emotions of the human breast, terror and pity included, they never effect this object by leaving a painful impression upon the mind of the spectator. The Hindus, in fact, have no Tragedy; a defect that subverts the theory that Tragedy necessarily preceded Comedy, because in the infancy of society the stronger passions predominated, and it was not till social intercourse was complicated and refined, that the follies and frivolities of mankind afforded material for satire. The theory is evidently more ingenious than just, for a considerable advance in refinement must have been made before plays were written at all, and the days of Æschylus were not those of the fierce and fiery emotions he delineates. In truth, however, the individual and social organisation of the native of India is unfavourable to the development of towering passion; and whatever poets or philosophers may have insinuated to the contrary, there is no doubt that the regions of physical equability have ever been, and still are, those of moral extremes.

The absence of tragic catastrophe in the Hindu dramas is not merely an unconscious omission; such catastrophe is prohibited by a positive rule, and the death of either the hero or the heroine is never to be announced. With that regard, indeed, for decorum, which even Voltaire thought might be sometimes dispensed with, it is not allowed in any manner "*ensanglanter la* scene," and death must invariably be inflicted out of the view of the spectators. Attention to *bienséance* is carried even to a further extent, and a number of interdictions are peculiar to the system of the Hindus. The excepted topics of a serious nature are, hostile defiance, solemn imprecations, exile, degradation, and national calamity; whilst those of a less grave, or comic character, are biting, scratching, kissing, eating, sleeping, the bath, inunction, and the marriage ceremony. Dramatic writers, especially those of a modern date, have sometimes violated these precepts; but in general the conduct of what may be termed the classical drama of the Hindus is exemplary and dignified. Nor is its moral purport neglected; and one of their writers declares, in an illustration familiar to ancient and modern poetry, that the chief end of the theatre is to disguise, by the insidious sweet, the unpalatable but salutary bitter, of the cup.

The extent of the Hindu plays is another peculiarity in which they differ from the dramatic writings of other nations; and even the *Robbers*, or *Don Carlos*, will suffer in the comparison of length. The *Mrichchhakati* would make at least three of the plays of Æschylus. In actual representation, however, a Hindu play constituted a less unreasonable demand upon the patience of an audience than an Athenian performance, consisting at one sitting of three Tragedies and a Farce. If the Hindu stage exhibited a long play, it exhibited that alone.

The compositions of the first class, or *Nátakas*, are comparatively frequent, and some of them are amongst the best specimens of the art. *Sakuntalá*, the *Mudrá-Rákshasa*, the *Veńí Sanhára*, *Anargha-Rághava*, and several others, belong to this order. The first is well known by the version of Sir William Jones; a translation of the second, and some accounts of the rest, will be found in the present collection.

2. The second species of *Rúpaka* is the *Prakarańa*, which agrees in all respects with the *Nátaka*, except that it takes a rather less elevated range. The fable is to be a pure fiction drawn from real life in a reputable class of society, and the most appropriate subject is love. The hero may be of ministerial rank, or a Brahman, or a merchant of respectability. The heroine may be a maid of family, or a courtesan. In the former case, the *Prakarańa* is termed *Śuddha*, or pure; in the latter,

Sankírńa, or mixed. By the *Veśyá*, or courtesan, however, we are not to understand a female who has disregarded the obligations of law or the precepts of virtue, but a character reared by a state of manners unfriendly to the admission of wedded females into society, and opening it only at the expense of reputation to women, who were trained for association with men by personal and mental acquirements to which the matron was a stranger. The *Veśyá* of the Hindus was the *Hetera* of the Greeks. Without the talents of *Aspasia*, or profligacy of *Laïs*, the *Vasantasená* of the first piece in this collection is a gentle, affectionate being, who, with the conventions of society in her favour, unites, as the *Hetera* often did, "accomplishments calculated to dazzle, with qualities of the heart which raise her above the contempt that, in spite of all precaution, falls upon her situation." The *Mrichchhakaṭí*, and *Málatí-Mádhava*, belong to the class of *Prakaraṇas*.

3. The *Bháńa*, according to the technical definition, is a monologue in one act, in which the performer narrates dramatically a variety of occurrences as happening either to himself or others. Love, war, fraud, intrigue, and imposition, are appropriate topics, and the narrator may enliven his recitation by a supposititious dialogue with an imaginary interlocutor. The language must be polished, and music and singing should precede and close the performance. The example quoted is the *Lílámadhukara*, but the only specimen met with is the *Sáradá Tilaka*, of which some account is given in the following pages. It is not impossible that ventriloquism assisted to give effect to the imaginary dialogue, as the art is not unknown in India.

4. The *Vyáyoga* is a dramatic representation of some military transaction, in which no part of the interest is derived from female participation; the sentiment of love is consequently excluded from it, and it admits of no comic intermixture. It is restricted to one act, one action, and a duration of one day, and the hero should be a warrior or demigod. The *Sáhitya-Darpaṇa* names the *Saugandhikáharaṇa* as an example, the *Daśa-Rúpaka* specifies the *Jámadagnya-Jaya*, the latter alluding either to the defeat of Kártavíryárjuna, or to the subjugation of the military tribe by the Brahmanical hero Paraśu-Ráma, the son of Jamadagni. The subject of the former would seem to be the rape of a princess named Saugandhiká, only that the

interest springing from such an event would contravene the rule that relates to female exclusion, and it may refer to the conflict between Vasishṭha and Viśwámitra for the all-bestowing cow. The *Dhananjaya-Vijaya* belongs to this class.

5. The *Samavakára* is the dramatic representation of some mythological fable in three acts; the business of the first is to occupy about nine hours; the second, three and a half; and the third, an hour and a half. The story of the piece relates to gods and demons, although mortals may be introduced. There is no individual hero, or the heroes may be as many as twelve, as Kṛishṇa and other divinities. The metre is that most usually employed in the *Vedas*, or the verses termed *Ushnih* and *Gáyatrí*. Although love may be touched upon, heroism should be the predominant passion; and the acts of enmity may be exhibited, both covert and avowed, such as ironical commendation and open defiance. Tempests, combats, and the storming of towns, may be represented, and all the pride and pomp of war, as horses, elephants, and cars, may be introduced. The example quoted, but which no longer exists in its dramatised form, is the *Samudra Mathana*, the Churning of the Ocean: a splendid subject for spectacle if well managed. We may doubt the success of the Hindu mechanicians in representing the mountain and the snake, the churning-staff and rope, or the agitations of the mighty main, from which sprang the personifications of health and beauty, and the beverage of immortality: this was, in all probability, clumsily contrived; but the gods and demons were well dressed and better acted, and with the patronage of a Rájá, the conflicts between the hosts of heaven and hell for the goddess of beauty and the cup of ambrosia, were no doubt got up with no want of numbers or of splendour. This entertainment must have been popular, as it was addressed more to the eye than the ear. As a mere spectacle it still exists, and in the western provinces the history of Ráma is represented in the dramatic form at the *Daśahara* on a vast, if not a magnificent scale. The followers of the contending chiefs, Ráma and Rávaṇa, amount sometimes to several hundreds: the battlements of Lanká, though of less durable materials, are of vast extent, and the encounters that take place are more like the mimic evolutions of real armies than a dramatic exhibition. It is scarcely necessary to add, that it occurs in the open air, usually

in a spacious plain, and with a want of order that ruins its dramatic effect. The most pleasing, as the best-conducted parts of the business, are the processions. The entry of Ráma and Sítá into Benares, in the year 1820, formed a richly picturesque and interesting scene.*

6. The *Dima* is a drama of a similar but more gloomy character than the last, and is limited to the representation of terrific events, as portents, incantations, sieges, and battles. It comprehends four acts. The hero should be a demon, demigod, or deity. The example named is the *Tripuradáha*, the destruction of the demon Tripura by Śiva, and conflagration of the three cities over which he ruled, and whence he derived his appellation.

7. The *Íhámriga* is a piece of intrigue in four acts, in which the hero is a god or illustrious mortal, and the heroine a goddess. Love and mirth are the prevailing sentiments. The heroine may be the subject of war or stratagem, and the devices of the hero may end in disappointment, but not in death. The example named is the *Kusumaśekhara-Vijaya*.

8. *Anka.* This is considered by some to be a piece in one act, but by others to be a supplementary act, serving as an introduction to a drama, or a more fully winding up of the story. The pathetic style should predominate: the hero may be a mortal; the subject should be well known. The example named is the *Sarmishthá-Yayáti*. A piece, termed *Yayáti-Charitra*, occurs amongst those noticed hereafter; but that is a *Nátaka*, and cannot therefore be here intended.

9. The *Vithí* is something similar to the *Bhána*: it is in one act, and may be performed by one actor, though the *Daśa-Rúpaka* admits of two. In either case it is a love-story carried on in comic dialogue, consisting of equivoque, evasion, enigma, quibble, jest, repartee, wilful misconstruction and misapplication, ironical praise, extravagant endearment, and jocose abuse. It is not very different, perhaps, in character from the *Fabulæ Atellanæ* of the Tuscans.

10. The *Prahasana* is a farcical or comic satire, and might be thought to have originated, like the old comedy, from the

* In Prinsep's Illustrations of Benares, part iii., are interesting representations of this scene and one which precedes it, the capture of Lanká.

Phallic Hymn. Unlike the Aristophanic comedy, however, it is not levelled at the many-headed mob, but in general at the sanctified and privileged orders of the community, as Ascetics, Brahmans, men of rank and wealth, and princes. The vices satirised in the two latter are those which emanate from an abuse of riches rather than of power, and are those of low luxury, not tyrannic despotism: the objects of satire in the former are sensuality and hypocrisy. It is in their extreme indelicacy that they resemble, although perhaps they scarcely equal, the Greek comedy; but they have not its redeeming properties, exuberant gaiety and brilliant imagination: they have some causticity and humour, but they are deficient in the high merits of poetry and wit. The *Hásyárńava*, *Kautuka-Sarvasva*, and *Dhúrta-Nartaka*, are existing specimens of this class of dramatic representation. According to the technical definitions of our authorities, the *Prahasana* is a drama in one act, intended to excite laughter. The story should be fictitious, and the hero may be an Ascetic, a Brahman, a king, or a rogue. The *dramatis personæ* are to be composed of courtiers, menials, mendicants, knaves, and harlots: the inferior persons are to speak low Prákrit, or a local dialect.

This terminates the first class of dramas: the second order is more numerous. It will be necessary to repeat the list, but it will not be essential to offer any detailed enumeration, as they tend to confirm what the foregoing remarks will have already suggested, that the Hindu writers multiply species very gratuitously, and make distinctions where no difference is discernible. In general, also, the descriptions will not admit of any illustration, as, except in the two first instances, the pieces cited as examples are not known to exist.

Uparupakas.

1. The *Náṭiká* is of two kinds, bearing an affinity in subject and personages, severally, to the *Náṭaka* and *Prakarańa*: in the latter case it is also termed *Prakarańiká*. The only difference from these forms is the length, the *Náṭiká* being restricted to four acts. The *Ratnávalí*, of which a translation is given, is a *Náṭiká*.

2. The *Troṭaka* may consist of five, seven, eight, or nine

acts: the business is partly human, partly celestial, as in the *Vikrama and Urvasí*.

3. The *Goshthí* is a piece in one act, with a *dramatis personæ* of nine or ten male, and five or six female characters. The subject is love. The example named is the *Raivata-madaniká*.

4. The *Saṭṭaka* is a marvellous story in any number of acts, but the language is to be wholly Prákrit. The *Karpúra-Manjarí* is an example of the class.

5. The *Náṭyarāsaka* consists chiefly of dancing and singing, and the subjects are love and mirth. It is in one act. The *Narmavatí* and *Vilásavatí* are cited as specimens.

6. The *Prasthána* is on the same subjects as the last, but the characters are of the lowest description: the hero and the heroine are slaves, and their associates outcasts. Song, music, and dancing, are its chief ingredients: it is in two acts. The *Śṛiṅgára-Tilaka* is an example. The appropriation of a specific drama to a particular class of people is highly characteristic of the social system of the Hindus.

7. The *Ullápya* is in one act; the subject mythological—the sentiments are love, mirth, and pathos: the dialogue is interspersed with songs. The example named is the *Deví-Mahá-deva*. This presents some analogy to the satiric drama of the Greeks, which was taken from mythology or heroic poetry, and differed chiefly from the Tragedies, which it followed, in a more lively strain and greater brevity, as well as in the introduction of songs and dances by Silenus and the Satyrs.

8. The *Kávya* is a love-story in one act, interspersed with poetical stanzas and musical airs. The *Yádavodaya* is an example.

9. The *Prenkhaṇa* is in one act, treating of war and dissension. The hero is of inferior rank, as in the *Báli Badha*.

10. The *Rásaka* is a comic entertainment in one act, with five characters. The hero and heroine are of elevated rank: the latter is of suitable merit, the former a fool. The *Aneka-múrtta* is a specimen.

11. The *Sanlápaka* is a drama in one, three, or four acts, the hero of which is a heretic. The subjects are controversy, deceit, violence, and war. The *Máyákápálika* is cited as an example; and possibly the *Prabodha-Chandrodaya*, the meta-

physical drama translated by the late Dr. Taylor, comes under this species.

12. *Srígadita* is an entertainment in one act, in which the goddess Srí, the goddess of prosperity or fortune, is introduced, or is imitated by the heroine. It is partly recited, and partly sung. An example of it is named the *Krídrasadsala*.

13. The *Silpaka* is in four acts. The scene is laid in a place where dead bodies are burned: the hero is a Brahman, and the confidant or *Pratinayaka* an outcast. Marvels and magic constitute the leading business of the piece. The *Kanakdeatí-Maddhava* is an example cited; and to borrow an illustration from the dramatic literature of Europe, we might class the *Freyschütz* under this head.

14. The *Vildsika* or *Lásika* is an entertainment in one act, of which love is the subject, and the general strain is comic or farcical. No example is cited.

15. The *Durmallika* is a comic intrigue in four acts, in each of which the friends of the hero and himself successively lead the business. The specimen named is the *Vindumatí*.

16. The *Prakaraníka* is here considered as a distinct class; but, as observed under the first head, this is usually considered only a variety of the *Nátiká*.

17. The *Hallísa* is an entertainment of singing and dancing, chiefly in one act, represented by one male and eight or ten female performers. The example named is the *Keliraivataka*; and the operatic ballets of Europe may afford some notion of the class.

18. The *Bhánika* is a comic piece in one act. It is not very clearly defined, but it seems to be something like the piece which, after undergoing various migrations from *Le Dépit Amoureux* of Molière, ended in the farce of *Lovers' Quarrels*—a representation of unfounded jealousies and mutual reproaches. The *Kámadulla* is the specimen named.

All these varieties are clearly reducible to but two, differing according to the loftier or lowlier tone of the composition, the more serious or comic tenor of the subject, and the regularity or irregularity of the construction. We might also conveniently transfer to them the definitions of the European stage, and class them under the heads of Tragedy, Comedy, Opera, Ballet, Burletta, Melodrama, and Farce. Their technical distribution is, however, very unimportant; and the enumeration of the distinctions, as originally recognised, is a matter of little interest, except as it conveys a satisfactory proof of the extent to which dramatic literature was once cultivated by the Hindus.

From this general sketch of the varieties of the Hindu Theatre, we shall now proceed to examine what in their notions constituted a play; under the heads of its Dramatic Arrangement; the Conduct of the Plot; the Characters of the Drama; the objects of Dramatic Representation and the means by which they were effected, or the Diction and Scenic Apparatus.

3. Dramatic Arrangement.

In the Hindu drama every piece opens with a prelude or induction, in which the audience are made acquainted with the author, his work, the actors, and such part of the prior events as it is necessary for the spectators to know. In its propitiation of the audience, and reference to past occurrences, it is analogous to the prologue of ancient and modern times, and, as far as spoken in character, accords with what have been termed the Prologues of Euripides, and those of Plautus. Being in dialogue, however, it is more correctly the induction of the old Comedy, which, although considered "out of date" by Beaumont and Fletcher, was not unfrequent amongst their contemporaries, as in *Cynthia's Revels*, the *Returne from Parnassus*, and especially the *Malcontent of Marston*, in which the interlocutors are the actors. The *Faust* of Goethe affords a specimen of an induction in the present day. In the Hindu theatre, however, the actors of the prelude were never more than two, the manager and one of his company, either an actor or actress, and it differs from the similar preliminary performances of other people by leading immediately into the business of the drama.

The first part of this introduction is termed the *Púrva-ranga*, and agreeably to Hindu prejudices, and the religious complexion of the occasions on which performances were represented, opens with a prayer, invoking in a benedictory formula the protection of some deity in favour of the audience. This is termed the *Nándí*, or that which is the cause of gratification to men and gods. This benediction may consist of one, two, or three stanzas. The elder writers rarely exceed two, but those of later date extend the *Nándí* to three or four, and in one instance, the *Veṇí-Saṃhára*, we have as many as six. Occasionally a short prayer is added to the benediction, or even substituted for it.

It does not very distinctly appear by whom the *Nándí* was spoken, for the general stage direction, *Nándyanté Sútradhárah*, "at the end of the *Nándí* the *Sútradhára*," seems to imply that it was not recited by this individual, the manager or conductor, the person who holds the thread or regulation of the business; but an aphorism of Bharata is cited, which says, "Let the *Sútradhára* recite the *Nándí* in a tone neither high nor low." If, however, he does not enter until it is recited, he must perform the recitation behind the scenes. Another text is cited from Bharata, which says, "Having read the *Nándí*, let the *Sútradhára* go off and the *Sthápaka* enter." And the *Sangíta-Kalpataru* has, "Let the *Sútradhára*, or some other person entering on the stage, pronounce the *Nándí*." The commentator on the *Mudrá-Rákshasa* observes, therefore, "that it is equally correct to supply the ellipse after *Nándyanté* by either *paṭhati* 'reads,' or *praviśati* 'enters:' in the former case the *Sútradhára* reciting the *Nándí* and then continuing the induction; in the latter, the benediction being pronounced by a different individual." It seems not unlikely that it was the intention of the original writers, although the commentators may not have understood it, to discriminate between the real and assumed personage of the *Sútradhára*, who spoke the benediction in his own character or as a Brahman, which he must have been, and then carried on the dialogue of the prelude as the manager of the theatrical corps. The *Sútradhára* was expected to be a man of no inferior qualifications; and according to the technical description of him, "he was to be well versed in light literature, as narrative, plays, and poetry: he should be familiar with various dialects; acquainted with the customs of different classes and the manners of various people, experienced in dramatic details, and conversant with different mechanical arts."

The prayer is usually often followed by some account of the author of the piece, which is always in a strain of panegyric, very different from the self-dispraising tone adopted by European dramatists, although no doubt more sincere. The induction must in most cases have been the work of the author of the play, but it may sometimes have been the composition of another hand. The introduction of the *Mrichchhakati* notices the death of the individual to whom the play is ascribed. In some places, the mention of the author is little more than the particularisation of his name.

The notice of the author is in general followed by a complimentary appeal to the favour of the audience, in a style with which we are perfectly familiar, and the manager occasionally gives a dramatic representation of himself and his concerns, as in the *Mrichchhakati* and *Mudrá-Rákshasa*, in a dialogue between him and one of his company, either an actor or an actress, who is termed the *Páripárświka*, or associate. The dialogue sometimes adverts to occurrences prior to the story of the piece, as in the *Uttara-Ráma-Charitra*, where the manager and actor are supposed to be inhabitants of Ayodhyá, and describe the departure of Ráma's guests, as if they had just witnessed it. In the *Vení-Sanhára*, too, it should appear that they are inmates of the Pándava camp; and in the *Mudrá-Rákshasa* the manager appears as an inhabitant of Pátaliputra. In other preludes the connexion is less immediate. In that of *Sákuntalá* the actress sings a song descriptive of the hot season, for the amusement of the audience; and in *Máluti and Mádhava* the manager and his companion declare the characters they are to play. In every case, however, the conclusion of the prelude, termed the *Prastávaná*, prepares the audience for the entrance of one of the dramatic personages, who appears either by simply naming him, as in *Sakuntalá*, where the manager abruptly exclaims, "Here comes the king Dushyanta," or by uttering something he is supposed to overhear, and to which he advances to reply, as in the *Mrichchhakati* and *Mudrá-Rákshasa*.

The piece, being thus opened, is carried on in the manner with which the theatres of Europe are familiar, or the division of scenes and acts.

The scene may be considered to be marked, as in the French drama, by the entrance of one character and the exit of another, for in general the stage is never left empty in the course of the act, nor does total change of place often occur. The rule, however, in this respect, is not very rigidly observed, and contrivances have been resorted to, to fill up the seeming chasm which such an interruption as a total change of scene requires, and to avoid that solecism which the entrance of a character, whose approach is unannounced, is considered.

Of these, two are personages: the interpreter and introducer; the *Vishkambhaka* and *Pravesaka*. These are members of the theatrical company, apparently, who may be supposed to sit by, and upon any interruption in the regular course of the piece, explain to the audience its cause and object. The *Vishkambha*, it is said, may appear at the beginning, in the middle, or at the end of an act: the *Pravesaka*, it is said, only between the acts. But this is contradicted by the constant practice, for in every place the *Pravesaka* indicates a change of scene. The duty of the *Pravesaka* was probably of a very simple nature, and he merely announced the change of scene and approach of a certain character. The *Vishkambha* had a more diversified duty, and besides filling up all the blanks in the story, he was expected to divert the audience by his wit and repartee, like the Arloquino Intromezzo, or the clowns of the Elizabethan period of our stage. The clumsiness of these supplementary performers seems not to have escaped the notice of the Hindu dramatists, and they are sometimes interwoven with the piece, as in the *Vedi-Sanhára*, where a scene between two goblins, who are seeking their banquet upon the field of battle, is considered to be chiefly intended to connect the business of the drama, and prepare the audience for the death of Droña, which they behold and describe; and the description of the combat between Lava and Chandraketu, in the *Uttara-Ráma-Charitra*, by the two spirits of air, is a similar and still happier substitute for an interpreter. The employment of the *Vishkambha* and *Pravesaka* is indicated by a simple naming of them, and what either is to do or say is left to the person who fills the character.

The act, or *Anka*, is said to be marked by the exit of all the personages: a definition which is equally applicable to the practice of the French theatre. Of the duration of the act we have already spoken, and it will have been seen in the enumeration of the different species of theatrical compositions, that the number of acts varies from one to ten. The *Hanuman-Nátaka* indeed has fourteen; but it will be seen by the abstract account of that drama, that it is a poem rather than a play, or at most a piece of patchwork, in which the fragments of an old play have been eked out by poetic narrative, and connected by the interposition of extraneous and undramatic matters. The precise division of Hindu plays into acts is a feature which serves to discriminate them from the Greek compositions, in which the division into acts was unknown, the only distinctions recognised being those of prologue, episode, and exode, regulated by the intervening songs of the chorus, to which we find nothing parallel in the regular plays of the Hindus. The division into acts appears to have been an arrangement invented by the Romans, from whom we can scarcely suspect the Hindus to have derived it.

The first act, or the *Ankamukha*, corresponds to the exposition, prologue, or protasis of the ancient theatre, and furnishes a clue to the subject of the whole story. This is in general ably done; as, for instance, in the *Mudrá Rákshasa*, the whole business of the last act of which is the development of contrivances intimated in the first. The first act of *Málatí and Mádhava* is entirely devoted to this object, with a minuteness of detail that is rather tedious, and reminds us of Puff's apology in the *Critic* for the language of the first scene of his play : " I was obliged to be plain and intelligible in the first scene, because there was so much matter of fact in it."

The ensuing acts carry on the business of the story to its final development in the last; and in general the Hindu writers are successful in maintaining the character of their exode, the business being rarely completed before the concluding act. The piece closes as it began, with a characteristic benediction or prayer, which is always repeated by the principal personage, and expresses his wishes for general plenty and happiness.

4. CONDUCT OF THE PLOT.

The business of every piece is termed its *Vastu*; its substance or thing, the *pragma* or *res*.

It is of two kinds, principal and secondary, or essential and episodical.

Every business involves five elements, the *Víja*, *Vindu*, *Patáká*, *Prakarí*, and *Káryu*.

The *Víja*, or the seed, is the circumstance from which the

business arises. The policy of the prime minister in the *Ratnávalí* is the seed, or remote cause, of the Rája's obtaining the princess.

The *Vindu*, which literally means a drop, is the unintentional development of some secondary incident, which furnishes a clue to the event—as when Ratnávalí learns accidentally that she has beheld the person of the Rája Vatsa, she recollects she was designed by her father to be his bride, which after a due course of interruption she becomes.

Patákí, a banner, perhaps intended to signify embellishment, an episode.

Prakarí, an episodical incident, or an event of limited duration and subordinate importance, in which the principal characters bear no part.

Kárya, is the end, or object, which being effected, the whole is effected, as the marriage of Vatsa and Ratnávalí.

The end or object of the business admits of five conditions: Beginning, Promotion, Hope of Success, Removal of Obstacles, Completion.

The series or combinations of incidents, the *Sandhis*, by which an object is ultimately attained, are also five.

The *Mukha* is the opening or preparatory course of incidents, by which the train of events to be afterwards developed is first sprung. Thus in *Málatí and Mádhava*, the hero and heroine have been thrown in each other's way by seeming accident, but in fact by the devices of their friends; and this lays the foundation of their love, and the occurrences of the play.

The *Pratimukha* is the metabasis, or secondary event, calculated to obstruct or promote the catastrophe, as the suspicion entertained by the queen, Vásavadattá, of her husband's love for Ságariká.

The *Garbha* is the covert prosecution of purpose, giving way in appearance to impediments, but in reality adhering to the original intention.

Vimarsha is the peripateia, in which an effect is produced contrary to its intended cause, or change in the course of the story, by which expectation is baffled, and an unforeseen reverse ensues. Sakuntalá, by her marriage with Dushyanta, has attained the summit of her desires, when she incurs the displeasure of

Durvásas, and is in consequence separated from the recollection of her lord.

The *Upasanhriti* or *Nirvahana*, is the catastrophe, or that to which all tends and in which all terminates.

This course assigned for the fable will be perhaps more intelligible if we apply the divisions to a drama of our own. In *Romeo and Juliet*, the ball at the house of Capulet may be considered the *Mukha*: the *Pratimukha* is the interview with Juliet in the garden: the *Garbha* is Juliet's apparent assent to the marriage with Paris: the *Vimarsha* is the despair of Romeo, consequent on a contrivance intended to preserve Juliet's faith. The catastrophe needs no elucidation.

Each of these divisions in the Hindu system comprehends a number of subdivisions, Angas, or members, to follow the description of which would be to exhaust any patience except Hindu. It will be therefore sufficient to observe, that they comprehend a variety of dramatic incidents, which the theatre of every nation abundantly presents, and which, in fact, have no limits but imagination and dramatic effect. The Hindus enumerate sixty-four; or twelve *Mukhángas*, twelve *Pratimukhángas*, thirteen *Garbhángas*, thirteen *Vimarshángas*, and fourteen *Nirvahaddngas*. We may cite one of each as an example.

Yukti is a *Mukhánga*: it means the connexion of purpose and result. Yogandharáyańa has introduced Ságariká to the queen, merely to put her in the way of the Rája, that he may see and love her. The business of the piece is founded on the result. We might say that the wager of Iachimo and Posthumus, and the visit of the former to the court of Cymboline, was an illustration of this element.

Parisarpa, a *Pratimukhánga*, implies the progressive narration of events. The Chamberlain relates in the *Veńi-Sanhára*, the death of Bhíshma and destruction of the Kauravas by Kŕishńa, as consequent upon the death of the son of the latter, Aniruddha. The description of the successive encounters of Macbeth and Banquo with the King of Norway and rebellious Thanes, by the bleeding soldier, is an instance of this variety.

Of the *Garbhángas*, *Abhútáharaśa*, may be understood to signify misprision of loss or evil. Thus when, in the *Veńi-Sanhára*, the messenger proclaims that Aswatthámán has been slain by

Kṛishṅa, it is supposed that the prince has fallen, but it turns out that the death of an elephant so named is intended. Thus Juliet first interprets the nurse's grief for Tybalt's death as occasioned by the death of Romeo.

One of the *Vimarshdagas* is *Dyuti*, provoking to combat, as in the scene between Arjuna and Bhíma, in the *Veṅí-Sanhára*. Examples of this are common enough in every drama. The scene between Dorax and Sebastian, in *Don Sebastian*, and that between Stukely and Lewson in *The Gamester*, are amongst the most powerful in the English language.

One of the members of the catastrophe is *Grahaṅa*, referring to a purpose held in view throughout. Thus Bhíma reminds Draupadí that she had been forbidden by him to tie up her dishevelled hair, as he had vowed to do it for her, when he had slain those who had subjected her to the indignity of untying the fillet which had bound it. The avowal made by Zanga, in the concluding scene of *The Revenge*, of the feeling by which he has been animated to destroy Alonzo, may be held to be illustrative of this variety.

We shall not pursue these technicalities any further. It is clear from what has been stated, that considerable artifice must have been employed by the Hindu dramatists, in the construction of their fable, to authorise such a complicated subdivision of its details.

5. CHARACTERS OF THE DRAMA.

Every description of composition has its appropriate hero and heroine, and in the ample range of the Hindu drama, every class of society contributes its members to support these personages. The hero may be a god or demigod, or a mortal, in the higher kinds of composition: he is drawn, in the latter case, from mythology, history, or fable, or is the creation of the author. As love enters largely into the business of the Hindu theatre, the attributes of the hero are defined with reference to his fitness for feeling and inspiring passion, and he is to be represented young, handsome, graceful, liberal, valiant, amiable, accomplished, and well-born. The chief technical classification of the *Náyaka*, or hero, is into *Lalita*, gay, thoughtless, and goodhumoured; *Sánta*, gentle and virtuous; *Dhíroddhíta*, high-spirited, but temperate and firm; *Uddhata*, ardent and ambitious. These are again subdivided, so as to make forty-eight species; and by considering them as diversified by mortal, semi-divine, or celestial origin, are multiplied to a hundred and forty-four kinds. It must be rather difficult for a writer to observe, amidst such a multiplicity, the rule laid down for his delineation of the manners of his hero: for whatever individual he adopts, he must take care to make him consistent with himself, and not to give him qualities incompatible with his organisation. Thus it is said that it is incongruous to ascribe liberality to the demon Rávaña; to unite piety and pride in the son of Jamadagni; and to accuse the high-minded Rāma of compassing the death of Bali by fraud. These blemishes, when they occur in the original legend, should be kept out of view by the dramatist. Some allowance, however, is made for "lover's perjuries," and a prince and hero may compromise his credit for dignity and veracity, in concealing from a jealous bride his *égaremens de cœur*.

Equal minuteness has been displayed in specifying the classes of *Náyikás* or heroines; and the extent to which females are partakers of scenic incident, affords an interesting picture of the relations of that sex in Hindu society. In the *Nátakas* and *Nátikás* we have the nymphs of heaven, the brides of demigods, the wives of saints, and female saints themselves, and the deified woods and rivers; in the plays of pure fiction, we have princesses and courtesans; and in the pieces of intrigue, the different inmates of the harem. The first class of females is the legitimate creation of poetry and mythology, the others are portraits from social life. The introduction of the unmarried female of high birth into the lighter scenes of common life, is an accession to which ancient comedy was a stranger. The unmarried girl of family is never introduced in person in the scenes of Plautus and Terence. In *Málatí and Mádhava*, we have Málatí and her friend Madayantiká; and in the *Ratnávalí*, Ságariká and the other damsels of the interior of the palace. It may be suspected, however, that the former piece presents a purer specimen of Hindu manners than the latter. It seems probable that the princes of India learnt the practice of the rigid exclusion of women in their harems from the Mohammedans, and that previously, although they were subject to many restrictions, they were allowed to go freely into public on public occasions, they were present at dramatic performances, they formed the chief part at bridal processions, they were permitted to visit the temples of the gods, and to perform their ablutions with little or no privacy in sacred streams; which last-named privileges they still retain, and to which Mohammedan women have no similar right. Even in later times, the presence of men other than a husband or a son, was far from prohibited in the inner apartments; and in the *Ratnávalí*, the minister of Vatsa, with his chamberlain and the envoy from Ceylon, are admitted to the audience of the Rájá in the presence of the queen and her attending damsels. In what may be considered heroic times, queens and princesses seem to have travelled about where and how they pleased; and in the *Uttara-Ráma-Charitra*, Sítá is sent to live by herself in the forests, and the mother of Ráma comes with little or no parade to the hermitage of Válmíki.

Although, however, the social restraints to which females were subjected, under the ancient Hindu system, were of a very different nature from those which Mohammedanism imposes, and were in all probability even less severe than those which prevailed in many of the Grecian states, they did no doubt operate to such an extent as to preclude women from taking any part in general society. This was more particularly the case with unmarried women; and we learn from several of the dramas, that it was a part of virtuous breeding for a virgin to decline conversation with a man, even with a lover. Thus Ságariká in the *Ratnávalí*, and Málatí in *Málatí and Mádhava*, can with difficulty be prevailed upon to address the objects of their affection. They answer to every question by proxy, and do not even trust their voices to their female companion above a whisper, when those they adore are present. Unmarried women, therefore, we may infer, might be in company with men and might bear their addresses, but would have violated decorum if they had ventured to reply. No restraint of the nature was imposed upon married women. S'akuntalá appears in the public court of Dushyanta and pleads her own cause; and Vásavadattá, in the *Ratnávalí*, enters unreservedly into communication with her father's envoy. The married ladies of the lighter pieces, indeed, exercise their wit upon their husband's particular confidant and friend, the Viddshaka, and the queen of Agnimitra and her foster sister Mekhalá, indulge themselves in practical jokes at Cháráyańá's expense.

The want of opportunity thus afforded to Hindu youth to appreciate the characters and dispositions of those to whom they were affianced, might be supposed to have subjected them to subsequent disgust and disappointment at home, and consequently compelled them to seek the gratification derived from female society elsewhere. Such has been the reason assigned for a similar practice amongst the Greeks. It may be doubted, however, whether this want of previous acquaintance was in any way the cause of the effect ascribed to it, for the practice was very universal, and disappointment could not have universally occurred. In all probability, it occurred less often than it does in European society, in which so much pains are taken to embellish talent, and in which conventional good breeding conceals defects. The practice rather originated in what was considered to be the perfection of female virtue. "She was the best of women of whom little could be said, either in the way of good or harm : she was educated to see as little, to hear as little, and inquire as little as possible, and the chief purposes of her married life were to perpetuate her race, and regulate the economy of the household." Her maximum of merit consisted in the assiduity with which she nursed her children and controlled her servants, and whilst thus devoted "to suckle fools and chronicle small beer," she might be a very useful, but certainly could not be a very entertaining companion.

The defective education of the virtuous portion of the sex, and their consequent uninteresting character, held out an inducement to the unprincipled members, both of Greek and Hindu society, to rear a class of females, who should supply those wants which rendered home cheerless, and should give to men hetera or female friends, and associates in intellectual as well as in animal enjoyment. A courtesan of this class inspired no abhorrence: she was brought up from her infancy to the life she professed, which she graced by her accomplishments, and not unfrequently dignified by her virtues. Her disregard of social restraint was not the voluntary breach of moral, social, or religious precepts: it was the business of her education to minister to pleasure, and in the imperfect system of the Greeks, she committed little or no trespass against the institutes of the national creed or the manners of society. The Hindu principles were more rigid; and not only was want of chastity in a female a capital breach of social and religious obligations, but the association of men with professed wantons was an equal violation of decorum, and, involving a departure from the purity of caste, was considered a virtual degradation from rank in society. In practice, however, greater latitude seems to have been observed; and in the *Mrichchhakati*, a Brahman, a man of family and repute, incurs apparently no discredit from his love for a courtesan. A still more curious feature is, that his passion for such an object seems to excite no sensation in his family nor uneasiness in his wife, and the nurse presents his child to his mistress, as to its mother; and his wife, besides interchanging civilities (a little coldly, perhaps, but not compulsively), finishes by calling her "sister," and acquiescing therefore in her legal union with her lord. It must be acknowledged that the poet has managed his story with great dexterity, and the interest with which he has invested his heroine prevents manners so revolting to our notions from being obtrusively offensive. No art was necessary, in the estimation of a Hindu writer, to provide his hero with a wife or two, more or less, and the acquisition of an additional bride is the ordinary catastrophe of the lighter dramas.

Women are distinguished as being *Swakíyá*, *Parakíyá*, and *Sámányá*—or the wife of an individual himself, the wife or daughter of another person, and one who is independent. Each of these is distinguished as *Mugdhá*, *Praudhá*, and *Pragalbhá*, or youthful, adolescent, and mature; and of each of these, again, there are many varieties, which it is needless to specify. We may observe, however, to the honour of the Hindu drama, that the *Parakíyá*, or she who is the wife of another person, is never to be made the object of a dramatic intrigue: a prohibition that would have sadly cooled the imagination and curbed the wit of Dryden and Congreve.

The incidental characters or conditions of a *Náyiká* are declared to be eight:—

1. The *Swádhínapatiká* is devoted to her husband.
2. The *Vásakasajjá* is a damsel full dressed in expectation of her lover.
3. The *Virahotkatthitá* mourns the absence of her lord.

4. The *Khaṇḍitā* is mortified by detecting a lover's infidelity.
5. The *Kalahāntaritā* is overcome with grief or anger at real or fancied neglect.
6. The *Vipralabdhā* is disappointed by her lover's failing his appointment.
7. The *Proshitabhartṛikā* is a female whose husband or lover is in a foreign country.
8. The *Abhisārikā* is a female who goes to meet her lover, or sends to seek him.

The *Alaṅkāras*, the ornaments or graces of women, and with which the *Nāyikā* should be delineated by the dramatic or poetic writer, are said to be twenty. Many of these are palpable enough: such as *Śobhā*, brilliancy or beauty, and youth ; *Mādhurya*, sweetness of disposition; *Dhairya*, steady attachment, &c. But there are some which, as characteristic of the Hindu system, may perhaps merit specification. *Bhāva* is a slight personal indication of natural emotion. *Hāva* is its stronger expression, as change of colour; and *Helā* is the decided manifestation of feeling. *Līlā* is mimicry of a lover's manner, language, dress, &c., for his diversion, or that of female companions. *Vilāsa* is the expression of desire evinced in look, act, or speech. *Vichchhitti* is neglect of dress and ornaments through mental agitation. *Vibhrama* is the wrong application of personal embellishments occasioned by hurry and anxiety. *Kilakiñchita* is mixed sensation, as the conflict between joy and grief, tenderness and resentment. *Moṭṭāyita* is the silent expression of returned affection. *Kuṭṭamita* is the affected repulse of a lover's endearments. *Vikṛita* is the suppression of the sentiments of the heart through bashfulness; and *Lalita* is the conviction of triumphant charms, and the sentiment of gratified love, as expressed by elegance of attire and complacency of deportment.

The *dramatis personæ*, with the exception of the hero and heroine, form the *aṅga* or the body of the characters. Of these the following are distinguished :—

The *Pīṭhamarda* is the friend and confidant of the hero, and sometimes the hero of a secondary action interwoven with the principal. Such is the case in the *Mālatī and Mādhava*, in which the love of Makaranda for Madayantikā proceeds parallel with that of Mādhava for Mālatī.

Another person of primary rank is the *Pratinâyaka*, the counterpart and antagonist of the hero. Such is Rávaṇa as opposed to Ráma, and Duryodhana to Yudhishṭhira.

Each of these may have his courtiers, ministers, officers, companions, and dependants; but there are two individuals, termed specifically the *Viṭa* and the *Vidúshaka*, that are peculiar in some degree to the theatre of the Hindus.

The character of the *Viṭa* is not very easily understood. It is necessary that he should be accomplished in the lighter arts, particularly poetry, music, and singing, and he appears indiscriminately as the companion of a man or woman, although, in the latter case, the female is the courtesan. He is generally represented on familiar and easy, and yet dependent, terms with his associate, and evinces something of the character of the Parasite of the Greek comedy, but that he is never rendered contemptible. It does not appear that he professes to teach the arts he practises, although it is not impossible that such was his employ, and that he was retained about the person of the wealthy and dissipated, as a kind of private instructor as well as entertaining companion. In lexicons, the person indicated by the *Viṭa* is a despicable being, of whose character no vestiges occur in the theatrical picture.

As Schlegel observes, every theatre has its buffoon, and the *Vidúshaka* plays that part in the theatre of the Hindus. He is the humble companion, not the servant, of a prince or man of rank; and it is a curious peculiarity, that he is always a Brahmin. He bears more affinity to Sancho Panza, perhaps, than any other character in western fiction, imitating him in his combination of shrewdness and simplicity, his fondness of good living, and his love of ease. In the dramas of intrigue, he exhibits some of the talents of Mercury, but with less activity and ingenuity, and occasionally suffers by his interference. In the *Mrichchhakati* he is further distinguished by his morality and his devotion to his friend. This character is always lively, and sometimes almost witty, although in general his facetiousness does not take a very lofty flight. According to the technical definition of his attributes, he is to excite mirth by being ridiculous in person, age, and attire.

The *Náyiká*, or heroine, has always her companion and confidante, and the most appropriate personage to fill this capacity is a foster sister. Where queens are the heroines, a favourite damsel discharges this duty. Female devotees play a leading part in several dramas as well as novels, and in that case are usually described as of the Bauddha sect. In the *Vrihat-Kathá* these pious ladies are usually painted in very unfavourable colours; but in *Málatí and Mádhava*, the old priestess, or rather ascetic, is represented as a woman of profound learning and sound morals, the instructress and friend of men who hold the highest offices in the state, and the instrument selected by them to secure the happiness of their children.

The subordinate characters of both sexes are derived from every class of society; and even the *Chándálas* find a place in the comedies of fiction. A strange enumeration is given of the male characters admissible as tenants of the interior of palaces, or Eunuchs, Mutes, Dwarfs, Foresters, and Barbarians. The attendance of females on the persons of kings is another national peculiarity, especially as it appears from the *Mudrá-Rákshasa*, that this practice was not confined to the inner apartments; for Chandragupta, although he does not appear in public so attended, goes thus accompanied from one palace to another.

6. OBJECTS OF DRAMATIC REPRESENTATION.

The purposes that are to be aimed at in dramatic composition are described as the same with those of poetic fiction in general: they are to convey instruction through the means of amusement; and, with this view, they must affect the minds of the spectators with the sentiments which they express. These sentiments are termed by the Hindus, *Rasas*, tastes or flavours, and they imply both the quality as inherent in the composition, and the perception of it as recognised by the reader or spectator. The *Rasas*, however, are considered usually as effects, not causes, and they are said to come from the *Bhávas*, conditions of the mind or body, which are followed by a corresponding expression in those who feel, or are supposed to feel them, and a corresponding impression on those who behold them. When these conditions are of a permanent or perdurable description, and produce a lasting and general impression, which is not disturbed by the influence of collateral or contrary excitements, they are, in fact, the same with the impressions: as desire or love, as the main object of the action is both the condition of the chief character, and the sentiment with which the spectator is filled. When the conditions are incidental and transitory, they contribute to the general impression, but are not confounded with it. They may, indeed, be contrary to it in their essence, without weakening or counteracting it; as a hero may, for public reasons, abandon his mistress without foregoing his love, and may perform acts of horror even in furtherance of his passion.

The *Bhávas* are therefore divided into *Sthåyin* or lasting, and *Vyabhichárin*, transitory or incidental. There are also other divisions, which we shall proceed to notice.

The *Sthåyi-Bhávas*, or permanent conditions, are, according to some authorities, eight; according to others, nine.

1. *Rati* is desire for any object, arising from seeing or hearing it, or having it present to the recollection.
2. *Hása* is laughter or mirth, distinct from the laughter of scorn.
3. *Soka* is sorrow at separation from a beloved object.
4. *Krodha* is the resentment of injurious treatment.
5. *Utsáha* is high-mindedness, or that feeling which prompts valour, munificence, or mercy.
6. *Bhaya* is the fear of reproach.
7. *Jugupsá* is aversion or disgust; the emotion which attends seeing, touching, or hearing of anything offensive.
8. *Vismaya* is the emotion produced by seeing, touching, or hearing of anything surprising.
9. *Sánta* is not always included in this enumeration: it implies that state of mind which contemplates all human events as transitory and insignificant.

Before adverting to the *Vyabhichári-Bhávas*, we must notice the other divisions, as they are essential accompaniments of both them and the *Sthåyi-Bhávas*. The *Bhávas* are distinguished as *Vibhávas*, *Anubhávas*, and *Sáttwika-Bhávas*.

The *Vibhávas* are the preliminary and accompanying conditions which lead to any particular state of mind or body, and the *Anubhávas* are the external signs which indicate its existence.

The *Sáttwika-Bhávas* are the involuntary expressions of emotion natural to a living being—as *Stambha*, paralysis; *Sweda*, perspiration; *Románcha*, erection of the hair of the body; *Swaravikára*, change of voice; *Vepathu*, trembling; *Varṇavikára*, change of colour; *Aśru*, tears; and *Pralaya*, immobility or helplessness. These, as the results of emotion, are the same with the *Anubhávas*.

The *Vyabhichári-Bhávas* are the most numerous; and in order to give a more accurate notion of them, as well as of this part of the system, we shall implicitly follow the guidance of the native authorities.

1. *Nirveda*, self-disparagement; *Vibhávas*, dissatisfaction with the world and desire to acquire holy knowledge; *Anubhávas*, tears, sighs, and appearance of mental dejection.

Example.—" Wandering round the world only wearies the wise, the abundance of learning engenders controversy, the notice of the great yields but humiliation, and the looks that gaze upon the lotus face lead only to the pangs of parting. Náráyańa was not propitiated at Prayága by me of little wisdom." (*Ram-Tarangińí*.)

2. *Gláni*, debility, inability to endure; *Vibhávas*, long sorrow, excess in exercise or pleasure, hunger and thirst; *Anubhávas*, inactivity, change of colour, and trembling of the limbs.

Example.—" Long and bitter sorrow withering her heart, like the tender bud of the lotus cut from its stem, has shrunk up her delicate frame, as the soft leaf of the *ketakí* is shrivelled by autumnal heat." (*Sarasvatikańtábharańa*, from the *Uttara-Ráma-Charitra*.)

3. *Sanká*, apprehension of encountering what is not desired, or doubt of obtaining what is wished; *Vibhávas*, another person's aversion or individual misconduct; *Anubhávas*, trembling, anxious looks and manner, concealment.

Example.—" She shrinks from every gaze, suspecting that her secret is discovered. If she observe two of her companions in conversation, she thinks they are talking of her; and if they laugh, she thinks herself the object of their mirth." (*Daśa-Rúpaka*, from the *Ratnávalí*.)

4. *Asúyá*, intolerance of another's superiority, and attempt to humiliate him; *Vibhávas*, irascibility, baseness; *Anubhávas*, angry expression, recapitulation of defects.

Example.—" The praise of the enemy of Madhu, pronounced in the assembly by the son of Páńdu, was insupportable to the Chedi monarch, for the mind of the arrogant cannot brook another's praise." (*Sáhitya-Darpańa*, from *Mágha*.)

Some writers consider *Irshyd* as synonymous with *Asúyd*; but one authority distinguishes it as a variety, and restricts the former to jealousy or intolerance of attention or respect shown to a rival, as,

Example.—"Go, shameless wretch, to her to whom you have transferred your homage, the crimson tincture of whose feet you wear as the embellishment of your forehead." (*Saraswatikantábharana.*)

5. *Mada*, intoxication, extravagant joy, and forgetfulness of sorrow; *Vibhávas*, drinking, &c.; *Anubhávas*, unsteadiness in movement, indistinctness of utterance, drowsiness, laughing, weeping.

Example.—"The tongue tastes the liquor, and our existence is wholly unprofitable: all the faculties are overwhelmed by the unreality of a shadow." (*Rasa-Tarangini.*)

6. *Srama*, weariness; *Vibhávas*, bodily exertion or excessive indulgence; *Anubhávas*, perspiration, languor, &c.

Example.—"There you reclined your form in repose upon my bosom, for vainly had my endearments sought to give relief to those tender limbs, beautiful in rest, and delicate as the soft fibres of the lotus stem, when wearied by the lengthened way." (*Dasa-Rúpaka*, from the *Uttara Ráma-Charitra.*)

7. *Alasya*, indolence, aversion to activity; *Vibhávas*, weariness, luxuriousness, pregnancy, meditation; *Anubhávas*, tardy and reluctant motion, stooping, yawning, becoming of a darker complexion.

Example.—"The daughter of the mountain, when heavy with her pleasing burden, was unable to prevent Hara from carrying off her necklace with her hands, and languidly raised her eye in smiles upon his theft." (*Rasa-Tarangini*, from the *Kumára-Sambhava.*)

8. *Dainya*, the depression of indigence and pain; *Vibhávas*, desertion, neglect, contempt; *Anubhávas*, hunger, thirst, ragged apparel, wretchedness of appearance.

Example.—"The husband, old and blind, reclines upon the platform; the dwelling is in ruins, and the rainy season is at hand. There are no good tidings of the son, and as the matron anxiously preserves the last drop of oil in the fragment of a broken jar, she looks at her pregnant daughter-in-law, and weeps." (*Dasa-Rúpaka.*)

9. *Chintá*, painful reflection, the absorption of the mind in unpleasant recollection; *Vibhávas*, the loss or absence of a desired object; *Anubhávas*, tears, sighs, change of colour, feverish heat.

Example.—"Whom do you think of, gentle and lovely maiden, as you lean your cheek upon your hand, around whose wrists the lotus fibre twines its cooling bracelet? from those long lashes drop a stream of pearly tears, to weave a lengthened necklace, far more bright than Hara's radiant smile." (Daśa-Rúpaka.)

10. *Moha*, perplexity, distraction, not knowing what is to be done or left undone; *Vibhávas*, terror, impetuosity, painful recollection; *Anubhávas*, giddiness, falling on the ground, insensibility.

Example.—"I know not whether this be pain or pleasure that I feel; whether I wake or sleep, whether wine or venom spread through my frame; thy touch has confounded all my faculties, and now I shake with cold, and now I burn with inward heat." (Daśa-Rúpaka, from the Uttara-Ráma-Charitra.)

11. *Smriti*, recollection; *Vibhávas*, the effort to remember, association of ideas; *Anubhávas*, contracting or drawing up the eyebrows, &c.

Example.—"Is this Mainâka that stops my way through the air? Whence is this audacity? Has he forgotten how he shrank from the thunderbolt of Indra?—Is it Tárkshya that thus presumes, who ought to know me, Rávana, the equal of his lord?—No, it is Jatáyu—oppressed by years, he comes to court his death." (Daśa-Rúpaka, from the Hanumán-Nátaka.)

12. *Dhriti*, concentration or repose of the mind, fortitude or content; *Vibhávas*, knowledge, power; *Anubhávas*, calm enjoyment, patient suffering.

Example.—"We are contented here with the bark of trees; you are happy in affluence: our satisfaction is equal, there is no difference in our conditions. He alone is poor whose desires are insatiable; but when the mind is satisfied, who can be called poor, who can be termed rich?" (Daśa-Rúpaka, from the Satakas of Bhartrihári.)

13. *Vridá*, shame, shrinking from praise or censure; *Vibhávas*, conscious impropriety, disgrace, defeat; *Anubhávas*, casting down the eyes, hanging down the head, covering the face, blushing.

Example.—"The eyes of Arjuna, suffused with starting tears, are fixed in sad dejection upon his bow; inflamed with rage, he mourns the death of Abhimanyu, slain by an unworthy enemy, but burns still more with shame to think it yet unrevenged! 'Alas, alas, my son!' are words that are swelling in his throat, but not suffered to find their way." (Saraswatikanthábharana, from the Veni-Sanhára.)

14. *Chapalatá*, unsteadiness, haste, repeatedly changing from

one thing to another; *Vibhávas*, envy, hatred, passion, joy; *Anubhávas*, angry looks, abuse, blows, following one's own inclination.

Example.—"When he heard that Ráma had taken up his bow, and announced with delight his expectation of the coming contest, after he had thrown a bridge over the sea and advanced to Lanká, the many hands of Rávaṇa dropped their shafts, as might be inferred from the rattling of the bracelets, which had been almost burst with exultation at the commencement of the war." (*Rasa-Tarangiṇí*, from the *Hanumán-Náṭaka*.)

15. *Harsha*, joy, mental exultation; *Vibhávas*, meeting with a lover or friend, the birth of a son, &c.; *Anubhávas*, horripilation, perspiration, tears, sobbing, change of voice.

Example.—"The matron to whose arms her lord returns in safety from the dangers of a journey over desert lands, wipes from her eyes the starting tear of joy as she thinks of the perils of the way. She brushes with her mantle from the faithful camel's loaded hair the heavy sand, and fills his mouth with handfuls of his favourite fodder." (*Dasa Rúpaka*.)

16. *Avega*, agitation or flurry, arising from unexpected or unpleasant events; *Vibhávas*, the approach of a friend or enemy, the occurrence of natural phenomena, and the proximity of imminent danger; *Anubhávas*, slipping, falling, tumbling, haste, inability to move, &c.

Example.—"Haste, haste, my arms!—Quick!—Caparison my steed!—Where is my sword? Bring me my dagger! Where is my bow, and where my mail? Such were the cries that echoed through the mountain caves, when, startled from their slumbers by the dream that thou hadst shown them, the enemy awoke in alarm." (*Dasa-Rúpaka*, from a play or poem of the author's own, which he has not named.)

17. *Jadata*, loss of faculty or activity, incapacity for every kind of business; *Vibhávas*, seeing, hearing, or encountering anything agreeable or disagreeable in excess; *Anubhávas*, silence, fixed look, apathetic indifference.

Example.—"1st *Rákshasa*. By whom have those mighty demons been slain, by Tridiras, Khara, and Dúshaṇa commanded?

"2d *Rákshasa*. By the ferocious warrior Ráma.

"1st *Rákshasa*. By him alone!

"2d *Rákshasa*. Who could believe it that did not see it? Amidst the din of battle, the numbers of our host were strewed headless corses on the plain, and plunging herons burrowed in the hollow of each severed neck.

"1st *Rákshasa*. If he be such as you describe, what can such as I attempt?" (*Dasa-Rúpaka*, from the *Uddhta-Rághava*.)

Example.—"When the monkey chiefs heard from Hanumat, upon his return, that they would be unable to cross the expanded bed of the ocean, they laughed at his report; but when they reached the shore, and first beheld the vast and ever-tossing main, they stood to gaze upon it like figures in a picture." (*Rasa-Tarangiṇí*, from the *Hanumaa-Nátaka*.)

18. *Garba*, arrogance, holding one's self superior to all men; *Vibhávas*, opinion of family, beauty, rank, and strength; *Anubhávas*, disrespect, frowns, freedoms, laughter, acts of prowess.

Example.—"Whilst I bear arms, what need of others' swords: that which cannot be accomplished by my falchion must be impossible for all." (*Sarasvatíkaṇṭhábharaṇa*, from the *Mahábhárata*.)

19. *Vishádá*, despair of success, anticipation of misfortune; *Vibhávas*, failure in acquiring wealth, fame, or offspring, and their loss; *Anubhávas*, sighing, palpitation, abstraction, anxious search for friends or patrons, &c.

Example.—"Táraká, what is this? Gourds sink in the stream, and stones are buoyant. The glory of the mighty monarch of the Rákshasas is effaced, and the child of a mortal triumphs. I have lived to see my kinsmen slain; the feebleness of age forbids the discharge of my functions. What now is to be done?" (*Daśa-Rúpaka*, from the *Víra-Charitra*.)

20. *Autsukya*, impatience; *Vibhávas*, expectation of a lover; *Anubhávas*, uneasiness, lassitude, sighs.

Example.—"The first watch is spent in agreeable diversions; the second, in weaving a wreath of lotus flowers, *champakas*, *ketakas*, *jasmines*; the third, in adjusting the golden bracelet, and chain, and ear-rings, and zone. But how, pretty damsel, is the last watch of the day to be passed?" (*Rasa-Tarangiṇí*.)

21. *Nidrá*, drowsiness, contraction of the mental faculties, or recession of their properties from the organs of sense; *Vibhávas*, fatigue of body or mind; *Anubhávas*, relaxation of the muscles, twinkling of the eyes, yawning, dosing.

Example.—"Still echo in my heart those gentle love-inspiring words my fawn-eyed maid breathed to-day, half indistinct and half articulate, when her eyes twinkled with drowsiness." (*Daśa-Rúpaka*.)

22. *Apasmára*, possession, demoniac or planetary influence; *Vibhávas*, impurity, solitude, excessive fear or grief, &c.; *Anu-*

bhávas, trembling, sighing, foaming, lolling out the tongue, falling on the ground in convulsions.

Example.—"When he beheld the Lord of Waters, furious and foaming, clinging to the earth and tossing high his mighty waves like arms, he thought him one possessed." (*Daśa-Rúpaka*, from *Mágha*).

23. *Supta*, sleep; *Vibhávas*, sleepiness; *Anubhávas*, closing of the eyes, immobility, and hard breathing.

Example.—"As the eyes of the foe of Mura close, and the breath plays upon his quivering lip, in the bowers on the Yamuná's bank, one smiling damsel steals away his robe, another the gem from his ear, and a third the golden bracelets from his arms." (*Rasa-Tarangiṇí*.)

24. *Vibodha*, the unfolding of the faculties, waking; *Vibhávas*, dissipation of drowsiness; *Anubhávas*, rubbing the eyes, snapping the fingers, shaking the limbs.

Example.—"May the glances of Hari preserve you, when he extends his dripping limbs, designing to quit his discus, pillow, and serpent couch amidst the ocean, and averts his half-opening eyes, red with long slumber, from the blaze of the lamps, set with gems." (*Saraswatíkaṇṭhábharaṇa*, from the *Mudrá-Rákshasa*.)

25. *Amarsha*, impatience of opposition or rivalry; *Vibhávas*, discomfiture, disgrace; *Anubhávas*, perspiration, redness of the eyes, shaking of the head, abusive language, blows.

Example.—"Shall the sons of Dhritaráshṭra go unpunished, and I survive? They have set fire to our dwelling, offered us poison for food, assumed our state, seized upon our wealth, and sought our lives, and have laid violent hands upon the robe and tresses of our common bride." (*Saraswatíkaṇṭhábharaṇa*, from the *Vení-Saṃhára*.)

26. *Avahitthá*, disguise, attempted concealment of sentiments by personal acts; *Vibhávas*, modesty, turpitude, importance; *Anubhávas*, acting, looking, and speaking in a manner foreign to the real object.

Example.—"Whilst thus the divine sage spoke, the beauteous Parvatí, standing by his side, held down her head with shame, and pretended to count the leaves of the lotus in her hand." (*Daśa-Rúpaka*, from the *Kumára-Sambhava*.)

27. *Ugratá*, sternness, cruelty; *Vibhávas*, promulgation of fault or crime, theft, evil disposition; *Anubhávas*, reviling, abusing, beating.

Example.—"Is not my unrelenting spirit known to all the world? One and twenty times did I destroy the martial race, and hewed to pieces the very infants in the womb; nor desisted till I had allayed the fires of a father's wrath, by ablution in the reservoir of blood which I had promised to his ghost." (*Dasa-Rúpaka*, from the *Vira-Charitra*.)

28. *Mati*, apprehension, mental conclusion; *Vibháva*, study of the Sástras; *Anubháva*, shaking the head, drawing up the brows, giving instruction or advice.

Example.—" Assuredly she is fit to be a Kshattriya's wife, for my mind feels her worthy of my love. The dictates of the soul are in all doubtful points the authority of the virtuous." (*Sarasvatíkaṇṭhábharaṇa*, from *Śakuntalá*.)

29. *Vyádhi*, sickness; *Vibhávas*, vitiation of the humours, effect of heat or cold, influence of the passions; *Anubhávas*, appropriate bodily symptoms.

Example.—" Her kindred are in tears, her parents in sorrowful abstraction, her friends are overcome with melancholy, her associates with affliction: the hope to her that to-day or to-morrow her sufferings will cease is despair to others, but she participates not in the pain of separation from the world." (*Dasa-Rúpaka*.)

30. *Unmáda*, absence of reflection or restraint: *Vibhávas*, loss of a beloved or desired object, reverse of fortune, morbid action or possession; *Anubhávas*, talking incoherently, laughing, weeping, or singing without cause.

Example.—" Vile Rákshasa, forbear; whither wouldst thou bear my beloved ! Alas! It is no demon, but a cloud. It is the bow of Indra, not the weapon of a distant foe; the rain-drops beat upon me, not hostile shafts; and that gleam of golden radiance is the lightning, not my love." (*Dasa-Rúpaka*, from *Vikrama and Urvaśí*.)

31. *Maraṇa*, death; *Vibhávas*, expiration, wounds, injuries; *Anubhávas*, falling on the ground, immobility.

Example.—" The female fiend, pierced through the heart by the resistless shafts of the blooming Ráma, poured through the nostrils a torrent of blood, and sought the dwelling of the lord of life." (*Sáhitya-Darpaṇa*, from the *Raghu-Vaṃśa*.)

32. *Trása*, fear without cause; *Vibhávas*, hearing frightful sounds, seeing alarming objects; *Anubhávas*, immobility, trembling, perspiration, relaxed muscles.

Example.—" As the fish played about their knees, the nymphs of heaven, their glances wild with terror and striking their hands together, looked upon each other fearfully." (*Sarasvatíkaṇṭhábharaṇa*, from the *Kirāta*.)

33. *Vitarka*, consideration, discussion; *Vibháva*, the percep-

tion of doubtful circumstances; *Anubhávas*, shaking the head, raising the eyebrows, &c.

Example.—"Has this been contrived by Bharata, misled by ambition, or has the second queen effected it through female levity? Both these notions must be incorrect. The prince is the hero's youngest brother; the queen, his parent and his father's wife. It is clear, therefore, that this unhappy event is the work of destiny." (*Dasa-Rúpaka*.)

This concludes the list of *Vyabhichári-Bhávas*, or incidental conditions, according to the best treatises on this subject; and as they assert, to the elementary rules of Bharata, in which they are enumerated. They are in many cases subtilised and subdivided in a manner which it is unnecessary here to notice. Their judicious delineation gives to poetic and dramatic composition its flavour or taste.

The *Rasas*, it is expressly stated, are so termed, from the analogy between mental and physical impressions. The conception of love or hatred, as derived from a drama, is fitly compared to the notion which such substances as may be sweet or saline convey of saltness or sweetness. The idea is not peculiar to Hindu literature; and the most polished nations of Europe agree in the employment of a term of similar literal and metaphorical import, as *taste, gusto, goût, geschmack*. A similar application of terms is traceable in Latin and Greek; and, as Addison observes, "this metaphor would have not been so general, had there not been a conformity between the mental taste and that sensitive taste which gives us a relish of every savour."

The *Rasas* reside in the composition, but are made sensible by their action on the reader or spectator. In the first case, they may be identified with the permanent conditions or *Bhávas*. It is more usual, however, to regard them as distinct—as the effects of the *Bhávas* and not of one nature with them. Their due appreciation depends upon the sensitiveness of the critic; but a spectator, who deserves the name, is defined by Bharata to be "one who is happy when the course of the drama is cheerful, melancholy when it is sorrowful, who rages when it is furious, and trembles when it is fearful," or, in a word, who sympathises with what he sees.

The *Rasas* are eight, according to Bharata: according to

some authorities there are nine. They are *Sringára*, love; *Hásya*, mirth; *Karuńá*, tenderness; *Raudra*, fury; *Víra*, heroism; *Bhayánaka*, terror; *Bíbhatsa*, disgust; and *Adbhuta*, wonder—the ninth is *Sánta*, or tranquillity. The serious part of this list is much more comprehensive than the Greek tragic *Rasas* of terror and pity; but, as anticipated by the Hindu critics, the whole might be easily extended. In reply to this, however, they say, that all other impressions may be classed under some of these, as paternal fondness comes under the head of tenderness, and avarice is an object of mirth; and the same argument may be urged in favour of the limitations of Aristotle. The fewer the classes, however, the more subtle is the ingenuity required to squeeze all the species into them, and so far the Hindu theory has an advantage over the Greek.

Sringára, or love, is a very leading principle in the drama of the Hindus: it is not, however, an indispensable ingredient, and many plays are wholly exempt from any trace of it. The love of the Hindus is less sensual than that of the Greek and Latin comedy, and less metaphysical than that of French and English tragedy. The loose gallantry of modern comedy is unknown to the Hindus, and they are equally strangers to the professed adoration of chivalric poetry; but their passion is neither tame nor undignified. It is sufficiently impassioned to be exempt from frigidity, and it is too tender to degrade the object of the passion; whilst, at the same time, the place that woman holds in society is too rationally defined for her to assume an influence foreign to her nature; and the estimation in which human life is held, is too humble, for a writer to elevate any mortal to the honours of a divinity. The condition of lovers is described as threefold: they may be in possession of each other's affections, and personally united; their passion may not have been mutually communicated, and their union not have taken place; and they may have been united and subsequently separated from each other. The first is called *Sambhoga*, the second *Ayoga*, and the third *Viprayoga*: or these kinds are reduced to two, and *Sambhoga* expresses successful, and *Vipralambha* unsuccessful love. The causes and consequences and modifications of these conditions are the subjects of much subtle definition, which it is not necessary to prosecute. Abundant illustration of the manner in which the passion is treated will be found in the following pages.

Víra is the *Rasa* of heroism; and heroic magnanimity is evinced in three ways: munificence, clemency, and valour. Where the latter is displayed, it must be calm, collected, and dispassionate: any indication of violence belongs to a different taste. The *Víra Charitra* affords an example of this *Rasa*, and the calm intrepidity of its hero presents a very favourable contrast to the fury of a Tydides, or the arrogance of a Rinaldo.

Bíbhatsa is the feeling of disgust inspired by filthy objects, or by fetid odours, or by low and virulent abuse. It is not the subject, it is believed, of any entire drama, but many scenes of this description occur, as the resort of Mádhava to the place of cremation, and the dialogue of the two demons in the *Feit Nathadra*.

Raudra is the sentiment of furious passion, expressed by violent gesticulation, threatening language, and acts of personal aggression. Examples of it occur only in detached characters, as in *Paraśurāma*, *Rāvaṇa*, and *Duryodhana*.

Hásya is mirth arising from ridicule of person, speech, or dress, either one's own or another's, and engenders laughter of various intensity: as *Smita*, which is only the expansion of the eyelids; *Hasita* displays the teeth; *Vihasita* is characterised by a gentle exclamation; *Upahasita* exhibits tears; in *Apahasita* the tears flow in excess; and *Atihasita* is "laughter holding both his sides." The two first kinds of merriment are the genteelest; the two next are rather vulgar, but pardonable; the two last are absolutely low, or "the vulgar way the vulgar show their mirth."

The *Adbhuta Rasa* is the expression of the marvellous. Wonder is the prevailing characteristic produced by uncommon objects, and indicated by exclamation, trembling, and perspiration, &c.

The *Bhayánaka* is the taste of terror: it is induced by awful occurrences, and exhibited by trembling, perspiration, dryness of mouth, and indistinctness of judgment.

Karuṇá is pity or tenderness excited by the occurrence of misfortunes: it is inspired by sighs and tears, mental unconsciousness or aberration, and is suitably illustrated by the delineation of depression, exhaustion, agony, and death.

The *Śānta Rasa* is very consistently excluded from dramatic composition, although it is allowed a place in moral or didactic poetry. It implies perfect quiescence, or exemption from mental excitement, and is therefore uncongenial to the drama, the object of which is to paint and inspire passion. The advocates for its exclusion suggest a compromise, and transfer it from the persons of the play to the audience, who are thus fitted for the impressions to be made upon them. It is highly proper, it is urged, that they should exhibit the *Śānta Rasa*, and sit in silent attention, their tempers perfectly passive, and their hearts free from every external influence.

Conformably to the genius of mythological classification, the *Rasas* are by some authorities considered to be personified of various hues, and subject to the influence of different divinities, as follows:—

Śringāra,	black,	subject to	Vishńu.
Hāsya,	white,		Rāma.
Raudra,	red,		Rudra.
Víra,	red,		Sakra.
Karuńá,	gray,		Varuńa.
Bhayānaka,	black,		Yama.
Bíbhatsa,	blue,		Mahākála.
Adbhuta,	yellow,		Brahmá.

The arrangement appears, however, to be modern, and little recognised.

The combinations of the *Rasas* with each other, their modifications, and the manner in which they are affected by the intermixture of the different *Bhávas*, furnish the Hindu writers on the subject with ample opportunity to indulge their passion for infinite minutiæ. It may be observed, however, that this rage for subtile subdivision is most remarkable in writers of recent date, and the oldest works, as the *Daśa-Rúpaka* for instance, are contented with a moderate multiplication of definitions. As to the dramatic writers themselves, they might possibly have been influenced in some degree by theoretical principles, and in the example of one of the most celebrated, *Bhavabhúti*, we have his three pieces severally appropriated, like Miss Baillie's plays of the Passions, to distinct emotions: *Málatí and Mádhava*, to the *Śringára Rasa*, or love; the *Víra Charitra* to heroism, or the *Víra Rasa*; and the *Uttara-Ráma-Charitra* to the *Karuná Rasa*, or tenderness. We have no reason to think, however, that he, or any of the elder writers, troubled themselves about trifles, or knew or regarded the multiplied laws which have been derived from their practice. It is not so much to illustrate the plays themselves, that the foregoing picture of the system founded on them has been sketched, as to afford a view of the theatrical criticism of the Hindus, and a notion of their mode of theorising. We cannot now question that they had a theory, which has been elaborated with great diligence, if not with much success, and which, although it comprises many puerilities, is not wholly a stranger to just principles or refined taste.

As connected with the *Rasas*, we may notice one more division, which is less liable than the preceding to the charge of unnecessary trifling; it rather affects the construction than the objects of the drama, but as part of the means by which its purposes are effected, may not be inconveniently noticed here. According to Bharata's aphorisms, there are four *Vrittis*, which may be rendered Styles of Dramatic Representation, implying the general character of the dialogue and incidents, and which are severally appropriate to different *Rasas* or passions. They are termed *Kausikí, Sátwatí, Árabhatí,* and *Bháratí*. The three first are suited respectively to the *Śringára, Víra,* and *Raudra Rasas;* the last is common to all. The three first chiefly concern the incidents and situations: the latter regards the dialogue, and signifies merely appropriate and elegant language. The discovery of a lady's love, by her having painted a picture of her lover, which she vainly endeavours to conceal from a friend, is an incident in the *Kausikí*, or playful and pleasing style. Inspiring dread of treachery by fabricated documents or supposititious proofs belongs to the *Sátwatí*, the grave and serious style; and combat, tumult, magic, and natural portents, are occurrences in the style termed *Árabhatí*, the awful and appalling.

7. Diction.

The language of the Hindu theatre offers many peculiarities, but they can scarcely be fully detailed without citing the original passages, and could only be duly appreciated by students of the Sanskrit language. It will be sufficient for our purpose, therefore, to advert to the principal characteristics.

According to the original aphorism of Bharata, "the poet is to employ choice and harmonious terms, and an elevated and polished style, embellished with the ornaments of rhetoric and rhythm." The injunction has not been disregarded, and in no department of Hindu literature are the powers of the Sanskrit language more lavishly developed. In the late writers, the style is generally so painfully laboured as to be still more painfully read; but in the oldest and best pieces, the composition, although highly finished, is not in general of difficult apprehension. The language of Kálidása is remarkably easy; so is that of Bhavabhúti, in the *Uttara-Ráma-Charitra*. In his other two plays, and especially in *Málatí and Mádhava*, it is more elaborate and difficult. The *Mrichchhakatí* presents fewer difficulties than any of the whole series. The *Mudrá-Ráksasa* is one of the most unintelligible.

The ordinary business dialogue of the Hindu dramas is for the greater part in prose, but reflections or descriptions, and the poetical flights of the author, are in verse. Every one of the many kinds of Sanskrit metre is employed on the latter occasion, from the *Anushtubh* to the *Dandaka*, or verse of four lines of eight syllables each, to that which contains any number of syllables from twenty-seven to one hundred and ninety-nine. Bhavabhúti occasionally indulges in this last metre; Kálidása seldom, if ever. His favourite form appears to be the *Áryá* or *Gáthá;* but none of the poets confine themselves to a particular description. The first thirty-five stanzas of *Śakuntalá* exhibit eleven kinds of metre; and in the scene quoted from *Málatí and Mádhava* by Mr. Colebrooke, in his Essay on Sanskrit and Prákrit Prosody, in the tenth volume of the Asiatic Researches, we have the like number, or eleven varieties, for the greater part of the most complex description. That this diversity of composition enhances the difficulty of understanding the Hindu plays may be admitted, but it likewise adds to the richness and melody of the composition. It is impossible to conceive language so beautifully musical, or so magnificently grand, as that of many of the verses of Bhavabhúti and Kálidása.

Another peculiarity of the Hindu plays is their employing different forms of speech for different characters. This is not, like the *patois* of the French comedies, or the Scotch of English dramas, individual and occasional, but is general and invariable. The hero and the principal personages speak Sanskrit, but women and the inferior characters use the various modifications of that language which are comprehended under the term Prákrit. As observed by Mr. Colebrooke, in regard to this mixture of languages, the Italian theatre presents instances in the prose comedies of Ruzzanti; and the coincidence is noticed by Mr. Walker, with reference to Sir William Jones's remarks, prefixed to his translation of *Sakuntalá*. But these five-act farces, the notion of which was probably borrowed from the *Pœnulus* of Plautus, hold but an insignificant place in the dramatic literature of Italy, and the employment of the Venetian and Bergamask dialects by Goldoni is only like the use of those of Somersetshire or Yorkshire on the English stage, except that it is rather more prominent and frequent. In no theatre, however, have we a mixture of languages exactly analogous to that invariable in the drama of the Hindus.

" *Prákrit*," Sir William Jones observes (Preface to *Sakuntalá*), "is little more than the language of the Brahmans melted down, by a delicate articulation, to the softness of Italian :" in which he is quite correct, as far as the Prákrit spoken by the heroine and principal female personages is concerned. Mr. Colebrooke, however, more correctly intimates, that the term *Prákrit* is of a more comprehensive nature, and is properly applicable to all the written and cultivated dialects of India. It may be doubted, however, if it is usually understood in this sense, and the term is applied in the *Prákrit* grammars to a variety of forms, which agree only in name with the spoken dialects. Thus the *Mágadhí*, by which name may be considered that dialect which is more ordinarily understood by *Prákrit*, is very different from the vernacular language of Magadh or Behar. The

Saurasení is by no means the same with the dialect of Mathura and Vrindavan, and the *Mahárāshṭrí* would be of little avail in communicating with the Mahrattas, or people of *Mahárāshtra*. The other species enumerated are equally incapable of identification with the dialects to which they might be supposed to refer.

According to the technical authorities, the different dialects employed are these:—The heroine and principal female characters speak *Saurasení*; attendants on royal persons speak *Mágadhí*; servants, Rajputs, and traders, *Ardha*—half or mixed *Mágadhí*. The *Vidushaka* speaks the *Práchí*, or eastern dialect; rogues use *Avantiká*, or the language of Ougein; and intriguers that of the Dekhan or Peninsula. The dialect of *Báhlika* is spoken by the people of the north, and *Drāvida* by the people of the Coromandel coast. The individuals named *Sakas* and *Sakáris* speak dialects of their own; and cowherds, outcasts, and foresters, use their respective forms of speech. Even the imps of mischief have their appropriate jargon, and the *Pisáchas* or goblins, when introduced on the stage, speak a dialect of Prákrit termed *Paisáchí*.

If these directions were implicitly followed, a Hindu play would be a polyglot that few individuals could hope to understand. In practice, however, we have rarely more than three varieties, or Sanskrit, and a Prákrit more or less refined. In point of fact, indeed, there is little real difference in the several varieties of Prákrit: they all agree in grammatical structure, and in the most important deviations from Sanskrit, and only vary in their orthoepy, the lower kinds employing the harshest letters and rudest combinations. The words are essentially the same in all, and all are essentially the same with Sanskrit, the difference affecting the pronunciation and spelling rather than the radical structure, and tending generally to shorten the words, and substitute a soft for a hard, and a slurred for an emphatic articulation. Thus *lavaṇa*, salt, becomes *loṇa*; *mayūra*, a peacock, becomes *mora*; *madhuka*, a kind of tree, becomes *mahwa*; *purusha*, a man, is *puriso*; *srigāla*, a jackal, is *sidla*; *yauvana*, youth, is *jovaṇa*; and *bhavati* becomes *hodi*. Prákrit is also averse to some forms of conjunct consonants, and either changes them to a simple reduplication or omits one of them: as *nagna*, naked, becomes *dugga;* *vatsa,* a child, *bachchha;* and *chandra,* the moon, *chanda.* In the aspirated letters, the aspirate alone is usually retained: as *gahíra,* for *gambhíra,* deep; *sahá,* for *sabhá,* an assembly. These will be sufficient to characterise the general nature of the changes by which Sanskrit becomes Prákrit, and which will sufficiently prove their identity. At the same time, in long and complicated sentences, the affinity is not always so obvious as it might be supposed, and the occurrence of Prákrit offers a difficulty in the perusal of Sanskrit plays which is not readily overcome without the aid of a commentary, in which the passages are always translated into Sanskrit. Prákrit admits of most of the prosody of Sanskrit, and a due proportion of it is always written in varied metre. Its grammatical construction is marked by some peculiarities, such as the want of a dual number and dative case, and the employment of but one conjugation. The lower species are especially characterised by a disregard of grammatical concords, and the use of a common termination for every modification of gender, number, and person.

There is one question of some interest attaching to the construction of the Prákrit, which merits a fuller inquiry than has been yet given to it, and on which this is not the place to dilate. Does it represent a dialect that was ever spoken? or is it an artificial modification of the Sanskrit language, devised to adapt the latter to peculiar branches of literature? The latter seems to be the most likely; for there would be no difficulty in the present day in writing it, although it is no longer spoken, and highly-finished specimens are to be found in plays which are modern productions. The *Vidagdha-Mádhava,* for instance, consists more than half of high Prákrit, and it was written less than three centuries ago. On the other hand, many of the modifications are to be found in the spoken dialects of Hindustan, and the rules of Prákrit grammar account for changes which without such aid it is difficult to comprehend. The simplification of the grammatical construction, by the disuse of the dual number and the reduced number of verbal conjugations, looks also like the spontaneous substitution of practical to theoretic perfection in actual speech, and may tempt us to think the Prákrit was once a spoken tongue. The subject is interesting, not only in a philological, but in a historical view;

for the sacred dialects of the Bauddhas and the Jainas are nothing else than Prákrit, and the period and circumstances of its transfer to Ceylon and to Nepaul are connected with the rise and progress of that religion which is professed by the principal nations to the north and east of Hindustan.

8. Scenic Apparatus.

The Hindus never had any building appropriated to public entertainments; they could not, therefore, have had any complicated system of scenery or properties. It appears from several of the dramas, that in the palaces of kings there was a chamber or hall known as the *Sangíta-Sálá*, the music saloon, in which dancing and singing were practised and sometimes exhibited; but there is no reference to any separate edifice for such purposes, open to the public, either gratuitously or at a charge, and such an institution would be foreign to the state of society in the East, which in many respects certainly was not advanced beyond that of the Middle Ages in Europe, when minstrels and mimes were universally strollers, and performed in the halls of baronial castles, or in booths at fairs. In England, even, there appears to have been no resident company of players, or permanent theatre, earlier than the reign of Elizabeth. Companies of actors in India must have been common at an early date, and must have been reputable, for the inductions often refer to the poets as their personal friends, and a poet of tolerable merit in India, under the ancient regime, was the friend and associate of sages and kings. The Hindu actors were never apparently classed with vagabonds or menials, and were never reduced to contemplate a badge of servitude as a mark of distinction. As to theatrical edifices, the manners of the people, and the nature of the climate, were adverse to their existence, and the spacious open courts of the dwellings of persons of consequence were equally adapted to the purposes of dramatic representation and the convenience of the spectators. We should never forget, in speaking of the Hindu drama, that its exhibition, as has been noticed in the preface, was not an ordinary occurrence, or an amusement of the people, but that it was part of an occasional celebration of some solemn or religious festival.

The writers on dramatic systems furnish us with no information whatever on this part of our subject, with one exception, and in the *Sangīta-Ratnākara*, alone, have we any allusion to the place in which performances were held. The description there given, indeed, rather applies to a place for the exhibition of singing and dancing; but it was, no doubt, the same with that in which dramatic representations took place, and the audiences were similarly composed on both occasions. The description is not very precise, but the following is the purport.

"The chamber in which dancing is to be exhibited should be spacious and elegant. It should be covered over by an awning, supported by pillars richly decorated and hung with garlands. The master of the house should take his seat in the centre, on a throne: the inmates of the private apartments should be seated on his left, and persons of rank upon his right. Behind both are to be seated the chief officers of the state or household, and poets, astrologers, physicians, and men of learning, are to be arranged in the centre. Female attendants, selected for their beauty and figure, are to be about the person of the principal, with fans and chowries, whilst persons carrying wands are to be stationed to keep order, and armed men as guards are to be placed in different directions. When all are seated, the band is to enter and perform certain airs; after which the chief dancer is to advance from behind the curtain, and after saluting the audience, scattering at the same time flowers amongst them, she will display her skill."

The direction for the appearance of the dancer here indicates the separation of the performers from the audience by a screen or curtain; and of this frequent proofs are afforded, by the stage directions in different plays. The stage itself was termed *Ranga Bhūmi* or *Nepathya;* but the latter term is also applied to the "within," as sounds or exclamations off the stage are said to occur, in the *Nepathya*. We might infer the distinction, also, from the instructions of *praviśati* and *niskkrāmati*, "enter and exit," which are invariably given; but they admit the possibility, as was the case in the early French theatre, of the actors, continually in view of the audience throughout, coming forward and withdrawing as required, without ever disappearing. It is often said, however, where a character makes his appearance under the influence of hurry or alarm, that he enters *apaṭīkṣhe-*

peda, with a toss of the curtain, throwing up or aside, apparently, the cloth suspended in the flat, instead of coming on regularly from the wing. It seems possible, also, that curtains were suspended transversely, so as to divide the stage into different portions, open equally to the audience, but screening one set of actors from the other, as if the one were within, and the other without a house or chamber. The first piece in the following collection often requires some such arrangement; unless, as is by no means unlikely, the whole was left to the imagination. It would appear, also, by the same piece, that part of the stage was raised, so as to form a terrace or balcony, as it was in Shakespeare's time in England.

The properties of the Hindu stage were, no doubt, as limited as the scenery, but seats, thrones, weapons, and cars with live cattle were used. The introduction of the latter is frequent, and could not always have been imaginary, being, as in the *Mrichchhakati* especially, indispensable to the business. Whether any contrivance was had recourse to, to represent the aërial chariots of the gods, is rather doubtful.

Costume was always observed, and various proofs occur of the personages being dressed in character. Females were represented in general by females; but it appears not to have been uncommon for men or lads to personate female characters, especially those of a graver character, like the Bauddha priestess in *Málati and Mádhava*.

There is no want of instruction for stage business, and we have the "asides" and "aparts" as regularly indicated as in the modern theatre in Europe. Even German precision is not unfrequently affected, and the sentiment with which the speaker is to deliver himself particularised. In directions for passing from one place to another, much is evidently left to the imagination, and the spectator must eke out the distance traversed by his own conceptions. There is often much want of dexterity in this part of the business, and a very little ingenuity would have avoided the incongruities produced. The defect, however, is common to the early plays of all theatres, and in Shakspeare we find some very clumsy contrivances. Thus, in *Richard the Second*, the king orders the trumpets to sound, whilst the council apparently discusses what is to be done with Hereford and Norfolk; and without any further intervention, Richard commands the combatants, who as well as the king and the peers have been all the time on the stage, "to draw near and list, what with our council we have done."

These are the only notices that can be offered of the theatrical representations of the Hindus, and although scanty, leave no doubt of their general character. The Hindu stage, in fact, is best illustrated by those labours which have been so successfully addressed to the history of the stage in Europe, to which, prior to the sixteenth century, it may be considered precisely analogous, with the advantages of attention to costume and female personation. We must not extend this analogy, however, to the literary merits of the two theatres, as much of that of the Hindus may compete successfully with the greater number of the dramatic productions of modern Europe, and offers no affinity to the monstrous and crude abortions which preceded the introduction of the legitimate drama in the west.

LIST OF HINDU PLAYS.

- * Mŕichchhakatí.
- Sakuntalá (translated by Sir William Jones).
- * Vikrama and Urvasí.
- † Málaviká and Agnimitra.
- * Uttara-Ráma-Charitra.
- * Málatí and Mádhava.
- † Mahávíra-Charitra.
- † Vení-Saṃhára.
- * Mudrá-Rákshasa.
- ‡ Udátta-Rághava.
- † Hanuman-Nátaka.
- * Ratnávalí.
- † Vidilhá-Sálábhanjiká.
- ‡ Bála-Rámáyaṇa.
- † Prachaṇḍa-Páṇḍava.
- ‡ Karpúra-Manjarí.
- ‡ Jámadagnya-Jaya.
- ‡ Samudra-Mathana.
- ‡ Tripuradáha.
- † Dhananjaya-Vijaya.
- ‡ Anargha-Rághava.
- † Sárada-Tilaka.
- † Yayáti-Charitra.
- ‡ Yayáti-Vijaya.
- ‖ Yayáti and Sarmishthá.
- † Dútángada.
- † Mŕigánkalekhá.
- † Vidagdha-Mádhava.
- † Abhiráma-Maṇi.
- † Madhuraniruddha.

- † Kaṃsa-Badha.
- † Pradyumna-Vijaya.
- † Srídáma-Charitra.
- † Dhúrtta-Narttaka.
- † Dhúrtta-Samágama.
- † Hásyárṇava.
- † Kautuka-Sarvaswa.
- Prabodha-Chandrodaya (translated by Dr. Taylor).
- ‖ Rámábhyudaya.
- ‖ Kunda-Mála.
- ‖ Saugandhikáharaṇa.
- ‖ Kusumaśekhara-Vijaya.
- ‖ Raivata-Madaniká.
- ‖ Narmavatí.
- ‖ Vilásavatí.
- ‖ Śringára-Tilaka.
- ‖ Deví-Mahádeva.
- ‖ Yádavodaya.
- ‖ Báli-Badha.
- ‖ Anekamurtta.
- ‖ Mayakapáliká.
- ‖ Krídárnsátala.
- ‖ Kanakavatí-Mádhava.
- ‖ Vindumatí.
- ‖ Kelinivataka.
- ‖ Kámadattá.
- ¶ Sankalpa-Súryodaya.
- ¶ Sudarsana-Vijaya.
- ¶ Vasantiká Pariṇaya.
- † Chitra-Yajna.

Those marked * are now translated, and some account is given of those marked † : the rest have not been procured.

Those marked ‡ are named in the *Daśa-Rúpaka*, and those marked || in the *Sáhitya-Darpaṇa*, as examples of the different kinds of dramatic composition. The three pieces marked ¶ were amongst the late Colonel Mackenzie's collection, and are known only in the south of India.

THE MRICHCHHAKATI,

OR

THE TOY-CART.

A Drama,

TRANSLATED FROM THE ORIGINAL

SANSKRIT.

PRELIMINARY NOTE.

THE uncertainty of the sounds to be given to the proper names that occur in the following pages will necessarily impair any satisfaction that their perusal may possibly afford. This difficulty may, however, be readily overcome by attention to a few simple rules.

The only letters to which any regard need be paid are the vowels *a, e, i,* and *u.*

A, i, and *u,* are distinguished as long or as short by an accent over the long vowel, as *a, á; i, í; u, ú.*

E, i, and *u,* whether long or short, are to be pronounced as in Italian, and so is the long or accented *á.*

The unaccented *a* has the sound of that letter in *adore, adorn, America,* or of *u* in *sun.* This is the most perplexing part of the system, but it rests on grounds that need not be detailed here. If written as pronounced, the names of the hero and heroine should be *Charoodutta* and *Vusuntusená,* instead of *Chárudatta, Vasantasená.*

The following recapitulation will afford a ready reference:

  a short or unaccented, as *u* in *sun;*
  á long or accented, as *a* in *far;*
  e, as *a* in *care;*
  i short or unaccented, as *i* in *kill;*
  í long or accented, as *ee* in *keel;*
  u short or unaccented, as *u* in *full;*
  ú long or accented, as *oo* in *fool.*

It is also necessary to observe, that the syllable *ka* at the end of a proper name is an optional addition; thus *Chandana* and *Chandanaka, A'rya* and *A'ryaka,* are the same.

INTRODUCTION.

THE drama of which the translation is now published is a work of great interest, both in the literary and national history of the Hindus.

Although not named by the authority from which we have principally drawn our general view of the Hindu dramatic system, the *Daśa-Rúpaka*, it is unquestionably alluded to in the text of that work, and we may therefore feel assured that this play was written earlier than the tenth century; there is every reason to infer much earlier.

The introduction of the *Mrichchhakaṭí* attributes the composition to a king named SÚDRAKA, and gives him a high character both in arms and letters: he lived, it is said, a hundred years and then burnt himself, leaving his kingdom to his son.

Over what kingdom SÚDRAKA ruled is not mentioned. The writer of the *Kámandakí* says it was *Avantí* or *Oujein;* tradition, especially in the *Dekhin*, includes him amongst the universal monarchs of India, and places him between CHANDRAGUPTA and VIKRAMÁDITYA, without specifying his capital. The late Col. Wilford (*As. Res.* vol. ix.) considers him the same with the founder of the *Ándhra* dynasty of *Magadha* kings, succeeding to the throne by deposing his master, the last of the *Kanwa* race, to whom he was minister; but these averments are very questionable. The circumstances are in fact attributed, it is said (p. 116), to a prince named BÁLIHITA, or SIPRAKA, or SINDHUKA, or (p. 103) MÁHAKARṆI—and the identification of SÚDRAKA with either or all of these, rests upon chronological data by no means satisfactorily established. From these (p. 100) it appears, that the first *Andhra* king of *Magadha* reigned 456 years earlier than the last, or PULIMAT, who, it is said, died A.D. 648 (p. 111), consequently the former reigned about A.D. 192. But it is stated, that in a work called the *Kumárikà-Khańḍa*, a portion of the *Skanda-Purána*, it is asserted that in the year of the *Kali* 3300—save 10—a great king would reign (it does not appear where) named SÚDRAKA. This date in our era is 190; the date of the first *Andhra* king, as mentioned above, is 192; *therefore* SÚDRAKA must be that king: a deduction which may possibly be correct, but which depends too much upon the accuracy of a work very little known, and upon a calculation that yet requires to be revised, to be considered as decidedly invalidating the popular notion, that SÚDRAKA preceded VIKRAMÁDITYA, and consequently the era of Christianity, by a century at least.

The attribution of a play to a regal author is not a singular occurrence. The *Ratnávalí*, as will be hereafter noticed, is ascribed to a bard of like dignity: whether truly or not, whether the monarch was not rather the patron than the poet, is immaterial to the chronology of the drama; as, if the work of SÚDRAKA'S reign, it may be considered as the oldest extant specimen of the Hindu drama, and a composition of respectable antiquity. The play contains abundant internal evidence of an ancient date.

The style, though not meagre, is in general simple and unartificial, and of a day evidently preceding the elaborate richness of Hindu writing, not to speak of the fantastic tricks and abuses which began to disgrace Sanskrit composition apparently in the ninth and tenth centuries. This may be considered a safe indication in a work of such pretence as one attributed to a regal bard; and although it could not be admitted alone as conclusive, yet, as associated with the name and date of SÚDRAKA, it is a strong confirmation of the latter, at least, being correct.

Another circumstance in favour of the antiquity of the drama is derived from a peculiarity in the language of one of the chief characters. SAṄSTHÁNAKA, the *Rája's* brother-in-law, affects literature, with which he has so little conversancy, that his citations of poetic personages and events are as erroneous as frequent. Now it is a remarkable circumstance that all his citations are from the *Rámáyaṇa* and *Mahábhárata*, and that he never alludes to the chief actors in the Paurâṅik legends, as *Dhruva, Daksha, Prahláda, Bali,* &c. There can be no good reason why he should not cite from a *Puráṇa* as well as from either of the poems which bear a similarly holy character, and it is not likely that the author of the drama, who was thoroughly familiar with the poems, should not have been acquainted with the *Puráṇas* if they had existed, or been equally in circulation: we have great reason therefore to suspect that the *Mṛichchhakatí* was written prior to the composition of the *Puráṇas*, or at least before the stories they contain had acquired by their aggregation familiar and popular currency.

Peculiarities in manners contribute to a similar conclusion, and the very panegyric upon SÚDRAKA, specifying his voluntary cremation when arrived at extreme old age, praises him for an act proscribed in the *Kali*, or present period of the world. By all current legal authorities, except the texts of the most ancient, suicide is prohibited everywhere except at *Prayága*, and is there allowed only under certain circumstances. The prohibition may be disregarded, it is true, but such a breach of the law could not with any decency have been made the theme of public eulogium by a Brahman in the Sanskṛit language, and therefore the event most probably preceded the law.

The subject of the piece, the love of a respectable Brahman for a courtesan, is also in favour of a period of some remoteness, although it may be allowed to mark a state of social demoralisation, a decline from the purity of Hindu institutions; at the same time, it seems probable that the practice of antiquity, as regarded the intercourse of the sexes, was much more lax than it pretends to be in modern days. The laws of MANU

8   INTRODUCTION.

recognise the cohabitation of a *Śúdrá* female with a Brahman, as an inferior kind of wife, or a handmaid. Now this association is prohibited in the *Kali* age, and its occurrence in the play, in which VASANTASENÁ, who may be supposed to be a *Śúdrá*, becomes the wife of CHÁRUDATTA, indicates a period anterior to the law prohibiting the marriage of a *Śúdrá* by a Brahman. The choice of such an event for the subject of a dramatic performance, renders it likely that such a prohibition could not have been then even contemplated.

The most unquestionable proof, however, of high antiquity, is the accuracy with which *Bauddha* observances are adverted to, and the flourishing condition in which the members of that sect are represented to exist. There is not only absolute toleration, but a kind of public recognition; the ascetic who renders such essential service to the heroine being recommended or nominated by authority, chief of all the *Vihára* or *Bauddha* establishments of *Ujjayin.*

At what period could this diffusion and prosperity of the *Bauddha* faith have occurred, and when was it likely that a popular work should describe it correctly? Many centuries have elapsed since Hindu writers were acquainted with the *Bauddhas* in their genuine characters. Their tenets are preserved in philosophical treatises with something like accuracy, but any attempt to describe their persons and practices invariably confounds them with the *Jainas.* The *Mrichchhakati* is as yet the only work where the *Bauddhas* appear undisguised. Now we know from the Christian writers of the second century, that in their days the worship of *Butta* or *Buddha* was very prevalent in India. We have every reason to believe, that shortly after that time the religion began to decline, more in consequence of the rise and growth of the Jains, probably, than any persecution of the *Bauddhas;* and as it is clear that the drama was written in the days of their prosperity, it follows that we cannot fairly assign it a later date than the first centuries of the Christian era.

From the considerations thus stated, we cannot but regard

the *Mrichchhakatí* as a work of considerable antiquity, and from internal evidence may very safely attribute it to the period when SÚDRAKA the sovereign reigned, whether that be reduced to the end of the second century after Christ, or whether we admit the traditional chronology, and place him about a century before our era.

The revolution in the government of *Ujjayin*, which forms an underplot in the piece, is narrated with so little exaggeration, that it is probably founded on fact. As the simple narrative of a simple event, it is the more entitled to our credence; and it is not at all unlikely that the Brahmans, offended by their sovereign PÁLAKA's public disregard of them, brought about a change of the government, employing a hermit and a cow-boy, or young peasant, as their instruments. This plain story is not improbably the origin of the obscure allusions which exercised the industry of Colonel Wilford, and in which, and in the purport of the word *A'rya*, the name of the cowherd in the play, and in general acceptation a title of respect, he thought he could trace a reference to the history of Christianity in India.—(*As. Res.* vol. x., Essay on the Sacred Isles of the West.) There is also an *A'rya* of some renown in the history of *Cashmir*, whom the same learned and laborious, but injudicious writer, identified with *Sálivahana*. The real character of that personage may now be more accurately appreciated.—(Essay on the History of Cashmir, *As. Res.* vol. xv. p. 84.)

The place which the *Mrichchhakatí* holds in the dramatic literature of all nations will, however, be thought matter of more interest by most readers than its antiquity or historical importance. That it is a curious and interesting picture of national manners every one will readily admit; and it is not the less valuable in this respect, that it is free from all exterior influence or adulteration. It is a portrait purely Indian. It represents a state of society sufficiently advanced in civilisation to be luxurious and corrupt, and is certainly very far from offering a flattering similitude, although not without some attractive features. There will probably be more variety of opinion on its merits as a literary composition, and its title to rank with the more polished dramas of the West may be called in question by competent judges. As observed by the spirited translator of Aristophanes, it is no longer the fashion for translators to direct the taste of their readers, and they must be left to condemn or approve for themselves. I shall therefore refrain from any further observations on this head; and if, in imitation of high authority, I venture to subjoin my own sentiments by way of epilogue, I shall do so as briefly as possible, and without any hope to bias the judgment of the public.

DRAMATIS PERSONÆ.

OF THE PRELUDE.

MANAGER. ACTRESS.

OF THE PLAY.

Men.

Chárudatta.—A Brahman of a wealthy and respectable family, reduced to poverty by his munificence, beloved by *Vasantasená.*

Rohasena.—The son of *Chárudatta,* a boy.

Maitreya.—A Brahman, the friend and companion of *Chárudatta,* the *Vidúshaka* or *Gracioso* of the piece, a character of mixed shrewdness and simplicity, with an affectionate disposition.

Vardhamána.—The servant of *Chárudatta.*

Sansthánaka.—The brother-in-law of the *Rájá,* an ignorant, frivolous, and cruel coxcomb.

The *Vita.*—The attendant, tutor, or parasite of the preceding.

Sthávaraka.—The servant of the Prince.

A'ryaka.—A cowherd and insurgent, finally successful.

Sarvilaka.—A dissipated Brahman, the friend of the preceding, in love with *Madaniká.*

The *Samváhaka.*—A man whose business it has been to rub and knead the joints, but who becomes a *Bauddha* mendicant or *Sramadáka.*

Máthura.—The keeper of a gaming-house.

Darduraka.—A Gambler.

Another Gambler.

Kardapáraka.—*Vasantasená's* servant.

The Judge.

The *Sreshlin*—or Provost.

The *Kápuska*.—Scribe or Recorder.
Chandanaka } Captains of the Town Guard.
Víraka
The *Vita*—or parasite attendant of *Vasantasená*.
Kumbhílaka.—A servant of *Vasantasená*.
Two *Chándálas*—or Public Executioners.
Officers of the Court.

Women.

The Wife of *Chárudatta*.
Vasantasená.—A courtezan, in love with *Chárudatta*, and beloved by him; the object also of *Sansthánaka's* addresses.
The Mother of *Vasantasená*.
Madaniká.—The attendant of *Vasantasená*, beloved by *Sarvilaka*.
Radaniká.—The servant of *Chárudatta's* house.

Persons spoken of.

Pálaka.—King of *Ujjayin*.
Rebhila.—A Musician.
The *Siddha* or Seer who has prophesied *A'ryaka's* triumph.

Passengers, Attendants, Guards, &c.

Scene, *Ujjayin*, the city and the suburbs.——Time, four days.

ACT I.

PRELUDE.

BENEDICTION.*

I. MAY that profound meditation of SAMBHU† protect you! (*the audience*) which is intent on BRAHMAN, the absorbing end of every effort of abstract vision; as he contemplates with the eye of wisdom, spirit, in himself, detached from all material instruments; his senses being restrained by holy knowledge, as he sits ruminating with suspended breath, whilst his serpents coil with the folds of his vesture round his bended knees.‡

---

* It is not said by whom this is uttered, and the Manager enters after it has been spoken.

† SAMBHU, a name of SIVA.

‡ This benediction alludes to the practices and notions of the *Pátanjala* modification of the *Sánkhya* philosophy, the *Yoga*, in which, by abstract meditation, *samadhi*, the fusion (*laya*) of individual with universal spirit, or *Brahmaa*, is to be effected, even in the body. Spirit is said to be detached from the instruments, *karanas*, the thirteen products of matter, or *mahat*, intellect; *ahankára*, consciousness; and the eleven organs of sense and action, which are enumerated amongst the categories of the *Sánkhya* system. The mode of effecting this union is by sitting in particular *asanas*, or postures; one of which is sitting on the hams with a cloth fastened round the knees and back, the *paryanka-bandhana*, or, as here termed, the *paryanka-granthi*, the bed-binding or bed-knot; also by suppressions of breath as long as practicable, *pránaswrodha*; by keeping the vision directed either on vacuity or inwardly, *sûnyekshana*; and by preventing as vigilantly as possible the wanderings of the senses. That this form of devotion may boast of considerable antiquity is evident from its being described and commended in the *Mahábhárata*, and being the prevailing system in the *Puránas*, especially those of a *Saiva* character, in some of which the origin

II. May the neck of *Nīlakaṇṭha*,* which resembles a dark cloud in hue, and which is decorated by the entwining arms of *Gaurī*,† as brilliant as the lightning, be ever your protection.

Enter MANAGER.

Enough: delay not longer to gratify the curiosity of this assembly. Saluting, therefore, this gentle audience, I apprise them that we are prepared to enact the drama entitled the *Toy-Cart*.‡

There was a celebrated poet whose gait was that of an elephant, whose eyes resembled those of the *chakora*,§ whose countenance was like the full moon, and who was of stately person and profound veracity; chiefest of the *Kshattriya* race and distinguished by the appellation of SÚDRA :|| he was well versed in the *Ṛig-* and *Sāma-Vedas*, in mathematical sciences, in the elegant arts, and the management of elephants.¶ By the favour of *Śiva* he enjoyed eyes uninvaded by darkness,

of the *Yoga* is ascribed to ŚIVA, who taught it in the person of ŚWETA, on the Himalaya mountains in the beginning of the *Kali age*. A peculiar and later modification of *Yoga* ascetism is manifest in the cavern temples and sculptures of Salsette, Elephanta, and Ellora.—See *As. Res.* vol. xvii. 183.

* A name of ŚIVA; the god with the dark-blue throat. The colour was the effect of the poison generated at the churning of the ocean which ŚIVA swallowed.

† The wife of ŚIVA.

‡ The term is literally *clay-cart*, a child's cart made of baked clay or earthenware, from *mṛid*, earth, and *śakaṭ*, a little cart. It refers to a toy belonging to the child of Chárudatta, which, as will be hereafter seen, plays an important part in the drama. The equivalent *Toy-Cart* is most familiar to our language, and is less equivocal than the literal translation. The play is termed a *prakaraṇa*, the second species of drama.

§ The Greek partridge.

‖ See the Introduction. The additional syllable *ka* is pleonastic.

¶ The *Hasti-likhā*: it is an accomplishment curiously characteristic of national manners. The proficiency of the Indians in this art early attracted the attention of Alexander's successors; and natives of India were so long exclusively employed in this service, that the term Indian was applied to every elephant-driver, to whatever country he might belong.—*Schlegel, Indische Bibliothek.*

and beheld his son seated on the throne: after performing the exalted *Aswamedha*,* having attained the age of a hundred years and ten days, he entered the fatal fire.† Valiant was he in war, and ready to encounter with his single arm the elephant of his adversary; yet he was void of wrath, eminent amongst those skilled in the *Vedas*, and affluent in piety: a prince was SÚDRAKA. In this drama, written by him, it is thus related.

In *Avanti*‡ lived a young Brahman of distinguished

---

* The emblematic sacrifice of a horse: one of the most solemn rites of Hindus in ancient times.

† That the practice of terminating life whenever burdened with age or infirmity was held, if not meritorious, to be justifiable, we know from the authorities which declare it to be so no longer. The *Nirnaya-Sindhu*, and other treatises on Hindu law, enumerate suicide on account of protracted life amongst the acts prohibited in the present age. These works are, however, comparatively modern; and that the practice of voluntary cremation was observed long subsequent to the beginning of the *Kali* era, we know from classical authority. The stories told by Herodotus of the Indians who put their infirm or aged relations to death, originated probably in some indistinct accounts of this usage. Megasthenes asserts that there was no fixed rule on this subject, and intimates that the sages of India reprehended the practice. Zarmanochegas (*Sramanáchárya*) burnt himself at Athens, "after the custom of his country;" and *Calanus* (*Kalyána*) mounted the funeral pile at Pasargadæ in the presence of the astonished Greeks, who were at a loss to consider the act as that of a sage or a madman, and were never of a mood to imitate such a model. Whether the rite was founded on positive prescription we are not aware, but instances of it are given in works of the highest character and of a weight little inferior to the inspired codes. In the *Rámáyana*, *Sarabhanga* the sage only delays his cremation until he has seen Ráma; after which, "having prepared the fire and offered oblations with the customary prayers, the pious and perfect *Sarabhanga* entered the flames."—*Aranya-Kánda*. The commentary on the drama states that the ceremony should be accompanied with the sacrifice called *sarvaswara*: it should probably be *sarvamedha*, prayers and oblations for universal success. The commentator is rather at a loss to explain how the author of the play announces his own death, and is disposed to ascribe it to his prophetic foresight acquired by astrological computation. There can be little doubt, however, that such part of the proems as relates to the personal history of the author is usually the work of another hand.

‡ The modern Oujein.

rank,* but of exceeding poverty; his name was CHÁRUDATTA. Of the many excellences of CHÁRUDATTA, a courtesan, VASANTASENÁ by name, became enamoured, and the story of their loves is the subject of king SÚDRAKA's drama, which exhibits the infamy of wickedness, the villainy of law, the efficacy of virtue, and the triumph of faithful love.

(*Walks round the stage.*)

Hey! the boards are deserted:† where can all the actors have vanished? Ah, I understand. Empty is the house of the childless—empty is the heart of one that has no friends;‡ the universe is a blank to the blockhead, and all is desolate to the poor. I have been chanting and reciting until my eyes ache, the pupils twinkling with hunger, like the seeds of the lotus shrivelled in the hot weather by the rays of a scorching sun.§ I will call one of my wenches, and see if there be anything in the house for breakfast. What ho there—Here am I! But I had better talk to them in a language they can understand.‖—What ho—I say! What with long fasting and loud shouting my limbs are shrivelled like dry lotus stalks. It is high time to take myself home, and see what is prepared for my coming. This is my mansion—I will go in.

* The *Sírthavaha* of the Brahmans. In many of the Hindu cities the different classes of the community of every rank still acknowledge certain of their members as their hereditary headmen or provosts—such is the house of *Sreshtin* or *Seth*: the title in common use is *Chaudri* or *Sirdar*. It is also to be inferred from this title, that *Chárudatta*, though a Brahman by birth, is a merchant by occupation.

† The *Sangíta-sálá*, a hall or chamber for music, singing, and dancing.

‡ This passage occurs in the *Hitopadésa* and *Panchatantra*, borrowed perhaps from the drama. The latter reads *hrídayasúnyanam*, instead of *chiradasúnyam*: the metre allows of either, and the construction of the sentence evidently requires the former.

§ The expression is, *Kshudhá mama akshiní kholakhaidyete*, which may be rendered as in the text, but cannot be translated, for the verb is made from the noun with more regard to the sound than the sense.

¶ Or in *Prákrit*, which is spoken always by the female characters; he accordingly proceeds in that dialect throughout the whole of the Prelude.

THE TOY-CART. 17

Enters.[*]

Hey day !—Some new frolic is going on in this mansion of mine. The ground, like a young damsel fresh from her toilet, wears a *tilaka* [†] smeared with the discoloured water of the rice that has been boiled in the iron kettle, and is perfumed with most savoury smells. Verily, my hunger increaseth. What, in the name of wonder, have my people found a treasure—or from the promptings of my appetite do I fancy everything smacks of boiled rice? If there be no breakfast for me at home, this hunger will be the death of me. Yet everything puts on a new face: one hussy is grinding perfumes, another is stringing flowers : [‡] the meaning of all this must be inquired into. Come hither one of you.

Enter ACTRESS.

Act. Here am I, sir.

Man. Welcome, welcome.

Act. What are your commands?

Man. Hark ye, girl, I have been bawling myself both hoarse and hungry : is there anything in the house for me to eat?

Act. There is everything, sir.

Man. Indeed ; and what is there?

Act. For example—there is rice, dressed or undressed, sugar, curds ; in short, there is sustenance for a century [§]— so may the gods comply with all your desires.

---

[*] *Pravisya avalokya cha :* Having entered and looked round. How the entrance is managed we are rather at a loss to conjecture, as no change of scene was probably attempted. In the spacious hall, however, in which the piece was acted, one part of the stage was in all likelihood supposed to represent the exterior, the other the interior of the dwelling.

[†] Or *tilataka*, a mark with some coloured substance made in the middle of the forehead.

[‡] The use of perfumes and garlands amongst the Hindus affords a parallel, both as an accompaniment to religious and convivial rites, to the usages of Athens and Rome.

[§] *Ajivra attavram vashudam.* Literally, the drug that confers immortality is to be eaten by the master.

VOL. I.

Man. Hark ye, my girl, is all this in my house, or do you jest?

Act. (*Apart.*) Oh, as he doubts, I will have a laugh at him. (*Aloud.*) Indeed and indeed, sir, there is all that I have mentioned—in the market.

Man. Ah, you hussy! May you be so disappointed. The deuce take you—you have hoisted me up like a ball on a turret top,* that I might tumble down again.

Act. Patience, sir, patience, I did but jest.

Man. Then what is the meaning of all this unusual preparation; this grinding of perfumes and stringing of chaplets? The ground is strewed with offerings of flowers of every dye.

Act. We hold a solemn fast to-day.†

Man. A fast, for what?

Act. That we may have a desirable master.‡

Man. In this world, or the next?

Act. Ah, in the next, to be sure.

Man. Here, gentles (*to the audience*), here is pretty usage: these damsels would engage a new manager in another world at my expense in this!

---

* The expression used does not seem to have been understood by the commentator. The words are, *turaśila lambuo* (S. *turaśida-lambuta*). The first is said to mean a long stick; the second, a column of clay fastened to one end of it, which, when raised mechanically to a given height, falls down by its own weight. A machine of this kind, a stick or bamboo resting on a fulcrum, with a weight at one end and a rope and bucket at the other, is used in some parts of India for drawing water. Or *turaśida* is explained a lofty part of a building; *lambuta*, one part of it, which having been carried up to be attached to the top of the *turaśida*, as a ball or pinnacle, falls down by accident. Neither of these explanations is very satisfactory, and the occurrence of such terms as these, of which the import must have been once familiar, but which is now uncertain, is a circumstance corroborative of the supposed antiquity of the composition.

† Every fast, when held as a religious observance on particular occasions, is a prelude to a feast.

‡ The Manager asks what is the name of the fast, every religious rite bearing its own appellation. The Actress replies, it is called the *Abhirúbabadi* or *Abhirúpapati*, which implies the meaning given in the text.

Act. Be appeased, sir. I have observed the fast, in order that I might have you again for my master in a future birth.

Man. That alters the case. But, pray, who directed you to hold this fast?

Act. Your particular friend, Chúrńavŕiddha.

Man. Oh, you son of a slave, I shall see you, Chúrńavŕiddha, some day or other, fast bound by king *Pálaka*, like the perfumed tresses of a new-married girl.

Act. Pardon us, dear sir; this fast was observed to secure the future felicity of our worthy Manager. (*Falls at his feet.*)

Man. Rise; enough. We must now consider by whom this fast is to be completed.

Act. We must invite some Brahman* of our own degree.

Man. Well, go, finish your preparations: I will seek the Brahman.

Act. I obey. [*Exit.*

MANAGER.

Alas! in such a flourishing city as *Ujjayin*, where am I to find a Brahman who is not of a superior rank to mine! (*Looking out.*) Yonder comes Maitreya, the friend of Chárudatta. I will ask him; he is poor enough. What, ho! Maitreya; condescend to be the first to eat in my house to-day.

MAITREYA (*behind the scenes*).

Call some other Brahman; I am particularly engaged.

Man. Food is provided; no enemy is in the way, and you shall have a present into the bargain.

Mait. (*Behind.*) I have already given you an answer. It is useless to disturb me.

Man. I shall not prevail upon him, and must therefore set off in quest of some other Brahman. [*Exit.*

---

* A Brahman should be invited to eat on these occasions before the household break their fast. The Manager and his family belong of course to the Brahmanical tribe.

(*The Scene* is supposed to represent a street on one side, and on the other the first court of Chárudatta's house: the outside of the house is also seen in the part next the street.*)

MAITREYA *enters the court with a piece of cloth in his hand.*

Truly, Maitreya, your condition is sad enough, and well qualified to subject you to be picked up in the street and fed by strangers. In the days of Chárudatta's prosperity, I was accustomed to stuff myself till I could eat no more, on scented dishes, until I breathed perfume; and sat lolling at yonder gateway, dyeing my fingers like a painter's, by dabbling amongst the coloured comfits, or chewing the cud at leisure like a high-fed city bull.† Now, in the season of his poverty, I wander about from house to house, like a lame pigeon, to pick up such crumbs as I can get. I am now sent by his dear friend Chúrńavŕiddha, with this garment that has lain amongst jasmine flowers till it is quite scented by them: it is for Chárudatta's wearing, when he has finished his devotions.—Oh, here he comes, he is presenting the oblation to the household gods.†

Enter CHÁRUDATTA *and* RADANIKÁ.

Chár. (*With a sigh.*)
    Alas! how changed; the offering to the gods,

---

* We have already observed that it does not seem probable that the Hindus ever knew what scenes were, and that they substituted curtains for them. In the present case, the whole machinery might have been a curtain intersecting the stage at a right angle to the flat, one side being the interior, the other the exterior of Chárudatta's house.

† The Hindus are accustomed at marriages and other ceremonials to let loose a bull, who thenceforward rambles about at will without an owner. No person would presume to appropriate a stray animal of this kind, and many think it a merit to feed him. In large towns, where these bulls are most abundant, they are generally in good case, and numerous enough to be very much in the way, although they are rarely mischievous. They seem to know their privileged character, and haunt the market-places and shops with an air of independence. At Benares, they are proverbially abundant, and that city is famed for its *rdarh*, *siarh*, and *sirhi*, or widows, bulls, and landing-places.

That swans and stately storks, in better time
About my threshold flocking, bore away,
Now a scant tribute to the insect tribe,
Falls 'midst rank grass, by worms to be devoured.*

(*Sits down.*)

Mait. I will approach the respectable Chárudatta. Health to you; may you prosper.

Chár. Maitreya, friend of all seasons, welcome; sit you down.

Mait. As you command. (*Sits down.*) This garment, perfumed by the jasmines it has lain amongst, is sent to you by your friend Chúrńavŕiddha, to be worn by you at the close of your devotions.

Chár. (*Takes it and appears thoughtful.*)

Mait. On what do you meditate?

Chár. My friend—

The happiness that follows close on sorrow,
Shows like a lamp that breaks upon the night:

---

* No house is supposed to be without its tutelary divinity, but the notion attached to this character is now very far from precise. The deity who is the object of hereditary and family worship, the *Kula-devatá*, is always one of the leading personages of the Hindu mythology, as Śiva, Vishńu, or Durgá, but the *Griha-devatá* rarely bears any distinct appellation. In Bengal, the domestic god is sometimes the *sálagrám* stone, sometimes the *tulasí* plant; sometimes a basket with a little rice in it, and sometimes a water-jar—to either of which a brief adoration is daily addressed, most usually by the females of the family. Occasionally small images of Lakshmí or Chańdí fulfil the office, or should a snake appear he is venerated as the guardian of the dwelling. In general, however, in former times the household deities were regarded as the unseen spirits of ill, the ghosts and goblins who hovered about every spot, and claimed some particular sites as their own. Offerings were made to them in the open air, by scattering a little rice with a short formula at the close of all ceremonies to keep them in good humour. Thus, at the end of the daily ceremony, the householder is enjoined by Manu "to throw up his oblation (*bali*) in the open air to all the gods, to those who walk by day and those who walk by night."—3, 90. Such is the nature of the rite alluded to in the drama. In this light, the household gods correspond better with the *genii locorum* than with the *lares* or *penates* of antiquity.

    But he that falls from affluence to poverty,
    May wear the human semblance, but exists
    A lifeless form alone.
Mait. What think you preferable then, death or poverty?
Chdr. Had I the choice,
    Death, and not poverty, were my election:
    To die is transient suffering; to be poor,
    Interminable anguish.

Mait. Nay, never heed. The loss of your wealth, lavished upon your kind friends, only enhances your merits; as the moon looks most lovely when reduced to the slender fragment that the draughts of the gods for half a month have left it.*

Chdr. I do not, trust me, grieve for my lost wealth:
    But that the guest no longer seeks the dwelling,
    Whence wealth has vanished, does, I own, afflict me.
    Like the ungrateful bees, who wanton fly
    The elephant's broad front, when thick congeals
    The dried-up dew,† they visit me no more.

Mait. The sons of slaves! your guest is ever ready to make a morning meal of a fortune: he is like the cow-boy, who, as if afraid of a gad-fly, drives his herds from place to place in the thicket, and sets them to feed always in fresh pasture.

Chdr. 'Tis true.—I think not of my wasted fortune.
    As fate decrees, so riches come and vanish.
    But I lament to find the love of friends
    Hangs all unstrung because a man is poor.

---

* The moon is supposed to be the reservoir of *amrita* or ambrosia, and to furnish the gods and manes with the supply. "It is replenished from the sun during the fortnight of the increase. On the full moon the gods adore that planet for one night, and from the first day all of them, together with the *pitris* and *rishis*, drink one *kala* or digit daily until the ambrosia is exhausted."—*Váyu-Purána.*

† At certain periods a thick dew exhales from the elephants' temples. The peculiarity, though known to Strabo, seems to have escaped naturalists till lately, when it was noticed by Cuvier.

And then with poverty comes disrespect;
From disrespect does self-dependence fail,
Then scorn and sorrow, following, overwhelm
The intellect; and when the judgment fails
The being perishes; and thus from poverty
Each ill that pains humanity proceeds.*

Mait. Ah well, it is but waste of thought to send it after the wealth-hunters; we have had enough of this subject.

Chdr. But poverty is aye the curse of thought.
It is our enemy's reproach; the theme
Of scorn to our best friends and dearest kin.
I had abjured the world and sought the hermitage,
But that my wife had shared in my distress.
Alas, the fires of sorrow in the heart
Glow impotent; they pain but burn not.
My friend, I have already made oblation
Unto the household gods—Go you to where
The four roads meet, and there present it
To the Great Mothers.†

Mait. Not I, indeed.

Chdr. Why not?

Mait. Of what use is it? You have worshipped the gods: what have they done for you? it is labour in vain to bestow upon them adoration.

Chdr. Speak not profanely. It is our duty.
                            And the gods
Undoubtedly are pleased with what is offered

---

* This passage occurs in the *Hitopadeśa*, with a slight variation.

† The *Mátrí* is the personified energy of a divinity, and in a figurative sense the mother of gods and men. The Mátrís are usually reckoned seven or eight, but in one enumeration they are made sixteen. The presentation of oblations to them as a regular and permanent rite is no longer known in Gangetic India. Tántrika ceremonies addressed to the sixteen Mátrís are not uncommon, but the rite in the text appears to be a matter of course, and seems to take the place of that enjoined by Manu to the *Pitris*, the manes or progenitors. "Turning to the south, let him present all the residue of his oblations to the *Pitris*."—3, 91.

In lowliness of spirit and with reverence,
In thought, and deed, and pious self-denial:
Go therefore and present the offering.

Maitr. I will not go, indeed; send somebody else. With me every part of the ritual is apt to get out of its place, and, as in the reflection of a mirror, the right becomes left and the left right. At this time of the evening, too, the royal road is crowded with loose persons, with cut-throats, courtiers, and courtesans:* amongst such a set I shall fare like the unhappy mouse, that fell into the clutches of the snake which was lying in ambush for the frog.† I cannot go, indeed. Why not go yourself? You have nothing to do but to sit here.

Chdr. Well, well—attend then whilst I tell my beads.

[*They retire.*

(*Behind the scenes.*) Stop, Vasantasená, stop!

Enter VASANTASENÁ *pursued by* SAMSTHÁNAKA, *the King's brother-in-law, the* VITA,‡ *and his own Servant.*

Vita. Stop, Vasantasená, stop! Why, losing your gentleness in your fears, do you ply those feet so fast, that should be nimble only in the dance? You run along like the timid deer from the pursuing hunter, casting tremulous glances fearfully around.

Samt. Stop, Vasantasená, stop! Why do you thus scamper away, stumbling at every step? Be pacified, you are in no danger. With love alone is my poor heart inflamed; it is burnt to a cinder, like a piece of meat upon the blazing coals.

Ser. Stop, lady, stop! Why, sister, do you fly? She runs along like a pea-hen in summer with a tail in full feather,

---

* This, besides its general bearing, announces the approaching entrance of Vasantasená and her pursuers, agreeably to the rule, that no character is to enter without previous intimation.

† If we are to consider the antiquity of this play as established, this passage bears testimony to the early currency of apologues in India.

‡ The *Vita* is the companion and minister of the pleasures of *Sankatha-naka*. See the remark made on this character in the introductory observations on the dramatic system of the Hindus, p. xlvii.

whilst my master follows her, like the young hound that chases the bird through the thicket.

Vita. Stop, Vasantasená, stop! You tremble like the young plantain tree, whilst the ends of your red vesture wanton on the wind. The seeds of the red lotus are put to shame by your glowing eyes, and the bed of orpiment, when first penetrated by the axe, is rivalled by the complexion of your cheeks.

Sams. Stop, Vasantasená, stop! Why do you thus fly from a liking, a love, a passion which you inflame? My nights you deprive of rest, and you avoid me by day. It is unavailing: you will trip and tumble into my hands as *Kunti* fell into those of *Rávana.**

Vita. Why, Vasantasená, do you grace my steps by leaving traces for them to obliterate? Like a snake from the monarch of the birds,† you glide away from me, but vain is your flight. I could outstrip the wind in such a chase, and shall I not overtake so delicate a fugitive?

Sams. Most worthy sir, I have invoked her by ten names. I have called her the taper lash of that filcher of broad pieces, *Káma;* the fish-eater, the figurante, the pug-nosed untamable shrew. I have termed her Love's dining-dish—the gulf of the poor man's substance—the walking frippery—the harlot—the hussy—the baggage—the wanton. I have addressed her by all these pretty names,‡ and yet she will have nothing to say to me.

---

* *Kunti* is the mother of the *Pándava* princes; *Rávana*, the giant king of *Lanká*, destroyed by *Ráma*. The former is a character of the *Mahábhárata*, the latter of the *Rámáyańa*. There is no sort of connexion between the two, and instead of *Kunti* it should have been *Sitá*, the wife of *Ráma*, whom *Rávana* carried off. It may be here remarked, that this confusion of persons and events is invariably repeated by *Samsthánaka*, who thus evinces both his ignorance and pretension.

† *Garuda*, the bird on which *Vishńu* rides, between whom and the serpent race is a deadly feud, originating in a dispute between their respective parents, *Kadrú* and *Vinatá*, the wives of *Kaśyapa.*

‡ To address a deity by a number of appellations is the readiest way to

Víta. Why, Vasantasená, do you fly us? The trembling pendants of your ears toss agitated against your cheeks, and make such music as the lute to a master's touch.* You fly like the female crane that starts away from the sound of thunder.

Sarv. Your ornaments jingle to your paces as you run from us, as Draupadí† fled from Ráma.‡ But I shall have you; I will dart upon yon like Hanumat§ upon Subhadrá,|| the lovely sister of Vítsedvasu.¶

Ser. Relent, relent, be gracious to the prince's friend; accept the flesh and the fish. When they can get fish and flesh, the dogs prey not upon carrion.

Víta. What should have so strangely alarmed you? Believe me, you look like the guardian goddess of the city, as round your slender waist sparkles with starlike gems that tinkling zone, and your countenance is pale with terror.

Sarv. As the female jackal is hunted by the dogs, so run you, and so we follow: you run along with your prey, and bear off from me both heart and pericardium.**

secure his good graces; so says the commentator. As to the names themselves, some latitude has been necessarily used in the translation, although an attempt has been made to convey some notion of their purport; the strain is not unlike that of our old comedies; the original is as follows: "*Bhátre! Bhátre! Esi Ńáṭaka-middi-bima bídiki, Mackchhátiki, Latiki, Ńtíki, Kulahdíki, Avatíki, Kámáha-manjutíki, Esí críohahá, Sarshaníḷai Vcaṇgahá, Vesii, Eve te daia-údaake maji kule, Ajjá bi mam narachhadi.*"

* Literally, such as is made by the touch of the *Víla* (*Vilajana-nakha-ghaṭíitcra rísá*), which indicates the particular art cultivated by this character.

† The wife of the *Páṇḍavas* and heroine of the *Mahábhárata*.

‡ The hero of the *Rámáyaṇa*.

§ The monkey friend of *Ráma*.

|| The sister of *Krishṇa*, carried off by *Arjuna*, as related in the *Mahábhárata*.

¶ This is probably intended for a blunder, instead of *Pándava*. *Vidvesvaru* is the name of a demigod of an inferior order, one of the *Gandharbas*, or choristers of *Indra's* heaven.

** *Saredikanani me kaiaoví kaianí*, "carrying off my heart and its envelopes," *vdikanam* being the *Práksit* of *vshlanam*.

' *Vas.* (*Calling for her female attendants.*) What ho! Pallavá, Parabhŕitiká.

Saṁs. (*In alarm to the Viṭa.*) Eh, sir, sir! men, men!

Viṭa. Never fear.

Vas. Mádhaviká, what ho!

Viṭa. Blockhead; she is calling her servants.

Saṁs. What, her women?

Viṭa. To be sure.

Saṁs. Who is afraid? I am a hero—a match for a hundred of them.

Vas. Alas, alas! my people are not within hail: I must trust to myself alone for my escape.

Viṭa. Search about, search about.

Saṁs. Vasantasená, what is the use of your bawling there for bud and blossom, or all spring together!* Who is to preserve you when I pursue? What could *Bhímasena* † do for you, or the son of *Jamadagni*, ‡ or the son of *Kunti*, § or *Daśakandhara* ‖ himself? I would take them, like *Duhśásana*, ¶ by their hair, and, as you shall see, with one touch of my well-sharpened sword off goes your head. Come, come, we have had enough of your running away. One who is desirous of dying cannot be said to live.

Vas. Good sir, I am only a weak woman.

Viṭa. True, therefore you may live.

Saṁs. True, you shall not die.

---

* Mistaking the names for *pallava*, a shoot, *mádhaviká*, a sort of creeper, and alluding to the latter's blossoming in the spring.

† The second of the sons of *Páńḍu*.

‡ *Paraśurāma*.

§ *Karńa*, or either of the *Páńḍava* princes.

‖ *Rávańa*, the ten-headed sovereign of *Lanká*.

¶ One of the *Kaurava* princes, who dragged *Draupadí* by the hair into the public court; an act of bitter insult to the *Páńḍava* princes, in revenge of which *Bhíma* vowed he would never be appeased till he had drunk the aggressor's blood. In the war that ensued he killed *Duhśásana*, and fulfilled his vow.

Vas. (*Apart.*) His very courtesy appals me. It shall be so. (*Aloud.*) Pray, sirs, why do you thus pursue me, or why address such language to me? Do you seek my jewels?

Vita. Fie, fie, what have we to do with your ornaments? Who plucks the blossoms of the creeper?

Vas. What is it, then, you require?

Sams. That I, who am a person of celestial nature, a mortal *Vâsudeva*,* obtain your affections.

Vas. Get you gone; you talk idly.

Sams. (*Claps his hands and laughs.*) What think you of that, sir? Hear how this gentle damsel regards me: she bids me go and rest myself, no doubt, after my fatigue in running after her;† but I swear by your head and my feet,‡ that I have gone astray neither in town nor village, but have kept close to your heels all the way, by the which I am wearied.

Vita. (*Apart.*) The blockhead! he misapprehends the whole. (*Aloud.*) Why, Vasantasená, you act quite out of character: the dwelling of a harlot is the free resort of youth: a courtesan is like a creeper that grows by the road-side—her person is an article for sale, her love a thing that money will buy, and her welcome is equally bestowed upon the amiable and disgusting. The sage and the idiot, the Brahman and the outcast, all bathe in the same stream, and the crow and the peacock perch upon the branches of the same creeper. The Brahman, the Kshattriya, the Vaisya, and all of every caste are ferried over in the same boat; and like the boat, the creeper, and the stream, the courtesan is equally accessible to all.

Vas. What you say, may be just, but, believe me, merit alone, not brutal violence, inspires love.

---

* *Krishna.*

† *Vasantasená's* exclamation was *khâtam*, an interjection of repugnance, or disgust. *Samsthánaka* assumes she said *tríâto*, or *Prikŕit, śánta,* weary. The quibble is lost in the translation, but that is of no very great importance.

‡ A very affronting adjuration.

Sams. Sir, sir, the truth is, that the baggage has had the perverseness to fall in love with a miserable wretch, one Chárudatta, whom she met in the garden of *Kámadeva's* temple : he lives close by here on our left, so take care she does not slip through our fingers.

Vita. (*Aside.*) Confound the fool, he lets out everything he ought to conceal. In love with Chárudatta—humph ! no wonder ; it is truly said, pearls string with pearls : well, let it be so, never mind this simpleton. (*Aloud.*) What say you, is the house of Chárudatta on our left ? the deuce it is.

Sams. Very true, I assure you.

Vas. (*Aside.*) Indeed ! the house of Chárudatta so near ! These wretches have unintentionally befriended me, and promoted a meeting with my beloved.

Sams. Sir, sir, Vasantasená is no longer visible ; she is lost in the dark, like an ink-cake in a pile of black beans.

Vita. It is very dark, indeed ! The gloom cheats my eyesight of its faculty ; my eyes open only to be closed by it ; such obscurity envelops everything, as if the heavens rained lamp-black : sight is as unavailing as the service of a worthless man.

Sams. I must search for Vasantasená.

Vita. Indeed ! (*Aloud.*) Is there not anything by which you may trace her ?

Sams. What should there be ?

Vita. The tinkling of her ornaments ; the odour of her perfumes ; and the fragrance of her garland.

Sams. Very true ; I can hear with my nostrils the scent of her garland spreading through the darkness, but I do not see the sound of her ornaments.*

---

* So in the "Midsummer's Night's Dream "—

   Bottom as Pyramus :

        "I see a voice: now will I to the chink,
         To spy an' I can hear my Thisby's face."

And in the same—

        "Eye of man hath not heard, nor ear seen," &c.

Vita. (*Apart, in the direction of Vas.*) Very well, Vasantasená. True, you are hidden by the gloom of the evening, like the lightning between gathering clouds, but the fragrance of your chaplet, the music of your anklets, will betray you,—do you hear?

Vas. (*To herself.*) I hear and comprehend. (*Takes off her garland and the rings from her ankles.*) If I am not mistaken, the private entrance is in this direction: by carrying my hands along the wall—(*feels for the door*)—ah, it is shut.

Chár. (*Within the court.*) My prayer* is finished; now, Maitreya, go, present the offering to the divine mothers.

Mait. I tell you I will not go.

Chár. Alas it does embitter poverty—
That then our friends grow deaf to our desires,
And lend a keener anguish to our sorrows.
The poor man's truth is scorned: the tender light
Of each mild virtue languishes; suspicion
Stamps him the perpetrator of each crime
That others are the authors of: no man seeks
To form acquaintance with him, nor exchange
Familiar greeting or respectful courtesy.
If e'er he find a place in rich men's dwellings
At solemn festivals, the wealthier guests
Survey him with disdainful wonder; and
Whene'er by chance he meets upon the road
With state and wealth, he sneaks into a corner,
Ashamed of his scant covering, till they pass,
Rejoicing to be overlooked. Believe me,
He who incurs the guilt of poverty
Adds a sixth sin to those we term most heinous.†
In truth, I mourn e'en poverty for thee,

---

* Literally, *japa*—inaudible repetition of prayer.

† The five great sins in the Hindu code are—stealing gold, drinking spirituous liquors, murder of a Brahman, adultery with the wife of a spiritual teacher, and association with a person guilty of either of these crimes.

Whose cherished dwelling is this wasting frame,
And oft I sadly wonder what asylum,
When this shall be no more, shall then receive thee.

Mait. Ah! well, if I must go, I must; but let your maid Radaniká go along with me.

Chár. Radaniká, follow Maitreya.

Rad. As you command, sir.

Muit. Here, Radaniká, do you take the offerings and the lamp, while I open the back-door. (*Opens the door.*)

Vas. (*On the outside.*) Luckily for me, the door is opened: I shall now get in. Ah the lamp. (*Brushes it out with her scarf, and enters.*)

Chár. What was that?

Muit. Opening the door let in a gust of wind, which has blown the lamp out: never mind—go on, Radaniká. I will just step into the house and re-light the lamp, and will be with you again immediately.

Sarhs. (*On the outside.*) What can have become of Vasantasená!

Vita. Search, search.

Sarhs. So I do, but cannot find her—I have her. (*Lays hold of the Vita.*)

Vita. Blockhead, this is I.

Sarhs. Stand out of the way then. (*Lays hold of the servant.*) Now then I have caught her.

Ser. No, your honour has caught me.

Sarhs. Here then, this way, this way, here, master, servant, servant, master, here, here, stand here.* (*Lays hold of Radaniká by the hair as she comes out.*) Ha, ha! now I have her indeed. I detected her endeavouring to escape by the scent of the garland. I have her fast by the hair, as *Chánakya* caught *Draupadí.* †

---

* We may suppose that some display of practical wit took place here.

† *Chánakya* was a celebrated statesman and writer on politics: he was the minister of *Chandragupta;* it is needless to add, he could not possibly be connected with the story of *Draupadí.*

Vita. Very well, young lady, very pretty; running after honest men's sons, in the pride of youth, with your head full dressed with flowers; you are caught in the fact.

Sams. You are the young girl, I believe, that was caught by the hair of the head: now call, and cry, and scream, and curse, and abuse *Siva, Sambhu, Sankara,* and *Iswara.**

Rad. (*In alarm.*) Bless me, gentlemen, what do you mean?

Vita. How now! the voice is that of another person.

Sams. Oh, sir, your female can change her voice when she will, as the cat mews in a different key when she attempts to steal cream.

Vita. Such a difference can scarcely be, and yet it is possible. Yes, it may be she has been taught to disguise her voice in the way of her profession, both for the purposes of deception and the articulation of the gamut.

Enter MAITREYA.

Mait. How funnily the lamp burns: it goes flutter, flutter, in the evening breeze, like the heart of a goat just caught in a snare. (*Seeing Radanika and the rest.*) Hey, Radanika!

Sams. Holloa, master—a man.

Mait. What is all this?—it is not right; not right at all—although Chárudatta be poor, yet strangers are not to come into his house without leave.

Rad. See here; Maitreya, here's disrespect to me.

Mait. Not you merely, but all of us. To me as well as you.

Rad. You, indeed—how can that be?

Mait. Why, have they been rude to you?

Rad. Rude indeed—to be sure, rude enough.

Mait. No, really.

Rad. Yes, really.

Mait. (*In wrath and taking up a stick.*) Then I will do for them: this is quite unbearable—every dog will bark in his own kennel, and why not a Brahman? With this dry bambu

---

* All names of Siva.

staff, as crooked as our fortunes, will I batter that head of thine, thou abominable villain.

Vita. Patience, patience! worthy Brahman.*

Mait. (*To him.*) Eh! this cannot be the offender. (*Turns to Samsthánaka.*) Oh! here he is. Oh, you king's brother-in-law! you abominable miscreant! have you no decency! Do not you know that, notwithstanding the worthy Chárudatta be poor, he is an ornament to Ujjayin, and how dare you think of forcing your way into his house and maltreating his people! There is no disgrace in an untoward fate; disgrace is in misconduct; a worthless man of wealth is contemptible.

Vitu. Worthy Brahman, pardon us, we mistook the person: we intended no affront, but looking for a female——

Mait. For her! (*Pointing to Radanika.*)

Vita. Heaven forbid!—No, no, for a girl her own mistress, who has run away. Searching for her, we lighted upon this damsel, and committed an unintentional indecorum. We beg your pardon, and submit ourselves to whatever you may please to ordain. (*Gives his sword and falls at Maitreya's feet.*)

Mait. You are a man of sense; arise. I knew not your quality when I addressed you so roughly; now I am aware of it, I shall treat you with proper politeness.

Vitu. You are entitled to our respect. I will only rise on one condition.

Mait. Declare it.

Vitu. That you will say nothing to Chárudatta of what has chanced.

Mait. I will not say anything to him on the subject.

Vitu. I will place your kindness, Brahman, on my head; armed with every excellence, you are invincible by arms.

Sams. What do you mean, my friend, by putting your hands together and falling at the feet of such a contemptible fellow?

* *Mahá-Bráhmana*, great Brahman, is the term used; it is also an expression of contempt, and is applied to those Brahmans who officiate for Sudras.

Vita. I am afraid.

Sams. Of what?

Vita. Of the eminent virtues of Chárudatta.

Sams. Very eminent, indeed, when they cannot afford his visitors a dinner.

Vita. Never mind that; he has become impoverished by his liberality: like the lake in the summer which is exhausted by relieving the thirst of the travellers; in his prosperity he was kind to all, and never treated any one with disrespect.

Sams. Who is this slave, the son of a slave? Is he a warrior, a hero? Is he *Páṇḍu*,* *Swetuketu*,† the son of *Rádhá*,‡ *Rávana*,§ or *Indradatta*?‖ Was he begotten on *Kuntí*, by *Ráma*, or is he *Aswatthámán*,¶ *Dharmaputra*,** or *Jaṭáyu*?††

Vita. No, you wiseacre, I will tell you who he is: he is Chárudatta, the tree of plenty to the poor, bowed down by its abundant fruit. He is the cherisher of the good, the mirror of the wise, a touchstone of piety, an ocean of decorum, the doer of good to all, of evil to none, a treasure of manly virtues, intelligent, liberal, and upright; in a word, he only is worthy of admiration: in the plenitude of his merits he may

---

* The brother of *Dhṛitaráshṭra*, and parent of the princes who are the heroes of the *Mahábhárata*. He was born of a fair complexion, whence his name, "The Pale." He left the kingdom of ancient Delhi to his brother, and retired to lead an ascetic life in the Himálaya mountains, where he died.

† *Swetaketu* was a sage, the son of *Uddálaka*, and is mentioned in the *Mahábhárata*.

‡ *Rádhá* was the wife of the charioteer of *Duryodhana*, and bred *Karńa* as her son, after he was exposed on the banks of the Yamuná by his own mother.

§ *Rávana* has already been noticed.

‖ *Indradatta* is a warrior in the *Mahábhárata*.

¶ *Aswatthámán* is the son of *Droṇa*, the military preceptor of the *Kaurava* and *Páṇḍava* princes; he fought in favour of *Dhṛitaráshṭra*.

** The son of *Dharma*, the ruler of *Tartarus*, is the elder of the Páṇḍava princes *Yudhishthira*.

†† This is a marvellous man-bird, the younger brother of *Sampáti* and son of *Garuḍa*: he attempted to rescue *Sítá* when carried off by *Rávana*, and was slain by him.

be said to live indeed; other men merely breathe. So come, we had better depart.

Saṁs. What, without Vasantasená?

Vita. Vasantasená is lost.

Saṁs. How lost?

Vita. Like the sight of the blind, the health of the sick, the wisdom of the fool, and the prosperity of the sluggard; like the learning of the dull and dissipated, and the friendship of foes.

Saṁs. Well, I will not go hence until I recover her.

Vita. You may as well. Have you never heard the saying:

  An elephant may be held by a chain,
   A steed be curbed by his rider's art;
  But even go hang, if you cannot gain
   The only bond woman obeys—her heart.

You may as well, therefore, come away.

Saṁs. Go, if you please; I shall stay where I am.

Vita. Very well, I leave you.   [*Exit.*

Saṁs. Let him go; who cares? (*To Maitreya.*) Now, you crow-foot pated pupil of mendicity, down with you.

Mait. We are cast down already.

Saṁs. By whom?

Mait. By destiny.

Saṁs. Get up then.

Mait. So we will.

Saṁs. When?

Mait. When fortune smiles.

Saṁs. Weep, weep.

Mait. So we do.

Saṁs. What for?

Mait. Our misfortunes.

Saṁs. Laugh, blockhead, laugh!

Mait. So we shall.

Saṁs. When?

Mait. When Chárudatta is again in prosperity.

Saṁs. Hark ye, fellow; do you carry a message from me

to the beggar Chárudatta. Say to him thus from me: A common wanton, hight Vasantasená, covered with gold upon gold, like the chief of a troop of comedians about to act a new play, saw you in the garden of *Kámadeva's* * temple, and took a fancy to you. Having put us to the trouble of using violence to secure her, she fled, and has taken refuge in your house. If you will give her up, and put her yourself into my hands without any litigation, her delivery shall be rewarded with my most particular regard; but if you will not put her forth, depend upon my eternal and exterminating enmity. Consider that a preserved pumpkin, a dried potherb, fried flesh, and boiled rice† that has stood for a night in the cold weather, stink when kept too long. Let him then not lose this opportunity. You speak well and distinctly; you must, therefore, speak my message so that I may hear you, as I sit in the upper terrace of my house, here adjoining. If you do not say what I have told you, I shall grind your head between my teeth, as I would a nut beneath my door.‡

* The temple of *Kámadeva* makes a great figure in all the dramas and tales of the Hindus of any antiquity. There was always a garden or grove attached to it, to which no sanctity, however, seems to have been ascribed, as was to those of Albunea or Dodona: it was rather the Daphne of the Hindu religion, the resort of the young of either sex at public festivals, and the scene of many love adventures: although the reserve, to which Hindu women were always subjected in public, rendered it no school for the Daphnaei Mores inspired by the shades of Antioch. All traces of the worship of *Kámadeva* have long since disappeared: his groves, indeed, could not possibly be frequented a moment after the intrusion of Mohammedan brutality.

† Allusion is made here to some circumstances of domestic economy, on which the Hindus of the present day can give no information, such cookery having long gone out of fashion, and no Dr. Kitchener having arisen in India to immortalise the culinary art. The stalk of the gourd, it is said, is covered with cow-dung to preserve it from insects. For the satisfaction of the curious the Prákrit of the original follows: it is a verse in the *Upajáti* measure—"*Kakbiluki gochhadalittarrálá; Sáke a śukkhe; talide hu mańśe; Bhatte a kemantialattitisiddhe; Láhe a brie do hu hodi pádi.*"

‡ Literally, as the kernel of the wood-apple below a door.—*Kabilla-tala-ppabitthań kabitthań gurień via, mańtaań de madanaddiliam.*

Mait. I will deliver your message.
Sans. Is the worthy Vita really gone? (*To the servant.*)
Serv. He is, sir.
Sans. Then, let us follow him quick.
Serv. Please to take your sword.
Sans. No, carry it after me.
Serv. This is your honour's sword.
Sans. Ah, very well, give it me. (*Takes it by the wrong end.*) I bear it on my shoulder, sleeping in its pink sheath;* and thus go I home as a jackal retires to his lair, followed by the yell of all the dogs and bitches of the village. [*Exit.*
Mait. My good Radanika, say nothing to Chárudatta about your having been insulted in this currish place, by that king's brother-in-law: he frets already about his affairs, and this business, I am sure, would double his vexation.
Rad. I am only Radanika, Maitreya; I can hold my tongue.
Mait. Nay, nay, not so. [*They retire.*
Chár. (*Within the house, to Vasantasená.*) Radaniká, my boy Rohasena must have enjoyed the breeze long enough; he will be chilled by the evening dews; take him in, and cover him with this cloth.
Vas. (*Apart.*) He mistakes me for one of the servants. (*Takes the cloth and smells it.*) Scented with jasmine flowers! Ha, then, he is not all a philosopher.† [*Retires.*
Chár. Radaniká, carry Rohasena to the inner apartments.
Vas. (*Apart*) Alas! my fortune gives me no admission to them.
Chár. What! No reply, Radaniká!—Alas! when a man has been unfortunate enough to have outlived his means, his best friends lose their regard, and old attachments change into dislike.

* Literally, of the colour of the flesh of the barkless radish.—*Niwaltkalasi mátátupeii rasásam.*

† Literally, his youth does not exhibit indifference.—*Anaddridam se jor. rasasá padikiardi.*

Enter MAITREYA *and* RADANIKÁ.

Mait. Here, sir, is Radaniká.

Chdr. Here—then who is this? Not knowing her, I have degraded her by the touch of my vestment.*

Vas. (Apart.) Degraded; no, exalted.

Chdr. She looks like the waning moon, half hidden by autumnal clouds; fie, fie, another's wife; this is not a meet object for my regards.

Mait. (Recognising Vasantasená.) A wife indeed, a pretty wife! Why, sir, this is Vasantasená, a lady, who, having had the felicity of seeing you in the gardens of *Kámadeva's* temple, has taken it into her head to honour you with her affection.

Chdr. (Apart.) Indeed; is this Vasantasená?
    What now avails it to return her love
    In my declining fortunes; let it sink
    Suppressed in silence, as a coward checks
    The wrath he dares not utter.

Mait. I have a message, too, from the king's brother-in-law.

Chdr. What?

Mait. Thus he says:† "A common wanton, hight Vasantasená, covered with gold upon gold, like the chief of a troop of comedians about to act a new play, saw you in the garden of *Kámadeva's* temple, and took a fancy to you. Having put us to the trouble of violence to secure her"——

Vas. "Violence to secure her!" Oh, I am honoured by such words.

Mait. "She fled, and has taken refuge in your house. If you will give her up, and put her yourself into my hands with-

---

* This instances the great reserve that separated the virtuous part of the sexes amongst the Hindus. To have touched the wife of another with the hem of the garment was a violation of her person. In the *Rája-Tarangiñí* the present of a fine vest to the Queen of Cashmir, which had been stamped with the seal of the donor, the King of Ceylon, and so far seemed to belong to him, is said to have occasioned a war between the princes.

† Like the missions in Homer, the messages are always repeated verbatim.

out litigation, her delivery shall be rewarded with my most particular regard; but if you will not put her forth, depend upon my eternal and exterminating enmity."

Chár. (*With disdain.*) He is a fool.

(*To himself.*) She would become a shrine—
 The pride of wealth
 Presents no charm to her, and she disdains
 The palace she is roughly bid to enter;
 Nor makes she harsh reply, but silent leaves
 The man she scorns, to waste his idle words.
Lady—I knew you not, and thus unwittingly
 Mistaking you for my attendant, offered you
 Unmeet indignity, I bend my head,
 In hope of your forgiveness.

Vas. Nay, sir, I am the offender, by intruding into a place of which I am unworthy; it is my head that must be humbled in reverence and supplication.

Mait. Very pretty on both sides; and whilst you two stand there, nodding your heads to each other like a field of long grass, permit me to bend mine, although in the style of a young camel's stiff knees, and request that you will be pleased to hold yourselves upright again.

Chár. Be it so; no further ceremony.

Vas. (*Aside.*) How kind his manner, how pleasing his expression! But it is not proper for me to remain longer: let me think. It shall be so. (*Aloud.*) Sir, respected sir, if truly I have found favour in your sight, permit me to leave these ornaments in your house; it was to rob me of them, that the villains I fled from pursued me.

Chár. This house, lady, is unsuited to such a trust.

Vas. Nay, worthy sir, you do not speak me true. Men, and not houses, are the things we trust to.

Chár. Maitreya, take the trinkets.

Vas. You have obliged me.

Mait. Much obliged to your ladyship. (*Taking them.*)

Chár. Blockhead, this is but a trust.

Mait. (To him apart.) What if they should be stolen?

Chár. They will be here but a short time.

Mait. What she has given us is ours.

Chár. I shall send you about your business.

Vas. Worthy sir, I could wish to have the safeguard of this your friend's company to return home.

Chár. Maitreya, attend the lady.

Mait. Go yourself; you are the properest person; attending her graceful form as the stately swan upon his mate. I am but a poor Brahman, and should as soon be demolished by these libertines as a meat-offering in the market-place by the dogs.

Chár. Well, well, I will attend her, and for further security on the road let the torches be prepared.

Mait. What ho! Vardhamána—*(enter Servant)*—light the flambeaus.

Vardh. (To him.) You dunderhead, how are they to be lighted without oil?

Mait. (Apart to Chárudatta.) To say the truth, sir, our torches are like harlots; they shine not in poor men's houses.*

Chár. Never heed; we shall not need a torch.

Pale as the maiden's cheek who pines with love,
The moon is up, with all its starry train—
And lights the royal road with lamps divine,
Whilst through the gloom its milk-white rays descend,
Like streamlets winding o'er the miry plain.

(They proceed.) This, lady, is your dwelling.†

[*Vasantasena makes an obeisance, and exit.*

Come, my friend, let us return—

---

* The original contains a pun upon the word *Sneha*, which means oil or affection—the one has no love, the other has no oil.

† Either the space appropriated to the stage was more spacious than we can conceive, or this progress to a dwelling evidently intended to be remote must be left in a great measure to the imagination. On the Greek stage the characters were not unfrequently supposed to be advancing from some distance whilst the chorus was singing, and in the Latin comedy a character

The road is solitary, save where the watch
Performs his wonted round : the silent night—
Fit season only for dishonest acts—
Should find us not abroad.
As to this casket, let it be your charge
By night, by day it shall be Vardhamána's.
Mait. As you command. [*Exeunt.*

is often spoken of as near at hand some time before he takes part in the dialogue. On the Spanish stage a transit of a similar nature was performed, as in "Courtesy, not Love;" where the first part of the scene lies amongst rocks and woods, and presently, without any apparent change, we find one of the characters say—

"How heedlessly have we advanced,
Even to the palace gates : and see where stand
Ladies in the balcony."

—"Horæ Hispanicæ."—*Blackwood's Magazine*, No. C.

END OF THE FIRST ACT.

ACT II.

Scene—VASANTASENA'S HOUSE.[*]

Enter a Female Attendant.

I AM sent to Vasantasená with a message from her mother, I will therefore enter and deliver it to her. Ah, there she sits. She seems uneasy, I must approach her.

(*Vasantasená discovered seated,[†] Madanika attending.*)

---

[*] The plan of this and subsequent scenes requires a similar arrangement as the first, or the stage to be divided transversely by a curtain, each being a double scene, or the inside and outside of the house. There might have not been even this ceremony, the characters whose business was over merely making way for the new comers, without leaving the stage, or being in any formal way separated from it. A case of this kind occurs in an old English play, *Monsieur D'Olive*, by Chapman, Act 3, Scene 1, where the Duke, Duchess, and train pass over the stage to see the Earl of Anne's unburied wife; pause and talk, yet take no notice of the Earl and his brother, who were in previous possession of the scene, and who remain on it when the rest depart, resuming their discourse as if nothing had occurred to interrupt them.

[†] In the original "enter seated," *âsanasthá praviśati*, a rather preposterous stage direction, but not without a parallel in the British drama. Thus in *The Pinner of Wakefield* : "Enter a shoemaker sitting upon the stage at work." In '*Tis pity She is a Whore*, Dodsley's edition, "Enter the Friar in his study, sitting in a chair." In the same piece, "Enter Giovanni and Annabella lying on a bed;" and in *The Lover's Melancholy*, "Enter Maleander on a couch." This sort of direction is constant in the old editions, and leaves it to be inferred that the characters had no alternative but to walk in and occupy the chair or bed, which latter the property man, as Malone observes, was ordered to thrust upon the stage when a bed-chamber was to be represented. The Greeks had some device for this purpose, although it does not appear very distinctly what. The Encyclema, as described by Julius Pollux, appears to have been a raised platform with a seat, and to have turned on a pivot, and the open side being made to face the audience, discovered the character sitting, as Euripides in the Acharnians and Sophocles in the clouds.

Vas. Well, girl, you must then——

Mad. Then—when—madam? You have given me no orders.

Vas. What said I?

Mad. You said, girl, you must then——

Vas. True.

Atten. (*Approaches.*) Madam, your mother desires that you will perform your ablutions and come to worship.

Vas. Tell my lady mother, child, that I shall not attend to-day; let the Brahman complete the ceremony.

Atten. As you command. [*Exit.*

Mad. Dear madam, affection, not malice, compels me to ask what you meant to say!

Vas. Why, Madanika, what think you of me?

Mad. I should guess from your being so absent that you are in love.

Vas. Well said, Madanika; you are a judge of hearts, it should seem.

Mad. Excuse me, but Love is a resistless god, and holds his holiday in the breast of youth: so tell me, what prince or courtier does my lady serve?

Vas. I pretend, Madanika, to be a mistress, not a slave.

Mad. What young and learned Brahman, then, is it that you love?

Vas. A Brahman is to be venerated, not loved.

Mad. It must be a merchant then, rich with the collected wealth of the many countries he has visited.

Vas. Nay, Madanika, it were very ill advised to fix my affections on a trader to foreign lands. His repeated absence would subject me to a life of incessant grief.

Mad. Neither a prince nor a courtier, a Brahman nor a merchant; who then can he possibly be?

Vas. Madanika, you were with me in the garden of Kámadeva's temple.

Mad. I was, madam.

Vas. Then why do you ask me, as if you knew nothing?

Mad. Ah! now I know—he in whose house you told me you had taken refuge.

Vas. How is he called?

Mad. He lives near the Exchange.*

Vas. I asked you his name.

Mad. His well-selected name is Chárudatta.

Vas. Right, Madaniká; right, girl, now you know all.

Mad. Is it so! (*Aside.*) But, lady, it is said that he is very poor.

Vas. I love him, nevertheless. No longer let the world believe that a courtesan is insensible to a poor man's merit.

Mad. Yet, lady, do the bees swarm in the mango-tree after it has shed its blossoms.

Vas. Therefore are they called wantons.†

Mad. Well, if he is the object of your affections, why not contrive an interview?

Vas. I have provided for it: the scheme must succeed; and although it is not easy to get access to him, yet it may be managed.

Mad. I suppose it was with this view that your ornaments were deposited in his hands?

Vas. You have a shrewd guess, wench.   [*They retire.*

Scene—A Street, with an open Temple; noise behind.

Halloa, sirs, halloa! Yon gambler has lost ten *suvarṇas*, and is running off without paying—stop him! stop him! Ah, I see you, there you go—stop! stop!

Enter the SAṂVÁHAKA *hastily.‡*

Curse on my gambling propensities; I am kicked by an ass, as it were by a she-ass just broke away from her first halter;

---

* *Sellhi-chattare paṭhiraṃdi* or *Sreshṭhi-chatware pratiraṃti.* He lives in the street of the Seths, or principal merchants and bankers.

† The original is a pun on the word *madhukaras*, honey-makers or beggars.

‡ A person employed to knead and chafe the limbs. The stage direction for his entrance implies a curtain. He enters, as the manuscripts of this

I am picked up by a pike * like *Ghatotkacha* by the dart of
Karńa;† no sooner did I see the master of the table‡ intent
upon the writings, than I started. Now I have got away
from them, where can I conceal myself? The gamester and

piece, both text and comment, have it, *apatâkshepa*, which might be rendered not putting aside the curtain, breaking through it in some part,
expressing hurry and fright; in other plays, however, the phrase is, more
correctly, *apatîkshepa*, throwing up the curtain; from *apati*, a screen, and
kshepa, throwing.

* The sense of this passage is rather obscure, but there can be no doubt
that puns are intended, and that *gaddaki* or *gardabhi*, meaning a she-ass,
as well as *śakti*, a dart or pike, imply something else in this place; perhaps
they signify the implements of play, cards, or dice. The commentator is
evidently at a loss, but is inclined to consider them to mean coins, which
is not impossible.

† The demon *Ghatotkacha* was killed by *Karńa*, with a lance given him
by *Indra*. The story is told in the *Mahábhárata*, and is translated in the
13th volume of the Asiatic Researches.

‡ The *Sabhika* is said in the *Mitákshará* to be a person who presides at
houses where assemblies are held for purposes of gambling, and who provides
the dice and all other materials. The *Agni-Puráńa*, which in the law chap-
ters is identically the same with the text of *Yájnyawalkya*, gives the following description of the *Sabhika's* duties and the laws of the gaming-table:—
"The *Sabhika* is entitled to five per cent. on money won at play, whenever
the sum exceeds one hundred; if it fall short of that amount, he is to receive
ten per cent. In return for the protection of the king, he shall pay to the
royal treasury a fixed proportion of his profits. It is his business to collect
from the unsuccessful party whatever sums they may have lost, and transfer
them to the winners; and it becomes him to do this civilly, and to adjust the
payment on liberal and lenient terms. In all licensed gaming-houses, where
the royal dues are regularly paid, the king should enforce the payment of all
sums lost, but he should not interfere with gaming-houses of a different class.
In all disputes, those who have been lookers-on are to be witnesses; and if
any foul play or false dice be proved against a gambler, he shall be branded
and banished the kingdom. The king shall appoint proper officers to attend
at gambling-houses, and secure all dishonest characters; the same rules are
applicable to cock-pits and other similar places, where animals are set to fight
for wagers." The legal sanction thus given to gambling is very different
from the sturdy and moral notions expressed by *Menu*, who directs kings to
prohibit such practices in their dominions, and even to punish with death
those who engage in them themselves or induce others to do so,—*Menu
Sanhita*, ix. 221-224,—but regulations of either tendency are manifest
indications of considerable progress in the vices of civilised society.

the master are at my heels. Here is an empty temple; I will walk backwards into it, and take my stand as its deity. (*Enters the temple.*)

   Enter MATHURA, *the keeper of the Gaming-house, and the*
        Gambler.

Mdth. Halloa, sirs! stop him, stop him.

Gam. Though you hide in hell, or take shelter with *Indra,* you shall not escape: *Rudra* himself cannot protect you. The keeper of the gaming-house is your only chance.

Mdth. Whither, you deceiver of a courteous publican, have you flown. You are shaking with fear, every limb of you; I know it by your irregular footmarks, as your feet have slipped and stumbled over the ground, blackening your family and fame.

Gam. So far he has run, but here the track is lost.

Mdth. Hey, the footmarks are all reversed. This temple had no image in it. Oh, the villain, he has walked backward into it.

Gam. Let us after him.

Mdth. Agreed. (*Enter the temple, and signify in dumb show to each other the discovery of the Samvdhaka.*)

Gam. Is this image, think you, of wood?

Mdth. No, it appears to me to be of stone. (*They shake and pinch the Samvdhaka.*) Never mind it, let us sit down and play out our game. (*They play.*)

Sam. (*Who gradually expresses an interest in watching the game.*) The rattling of the dice are as tantalising to a man without a penny, as the sound of a drum to a king without a kingdom. I shall not play, I know. Gambling is as bad as being pitched from the top of mount *Meru:* and yet, like the *Coïl's* song, the sound of the dice is really bewitching.

Gam. The throw is mine.

Mdth. No, no, it is mine.

Sam. (*Forgetting himself and jumping off the pedestal.*) No, no, it is mine.

Gam. The man is taken.

Mdth. (*Seizing the Samedhaka.*) Now, you scoundrel, we have you; where are the ten *suvarnas?* *

Sam. I will pay them in the course of the day.

Mdth. Pay them now.

Sam. Have patience, and you shall be paid.

Mdth. I must be paid immediately.

Sam. Oh, dear, oh, lord, my head. (*Falls down as in a swoon. They beat him.*)

Mdth. You are fast now in the gaming ring.†

Sam. (*Rising and expressing pain.*) It is very hard that you will not give me a little time; where am I to get the money?

Mdth. Give me a pledge then.

Sam. Very well. (*Taking the Gamester aside.*) I tell you what, I will pay you half the money if you will forgive the rest.

Gam. Agreed.

Sam. (*to Mdthura, aside.*) I will give you security for half the debt, if you cry quits for the other half.

Mdth. Agreed.

Sam. (*To the Gamester aloud.*) You let me off half the debt?

Gam. I do.

---

* A *suvarna* is a weight of gold which, according to different data, varies from 108 grains to 227. As the same with the tola in common use it should be 224½ grains; but the original authorities should perhaps be our guides in this place, and we may reckon the *suvarna* at the lower weight of 108 grains. It may be estimated in value at about rupees 8·11, or 18s. 6d. It is here evidently intended to represent a coin as well as a weight, like our ancient penny and pound. It does not follow, because coins were weights, that therefore they could not be coins, and such an inference is contradicted by the history of all money. Pansanias probably made some such mistake when he asserted that "the Indians, although their country abounded with metals, had no coins." That they had coins is proved not only by the sense of the term *suvarna* here, but by the probable sense of the words *suddhati* and *sakti*, noticed above, and that of the *sinaka* in page 25 (last note), which, according to the comment, means pieces bearing the figure of *Siva.*

† Literally *jédiarumaddali'e badtho si.* The meaning of *moddali* here is no doubt technical, and its precise import is not understood.

Sam. And you give up half? (*To the Sabhika.*)
Mâth. Yes, I do.
Sam. Then, good morning to you, gentlemen. (*Going.*)
Mâth. Halloa, not so fast, where are you going?
Sam. See here, my masters—one has forgiven me one-half, and the other has let me off another half; is it not clear that I am quits for the whole?
Mâth. Hark ye, my friend, my name is Mâthura. I know a thing or two, and am not to be done in this way: so down directly with the whole sum.
Sam. Where am I to get it?
Mâth. Sell your father.
Sam. Where is my father?
Mâth. Sell your mother.
Sam. Where is she?
Mâth. Sell yourself.*
Sam. Well, well, be pacified, take me upon the highway.
Mâth. Come along. (*They proceed.*) What ho, good worthy friends; pray, some one buy me of this gambler for ten suvarnas.
Passenger.† What noise is that?
Sam. I will be your servant, your slave. Gone, and no reply—well, try again: who buys, who buys; will no one buy me of this gambler for ten suvarnas? He has passed and not said a syllable! Ah, luckless me, ever since the noble Chârudatta came to poverty, I prosper only in misfortunes.
Mâth. Come, come—give me the money.
Sam. How should I give it? (*Falls and is dragged along by Mâthura.*) Murder, murder! help—protect me.

---

* A creditor is authorised by the old Hindu law to enforce payment of an acknowledged debt by blows, the detention of the debtor's person, and compelling him to work in his service; this treatment of the Samvyavahârin, therefore, however barbarous, is perfectly legal.

† *Akâśe* is the stage direction, a voice in the air; but this stage direction supposes a very thin company: none to act mob.

THE TOY-CART.

Enter DARDURAKA.

Gambling is to the gamester an empire without a throne; he never anticipates defeat, but levies tribute from all, and liberally disburses what he obtains; he enjoys the revenues of a prince, and counts the opulent amongst his servants; money, wife, friends, all are to be won at the gaming-table, and all is gained, all possessed, and all lost at play. Let me see: *Tray* carried off everything; *Deuce* set my skin crawling; *Ace* settled the point, and *Doublets** dished me completely. Ha!

---

* The terms here used in the original are not familiar to the Hindus of the present day. They are *Treta*, *Pdwara*, *Nardita*, and *Kata*; for these the commentary substitutes *Tipá*, *Dad*, *Náddi*, and *Pérá*, or Three, Two, Ace, and Four. If correct, the game alluded to is a kind of Hazard: it is played upon a table or cloth with four compartments, called severally *Náddi*, *Dad*, *Tipá*, and *Chouk* or *Pérá*, and by any number of players. Each stakes, upon one or other of the compartments, whatever sum the caster will set him in. The caster has sixteen cowries, which he shakes in his hands and throws on the ground; those that fall with the valve uppermost are counted, and according as they correspond to either of the divisions, that division sweeps the table. The mode of counting them refers to the favourite mode of telling off articles in India by four; and the numbers of one, two, &c., are not only those numbers simply, but the same in excess above four and its multiples; thus *Náddi* or Ace is counted by one, five, nine, or thirteen cowries; *Dad* or *Deuce*, by two, six, ten, and fourteen; *Tipá* or *Tray*, by three, seven, eleven, and fifteen; and *Pérá*, by four, eight, twelve, and sixteen. There is reason to doubt, however, whether the commentator is correct, and the word *Nardita* presents some trace of the word *Nerd*—the game presented to the Indians by the Persians in exchange for chess; invented, according to *Firdusi*, by *Buzerjemehr*; but improved by him, according to other traditions noticed by the author of the *Burhankati*. The Arabic authorities quoted by Hyde refer it to *Shapur*, or his son *Ardeshir*, of the Sasanian dynasty; but, as he observes, the invention is more usually ascribed to Palamedes at the siege of Troy. It is undoubtedly an ancient game, and was probably familiarly known to all the eastern nations long before the time of *Nushirwan*; the Indians as well as others; and if they invented chess, they might very naturally have elaborated it out of this game, their *Chouper* or *Chaturanga*, a word which seems to be the original of *Shatreng* or *Shatrenj*, *Zatrikion*, *Echecs*, *Scacchi*, *Chess*, and which is applicable to the game as played with *four* bodies or armies. Sir William Jones was informed that Indian chess was so played; but there is no satisfactory proof of this, and it may be doubted whether any other game of tables than *Chouper* is traceable in Sanskrit works.

here's my acquaintance, the keeper of the gaming-house, Máthura: I cannot avoid him, so I will wrap myself up so as not to be known. Eh! this vest is rather threadbare; it is embellished with sundry holes. It makes but a sorry covering, and looks best folded up. (*Folds up his uppercloth after examining it, and puts it under his arm.*) Never mind him; what can he do to me? I can stand with one foot on the ground, and the other in the air, as long as the sun is in the heavens.

Máth. Come, come; your money.

Sam. Whence is it to be got?

Dar. What is going on here?

Passen. This gambler is getting a thrashing from the *Sabhika*, and nobody will take his part.

Dar. Indeed! then I must interfere, I see. (*Approaches.*) Make way here; heigh, sirs: Máthura, that rogue, and the Samváhaka; the wretch, whose head is hanging below his heels at sunset, whose back is variegated with stripes and bruises, and whose legs are daily nibbled by the dogs; what has he, with his lank emaciated carcase, to do with gambling? I must appease Máthura. Good day, Máthura.

Máth. Good day, good day.

Dar. What are you at here?

Máth. This fellow owes me ten *suvarńas*.

Dar. A trifle, a trifle.*

Máth. (*Snatching Darduraka's ragged cloth from him.*) See here, my masters; here is a pretty fellow, in a ragged robe, to call ten *suvarńas* a trifle.

Dar. Why, you blockhead, how often do I stake ten suvar-

There is a striking resemblance between the *Pásas* of the Hindus and *Pessoi* of the Greeks, the latter of which Hyde identifies with dice used in the *Nerdiladium*. Wodhull, the translator of Euripides, adopts the same version, and their authority is preferable to that of Pope, who renders it *Chess*, but makes it out something very different in his note on the passage.

* Literally, a morning meal, a breakfast, *Kalpararitam*.

dus on a throw. What is a man to do with his money? carry it in his waistband!* But you; you are villain enough, for the sake of ten *suvarnas*, to demolish the five senses of a man.

Máth. Keep your *suvarnas* for your morning meal, if you like: this is my property.

Dar. Very well; hear me! Give him other ten *suvarnas*, and let him play you for the whole.

Máth. How so?

Dar. If he wins, he shall pay you the money.

Máth. And if he lose?

Dar. Then, he shall not pay.

Máth. Go to; you talk nonsense. Will you give it? My name's *Máthura*; I am a cheat, and win other men's money unfairly: what then? I am not to be bullied by such a black-guard as you.

Dar. Whom do you call a blackguard?

Máth. You are a blackguard.

Dar. Your father was a blackguard. (*Makes signs to the Samvahaka to escape.*)

Máth. You son of a slave!† are you not a gambler yourself?

Dar. Me! do you call me a gambler?

Máth. Enough, enough. Come, do you pay the ten *suvar-nas*. (*To the Samvahaka.*)

Sam. I will pay them to-day. [*Máthura drags him along.*

Dar. You villain! no one shall maltreat the poor in my presence.

  [*Máthura gives the Samvahaka a blow on the nose; it
  bleeds; the Samvahaka, on seeing his blood, faints
  and falls on the ground. Darduraka approaches, gets*

---

* The natives of India commonly carry money tied up in one end of a cloth, which is bound round their loins, or sometimes thrown over their shoulders.

† *Gonirís-putta*, which the commentator explains *gaṇiká-* or *viṇyá-putra*: this term of abuse is of all perhaps most widely disseminated, and in the languages of Spain and England is as native a in Prákṛit.

between him and Máthura, and a scuffle ensues: they pause.

Máth. You villain! you son of a slave! you shall suffer for this.

Dar. You fool! you have assaulted me on the king's highway; you shall see to-morrow, in court, whether you are to beat people in this manner.

Máth. Ah, ha! yes, yes, I shall see; depend upon it.

Dar. How so! how will you see?

Máth. How! why, so, to be sure. (*Thrusting his face forward.*) [*Dardurака throws a handful of dust into his eyes; Máthura cries out with pain and falls; the Samárdhaka recovers, and according to Dardurака's gesticulations makes his escape.*

Dar. Máthura is a man of some weight here, that's certain; I had better therefore take myself off. My friend Sarvilaka told me that a cunning man has prophesied to a cowherd, named Áryaka, that he shall be king, and people like myself are flocking to him accordingly: my plan is to join him with the rest. [*Exit.*

Scene—VASANTASENÁ'S HOUSE (*outside and inside*).

Enter the SAMVÁHAKA, *wandering about.*

(*Interior.*) The door of this house is open; I will enter it. (*Enters and sees Vasantasená.*) Lady, I seek protection.

Vas. It is offered you; fear nothing. Madaniká, shut the door. What do you fly from?

Sam. A creditor.

Vas. Secure the door. (*To Madaniká.*)

Sam. (*To himself.*) She seems to be as much afraid of a creditor as myself; so much the better; he that takes a burthen suited to his strength will not slip by the way, nor perish in the thicket. My situation is duly known here, it seems.

Enter (outside of the House) MÁTHURA *and the* GAMBLER.

Máth. (*Rubbing his eyes.*) The money, I say; I will have the money.

Gam. Sir, whilst we were struggling with Darduraka, the other rogue has run off.

Máth. The villain! but I have flattened his nose for him; we shall track him by the blood.

Gam. He has entered here. (*Stops at Vasantasená's door.*)

Máth. The ten *suvarńas* are gone.

Gam. Let us complain to the prince.

Máth. In the meantime the scoundrel will come forth and escape. No; let us wait here; we shall have him yet.

Inside of the House.

Vas. (*Makes signs to Madaniká.*)

Mad. (*To the Samvàhaka.*) My mistress, sir, wishes to know whence you are; who you are; what you are; and what you are afraid of.

Sam. I will tell you. I was born, lady, at Pátaliputra; I am the son of a householder, and follow the profession of a Samvàhaka.

Vas. Were you trained to this effeminate occupation?*

Sam. I learnt the practice, lady, to get a livelihood.

Mad. So far so good. Proceed.

Sam. Whilst living in my father's house, I heard travellers talk of distant countries, and felt curious to visit them myself. Accordingly, I came to Ujjayin, where I entered into the service of a distinguished person, whose like for an engaging figure and courteous speech never yet acknowledged kindness or forgot offence—enough said; he only values his consequence as it enables him to do good and cherish all who seek his protection.

---

* She calls it a *sukumára-kalá*, a very soft art; perhaps not intending the exact sense which, in conformity with European ideas, is attached to it in the translation.

Mad. Who is this that so graces Ujjayin, having stolen the good qualities my lady loves?

Vas. Right, Madanika, my heart suggests to me the same inquiry.

Mad. Proceed.

Sam. This gentleman having by his munificent bounty——

Vas. Lavished all his wealth.

Sam. How should your ladyship know? I have not yet told you this.

Vas. I need no telling: worth and wealth are rarely found together. The pool is full to the brim, whose water is unfit for drinking.

Mad. Oblige us with his name.

Sam. To whom is the appellation of that earthly moon unknown, entitled to universal eulogium? his habitation is near the Exchange; his name is Chárudatta.

Vas. (*Springs from her seat.*) Girl, girl, a seat. This house is yours, sir; pray be seated. A fan! wench—quick; our worthy guest is fatigued.*

Sam (*To himself.*) Such respect from the simple utterance of Chárudatta's name! Bravo! excellent Chárudatta! you in this world live; other men only breathe. (*Falls at Vasantasena's feet.*) Pray, lady, resume your seat.

Vas. (*Sitting down.*) Where is your wealthy dun?

Sam. He is truly wealthy,† who is rich in good acts, although he own not perishable riches. He who knows how to honour others, knows how his honour may be best deserved.

Vas. Proceed.

---

* This might be thought a little extravagant, but it is not without a parallel in European flattery, and from motives less reputable. Lewis XIV. having one day sent a footman to the Duke of Monbazon with a letter, the duke, who happened to be at dinner, made the footman take the highest place at his table, and afterwards accompanied him to the court-yard, because he came from the king.

† The connexion of the reply with Vasantasena's question turns upon the word *Dhanika,* which means a rich man as well as a creditor.

Sarh. I was made by that gentleman one of his personal attendants; but in his reduced circumstances being necessarily discharged, I took to play, and by a run of ill-luck have lost ten *suvarnas*.

Mdth. (*Without.*) I am robbed! I am plundered!

Sarh. Hear, lady, hear; those two gamblers are lying wait for me; what is your ladyship's will?

Vas. Madanika, the birds are fluttering about and rustling in the leaves of the adjoining tree; go to this poor fellow's pursuers, and say to them that he sends them this jewel in payment.

Mad. As you command. [*Exit.*

Outside of the House.

Mdth. I am robbed!

MADANIKA *enters by the side door unobserved.*

Mad. These two, by their casting such anxious looks up to the house, their agitation, their close conference, and the diligence with which they watch the door, must be the gambler and the keeper of the gaming-house. I salute you, sir.

Mdth. Joy be with you, wench.

Mad. Which of you two is the master of the gaming-house?

Mdth. He, my graceful damsel, whom you now address with pouting lip, soft speech, and wicked eye; but get you gone; I have nothing for you.

Mad. If you talk thus, you are no gambler. What! have you no one in your debt?

Mdth. Yes, there is a fellow owes me ten *suvarnas:* what of him?

Mad. On his behalf, my mistress sends—nay, I mistake—he sends you this bracelet.

Mdth. Ha, ha! tell him I take this as a pledge, and that he may come and have his revenge when he will.

[*Exeunt severally.*

Inside of the House.

Enter MADANIKÁ.

They have gone away, madam, quite pleased.

Vas. Now, my friend, depart, and relieve the anxiety of your family.

Sam. If there be anything, lady, in which I can be of use to you, employ me.

Vas. There is a higher claim upon your service; you should still be ready to minister to him by whom you were once employed, and on whose account your skill was acquired.

Sam. The lady discards me; how shall I requite her kindness! (*Aloud.*) Lady, as I find my profession only begets disgrace, I will become a Bauddha mendicant;* I tell you my design, and beg you will keep it in your recollection.

Vas. Nay, friend, do nothing rashly.

Sam. I am determined, lady. (*Going.*) In bidding adieu to gambling, the hands of men are no longer armed against me: I can now hold up my head boldly as I go along the public road. (*A noise behind the scenes.*) What is the matter now?

(*Behind the scenes.*) Vasantasená's hunting elephant has broken loose.

Sam. I must go and see this furious beast;—yet why should I, as I purpose a pious life? [*Exit.*

A continued clamour without till KARNAPÚRAKA *enters hastily.*

Kar. Where is my lady?

---

* Literally a *Sákya-sramanaka, takhaśśamanaka.* The expression is rather remarkable, for it decides an important point in the religious history of the Hindus. The *Sarmanes* or *Germanes* of the days of *Alexander* have been supposed to be *Bauddha* ascetics only. Mr. Colebrooke, however, has shown that the term *Sramano* is not restricted to the *Bauddha* sect, but is equally applicable to any ascetic; and although the probable original of *Sarmanes* and *Sramoneous,* and usually expressing a *Bauddha,* it does not necessarily bear that import. This assertion is here confirmed, as the author thinks it necessary to add *Sákya* to *Sramanaka,* to imply a mendicant the follower of *Sákya Muni,* or last living *Buddha.*

Mad. You unmannerly fellow! what ails you? Cannot you see your mistress and address her fittingly?

Kar. Lady, I salute you.

Vas. Karnapúraka, you seem highly pleased with something; what is it?

Kar. You have lost a great deal to-day in not witnessing your humble servant's achievement.

Vas. What achievement?

Kar. Only hear. Your ladyship's fierce elephant Khuñtamornka* killed his keeper and broke his chain; he then scoured off along the high road, making a terrible confusion. The people shouted and screamed, "Carry off the children, get up the trees, climb the walls, the elephant is coming!" Away went girdles and anklets; and pearls and diamonds were scattering about in all directions. There he was, plunging about in Ujjayin, and tearing everything to pieces with his trunk, his feet, and his tusks, as if the city had been a large tank full of lotus flowers. A mendicant came in his way; the elephant broke his staff, water-pot, and platter, sprinkled him with water from his trunk, and held him up between his tusks; all cried out, "The holy man will be killed."

Vas. Alas! alas!

Kar. Don't be alarmed; only hear. Seeing him thus at large, and handling the holy man so roughly, I, Karnapúraka, my lady's humblest slave, determined to rescue the mendicant and punish my gentleman; so I quickly snatched up an iron bar, and approaching him sidelong,† made a desperate blow at the animal.

Vas. Go on.

---

* The name of the elephant *Khuñdamorcka*, which is given in the text, is said to be a Mahratta compound, signifying the breaker of the post to which he is chained.

† *Vámachalanéna jáda-lekhanam upphania*, drawing a gaming-letter with the left foot, is the literal expression, the exact sense of which is not explained by the commentator.

Kar. Dig as he was, like the peaks of Vindhya, I brought him down and saved the saint.

Vas. You have done well.

Kar. So everybody said, "Well done, Karnapúraka, well done!" for all Ujjayin, in a panic, like a boat ill-laden, was heaped on one spot, and one person, who had no great matter of dress to boast of himself, turning his eyes upwards, and fetching a deep sigh, threw his garment over me.

Vas. Does it smell of jasmines?

Kar. The smell of the elephant's frontal moisture is still in my nostrils; so I cannot tell how the garment smells.

Vas. Is there any name on it? see, see!

Kar. Here are letters; your ladyship will best be able to read them.*

Vas. (*Reads.*) Chárudatta! (*Throws the cloth round her with delight.*)

Mad. How well the garment becomes our mistress, does it not?

Kar. (*Sulkily.*) Yes, it becomes her well enough.

Vas. Karúnpúraka, be this your recompense. (*Gives him an ornament.*)

Kar. (*Puts it to his head and bows.*) Now indeed the garment sets as it should do.

Vas. Where did you leave Chárudatta?

Kar. Going home, I believe, along this road.

Vas. (*To Madanikd.*) Quick, girl, quick; up on this terrace, and we may yet catch a glimpse of him. [*Exeunt.*

* The art of marking on linen was therefore known to the Hindus.

END OF THE SECOND ACT.

ACT III.

CHÁRUDATTA'S HOUSE (*outside and inside*).

Enter VARDHAMÁNA (*inside*).

A WORTHY kind master, even though he be poor, is the delight of his servants; whilst a morose haughty fellow, who has only his wealth to boast of, is a constant vexation. There is no changing nature; nothing can keep an ox out of a field of corn, nor stop a man who covets another's wife. There is no parting a gamester from the dice, and there is no remedy for an innate defect. My excellent master has gone to a concert. It is not quite midnight, I suppose. I need not expect his return yet awhile; I shall therefore take a nap in the hall. (*Sleeps.*)

Enter (*outside*) CHÁRUDATTA *and* MAITREYA.

Chár. Excellent, excellent indeed; Rebhila sang most exquisitely.

Although not ocean-born, the tuneful *vínâ* *
Is most assuredly a gem of heaven—

---

* The Hindu lute. A description of it may be seen in the first volume of the *Researches*; it is an instrument of much sweetness and compass, but little power. At the churning of the ocean by the gods and demons, various persons and articles were recovered from the deep; these are called *ratnas*, or gems, and the popular enumeration of them is fourteen—or *Lakshmí* the Goddess of Beauty, *Dhanwantari* the physician of the Gods, the *Apsarasas* or Nymphs of Indra's heaven, *Surá* the Goddess of Wine, the Moon, the Jewel worn by Krishńa, the all-bestowing Tree, the Cow of Abundance, the Elephant of Indra, his Steed, Poison, and Ambrosia: the other two are the Bow of Vishńu and his *Sankha*, or Shell; but they are not generally included in the Pauranic lists, and even the Bhágavata- and

Like a dear friend, it cheers the lonely heart,
And lends new lustre to the social meeting.
It lulls the pain that absent lovers feel,
And adds fresh impulse to the glow of passion.

Mait. Come, sir, let us get home.

Chdr. In truth, brave Rebhila, 'twas deftly sung.

Mait. Now, to me, there are two things at which I cannot choose but laugh, a woman reading Sanskṛit, and a man singing a song: the woman snuffles like a young cow when the rope is first passed through her nostrils;* and the man wheezes like an old Pandit who has been repeating his bead-roll till the flowers of his chaplet are as dry as his throat: to my seeming it is vastly ridiculous.

Chdr. What, my good friend, were you not pleased to-night with Rebhila's fine execution?—

Smooth were the tones, articulate and flowing
With graceful modulation, sweet and pleasing,
And fraught with warm and passionate expression;
So that I often thought the dulcet sounds
Some female, stationed covertly, must utter.
Still echoes in my ears the soothing strain,
And as I pace along, methinks I hear
The liquid cadence and melodious utterance.
The *rís's* sweet notes, now gently undulating,
Now swelling high, now dying to a close—

Vishṇu-Purāṇa omit them. In one place the Padma-Purāṇa gives but eleven, omitting the *Kaustubha* or gem of Kṛishṇa; in another, the *Uttara-Khaṇḍa*, it enumerates nine, and the list is rather peculiar. It runs: Poison; the Goddess of Misfortune; the Goddess of Wine; Sloth; the Apsarases; the Elephant of Indra; Lakshmí; the Moon; the Tulasí plant. The *Mahábhárata* specifies but nine; omitting the Cow and Tree of Plenty and the beauties of Swarga.

* The rein in draft-cattle is passed through the cartilaginous septum of the nose. The fashion seems to have been a European one in former times: thus Iago says of *Othello*—

"He will as tenderly be led by the nose,
As asses are."

Sporting awhile in desultory descant,
And still recurring to the tasteful theme."

Mait. Come, my friend, the very dogs in the high road through the market-place are fast asleep; let us go home. See, see, the moon descends from his mansion in the skies, making his way through the darkness.

Chár. True have you said. From his high palace bowed,
And hastening to his setting, scantly gleams
The waning moon, amidst the gathering gloom;
In slender crescent, like the tusk's fine point,
That peers above the darkening wave, where bathes
The forest elephant.

Mait. Here we are at home. Holloa! Vardhamána, arise and open the door.

Vardh. (*Within.*) Hark, I hear Maitreya's voice: Chárudatta is returned; I must let him in. (*Opens the door.*) Sir, I salute you; you also Maitreya. Here are the couches ready spread; please you to repose. (*They enter and sit.*)

Mait. Vardhamána, tell Radaniká to bring water for the feet. †

Chár. Nay, nay, disturb not those who are asleep.

Vardh. I will bring water, and Maitreya here can wash your feet.

Mait. Do you hear, my friend, the son of a slave? he is to hold the water, and he sets me, who am a Brahman, to wash your feet.

---

* Some liberties have been here unavoidably taken with the text, for the precise force of several of the technical terms employed it is impossible to render without a familiarity with the musical theory of the Hindus, to which the translator makes no pretence. It is believed, however, that the deviation from their general tenor is not very excursive.

† Washing the feet upon a person's return home has always been the common practice of the oriental nations: it was equally the practice of the Greeks: thus *Philoxleon* in the *Wasps*—

"Next my girl, sprightly nymph, brings her napkin and lymph,
Feet and ankles are quick to ablution."

Chár. Do you, Maitreya, hold the water; Vardhamána can perform the rest.

Vardh. Come then, worthy Maitreya, pour out the water. (*Vardhamána washes Chárudatta's feet, and is going.*)

Chár. Nay, Vardhamána, wash the feet of the Brahman.

Mait. Never mind; it is of little use; I must soon go tramping over the ground again, like a jackass.

Vardh. Most worthy Maitreya, you are a Brahman, are you?

Mait. To be sure I am; like the boa amongst serpents, so am I, a Brahman amongst Brahmans.

Vardh. I cry you mercy: that being the case, I will wash your feet. (*Does so.*) Now, Maitreya, this gold casket, of which I have had the charge by day, it is your turn to take care of. (*Gives it to him, and exit.*)

Mait. So; it is safe through the day. What! have we no thieves in Ujjayin, that no one could have carried off this vile pilferer of my rest: pray let me carry it into the courtyard.

Chár. Impossible, it has been left in trust;
And is not to be parted with to any
But the right owner; Brahman, take heed to it. (*Lies down.*)
Still do I hear the soothing strain.

Mait. Pray, sir, is it your intention to go to sleep?

Chár. Assuredly.
I feel the drowsy deity invade
My forehead, and descend upon my eyelids.
Sleep, like decay, viewless and variable,
Grows stronger in its triumph o'er our strength.

Mait. Very true, so let us go to sleep. (*They sleep.*)

Enter SARVILAKA (*outside*).

Creeping along the ground, like a snake crawling out of his old skin, I effect with slight and strength a passage for my cowering frame. (*Looking up.*) The sovereign of the skies is in his decline: 'tis well. Night, like a tender mother, shrouds with her protecting darkness those of her children whose prowess assails the dwellings of mankind, and shrinks from an encounter with the servants of the king. I have made a breach in the garden wall, and have got into the midst of the garden. Now for the house. Men call this practice infamous, whose chief success is gained from the sleep of others, and whose booty is won by craft. If not heroism, it is at least independence, and preferable to the homage paid by slaves. As to nocturnal attacks, did not *Aswatthaman* long ago overpower in a night-onset his slumbering foes?" Where shall I make the breach? what part is softened by recent damp? where is it likely that no noise will be made by the falling fragments? where is a wide opening most practicable which will not be afterwards visible? in what part of the wall are the bricks old, and corroded by saline exudations?† where can I penetrate without encountering women?‡ and where am I likely to light upon my booty? (*Feels the wall.*) The ground here is softened by continual sprinkling with water and exposure to the sun, and is crusted with salt. Here is a rat-hole. The prize is sure: this is the first omen of success the sons of *Skanda* have laid down. Let me see: how shall I proceed? The god of the golden spear§ teaches four modes of breaching a house: picking out burnt bricks, cutting through unbaked ones, throwing water on a mud wall, and boring through one of wood. This wall is of baked bricks: they must be picked out, but I must give them a sample of my skill. Shall the breach be the lotus blossom, the full sun or the new moon, the lake, the

* This exploit forms the subject of a section of the *Mahábhárata*, the *Sauptika-Parvan*.

† These considerations, and much of what follows, are agreeably to the Thief's Manual, which is said to exist in Samskrit, or a work on the *Chaurya-Vidyá*, the Science of Thieving, ascribed to *Yogáchárya*, who was taught the science by no less a person than the god *Kárttikeya*, resembling, in respect to the objects of this patronage, the Grecian Mercury.

‡ To be avoided either out of delicacy towards the sex or as a bad omen.

§ *Kárttikeya.*

swastika,* or the water-jar? It must be something to astonish the natives. The water-jar looks best in a brick wall;—that shall be the shape. In other walls that I have breached by night, the neighbours have had occasion both to censure and approve my talents. Reverence to the prince *Kárttikeya*, the giver of all good; reverence to the god of the golden spear; to *Bráhmaṇya*, the celestial champion of the celestials; the son of fire.† Reverence to *Yogáchárya*, whose chief scholar I am, and by whom well pleased was the magic unguent‡ conferred upon me, anointed with which, no eye beholds nor weapon harms me. Shame on me! I have forgotten my measuring-line, —never mind, my Brahmanical thread will answer the purpose. This thread is a most useful appendage to a Brahman, especially one of my complexion: it serves to measure the depth and height of walls, and to withdraw ornaments from their position; it opens a latch in a door as well as a key, and is an excellent ligature for the bite of a snake. Let us take measure, and go to work: so, so—(*extracting the bricks*)—one brick alone remains. Ha! hang it; I am bitten by a snake—(*ties the finger with the cord*)—'tis well again,—I must get on. (*Looks in.*) How! a lamp alight! the golden ray streaming through the opening in the wall shows amidst the exterior darkness, like the yellow streak of pure metal on the touchstone. The breach is perfect; now to enter.§ There is no one. Reverence to *Kárttikeya*. (*Enters.*) Here are two men asleep; let me set the outer door

---

* A magical diagram so called.

† These are all epithets of *Kárttikeya*, who in his military character corresponds to the Grecian Mars. He seems to have lost his reputation as the patron of thieves, who more usually worship some of the forms of *Durgá*.

‡ *Yogarochana*. *Yoga* here is abstract devotion, for the purpose of obtaining supernatural power. What the article is may be doubted, but *rochaná* may be rendered unguent.

§ He talks in the text, however, of sending in a deputy first; the term is *pratipurusha*, a pro man or substitute: it is questionable, however, what is precisely meant here, especially as no further allusion is made to such a character: it is probably a slip of the author.

open to get off easily if there should be occasion; how it creaks! it is stiff with age; a little water will be of use. (*Sprinkles the floor.*) Nay, not so, it makes too much noise pattering on the ground. (*Supports the door with his back, and opens it.*) So far, so well. Now, are these true sleepers or only counterfeits? (*He tries them.*) They are sound: the breathing is regular and not fluttered; the eye is fast and firmly shut; the body is all relaxed; the joints are loose, and the limbs protrude beyond the limits of the bed. If shamming sleep, they will not bear the gleam of the lamp upon their faces. (*Passes the lamp over their faces.*) All is safe. What have we here? a drum, a tabor, a lute, pipes; and here are books. Why, zounds, I have got into the house of a dancer or a poet. I took it for the dwelling of some man of consequence, or I should have let it alone. Is this poverty, or only the show of poverty? fear of thieves, or dread of the king? Are the effects hid underground? Whatever is underground is my property. Let us scatter the seed, whose sowing leaves nothing undiscernible. (*Throws about seeds.*) The man is an absolute pauper, and so I leave him. (*Going.*)

Mait. (*Dreaming.*) Master, they are breaking into the house. I see the thief. Here, here! do you take care of the gold casket.

Sar. How! does he perceive me? does he mock me with his poverty? he dies. (*Approaching.*) Haply he dreams. (*Looking at Maitreya.*) Eh! sure enough, there is in the light of the lamp something like a casket wrapped up in a ragged bathing-gown; that must be mine. No, no; it is cruel to ruin a worthy man, so miserably reduced already. I will even let it alone.

Mait. (*Dreaming.*) My friend, if you do not take the casket, may you incur the guilt of disappointing a cow, and of deceiving a Brahman.

Sar. These invocations are irresistible: take it I must. Softly: the light will betray me. I have the fire-flapping insect to put it out. I must cast it into the lamp. (*Takes out the insect.*) Place and time requiring, let this insect fly. It hovers round the wick—with the wind of its wings the flame is extinguished. Shame on this total darkness, or rather shame on the darkness with which I have obscured the lustre of my race! how well it suits that Sarvilaka, a Brahman, the son of a Brahman, learned in the four *Vedas*, and above receiving donations from others, should now be engaged in such unworthy courses! And why? For the sake of a harlot, for the sake of Madaniká. Ah, well! I must even go on, and acknowledge the courtesy of this Brahman.

Mait. (*Half-awake.*) Eh, my good friend, how cold your hand is!

Sar. Blockhead! I had forgotten, I have chilled my hand by the water I touched; I will put it to my side. (*Chafes his left hand on his side and takes the casket with it.*)

Mait. (*Still only half-awake*). Have you got it?

Sar. The civility of this Brahman is exceeding! I have it.

Mait. Now like a pedlar that has sold all his wares, I shall go soundly to sleep. (*Sleeps.*)

Sar. Sleep, illustrious Brahman! May you sleep a hundred years! Fie on this love! for whose dear sake I thus bring trouble on a Brahman's dwelling—nay, rather call down shame upon myself; and fie! and fie! upon this unmanning poverty, that urges me to acts which I must needs condemn. Now to Vasantasena to redeem my beloved Madaniká with this night's booty. I hear footsteps; should it be the watch—what then!— shall I stand here like a post?—no, let Sarvilaka be his own protection. Am I not a cat in climbing, a deer in running, a snake in twisting, a hawk in darting upon the prey, a dog in baying man, whether asleep or awake! In assuming various forms am I not *Máyá** herself, and *Saraswati*† in the gift of tongues? A lamp in the night, a mule in a defile, a horse by land, a boat by water, a snake in motion, and a rock in

---

* The personification of Illusion and unreality.

† The wife of *Brahmá*, and goddess of learning and the arts.

stability! In hovering about I compete with the king of birds, and in an eye to the ground, am keener than the hare. Am I not like a wolf in seizing, and like a lion in strength?

Enter RADANIKÁ.

Bless me! what has become of Vardhamána? He was asleep at the hall door, but is there no longer. I must wake Maitreya. (*Approaches.*)

Sar. (*Going to stab her.*) Ha! a woman! she is safe, and I may depart. [*Exit.*

Rad. Oh, dear me! a thief has broken into the house, and there he goes out at the door. Why, Maitreya! Maitreya! up, up, I say. A thief has broken into the house, and has just made his escape.

Mait. Eh, what do you say, you foolish toad? a thief made his escape?

Rad. Nay, this is no joke—see here.

Mait. What say you, hey, the outer door opened? Chárudatta, friend, awake! a thief has been in the house and has just made his escape.

Chár. This is not an hour to jest.

Mait. It is true enough, as you may satisfy yourself.

Chár. Where did he get in?

Mait. Look here. (*Discovers the breach.*)

Chár. Upon my word, a not unseemly fissure; the bricks are taken out above and below; the head is small, the body large: there is really talent in this thief.

Mait. The opening must have been made by one of two persons; by a novice, merely to try his hand, or by a stranger to this city; for who in Ujjayin is ignorant of the poverty of our mansion?

Chár. No doubt, by a stranger—one who did not know the condition of my affairs, and forgot that those only sleep soundly who have little to lose. Trusting to the external semblance of this mansion, erected in more prosperous times, he entered full of hope, and has gone away disappointed.

What will the poor fellow have to tell his comrades? I have broken into the house of the son of the chief of a corporation, and found nothing.

Mait. Really, I am very much concerned for the luckless rogue. Ah, ha! thought he, here is a fine house; now for jewels, for caskets. (*Recollecting.*) By the by, where is the casket? oh yes, I remember. Ha, ha! my friend, you are apt to say of me, that blockhead Maitreya! that dunderhead Maitreya! but it was a wise trick of mine to give the casket to you: had I not done so, the villain would have walked off with it.

Chdr. Come, come, this jesting is misplaced.

Mait. Jesting—no, no; blockhead though I be, I know when a joke is out of season.

Chdr. When did you give the casket to me?

Mait. When I called out to you, "How cold your hand is!"

Chdr. It must be so. (*Looking about.*) My good friend, I am much obliged by your kindness.

Mait. Why: is not the casket stolen?

Chdr. It is stolen.

Mait. Then what have you to thank me for?

Chdr. That the poor rogue has not gone away empty-handed.

Mait. He has carried off what was left in trust.

Chdr. How! in trust, alas! (*Faints.*)

Mait. Revive, revive, sir! though the thief has stolen the deposit, why should it so seriously affect you?

Chdr. Alas! my friend, who will believe it stolen?
 A general ordeal waits me. In this world
 Cold poverty is doomed to wake suspicion.
 Alas! till now, my fortune only felt
 The enmity of fate; but now its venom
 Sheds a foul blight upon my dearer fame.

Mait. I tell you what. I will maintain that the casket was never entrusted to us. Who gave it, pray? who took it? where are your witnesses?

Chár. Think you I can sanction thus a falsity?
No, no; I will beg alms, and so obtain
The value of the pledge, and quit its owner;
But cannot condescend to shame my soul
By utterance of a lie. [*Exit.*
Rad. I will go and tell my mistress what has happened.
[*Exit.*

Scene—Another Room.

Enter the WIFE *of* CHÁRUDATTA *and* RADANIKÁ.*

Wife. But indeed is my lord unhurt? is he safe, and his friend Maitreya?

Rad. Both safe, madam, I assure you, but the ornaments left by the courtesan are stolen.

Wife. Alas, girl! what say you? My husband's person is unharmed: that glads me. Yet better had his person come to harm than his fair fame incur disparagement. The people of Ujjayin will now be ready to suspect that indigence has impelled him to an unworthy act. Destiny, thou potent deity, thou sportest with the fortunes of mankind, and renderest them as tremulous as the watery drop that quivers on the lotus leaves. This string of jewels was given me in my maternal mansion: † it is all that is left to us, and I know my husband, in the loftiness of his spirit, will not accept it from me. Girl, go call the worthy Maitreya hither. [*Exit.*

RADANIKÁ *returns with* MAITREYA.

Mait. Health to you, respected lady.
Wife. I salute you, sir. Oblige me by facing the east.
Mait. You are obeyed.
Wife. I pray you accept this.
Mait. Nay, not so.

---

* The close of the last scene, the present scene, and the first part of the ensuing, offer a favourable picture of the domestic character of the Hindus. Radaniká has been rather rapid in her communication.

† One of the sources of the wife's peculiar wealth over which the husband has no control.

Wife. I fasted on the *Ratnashashthi*,* when, as you know, wealth must be given to a Brahman. My Brahman had been provided elsewhere, and I beg therefore that, in his stead, you will accept this string of jewels.

Mait. Very well; I will go and state the matter to my friend.

Wife. Thanks, Maitreya; but take heed, do not put me to shame. [*Exit.*

Scene—*The Hall.* CHÁRUDATTA *discovered.*

Chár. Maitreya tarries long; in his distress I hope he does not purpose aught unfitting.

Enter MAITREYA.

Mait. Here am I, sir, and bring you this. (*Gives the string of jewels.*)

Chár. What is this?

Mait. The fruit borne by the excellence of a wife worthy of her husband.

Chár. Is this the kindness of the Brahman's wife?
Out on it!—that I should be reduced so low
As, when my own has disappeared, to need
Assistance from a woman's wealth. So true
It is, our very natures are transformed
By opulence: the poor man helpless grows,
And woman wealthy acts with manly vigour.—
'Tis false; I am not poor:—a wife whose love
Outlives my fortune; a true friend who shares
My sorrows and my joy; and honesty
Unwarped by indigence, these still are mine.
Maitreya, hie thee to Vasantasená,
Tell her the casket, heedlessly impledged,
Was lost by me at play, but in its stead
I do beseech her to accept these jewels.

---

* A vow is probably implied: the occasion is not at present in the ritual; the term *shashthi* implies it was some observance held on the sixth day of the lunar fortnight.

Mait. I will do no such thing. What! are we to part with these gems, the quintessence of the four oceans, for a thing carried off by thieves, and which we have neither eaten nor drank, nor touched a penny for?

Chdr. Not so; to me, confiding in my care
And honesty, the casket was entrusted;
And for that faith, which cannot be o'ervalued,
A price of high amount must be repaid.
Touching my breast, I therefore supplicate,
You will not hence, this charge not undertaken.
You, Vardhamána, gather up these bricks
To fill the chasm again; we'll leave no trace
To catch the idle censure of men's tongues.
Come, come, Maitreya, rouse a liberal feeling,
Nor act in this a despicable niggard.

Mait. How can a pauper be a niggard? he has nothing to part with.

Chdr. I am not poor, I tell thee, but retain
Treasures I prize beyond whate'er is lost.
Go then, discharge this office, and meanwhile
I hail the dawn with its accustomed rites. [*Exit.*

END OF THE THIRD ACT.

ACT IV.

VASANTASENÁ'S HOUSE.

Enter Female Attendant.

I am sent to the lady Vasantasená by her mother: oh, here she is, looking on a picture, and engaged in conversation with Madaniká.

Enter VASANTASENÁ *as described.*

Vas. But, Madaniká, is this a good likeness of Chárudatta?
Mad. Very good.
Vas. How do you know?
Mad. I conclude so, madam, from the affectionate looks which you bestow upon it.
Vas. How, wench, do you say this in the language of our profession?
Mad. Nay, madam, surely even one of us is not incapable of speaking truth.
Vas. The woman, wench, that admits the love of many men is false to them all.
Mad. Yet, madam, when the eyes and thoughts are intent but on one object, it is very unnecessary to inquire the cause.
Vas. But tell me, girl, do I not seem ridiculous to my friends?
Mad. Nay, not so, madam; a woman is secure of the sympathy of her companions.

Attendant advances.

Att. Madam, your mother desires you to ascend your litter and repair to the private apartments.
Vas. To meet my Chárudatta.

Att. The person, madam, who has sent the chariot has sent very costly ornaments.*

Vas. Who is he?

Att. Samsthánaka, the Rája's brother-in-law.

Vas. Begone, let me not hear him named.

Att. Forgive me, madam; I but deliver my message.

Vas. The message is odious.

Att. What reply am I to convey to your lady mother?

Vas. Tell her, if she would not have me dead, she must send me no more such messages.

Att. I shall obey. [*Exit.*

The Outside of the House—A Garden.

Enter SARVILAKA (*below*).

Sar. My course is like the moon's, and with the dawn
Declines its fading beams: my deeds have shamed
The lazy night, have triumphed over sleep,
And mocked the baffled vigilance of the watch.
Yet I am scant secure, and view with terror
Him who appears to track my rapid steps,
Or seems to hasten where I rest my flight.—
Thus guilty conscience makes me fear, for man
Is ever frightened by his own offences. †
'Tis for Madaniká's dear sake alone
I perpetrate this violence, as I shun
The leader and his train, avoid the mansion
A woman sole inhabits, or I stand
Still as the door-post, while the town-guard passes,
And with a hundred tricks thus make the night
As full of action as the busy day.

Vas. (*Within.*) Here, girl, take the picture, lay it on my couch; and here, bring me my fan.

---

* Literally, ornaments to the value of ten thousand *suvarnas*.

† It might be rendered, "Thus conscience does make cowards of us all." Tad sarvam talayati dúshito 'ntaritmá svair doshair bhavati hi sankito manushyah.

Mad. I obey. [*Exit Madanikā.*
Sar. This is the dwelling of Vasantasenā. (*Enters.*) Where can Madanikā be found?

MADANIKĀ *enters with the fan.*

Sar. Ah, here she comes, as graceful as the bride
Of love, and soothing to my burning heart
As sandal to the fevered flesh. Madanikā!
Mad. Eh! S'arvilaka! health to you. Whence do you come?
Sar. I will tell you.

Enter VASANTASENĀ (*above*).

Vas. (*Above.*) Madinakā tarries long; where can she be? (*Looks from the window.*) How! she is engaged in conversation with a man: her eyes are fixed intently upon him, and seem to quaff overflowing drafts of love; they appear to understand each other. He woos her probably to be his companion: well, be it so; never be genuine affection thwarted. I will wait her leisure.

Mad. Well, S'arvilaka, proceed. (*He looks cautiously round.*) Why do you thus examine the place? You seem alarmed.
Sar. I have a secret to entrust you with; are we alone?
Mad. Quite.
Vas. A secret! then I must not listen longer.
Sar. Tell me, Madanikā, what cost procures
Your manumission of Vasantasenā?
Vas. He names me; the secret then regards me, and I must be a party in it; behind this window I can overhear him unobserved.
Mad. My lady has often declared, S'arvilaka, that she would liberate us all without price if she were her own mistress; but where is the wealth with which you are to purchase my freedom?
Sar. To tell you sooth, my poverty and love
Have urged me to an act of violence.
Vas. How has this act transformed his otherwise goodly appearance!

Mad. Ah! Sarvilaka, for a transitory enjoyment you have endangered two valuable things.

Sar. And what are they?

Mad. Your person and your reputation.

Sar. Silly girl! fortune favours force.

Mad. (*Ironically.*) Your conduct is without blame; the violence you have committed on my account is no doubt quite proper.

Sar. It may be venial, for I have not plundered
A lovely woman graced with glittering gems,
The blossoms of a creeper. I have not filched
A Brahman's gold, for purposes of piety
Collected, nor from the heedless nurse
Have I borne off the innocent babe for hire.
I have well weighed whate'er I have committed.
Apprise your mistress, then, these gems are hers,
That seem as they were made on purpose for her,
If she will yield you up, but let her keep them
Carefully concealed.

Mad. An ornament that must never be worn is but ill suited to my mistress. But come, let me see these trinkets.

Sar. Behold them.

Mad. I have certainly seen them before: where did you get them?

Sar. That concerns not you; ask no questions, but take them.

Mad. (*Angrily.*) If you can place no confidence in me, why seek to make me yours?

Sar. I was informed, then, that near the Bazar resided the chief of his tribe, one Chárudatta.

VASANTASENÁ *and* MADANIKÁ *both faint.*

Sar. Madaniká, revive! what ails the wench?
Her limbs are all unstrung, her looks are wild.
Why, girl, is this your love? is then so terrible
The thought to share your destiny with mine?

70   THE TOY-CART.

Mad. Avoid me, wretch! Yet stay, I dread to ask. Was
no one hurt or murdered in that mansion?
    Sar. I touch not one who trembles or who sleeps.
    Unharmed by me were all in that abode.
Mad. In truth?
Sar. In very truth.
Vas. Do I yet live?
Mad. This is indeed a blessing.
Sar. (*With jealous warmth.*)
    You seem to take strange interest in this business.
    'Twas love of you that urged me to the act—
    Me, sprung of virtuous and of pure descent.
    Spurred by my passion, I have offered you
    A life of credit and a faithful heart;
    And this is my reward—to be reviled,
    And find your cares devoted to another.
    In vain the lofty tree of flowering youth
    Bears goodly fruit, the prey of harlot birds.
    Wealth, manhood, all we value, are consumed
    By passion's fierce ungovernable fire.
    Ah! what a fool is man, to place his trust
    In woman or in fortune, fickle both
    As serpent-nymphs! Be woman's love unwoo'd,
    For humble love she pays with scorn. Let her
    First proffer tenderness, and whilst it lasts
    Be kind, but leave her as her fondness cools.
    'Tis wisely said, for money woman weeps
    And smiles at will, and of his confidence,
    The man she trusts not, craftily beguiles.
    Let then the youth of merit and of birth
    Beware the wanton's charms, that baleful blow
    Like flowers on charnel ground; the ocean waves
    Are less unsteady, and the varying tints
    Of eve less fleeting than a woman's fondness.
    Wealth is her aim; as soon as man is drained
    Of all his goods, like a squeezed colour bag,

She casts him off. Brief as the lightning's flash
Is woman's love. Nay, she can look devotion
To one man whilst another rules her heart,
And even whilst she holds in fond embrace
One lover, for his rival breathes her sighs.
But why expect what nature has withheld?
The lotus blooms not on the mountain's brow,
Nor bears the mule the burthen of the horse;
The grain of barley buds not into rice,
Nor dwells one virtue in the breast of woman.*
Fool that I was, to let that wretch escape;
'Tis not too late, and Chárudatta dies. (*Going.*)

Mad. (*Catching hold of him.*) You have talked a great deal of stuff, and are angry without rhyme or reason.

Sar. How, without reason?

Mad. These ornaments are in truth the property of Vasantasená.

Sar. Indeed!

Mad. And were left by her in deposit with Chárudatta.

Sar. For what purpose?

Mad. I will tell you. (*Whispers.*)

Sar. I am overcome with shame. The friendly branch
. That gave me shadow when oppressed with heat,
My heedless hand has shorn of its bright leaves.

Vas. I am glad that he repents: he has acted without reflection.

Sar. What is to be done?

Mad. You are the best judge.

---

* In generalising some of these asperities the author is made to appear more of a misogynist than he really is; some of the aspersions are, however, addressed to the whole sex, and the application of the rest is not without countenance. The Hindu poets very rarely dispraise women; they almost invariably represent them as amiable and affectionate. In this they might give a lesson to the bards of more lofty nations, and particularly to the Greeks, who both in tragedy and comedy pursued the fair sex with implacable rancour. Aristophanes is not a whit behind Euripides, although he ridicules the tragedian for his ungallant propensities.

Sar. Nay, not so.
    Nature is woman's teacher, and she learns
    More sense than man, the pedant, gleans from books.
Mad. I should advise you then, go and return these ornaments to Chárudatta.
Sar. And what if he deliver me up to justice?
Mad. There is no heat from the moon.
Sar. I heed not of his gentleness, and brave
    Unshrinkingly the consequence of all
    I dare to do—but this, this act I blush for;
    And of such petty scoundrels as myself
    How must the prince dispose? No—no,
    We must devise some other means.
Mad. I have.
Vas. What can she suggest?
Mad. You shall pass yourself off as a messenger from Chárudatta, sent to restore these trinkets to my lady.
Sar. And what results?
Mad. You will be no thief; Chárudatta will sustain no loss, and my lady recover her own property.
Sar. This is downright robbery, carrying off my booty.
Mad. If you do not relinquish it, that will be much more like robbery.
Vas. Well said, Madaniká; you advise as a faithful friend.
Sar. I have gained much by asking your advice.
    When there is no moon at night, 'tis difficult
    To get a guide that may be safely followed.
Mad. Stay here,* whilst I give notice to my mistress.
Sar. Be it so.
Mad. (*Approaches Vasantasená.*) Lady, a Brahman attends you from Chárudatta.
Vas. How do you know his mission?
Mad. Do I not know my own affairs?

---

* In the original *masmín kámadevagehe*. In this dwelling of Kámadeva, a chamber or open porch probably, with the figure of the Hindu Cupid.

Vas. (*Smiling.*) Very true; let him advance, Madaniká.
[*She descends, and brings Sarviláka forward as Vasantasená enters below.*]

Sar. Lady, I salute you; peace be with you.

Vas. I salute you. Pray be seated. (*Sits.*)

Sar. The respected Chárudatta informs you, that as his house is very insecure, he is apprehensive this casket may be lost, and therefore begs you will take it back again. (*Gives it to Madaniká and is going.*)

Vas. Stay; I have a favour to request. Let me trouble you to convey to the worthy sender something from me.

Sar. (*Aside.*) Who the deuce is to give it to him? (*Aloud.*) What am I to take?

Vas. Madaniká.

Sar. I understand you not.

Vas. I understand myself.

Sar. What mean you?

Vas. The truth is, it was agreed between Chárudatta and me, that the person by whom he should send back these jewels should receive Madaniká as a present from me on his account: you are therefore to take this damsel, and thank Chárudatta for her. You understand me now.

Sar. (*Apart.*) She knows the truth; that is clear. No matter (*Aloud.*)

    May all prosperity bless Chárudatta.
    'Tis politic in man to nurture merit,
    For poverty with worth is richer far
    Than majesty without all real excellence.
    Nought is beyond its reach; the radiant moon
    Won by its worth a seat on *Siva's* * brow.

Vas. Who waits? bring forth the litter.†

Sar. It attends. (*The carriage comes on.*)

Vas. My dear girl, Madaniká, ascend the litter; I have given you away: look at me well; do not forget me.

---

* The god *Siva* wears the crescent moon as the ornament of his forehead.

† A small covered carriage on two wheels, drawn by oxen.

Mad. (Weeping.) I am discarded by my mistress. *(Falls at her feet.)*

Vas. Nay, wench, rise, it is now my place to stoop to you; go take your seat, and keep me ever in your recollection.

Sar. Lady, may every good attend you! Madaniká, with grateful looks survey your bounteous benefactress; bow your head in gratitude to her to whom you owe the unexpected dignity that waits upon the title and the state of wife.*

[*They salute* VASANTASENÁ *as she departs, and ascend the car.*

(Behind.)

Who hears! who hears! the Governor commands. In consequence of a reported prophecy, that the son of a cowherd, named Áryaka, shall ascend the throne, his majesty Pálaka has deemed it expedient to apprehend him, and detain him in confinement. Let all men therefore remain quietly in their houses, and entertain no alarm.

Sar. How! the king has seized my dear friend Áryaka, and I am thinking of a wife!

This world presents two things most dear to all men;
A friend and mistress; but the friend is prized
Above a hundred beauties. I must hence,
And try to liberate him. *(Alights.)*

Mad. Stay but a while, my dearest lord; consign me first to reputable friends, then leave me, if it must be so.

Sar. You speak my thoughts, love. Hark ye. *(To the servant.)* Know you the residence of Rebhila,
The chief of the musicians?

Serv. I do, sir.

* *Vadhátabdúragnsúthana*, the covering of the title of wife. At the same time Madaniká is of course only a wife for the nonce, or rather of an inferior degree; an *amie de maison*, or a gentle concubine. In India these left-hand marriages are common amongst both Hindus and Mohammedans, and are considered by no means disreputable. It would be impossible to contract any other with a woman of Madaniká's past life and servile condition. On the ground of disparity of rank, left-hand marriages are still sanctioned in Germany, but they seem not essentially different from those here alluded to.

Sar. Convey my lady thither.
Serv. As you command.
Mad. I obey. Farewell. For my sake, be not rash.
[*Exit.*

Sar. Now then to rouse the friends of Áryaka,
Our kindred and associates—all who deem
The king has wronged their will, and all who trust
The prowess of their arms. We will redeem
Our chief from bonds, as by his faithful minister
Udayana* was rescued.
This seizure is unjust, it is the deed
Of a most cowardly and treacherous foe ;
But we shall soon release him from such grasp,
Like the fair moon from *Ráhu's* jaws set free.†
[*Exit.*

Vasantasená's Dwelling (inside).

Enter A Female Attendant, *meeting* VASANTASENÁ.

Att. Lady, you are fortunate, a Brahman from Chárudatta.
Vas. This is indeed a lucky day. Receive him with all

---

* Udayana or *Vatsa* is a celebrated character in Hindu fiction. He was the son of Sahasráníka and grandson of Satáníka, who transferred the capital of Upper India from Hástinapur to Kausámbí. Satáníka was the son of Janamejaya, the great grandson of Arjuna. *Vatsa* was named Udayana from being educated on the Eastern or Udaya mountain by the sage Jamadagni. When arrived at maturity, he was decoyed into captivity by Chandasena, king of Ujjayin. He was liberated by his minister Yogandharáyana, and in his escape carried off *Vásavadattá*, the daughter of his captor. His adventures are recorded in the *Vásavadattá*, a poem by Subhándhu, and in the Vrihat-Kathá. They have been translated from the latter and published in the *Calcutta Quarterly Magazine* for June 1824. All the parties will become more familiar to us hereafter, as *Vatsa* is the hero of the Ratnávalí, translated in the following pages.

† *Ráhu* is the ascending node, personified as the head of the Dragon, who is supposed, in the mythological astronomy of the Hindus, to seize upon the moon, and thus occasion eclipses. According to the *Mahábhárata*, Ráhu was one of the *Asuras*, or demons, who at the churning of the ocean crept amongst the gods and stole a draught of *amrita* or ambrosia. The intruder was detected by the Sun and Moon, who pointing him out to Vishńu, that deity decapitated the demon: hence his immortality and his enmity to the planets.

VOL. I. F

respect; request him to enter, and call the Chamberlain* to attend him.

All. As you command. [*Exit.*

Outside of the House.

Enter MAITREYA *and the* BANDHULA.

Mait. Here's honour! The sovereign of the *Rákhasas*, *Rávańa*, travels in the car of *Kuvera*, obtained by the force of his devotions; but I, who am a poor Brahman, and no saint, yet I am conveyed about by lovely damsels.

All. This is the outer door, sir.

Mait. A very pretty entrance, indeed. The threshold is very neatly coloured, well swept and watered; the floor is beautified with strings of sweet flowers; the top of the gate is lofty and gives one the pleasure of looking up to the clouds, whilst the jasmine festoon hangs tremblingly down, as if it were now tossing on the trunk of *Indra's* elephant. † Over the doorway is a lofty arch of ivory; above it again wave flags dyed with safflower, their fringes curling in the wind, like fingers that beckon me, "come hither." On either side, the capitals of the door-posts support elegant crystal flower-pots, in which young mango-trees are springing up. The door panels are of gold, stuck, like the stout breast of a demon, with studs of

---

* The word so rendered is *bandhula*, an explanation of which is offered in the text a little further on.

† This garland was the cause of very important events. According to the *Brahma-Vaivarta-Purána*, it was given to Indra by a choleric sage named *Durvásas*, who received it from a Vidyádharí: attaching little value to the gift, the god tossed it to his elephant, and the elephant threw it to earth. *Durvásas*, highly offended, pronounced that Indra and all the three worlds under his supremacy should be deprived of their *Sri*, fortune or prosperity: in consequence, the world fell into decay, sacrifices ceased, and the gods were enfeebled. Everything would have perished, if the goddess had not been recovered. To re-obtain her, the gods and demons, by the advice and with the aid of Vishńu, churned the ocean :—"Such mighty matters spring from trivial things."

adamant.* The whole cries "away" to a poor man, whilst its splendour catches the eye of the wisest.

All. This leads to the first court.† Enter, sir, enter.

(*They enter the first Court.*)

Mait. Bless me! why here is a line of palaces, as white as the moon, as the conch, as the stalk of the water-lily—the stucco has been laid on here by handfuls; golden steps, embellished with various stones, lead to the upper apartments, whence the crystal windows, festooned with pearls, and bright as the eyes of a moon-faced maid, look down upon *Ujjayin*. The porter dozes on an easy-chair as stately as a Brahman deep in the Vedas; and the very crows, crammed with rice and curds, disdain the fragments of the sacrifice,‡ as if they were no more than scattered plaster. Proceed.

All. That is the second court. Enter.

(*They enter the second Court.*)

Mait. Oh, here are the stables; the carriage oxen are in good case, pampered with *javasa*§ I declare; and straw and oil-cakes are ready for them; their horns are bright with

---

* The correctness of the comparison is more evident in the original, where the word *vajra* implies both a diamond and the thunderbolt of Indra, with which he pierces the breasts of his foes.

† The interior of the houses at Pompeii conveys same idea of an Indian house, which like them is a set of chambers, of one or two stories, surrounding a central unroofed square. A house of a superior description is merely denoted by the superior extent of this square, and by its comprising a set or series of them, as in the text. The several entrances were in representation left, we may presume, to the imagination of the audience; something after the fashion which Sir Philip Sydney describes: "Now you shall have three ladies walk to gather flowers, and then you must believe the stage to be a garden. By and by we hear news of shipwreck in the same place; then we are to blame, if we accept it not for a rock. Upon the back of that comes out a hideous monster with fire and smoke; and then the miserable beholders are bound to take it for a cave; while, in the meantime, two armies fly in, represented with swords and bucklers, and then what hard heart will not receive it for a pitched field."

‡ The last portion of the offering of rice, &c., thrown into the air for the spirits of ill, the *Bali*, of which notice was taken in the first scene.

§ A species of hedysarum.

grease. Here we have a buffalo snorting indignantly, like a Brahman of high caste whom somebody has affronted; here the ram* stands to have his neck well rubbed, like a wrestler after a match; here they dress the manes of the horses; here is a monkey tied as fast a thief;† and here the *mahauts*‡ are plying the elephants with balls of rice and *ghee*. Proceed.

Att. This, sir, is the third gateway.

(*They enter the third Court.*)

Mait. Oh, this is the public court, where the young bucks of *Ujjayin* assemble; these are their seats, I suppose—the half-read book lies on the gaming-table, the men of which are made of jewels. Oh, yonder are some old hangers-on, lounging about with many-coloured pictures in their hands, and skilled in the peace and war of love. What next?

Att. This is the entrance to the fourth court.

(*They enter the fourth Court.*)

Mait. Oh, ho! this is a very gay scene: here the drums, whilst beaten by taper fingers, emit, like clouds, a murmuring tone; there the cymbals beating time, flash as they descend like the unlucky stars§ that fall from heaven. The flute here breathes the soft hum of the bee, whilst here a damsel holds the *vīnā* in her lap, and frets its wires with her finger-nails, like some wild minx that sets her mark on the face of her offending swain: some damsels are singing, like so many bees intoxicated with flowery nectar; others are practising the graceful dance, and others are employed in reading plays and

---

* Rams in India are commonly trained to fight.

† Monkeys are kept in stables as a sort of scape-goats apparently: hence the Persian proverb current in Hindustan, "The misfortune of the stable on the head of the monkey:" *Bilai tarikh ber seri maimun*.—Roebuck's Proverbs.

‡ Elephant-driver; the Sanskrit is *Mahámátra*. The balls alluded to are the common food of the elephants.

§ The phrase is, the stars that have lost their virtue, *kshīṇapuṇyā tārakā*. The notion is, that the stars are individuals raised to that honour for a time proportioned to the sum of their merits; this being exhausted, they descend to earth, often visibly, as in the case of shooting-stars.

poems.* The place is hung with water-jars, suspended to catch the cooling breeze. What comes next?

All. This is the gate of the fifth court.

(*They enter the fifth Court.*)

Mait. Ah, how my mouth waters! what a savoury scent of oil and assafœtida! The kitchen sighs softly forth its fragrant and abundant smoke—the odours are delicious—they fill me with rapture. The butcher's boy is washing the skin of an animal just slain, like so much foul linen; the cook is surrounded with dishes; the sweetmeats are mixing; the cakes are baking. (*Apart.*) Oh that I could meet with some one to do me a friendly turn; one who would wash my feet, and say, eat, sir, eat. (*Aloud.*) This is certainly *Indra's* heaven; the damsels are *Apsarasas*, the *Bandhulas* are *Gandharbas*. Pray, why do they call you *Bandhulas*?

All. We inhabit the dwellings of others and eat the bread of the stranger: we are the offspring of parents whom no tie connects: we exercise our indescribable merits in gaining men's money, and we sport through life as free and unrestrained as the cubs of the elephant.

Mait. What do we come to next?

All. This is the sixth entry.

(*They enter.*)

Mait. The arched gateway is of gold and many-coloured gems on a ground of sapphire, and looks like the bow of *Indra*† in an azure sky. What is going forward here so busily? It is the jeweller's court: skilful artists are examining pearls, topazes, sapphires, emeralds, rubies, the lapis-lazuli, coral, and other jewels; some set rubies in gold, some work gold ornaments on coloured thread, some string pearls, some grind the lapis-lazuli, some pierce shells, and some cut coral. Here we have perfumers drying the saffron bags, shaking the musk bags, expressing the sandal-juice and compounding essences.

* Reading, *Nâlyaiś solfingiram*.
† The rainbow.

Whom have we here? fair damsels and their gallants, laughing, talking, chewing musk and betel, and drinking wine. Here are the male and female attendants, and here are miserable hangers-on—men that neglected their own families and spent their all upon the harlot, and are now glad to quaff the drainings of her wine-cup.

All. This is the seventh court. Enter.

(*They enter the seventh Court.*)

Mait. This is the aviary—very handsome indeed! The doves bill and coo in comfort; the pampered parrot croaks like a Brahman *pandit*, stuffed with curds and rice, chanting a hymn from the Vedas; the *Maina** chatters as glibly as a housemaid issuing her mistress's command to her fellow-servants, while the *Kóil*,† crammed with juicy fruit, whines like a water-carrier. The quails fight; the partridges cry; the domestic peacock dances about delighted, and fans the palace with his gem-emblazoned tail, as if to cool its heated walls; the swans,‡ like balls of moonlight, roll about in pairs, and follow each graceful maid, as if to learn to imitate her walk, whilst the long-legged cranes§ stalk about the court, like eunuchs on guard. I declare the lady lives here amongst the winged race as if she tenanted *Indra's* garden. Well, where do you go now?

All. Enter, sir, the eighth court.

(*They enter.*)

Mait. Pray, who is that gentleman dressed in silken raiment, glittering with rich ornaments, and rolling about as if his limbs were out of joint?

All. That, sir, is my lady's brother.

Mait. Humph—what course of pious austerity in his last life made him Vasantasená's brother? Nay, not so; for after

---

* The *Madanasárikí*, the talking Maina or Malnate, Indian Stare or Grakle (Gracula religiosa).

† The Indian cuckoo (Cuculus Indicus).

‡ The *rájahansas*; the term is also applied to the flamingo.

§ The *sárasa*, or Indian crane.

all, though smooth, bright, and fragrant, the *champa** tree that grows on funeral ground is not to be approached. And pray, who is that lady dressed in flowered muslin?†—a goodly person truly; her feet shining with oil thrust into a pair of slippers: she sits in state, high on a gorgeous throne.

Att. That is my lady's mother.

Mait. A portly old hag, indeed: how did she contrive to get in here? Oh, I suppose she was first set up here, as they do with an unwieldy *Mahádeva*, and then the walls were built round her.‡

Att. How now, slave! What! do you make a jest of our lady, affected, too, as she is with a quartan ague!

Mait. A what? O mighty Fever, be pleased to afflict me with a quartan, if such are its symptoms!

Att. You will die, slave.

Mait. No, hussey; better that this bloated porpoise, swelled up with wine and years, die; there will then be a dinner for a thousand jackals. But no matter; what do you know about it? I had heard of Vasantasená's wealth, and now I find it true; it seems to me that the treasures of the three worlds are collected in this mansion. I am in doubt whether to regard it as the dwelling of a courtesan or the palace of *Kuvera*.§ Where is your lady?

Att. She's in the arbour. Enter.

(*They enter the Garden.*)

Mait. A very lovely scene! the numerous trees are bowed down by delicious fruit, and between them are silken swings

---

* A handsome tree with fragrant blossoms (Michelia champac).

† *Phulla-paṭdraṇ-pdadd*, for *Puṣpa-patṭvraka-pratrita*, dressed in a garment of or with flowers, which the commentator explains to mean worked muslin: *Sakāma-sūtra-puṣpādi kṛtrimādi patra bharmāṭi sa tathā puṣpa-paṭa-prasādhikā.* The cloth on which artificial flowers are worked in fine thread is well known as *Puṣpapāṭá*, flowered cloth.

‡ The stone emblems of this deity are sometimes of great bulk and weight.

§ The God of Wealth.

constructed for the light form of youthful beauty: the yellow jasmine, the graceful *mádhaví*,* the full-blossomed *mallikâ*,† the blue clitoria, spontaneous shed their flowers, and strew the ground with a carpet more lovely than any in the groves of *Indra*; the reservoir glows with the red lotus blossoms, like the dawn with the fiery beams of the rising sun; and here the *asoka*‡ tree, with its rich crimson blossoms, shines like a young warrior bathed with the sanguine shower of the furious fight. Where is your lady?

Att. Look lower, and you will see her.

Mait. (*Approaching Vasantasená.*) Health to you, lady.

Vas. (*Rising.*) Welcome, Maitreya; take a seat.

Mait. Pray, keep you yours. (*They sit.*)

Vas. I hope all is well with the son of the *Sárthavaha*.§

Mait. Is all well with your ladyship?

Vas. Undoubtedly, Maitreya; the birds of affection gladly nestle in the tree, which, fruitful in excellence, puts forth the flowers of magnanimity and the leaves of merit, and rises with the trunk of modesty from the root of honour. ||

Mait. (*Apart.*) Figurative indeed. (*Aloud.*) What else?

Vas. What brings you hither? ¶

Mait. I will tell you:—Chárudatta presents his respects to you.

Vas. With respect I receive his commands.

Mait. He desires me to say, that he has lost your golden casket; it was implodged by him at play, and the keeper of

---

* Jasminum grandiflorum.
† Jasminum zambac.
‡ A tree with red blossoms, Jonesia asoka.
§ The head of his tribe.
‖ This is a passage of a very unusual character in Sanskrit composition, and is rather in the style of Persian than Indian writing: it has, however, more of the allegory than is common to Persian poetry, in which, though the metaphors follow one another without intermission, they are independent and unconnected.
¶ It is a singularity that so far in the scene Vasantasená speaks Sanskrit,

the tables, a servant of the prince, is gone, no one knows whither.

Att. Lady, you are in luck; the grave Chárudatta turned gambler.

Vas. (*Apart.*) How! the casket has been stolen, and he says it was lost at play. Yet even in this I love him.

Mait. As the accident cannot now be helped, he requests, in lieu of the casket, you will accept this string of diamonds.

Vas. (*Apart.*) Shall I show him the ornaments? (*Considering.*) No, not so.

Mait. Will you not receive this equivalent?

Vas. (*Smiling.*) Why not, Maitreya? (*Takes and puts it to her heart.*) But how is this? do drops of nectar fall from the mango-tree after it has shed its blossoms? My good friend, tell that sad gambler, Chárudatta, that I shall call upon him in the evening.

Mait. (*Apart.*) So, so; she intends to get more out of him, I suppose. (*Aloud.*) I shall so inform him, madam. (*Apart.*) I wish he was rid of this precious acquaintance. [*Exit.*

Vas. Here, girl, take the jewels and attend me to Chárudatta.

Att. But look, madam, look! a sudden storm is gathering.

Vas. No matter.

Let the clouds gather and dark night descend,
And heavy fall unintermitted showers;
I heed them not, wench, when I haste to seek
His presence, whose loved image warms my heart.—
Take charge of these, and lightly trip along. [*Exit.*

END OF THE FOURTH ACT.

ACT V.

CHÁRUDATTA'S GARDEN.

Enter CHÁRUDATTA (*looking up*).

A HEAVY storm impends: the gathering gloom
Delights the peafowl* and distracts the swan,†
Not yet prepared for periodic flight;
And these deep shades contrast with sad despondence
The heart that pines in absence.‡ Through the air,
A rival Keśava,§ the purple cloud
Rolls stately on, girt by the golden lightning,

---

* These birds are the invariable accompaniments of the rainy season, as observed in my translation of the Cloud Messenger. It is unnecessary to cite the parallel passages, as the idea recurs often enough in this act, in which all the commonplaces of Hindu poetry relating to the "Rains" are exhausted; a few of the repetitions have been purposely omitted.

† Rather the wild gray goose, which bird is supposed to migrate annually to the Himalaya mountains, particularly to the Mánasarovara lake, whence it is termed Mánasaukas, the dweller of Mánasa. Mr Moorcroft, in his adventurous visit to this lake in 1812, found these birds in vast flocks along the beach and on the water; and concluded from what he saw that they were accustomed to frequent the lake and breed in the surrounding rocks, when the swell of the rivers of Hindustan and the inundation of the plains conceal their usual food.

‡ The time just previous to the commencement of the rainy season is the period at which Indian travellers may be expected home, not only because the weather is then favourable, but because after the rains have set in, the roads are broken up, and travelling becomes difficult and unpleasant. Hence the Hindu poets always speak of this season as one at which lovers, till then separated, meet again.

§ A name of Krishńa, *Crisivus*, alluding, as generally supposed, to his graceful tresses, but, according to the *Mahábhárata*, from his being an incarnation of one of the hairs of Vishńu.

As by his yellow garb, and bearing high
The long white line of storks, the God's pure shell :*
From the dark womb, in rapid fall descend
The silvery drops, and glittering in the gleam,
Shot from the lightning, bright and fitful, sparkle
Like a rich fringe rent from the robe of heaven.
The firmament is filled with scattered clouds,
And, as they fly before the wind, their forms,
As in a picture, image various shapes,
The semblances of storks and soaring swans,
Of dolphins and the monsters of the deep,
Of dragons vast, and pinnacles, and towers.
The spreading shade, methinks, is like the host
Of *Dhritarashtra* † shouting loud in thunder.
Yon strutting peacock welcomes its advance,
Like proud *Duryodhan*, vaunting of his might:
From its dread enmity, the *Koïl* ‡ flies,
Like luckless *Yudhishthira*, § by the dice
Bereaved of power, and scatter wild the swans,
Like the proscribed and houseless *Pándavas*,
Wandering from home and every comfort far,
Through paths untrod, till then, and realms unknown.
Maitreya long delays. Will not to-day
Apprise me of the issue of his visit?   (*Retires.*)

Enter MAITREYA.

What a rapacious, mean wretch is this harlot! Scarcely a word did she say, but, without any ceremony, pounced upon the necklace. With all her pomp and parade, she could not say to me, my good friend, Maitreya, take a little refreshment; not

---

* The *šaṅkha* or conch shell is borne by Vishńu in one of his hands.
† The father of *Duryodhana* and the other Kuru princes, whose war with their cousins, the sons of Páńdu, is the subject of the *Mahábhárata*.
‡ The Indian cuckoo.
§ The eldest of the sons of Páńdu, who with his brothers was banished from the realm of his forefathers and spent some time in the forests towards the South of India.

even so much as to offer me a draught of water—her wealth is positively all thrown away upon her. It is very true, there is no lotus that has not a stalk; no trader that is not a cheat; there is not a goldsmith that is not a thief; there never was a village meeting without a quarrel; and there never will be a harlot without rapacity: these are things that always go together. I shall therefore dissuade my worthy friend from his infatuation. Ha! yonder I see him in the garden. Health and prosperity to Chárudatta!

Chár. (*Comes forward.*) Welcome, my good friend; Maitreya, sit down.

Mait. I am seated. (*Sits.*)

Chár. Now, my friend, your news?

Mait. It is all over.

Chár. How so? does she refuse the proffered gems?

Mait. We have no such luck; she put her soft hands to her forehead, and then laid hold of the necklace.

Chár. Then, why do you complain?

Mait. Why? reason enough. We have made a pretty job of it; to lose a necklace worth the four seas, for a thing of little value, and one we neither ate, nor drank, and which a thief carried off.

Chár. You reason idly.

The pledge was here deposited in trust,
And for that trust a costly price was due.

Mait. I have another cause of complaint. She made signs to her damsels, and they covered their faces with their veils and made me their merriment. I beg, therefore, that you will desist from such unbecoming intercourse. A courtesan is like a thorn that has run into your foot; you cannot even get rid of it without pain; and it is indisputably true, that wherever a harlot, an elephant, a scribe,* a mendicant, a

* The *Káyastha* or *Kayth*, whose profession is writing and accounts. Men of this tribe were usually employed by the Hindu princes in the collection and record of their revenues, and their character for a spirit of extortion became proverbial. They appear to have been particularly obnoxious to the Brahmans.

spy, or a jackass, find admission, they are sure to do mischief.

Chár. Enough of this unmerited reviling.
My fallen fortunes are a sure protection.
The fiery steed bounds fleetly o'er the plain
Till fading breath retards his lagging course;
So man's desires first urge his heedless path,
But soon exhausted shrink into his bosom.
Believe me, friend, a female of this order,
A true wealth-hunter, troubles not the poor:
(*Apart.*) She, she, alone, bestows her love on merit.
(*Aloud.*) We are by wealth abandoned, and by her.

Mait. (*Apart.*) This love is the devil: he turns up his eyes and sighs from the very bottom of his heart. I see plainly my advice to him to conquer his passion only serves to confirm it. (*Aloud.*) She desired me to say, she intends paying you a visit this evening. I suspect she is not satisfied with the necklace, and intends to demand something more valuable.

Chár. Well, let her come; she shall depart contented.

Enter KUMBHILAKA, *Vasantasená's Servant.*

I wish every one to take notice, that the harder it rains, the more thoroughly do I get ducked, and the colder the wind that blows down my back, the more do my limbs shiver. A pretty situation for a man of my talents; for one who can play the flute with seven holes, the *vîná* with seven strings, can sing like a jackass, and who acknowledges no musical superior, except perhaps *Tamburu*** or *Nárada.*† Vasantasená sends me to Chárudatta's house. (*Advances.*) There is Chárudatta in the garden, and that dunderhead Maitreya with him. I must throw out a signal to him. (*Throws a clod of earth at Maitreya.*)

Mait. Holloa! who pelts me with a pellet, like a *kapittha*‡ tree in an orchard?

---

* An attendant upon *Kuvera*, and one of the chief *Gandharbas* or choristers of heaven.

† The son of Brahmá, the inventor of the Indian lute.

‡ The elephant or wood apple (Feronia elephantum).

Chár. It was probably thrown down in their sport by the pigeons that tenant the top of the garden wall.

Mait. Wait a while, you saucy son of a slave, and with this stick I will knock you off the wall, like a ripe mango from the tree.

Chár. Sit down, sit down; fright not the gentle bird, nor chase him from his mate.

Kum. The blockhead! he sees the pigeons and cannot see me. I must give him another salutation. (*Throws another clod.*)

Mait. Hey, again! (*Looks up.*) O Kumbhilaka! is it you? Wait a while, and I will come to you. (*Goes to the door.*) Come in; how fares it?

Kum. I salute you, sir.

Mait. And what brings you here in such foul weather?

Kum. She sent me.

Mait. And who is she?

Kum. She—she—she.

Mait. She—she—she! What are you sputtering about, like an old miser when things are dear? Who—who—who?

Kum. Hoo—hoo—hoo! What are you too-whooing about, like an owl that has been scared from a sacrifice?*

Mait. Speak out, man, intelligibly.

Kum. I will; but first I'll give you something to guess.

Mait. I shall give you a box of the ears, I believe.

Kum. Never mind that. In which season, pray, does the mango blossom?

Mait. In the season of *Grishma*† to be sure, you blockhead!

Kum. Blockhead yourself! it does no such thing.

Mait. Hey, how is that? I must ask my friend. Stop a moment. (*Goes to Chárudatta.*) Pray, sir, in which season does the mango blossom?

---

* In the original, Kumbhilaka says *Eid id*, to which Maitreya replies, *id, eid, id*. Kumbhilaka's answer is, What are you barking about, like the lover of Indra's sacrifice (a dog)?

† The hot season.

Chdr. Why, you simpleton, in *Vasanta*.*

Mait. (*To Kumb.*) Why, you simpleton, the mango blossoms in *Vasanta*.

Kum. Very well. Now answer me one more question: Who guards wealthy towns?

Mait. Why, the town guard, to be sure.

Kum. No; that is not it.

Mait. No? Let me see. (*Aside.*) I must consult Chárudatta. Pray, sir, who guards wealthy towns?

Chdr. The Sená† undoubtedly.

Mait. (*To Kum.*) The Sená undoubtedly.

Kum. Very well; now put your answers together; quick, quick!

Mait. Ha, I have it! Vasantasená.‡

Kum. She is here.

Mait. I must apprise my friend. Sir, we have a dun§ here.

Chdr. Here? a dun in my house?

Mait. I do not know anything about the house, but there is one at the door. Vasantasená is arrived.

Chdr. Nay, now you jest?

Mait. If you do not believe me, ask this fellow. Here, you Kumbhilaka!

Kum. (*Advancing.*) Sir, I salute you.

---

* Spring. It is necessary to keep the original words here, and in what follows.

† The army or military.

‡ This is sad quibbling, but may be vindicated by the example of much loftier genius; it is sufficient to show, also, that the regular charade—for it is nothing else—is neither of modern nor western invention. There is some further quibbling in the text. Maitreya puts his answer together *Sená Vasanta*, and the wit lies in punning and blundering on *parivartaya*, turn round or transpose, and *pada* a foot or an inflected word. The very term might be suspected of etymological affinity to the English "Pun," being *paśna*, the Prákrit form of *praśna*, a question, Kumbhilaka commencing his *facetiæ* with *Ale, paśhaḿ de daiśám*, I will give you a question.

§ *Dhanika*, a creditor, a dun.

Chdr. You are welcome; tell me, is Vasantasená here?
Kum. She is, sir.
Chdr. Never be grateful message unrewarded; this for your pains. (*Gives him his garment.*)
Kum. (*Bows.*) I shall inform my mistress.   [*Exit.*
Mait. Now, I hope you are satisfied. To come out in such weather; you can have no doubt what brings her.
Chdr. I do not feel quite confident.
Mait. Depend upon it, I am right; the casket was worth more than the necklace, and she comes for the difference.
Chdr. (*Apart.*) She shall be gratified.   (*They retire.*)

(*Outside of the Garden.*)
Enter VASANTASENÁ *splendidly dressed, attended by the* Vita, *a female servant, and one carrying a large umbrella.**

Att. Lady, upon the mountain's brow, the clouds
Hang dark and drooping, as the aching heart
Of her who sorrows for her absent lord;
Their thunders rouse the peafowl, and the sky
Is agitated by their wings, as fanned
By thousand fans with costly gems inchased.
The chattering frog quaffs the pellucid drops
That cleanse his miry jaws. The peahen shrieks
With transport, and the *Nípa* freshly blooms.
The moon is blotted by the driving scud,
As is the saintly character by those
Who wear its garb to voil their abject lives;
And like the damsel whose fair fame is lost
In ever-changing loves, the lightning, true
To no one quarter, flits along the skies.
Vas. You speak it well, my friend: to me it seems—
The jealous night, as with the gloom she wantons,
Looks on me as a rival bride, and dreading
I may disturb her pleasures, stops my path
And bids me angrily my steps retrace.

* We have now an cumulatively poetical description of the rainy season.

THE TOY-CART.

All. Reply with courage, chide her to submission.
Vas. Reviling is the weakness of our sex,
And but of small avail,—I heed her not.
Let the clouds fall in torrents, thunder roar,
And heaven's red bolt dash fiery to the ground,
The dauntless damsel faithful love inspires,
Treads boldly on, nor dreads the maddening storm.
Vita. Like an invading prince, who holds his court
Within the city of his humbled foe,
Yon mighty cloud, advancing with the wind,
With store of arrowy shower, with thundering drums,
And blazing streamers, marches to assail
In his own heavens the monarch of the night.
Vas. Nay, nay, not so; I rather read it thus:
The clouds, that like unwieldly elephants
Roll their inflated masses grumbling on,
Or whiten with the migratory troop
Of hovering cranes, teach anguish to the bosom.
The stork's shrill cry sounds like the plaintive tabor
To her who, while she wanders o'er its parchment,
Is lost in musings of her lord's return,
And every tone that hails the rainy season,
Falls on her heart like brine upon a wound.
Vita. Behold, where yonder ponderous cloud assumes
The stature of the elephant, the storks
Entwine a fillet for his front, and waves
The lightning, like a *chouri* o'er his head.
Vas. Observe, my friend, the day is swallowed up
By these deep shades, dark as the dripping leaf
Of the tamála tree, and, like an elephant
That cowering shuns the battle's arrowy sleet,
So shrinks the scattering ant-hill from the shower.
The fickle lightning darts such brilliant rays,
As gleam from golden lamps in temples hung,
Whilst, like the consort of an humble lord,
The timid moonlight peeps amidst the clouds.

Vita. There, like a string of elephants, the clouds
In regular file, by lightning fillets bound,
Move slowly at their potent god's commands.
The heavens let down a silver chain to earth.
The earth, that shines with buds and sheds sweet odours,
Is pierced with showers, like diamond-shafted darts
Launched from the rolling mass of deepest blue,
Which heaves before the breeze and foams with flame;
Like ocean's dark waves by the tempest driven,
And tossing high their flashing surge to shore.*

Vas. Hailed by the peafowl with their shrillest cries,
By the pleased storks delightedly caressed,
And by the provident swans with anxious eye
Regarded, yonder rests one threatening cloud
Involving all the atmosphere in gloom.

Vita. The countenance of heaven is close concealed,
By shades the lightning scant irradiates.
The day and night confusedly intermix,
And all the lotus eyes of either close,
The world is lulled to slumber by the sound
Of falling waters, sheltered by the clouds
That countless crowd the chambers of the sky.

Vas. The stars are all extinct, as fades the memory
Of kindness in a bad man's heart. The heavens
Are shorn of all their radiance, as the wife
Her glory loses in her husband's absence.
In sooth, I think the firmament dissolves:
Melted by Indra's scorching bolt it falls
In unexhausted torrents. Now the cloud
Ascends—now stoops—now roars aloud in thunder—
Now sheds its streams—now frowns with deeper gloom,
Full of fantastic change, like one new raised

---

* I have in this place, and in a few others, expanded the expression, in order to convey more accurately the idea intended by the simpler phraseology of the original.

By fortune's fickle favours.

Vitu.   Now the sky
With lightning flames, now laughs with whitening
    storks—
Now glows with *Indra's* painted bow, that hurls
Its hundred shafts—now rattles with his bolt—
Now loud it chafes with rushing winds, and now
With clustering clouds that roll their spiry folds
Like sable snakes along—it thickens dark,
As if 'twere clothed with vapours, such as spread
When incense soars in curling wreaths to heaven.

Vas. Shame on thee, cloud, that seekest to affright me
With thy loud threats, and with thy watery shafts
Wouldst stay my progress, hastening to my love.'
Indra! I violate no vows to thee,
That thou shouldst thunder angrily reproof;
It ill becomes thee to obstruct my path.
Draw off thy clouds in pity to my passion,
If ever thou wert conscious of affection,
And for *Ahalyá** wore a husband's form.
Or be it so—rage on—still pour thy deluge,
And launch thy hundred-shafted bolt, in vain.
Thou canst not stop the faithful maid that flies
To lose her terrors in a lover's arms.
If the clouds roar—e'en be it so—it is
Their nature—all of man is ever savage.
But gentle lightning, how canst thou not know
The cares that agitate the female bosom?†

Vita. Enough—she now befriends us, like a lamp
That glows in *Indra's* palace, like a banner,
Whose white folds wave upon a mountain's brow,

---

* *Indra* having fallen in love with *Ahalyá*, the wife of the sage *Gautama*, and finding her not to be won to his purpose, deceived her by the Amphitryonic device of assuming her husband's shape.

† The clouds are male personifications, the lightning is a nymph.

Or like the gold cord on *Airávat's** breast,
She gleams and shows you where your lord resides.
Vas. Is this the mansion?
Vita. It is; I will announce your coming.
Ho there! inform the worthy Chárudatta,
A lady at his door awaits; her locks
Are drenched with rain, her gentle nerves are shaken
By angry tempests, and her delicate feet
By cumbering mire and massy anklets wearied,†
She pauses to refresh with cooling streams.
Chár. (*To Maitreya.*) Hear you, my friend?
Mait. As you command. (*Opens the door.*)
    Health to you, lady.
Vas. Sir, I salute you. . (*To the Vita.*) Here, let the umbrella-bearer wait upon you.
Vita. (*Apart.*) A hint for me, I take it, to withdraw. I shall obey you. [*Exit.*
Vas. Now, good Maitreya, where is our gambler?
Mait. (*Apart.*) Gambler indeed! my friend is much honoured by the appellation. There he sits, madam, in the arbour.
Vas. In the arbour—is it dry?
Mait. Quite; there is nothing to eat or drink in it: enter, enter.
Vas. (*To her Servant.*) What shall I say?
Ser. Gambler, good evening to you.
Vas. Shall I be able?
Ser. Opportunity will give you courage.
Mait. Enter, lady, enter.
Vas. (*Enters, and approaching Chárudatta, throws flowers at him.*) Gambler, good evening to you.
Chár. (*Rising.*) Vasantasená!
Lady, believe me, every day has passed

---

* The elephant of Indra.

† It may be scarcely necessary to observe that heavy rings, usually of silver set with a fringe of small bells, are worn by Hindu ladies upon their ankles.

Most heavily, and sleepless dragged my nights,
But now your charms appear my cares are over,
And this glad evening terminates my sorrows.
Then welcome, welcome to my bower—be seated.

Mait. Take a seat, madam. (*They sit.*)

Chdr. Maitreya, from the flowers that grace her ear
Surcharged with rain, the drops have trickled down
And bathed her bosom, like a young prince installed
The partner of imperial honours.* Haste and bring
A vest of finest texture to replace
This chilling robe.

Fem. Att. Stop, Maitreya, I will assist my mistress if you please. (*Does so.*)

Mait. (*To Chárudatta.*) Now, sir, shall I inquire the object of this visitation?

Chdr. Do so.

Mait. And now, madam, may I ask what has brought you out, on such a vile, dark, rainy evening?

Att. Lady, here's a smart Brahman!

Vas. Nay, an able one, so call him.

Att. My mistress, sir, wished to be informed of the real value of the necklace that you brought her.

Mait. There, I said so. (*To Chárudatta.*)

Att. The reason why she wishes to know is that she has pledged it at play, and the keeper of the tables, being a servant of the prince's, is gone on some duty, and is not to be found.

Mait. Umph, tit for tat.

Att. Until he can be heard of, and the necklace be redeemed, be pleased to accept in lieu of it this golden casket. (*Gives him the casket stolen by Sarvilaka. Maitreya examines it.*) You examine it very closely; one would suppose you had seen it before.

---

* Therefore sprinkled with holy water.

Mait. It is very curious: the cunning of the workman beguiles my eyes.

Att. No, your eyesight is defective, it is the very same.

Mait. Indeed! my worthy friend, here is the gold casket again that was stolen from our house.

Chdr. No, no, it is but a requital
Of our attempt to substitute a change
Of that entrusted to us; this is the truth,
Howe'er the casket may appear the same.

Mait. It is the same! I swear it, as I am a Brahman.

Chdr. I am glad of it.

Mait. Shall I ask how they came by it?

Chdr. Why not?

Mait. (*Whispers the Attendant.*) Is it so indeed?

Att. (*Whispers Maitreya.*) It is indeed.

Chdr. What is?—why leave us out?

Mait. (*Whispers Chárudatta.*) This it is indeed.

Chdr. (*To the Attendant.*) Is this indeed, my girl, the golden casket?

Att. It is the same, sir.

Chdr. A pleasing speech with me should never go
Without fit recompense,—accept this ring. (*Looks at his hand; finds he has no ring; expresses shame.*)

Vas. How well he merits wealth.

Chdr. (*Apart.*) How can that man be said to live, who lives
A pauper, and whose gratitude and wrath
Are barren both. The bird whose wings are clipped—
The leafless tree—the desiccated pool—
The desolate mansion, and the toothless snake—
Are all meet emblems of the hapless wretch
Whose festive hours no fond associates grace,
And brightest moments yield no fruit to others.

Mait. (*To him.*) Enough, enough, there is no good in fretting. (*Aloud.*) But, lady, I shall thank you to restore me my bathing-gown, in which the casket was wrapped at the time it was stolen.

Vas. And now, worthy Chárudatta, believe me, when the casket was stolen, it was quite unnecessary to send me this equivalent.

Chdr. Had I not sent it, lady, who had trusted me !—
    I and my wealth in most men's eyes are equal,
    And poverty will ever be suspected.

Mait. A word, damsel ; do you mean to take up your abode here?

Att. Fie, Maitreya, how you talk!

Mait. My good friend, the clouds are collecting again, and the heavy drops drive us from our easy seats.

Chdr. 'Tis true, they penetrate the yielding clouds
    As sinks the lotus stalk into its bed
    Of plashy mire, and now again they fall
    Like tears celestial from the weeping sky
    That wails the absent moon.
    The clouds, like *Baludeva's* vesture, dark,
    Profusely shed a shower of precious pearls
    From *Indra's* treasury—the drops descend
    Rapid and rattling, like the angry shafts
    From *Arjun's* quiver, and of like purity
    As are the hearts of holy men.
    See, lady, how the firmament, anointed
    With unguent of the black tamála's hue,
    And fanned by fragrant and refreshing gales,
    Is by the lightning tenderly embraced,
    As the loved lord whom fearlessly she flies to.

    [*Vasantasená gesticulates affection, and falls into Chárudatta's arms.*

Chdr. (*Embracing her.*)
    Louder and louder still roar on, ye clouds !
    To me the sound is music, by your aid
    My love is blessed, my heart expands with hope.

Mait. (*As to the cloud.*) You foul-faced rascal, you are a worthless reprobate, to have so scared her ladyship by your lightnings.

Chár. Reprove it not, for let the rain descend,
The heavens still lour, and wide the lightnings launch
A hundred flames; they have befriended me,
And given me her for whom I sighed in vain.
Happy, thrice happy, they whose walls enshrine
The fair they worship, and whose arms enfold
Her shivering beauties in their warm embrace.
Look, love, the bow of Indra arches heaven;
Like outspread arms, extended with fatigue,
It stretches forth; the yawning sky displays
Its lightning tongue—its chin of clouds hangs low—
All woo us to repose—let us retire: the drops
Fall musical, and pattering on the leaves
Of the tall palm, or on the pebbly ground,
Or in the brook, emit such harmony
As sweetly wakens from the voice and lute.   [*Exit.*

END OF THE FIFTH ACT.

ACT VI.

CHÁRUDATTA'S HOUSE,

Inside and Outside as before.

Inside.—Enter Female Servant.

Hey-day! does not my lady mean to rise this morning? I shall make bold to call her. Madam!

Enter VASANTASENÁ.

Look, madam, it is day.

Vas. How! why the morning dawns as darkling as if it still were night.

Ser. It is morning to us, though it may be night to you, madam.

Vas. Where is your gambler?

Ser. Chárudatta, madam, having given his orders to Vardhamána, is gone to the old flower garden *Pushpakaranda*.

Vas. What orders gave he?

Ser. To get your litter ready.

Vas. Whither am I to go?

Ser. Whither Chárudatta is gone.

Vas. Very well, girl, I have scarcely yet beheld him; to-day will gratify me with his sight. What! did I find my way into the inner apartments?

Ser. Not only that, madam, but into every one's heart.

Vas. I fear me his family are vexed.

Ser. They will be vexed then only when——

Vas. When?

Ser. When you depart.

Vas. Then is it my place first to be afflicted. Here, girl, take this necklace to my respected sister,* and say from

---

* That is, to Chárudatta's wife.

me, I am Chárudatta's handmaid and your slave, then be this necklace again the ornament of that neck to which it of right belongs.

Ser. But, lady, Chárudatta will be displeased.

Vas. Go, do as I bid you; he will not be offended.

Ser. As you command. [*Exit, and returns presently.*

Madam, thus says the lady: you are favoured by the son of my lord; it is not proper for me to accept this necklace. Know that the only ornament I value is my husband.

Enter RADANIKÁ *and* CHÁRUDATTA'S CHILD.

Rad. Come along, my child, let us ride in your cart.

Child. I do not want this cart; it is only of clay—I want one of gold.

Rad. And where are we to get the gold, my little man? Wait till your father is rich again, and then he will buy you one: now this will do. Come, let us go and see Vasantasená. Lady, I salute you.

Vas. Welcome Radaniká. Whose charming boy is this? although so ill-attired, his lovely face quite fascinates me.

Rad. This is Rohasena, the son of Chárudatta.

Vas. (*Stretching out her arms.*) Come here, my little dear, and kiss me. (*Takes him on her lap.*) How like his father!

Rad. He is like him too in disposition. Chárudatta dotes on him.

Vas. Why does he weep?

Rad. The child of our neighbour had a golden cart, which this little fellow saw and wanted. I made him this of clay, but he is not pleased with it, and is crying for the other.

Vas. Alas, alas, this little creature is already mortified by another's prosperity. O fate! thou sportest with the fortunes of mankind, like drops of water trembling on the lotus leaf. Don't cry, my good boy, and you shall have a gold cart.

Child. Radaniká, who is this?

Vas. A handmaid purchased by your father's merits.

Rad. This is your lady mother, child.

Child. You tell me untruth, Radaniká; how can this be my mother when she wears such fine things?

Vas. How piteous a speech for so soft a tongue! (*Takes off her ornaments in tears.*) Now I am your mother. Here, take this trinket and go buy a gold cart.

Child. Away, I will not take it, you cry at parting with it.

Vas. (*Wiping her eyes.*) I weep no more. Go, love, and play. (*Fills his cart with her jewels.*) There go, get you a golden cart. [*Exit* RADANIKÁ *with* CHILD.

Outside.—Enter VARDHAMÁNA *with the litter.**

Radaniká, let the lady know the carriage waits for her at the private door.

Inside.—Enter RADANIKÁ.

Lady, the covered litter attends you at the back-door.

Vas. Stay a moment whilst I prepare myself.

Rad. Stay a moment, Vardhamána, the lady is not quite ready.

Var. And I have forgotten the cushions of the carriage. Wait till I bring them. These oxen are not steady enough to be left; I will drive back and return presently.

[*Exit with the car.*

Vas. (*Inside.*) Bring me my things, girl, I can put them on myself. (*Dressing.*)

Outside.—Enter STHÁVARAKA, *the Servant of Samsthánaka, with a carriage.*

I am ordered by the king's brother-in-law, my master, to take this vehicle with all speed to the old flower-garden, Pushpakarandá. Come up, come up. (*Looking.*) Why, the road is blocked with country carts. Holloa there! get out of

---

* A car of two wheels drawn by oxen and enclosed with curtains. The introduction of this kind of stage property is so constant and essential, that it must have been real, and shows that the place appropriated to the representation must have been level and spacious. It renders it probable that the open court within the house was the spot where the drama was exhibited.

the way. What says he, whose carriage is it? Samsthánaka's, the king's brother-in-law; quick, quick! clear the road. (*Drives on.*) Who should that be, that looked at me so curiously, and then stole off down another road, like an unlucky gambler that runs away from the table-keeper!* No matter; I must get on. Holloa you! out of the way there! What! Come and give you a turn of the wheel: it sticks, does it! It is very likely that the king's brother-in-law's man shall assist you to a twist of the wheel. Oh, it is a poor miserable rustic, and alone too. Well, I will lend you a hand. This is Chárudatta's postern door. I can leave the carriage here in the meantime so, stop there, I will be with you.

[*Exit, leaving the carriage at the door.*

Ser. (*Inside.*) I hear the wheels: the carriage is returned, madam.

Vas. Quick, quick! I feel strangely flurried;—open the door.

Ser. 'Tis done.

Vas. Go you to rest.

Ser. As you command. [*Exit.*

Vas. (*Goes forth and ascends Samsthánaka's carriage.*) My right eye twinkles;† never mind, meeting Chárudatta will prove it causeless. (*Draws the curtains.*)

Re-enter STHÁVARAKA.

I have helped him, and now have a clear road. (*Mounts and proceeds.*) Why, the vehicle is heavier than it was, or it appears so to me, because I am tired with helping yonder cart. No matter, I must proceed;—come up.

(*Behind the scenes.*)

Who ho, there, guards! look to it; be vigilant—sleep not at your posts; the cowherd has burst his bonds, slain his gaoler, and broken from his prison; he is now in flight—seize him! seize him!

---

* This is to prepare the entrance of *Aryaka*, who has just fled from prison.

† An unlucky omen for a woman, lucky for a man.

Sthd. Here's a precious uproar! I had better get clear of it.
[*Exit with the car.*]

Enter ARYAKA *as in flight.*

I have swam thus far to shore, and from the wave
Of fell captivity, the tyrant Pálaka
Had plunged me into, once more have escaped.
Like a tame elephant from his stall broke loose,
I drag along with me my ruptured chain.
Sarvilaka, my friend, to thee I owe
My freedom and my life. Condemned to pine
In the dark dungeon, where the monarch's fears,
Awakened by the sage's prophecies,
Cast me to die, dragged from my humble home. (*Weeps.*)
What crime have I committed, to be sought
Thus like a venomous snake, to be destroyed !
If such my destiny, as is foretold,
In what consists my guilt? be fate accused—
Fate is a power resistless, and a king
Alike demands our homage. Who contends
With force superior? mine is to submit.
Yet for my life I fly—ah ! whither now
Shall I find refuge? See, yon door invites me !
Some good man's gate is open, and like me
Its withered fortunes, for the bolt is broken,
And the broad valves are shattered and decayed :
It calls me kinsman, and it proves my friend.

VARDHAMÁNA *returning with Chárudatta's carriage* (*without*).
Come up, come up !

(ARYAKA *listening.*)

A carriage, and it comes this way.
If it should be a village car, not freighted
With passengers uncourteous, or a vehicle
For women, but its fair load not received,
Or be it travelling from the town, and fit
For decent occupancy—be it but empty
And unattended, and my fate befriends me.

Enter VARDHAMÁNA *with the carriage.*

What ho! Radaniká, I have got the cushions, and the car is ready: so inform the lady Vasantasená; tell her to ascend, that I may set off for *Pushpakarańḍaka.*

Ary. It is a courtezan's, and travelling outwards;
'Tis fortunate—I mount. (*Advances.*)

Vard. (*Listening and hearing the ringing of Áryaka's chain.*) I hear the sound of the anklets, she is hoar. Get up quick, lady; get up behind; the cattle are impatient, I must not leave them.

ÁRYAKA *ascends.*

Vard. The sound has ceased, and the carriage is heavier than it was: her ladyship must be seated, so here goes.

[*Exit with the car.*

Scene—Another Street.

Enter VÍRAKA, *Captain of the Watch, attended.*

Halloa! Jaya, Jayamána, Chandanaka, Mangala, Pushpabhadra, and the rest, follow quick, and we shall catch the villain, though he has broken his prison and the king's slumbers. Here, fall in; go you to the east gate, you to the west, you to the south, you to the north: on this pile of broken bricks, Chandanaka and I will stop and look about us. What ho, Chandanaka!

Enter CHANDANAKA *attended, in a bustle.*

What ho! Víraka, Visalya, Bhímángada, Daṅḍakála, Daṅḍakára, quick, quick! never let the king's fortune move off into another family: away with you, search the streets, the roads, the gardens, the houses, the stalls, the markets, and let no auspicious corner pass unexamined;—away! (*Exeunt guard.*) Well, Víraka, what say you? will any one convey this runaway cowboy out of peril? Verily, whoever dares to carry him off whilst Chandanaka lives, had better have had at his birth the Sun in the eighth mansion, the Moon in the fourth, Venus in the sixth, Mars in the fifth, Jupiter in the sixth, and Saturn in the ninth.*

Vir. He must have had assistance, no doubt, valiant Chandanaka; but, by your heart, I swear that he escaped before dawn.

Enter VARDHAMÁNA *with the car and* ÁRYAKA *concealed.*

Chan. What ho, there! see, see, a covered litter passes along the high road; inquire whose it is and whither going.

Vir. What ho, driver! stop and answer. Whose vehicle is this; who is inside; and where are you going?

Var. The carriage belongs, sir, to the worthy Chárudatta; the lady Vasantasená is inside, and I am carrying her to the old flower-garden to meet Chárudatta there.

Chan. Let him pass.

Vir. Without inspection?

Chan. Undoubtedly.

Vir. On what surety?

Chan. Chárudatta's.

Vir. And who is Chárudatta, or who is Vasantasená, that the carriage is to pass free?

Chan. Do you not know who they are? If you know not Chárudatta and Vasantasená, you know not the moon and moonlight when you see them together in the skies. Who is there that is not acquainted with that moon of mildness, that lotus of merit, that liberator from sorrow, that pearl, the essence of the four oceans, Chárudatta? Both are of the highest respectability, the boast and pride of the city, the lovely Vasantasená and virtuous Chárudatta.

Vir. Phoo, phoo! I know them well enough, but in the discharge of my duty my own father must be a stranger.

Aryaka. (*In the car.*) Yon Víraka has ever been my foe,

---

* This appears to be the literal import of the passage; its astrological signification is not so clear. According to the commentary, these planetary conjunctions forbode severally pain, colic, fatuity, consumption, sorrow, and indigence.

Chandanaka my friend; the two are ill
Associated in a common duty.
One fire the marriage ceremony asks,
Another serves to light the funeral pile.*

Chan. Well, careful captain, high in the king's confidence, do you then look into the carriage; I will look to the cattle.

Vir. Nay, you are in command and confidence as well as I am; do you inspect it.

Chan. What I see is in fact seen by you.

Vir. Not only by me, but by the king himself.

Chan. Holloa, you! stop the car.

Ary. Unfortunately, I am discovered; I have no sword;
Like Bhíma then I must employ my hands;
Better to die than be again a captive.
Yet, hold, it is not yet despair.

CHANDANAKA *looks into the car.*

Ary. Protection:—I am at your mercy.

Chan. Fear not, who seeks protection will obtain it.

Ary. Fortune forsakes, tribe, family, and friends
Discard, and all men scorn the coward slave
Who fears to grant protection to the wretched.

Chan. How! Áryaka!

---

* Where a perpetual flame is maintained, it lights the fire round which the bride and bridegroom step at the marriage ceremony, and the funeral pile of either; but the household fire is preserved only by a particular sect, the *Agnihotras*, and the great body of the people have nothing of the kind. In this case they distinguish between the sources whence they obtain the kindling flame according to the purposes of its application, and the fire of the marriage rite is taken from the hearth of a respectable person, or from a fire lighted on some auspicious occasion, whilst for the funeral pile "any unpolluted fire may be used. It is only necessary to avoid taking it from another pile, or from the abode of an outcast, of a man belonging to the tribe of executioners, of a woman who has lately borne a child, or of any person who is unclean."—*Colebrook on the Religious Ceremonies of the Hindus: Asiatic Res.*, vii. 241. Notwithstanding these exceptions, it is the common practice of the Hindus of ordinary rank in the western provinces to procure fire from an outcast to light the funeral pile.

Like the poor bird that, flying from the hawk,
Falls in the fowler's net, art thou my prize,*
And, luckless wretch, appliest to me for aid!
He is in Chárudatta's car, his crime
Is none; Sarvilaka, to whom I owe
My own life, is his friend; but then—
My duty to the prince. What's to be done!
E'en be it so—I told him not to fear;
The words have passed my lips   I must befriend him,
Come on't what will: the succour once assured,
Must be extended, though the end be ruin.†

(*Returning.*) I have seen—Áryá—Áryá Vasantasená, and she says right; it is indecorous to detain her on the road when she has an appointment with Chárudatta.

Vír. Excuse me, Chandanaka; I have some doubts in the matter.

Chan. How so!

Vír. You seem flurried, and it was with some indistinctness you call out first Árya, then corrected yourself, and said Áryá Vasantasená.‡ I have some strange misgivings.

Chan. Misgivings, indeed! why, you know, we of the South are not very nice in our articulation, and are apt to con-

---

* Another instance of the familiar use of apologues.

† The importance attached to the duty of affording protection to those who solicit it is repeatedly urged in the Hindu writings: thus in the Hitopadésa:

"What even are called here great gifts, such as donations of land, gold, cattle, and food, are all inferior to the gift of protection, and he who affords succour to the helpless that fly to him for aid, obtains a reward equal to that of performing the *Aswamedha* sacrifice, which confers the enjoyment of every desire."—*Hit.*

This feeling seems to have pervaded the heroic times both of Greece and Rome, and to have secured Admetus an asylum at the court of Cræsus, and Coriolanus a refuge in the halls of Aufidius.

‡ The difference of masculine and feminine terminations, *Árya* and *Áryá*, the first being either the same with *Áryaka*, a name, or "the respectable," as applied to a man; the second means the same as applied to a woman.

VOL. I.   M

found sounds. Being accustomed to speak the dialects of a number of barbarous and other outcast tribes,* it would be all the same to us, whether it was Árya or Áryá, masculine, feminine, or neuter.

Vír. Ah, well—I shall take a look myself: such are the prince's orders—he knows he can trust me.

Chan. And am I not trusted by him?

Vír. True, but I must obey his orders.

Chan. (Apart.) If it is known that the cowherd was seized in Chárudatta's carriage, *he* will be involved in the punishment. I must give my friend here a specimen of Carnatic eloquence. *(Aloud.)* Hark ye, Víraka, I have already inspected the carriage; why are you to inspect it again? who the deuce are you, I should like to know?

Vír. And who are you, pray?

Chan. I'll tell you: one entitled to your most profound respect: you should recollect your caste.

Vír. My caste, what is it then?

Chan. Oh, I do not wish to say.

Vír. Say, say if you like, and if you don't like it, leave it alone.

---

* The original specifies the countries, and the list is not only curious in itself, but it is worthy of remark, on account of the character of *Mlechchhas* or barbarous tribes (that is to say, other than Hindu) being assigned to people who are chiefly, if not wholly, natives of Southern India. We might suppose that the nations of the Peninsula were not universally Hindus at the period when this play was written; they must, however, have received the religion, not only of the Vedas, but even of the Puránas, before the Christian era, as the name of Cape Comari proves; so called, according to Arrian, from a temple dedicated to a goddess, or in fact to *Kumari*, a name of *Párvati* or *Umá*, the virgin bride of Siva. The countries specified are *Khasa, Khattibhatta, Kadattha, Acilaka, Karúáta* (Carnatick), *Karña, Pritrarata, Andhra* (Telingana), *Vida* (Virat or Berar), *Chúda* (Coromandel), *Viña, Barbara, Kheratidaa, Mukha, Madhughdta.* Most of these we cannot identify; they are very possibly distorted by the copyists. Their general application to the South is, however, not only indicated by the few which are recognisable, but by Chandanaka calling himself a *Dakhinatta* or *Dakshinátya*, a dweller of the South.

THE TOY-CART.

Chan. I do not wish to shame you; let it be; it is not worth while to break a wood apple.

Vir. Nay, I insist.

[*Chan.* intimates by signs that Viraka is a Chandr, or worker in leather.

Vir. It is false—I deny it.

Chan. You were wont to carry a dead jackal in your hand,* to replace dislocated joints, and to flourish a pair of shears; and you are now a general. A very pretty general!

Vir. You are a most high and mighty hero, no doubt, far above your real origin.

Chan. What was my origin?

Vir. Excuse me.

Chan. I defy you,—my caste is as pure as the moon.

Vir. No doubt; vastly pure, when your mother was a tabor, your father a kettle-drum, and your brother a tamborine;† but you—you are a general.

Chan. I a *Chamdr*, I Chandanaka, a *Chamdr*; mighty well, mighty well! Look, by all means.

Vir. Ho, driver! Stay till I inspect the car.

---

* Whose skin he is about to employ. The second attribute of this caste is rather derogatory to surgical science, if it be correctly rendered, which is not certain; the expression is *Purishanî kuchcha gatthiardhabano—Purushânâm kuchagranthisañsthâpakaḥ*; the rectifier of men's crooked joints.

† Instruments covered with skins and made by out-castes. The expressions for the last are *Dummuka karada-abhidâ* (*Durmukha-karataka-bhidâ*). *Karata* has various meanings, one of which, a musical instrument, may apply, especially as the like designations are given to the parents. The chief difficulty is the not knowing what sort of instrument, but conformably to the main purport of the speech it must be a kind of drum. A consideration of some importance, however, is the possibility of *karataka* being intended for the jackal of the *Hitopadesa* so named. The animal is associated with the *Chamdr* in the speech of Chandanaka, and a similar allusion may be intended here. How this would affect our speculations as to the date of the play is another question. It does not necessarily involve any difference of opinion, as the apologue may be of considerable antiquity, and prior to the Christian era. There is no doubt of its being widely diffused a few centuries subsequent.

(*Viraka approaches it; Chandanaka seizes him by the hair, drags him back, throws him down and kicks him.*)

Vir. (*Rising.*) What do you mean by this treatment of me!—but I will have vengeance. If I have not your head severed from your body, and your limbs quartered and exposed in the public place, I am not Víraka.*   [*Exit.*

Chan. Away to the palace, or the court. Complain; I care not. Who will heed such a dog as you? (*To Vardhamána.*) Quick, and if any one stops you, say the carriage has been inspected by Víraka and Chandanaka. Lady Vasantasená, I give you this as a passport. (*Gives Áryaka a sword.*)

Áry. My right arm throbs as I receive the weapon.
Fortune is friendly to me. I am safe.

Chan. The Árya † will remember Chandana.
I ask not this for favour, but in love.

Áry. Fate has this day made Chandana my friend.
If the saint's prophecy should be fulfilled,
I will remember well how much I owe him.

Chan. May every deity ‡ befriend your cause;
And may your enemies before you fall,
Like *Sumbha* and *Nisumbha* by the wrath
Of the resentful goddess.§   Drive on.
            [*Exit Vardhamdna with Car.*

---

* A rather unworthy mode of resenting the affront, especially the profession and rank of the speaker being considered: the affront itself is very unbecoming a hero and a general. The scene is a curious, and no doubt accurate, picture of manners amongst the Hindus.

† A title of respect.

‡ The original specifies the deities invoked, or *Siva, Vishnu, Brahmá,* the Sun and the Moon.

§ Durga, by whom the two demons, *Sumbha* and *Nisumbha,* were destroyed, as related in the fifth and following sections of the *Chandipath,* a section of the *Márkandeya Purána;* also in the *Vámana* and other Puránas. Agreeably to our notion of the priority of the play to the Puránas, there should be other authority for the story, but it has not been found in the *Mahábhárata*.

Chan. (*looking after it*). Ha! yonder I see my friend Sarvilaka follows the carriage. Well, may they prosper. Viraka will now to the prince and tell how he has been handled: I must collect my friends and relatives, and follow him without delay. [*Exit.*

END OF THE SIXTH ACT.

ACT VII.

THE GARDEN PUSHPAKARANDA.

Enter CHÁRUDATTA *and* MAITREYA.

Mait. How bravely the old garden looks.
Chár. 'Tis true; like wealthy merchants are the trees
    Who spread in clustering flowers the choicest wares;
    Amongst them busily the bees are straying
    To gather tribute for the royal hive.
Mait. Here is a fine block of stone; sit down on it.
Chár. (*Seated.*) Vardhamána tarries long.
Mait. I told him to make all possible haste.
Chár. Then why so tardy? Or the car rolls heavily:
    Or it has broken down upon the way;
    Or the old traces have been snapped; or lies
    A tree across their path; or have they strayed
    Another road, or are the beasts untractable?
    Or have—oh, here he comes.
        Enter VARDHAMÁNA *with the Car.*
    Come up.
Áry. (*In the car.*)
    Fled from the monarch's myrmidons, and cramped
    By this vile fetter round my foot, I owe
    My safety to this vehicle—where, like the cuckoo *
    Nursed in a stranger nest, I find concealment.
    Now, far beyond the city, I am safe.
    Shall I alight, and seek to gain a refuge

---

* The Hindus believe that the *koil*, the Indian cuckoo, deposits its eggs in the nest of the crow, and leaves them there to be hatched.

Amidst the dark recesses of these groves,
Or shall I dare encounter with the owner
Of this befriending car? 'Twere far more grateful
To meet with Chárudatta, than to hear
His pity only as I darkling lurk
Among these shades. My new acquired liberty
Will yield him pleasure, and my wasted form
Will grow once more to vigour from the interview.

Var. This is the place:—what ho! Maitreya.

Mait. Welcome, Vardhamána; I have been looking out for you.

Var. Well, here I am; and so is Vasantasená.

Mait. But, you son of a slave, what has detained you so long?

Var. Do not be angry, Maitreya. I was obliged to go back to find the cushions which I had at first forgot.

Chdr. Well, well.—Maitreya, assist Vasantasená to alight.

Mait. What! has she got fetters on her feet, that she cannot come down by herself? (*Goes to the car and looks in.*) Holloa! what have we here?* This is not Vasantasená—it is Vasantasena, I suppose.

Chdr. Refrain your mirth, my friend; love ill-sustains
The least delay. I help her to alight. (*Rises.*)

Ary. Here comes the worthy Chárudatta;
Cheering his voice, and gentle is his aspect:
I need not fear.

Chdr. (*Looking in.*) How! who is this?
His arms are like the elephant's vast tusks—
His breasts, his shoulders, brawny as the lion's—
His eyes are coppery-red and roll in anger—
How should a person of such goodly presence
Dear fetters on his limbs? Who art thou, say?

Ary. My name is *Aryaka:* to tend the herds

---

* The masculine form of the name soon, *Vasantasenas* est, non *Vasantasena.*

The duty I was born to; and to thee
I hither come, a suppliant for protection.
Chdr. Art thou that *Aryaka*, our prince's fears
Dragged from his humble station to a prison?
Ary. The same.
Chdr. Fate, that has brought thee hither, is thy friend.
My life I may resign, but cannot turn
Away from one who sues to me for refuge.
Vardhamána, remove those fetters.
Var. (*Obeys.*) The chains are off, sir.
Ary. (*To Chdr.*) And chains more lasting by this aid imposed.
Mait. Then now pray take yourself off too. Come, my good friend, now this gentleman is at large, I think we had better get home as quick as we can.
Chdr. Fie on thy speech! what need of haste?
Ary. Excuse* me, Chárudatta, that I mounted,
Nor sought permission first, into this car.
Chdr. You have graced me by such courtesy.
Ary. Have I your leave to leave you?
Chdr. It is yours.
Ary. I will descend.
Chdr. Nay, friend, not so.
Your steps still labour from the weighty bond
So recently removed: besides, the car
Will unsuspected bear you on your way
Beyond our boundaries—pray keep your seat.
Ary. As you direct.
Chdr. Auspicious be your way
To join your friends.
Ary. I hope I leave one here.
Chdr. 'Tis one who hopes to be remembered by you
In other times.
Ary. Can I forget myself?
Chdr. The gods protect your path.

---

* A very civil and nationally characteristic dialogue ensues.

Ary. It is to you
 I owe my safety.
Chdr. Not so, you owe it
 To your bright fortunes.
Ary. Of the which, indeed,
 I hold you as the cause.
Chdr. But Pálaka
 Must still be heeded; and around he sends
 A numerous guard, who may detain your steps.
 Use no delay; but with all speed depart.
Ary. To meet again. [*Exit.*
Chdr. The deed that I have done will little please
 The king, should it be known; and kings behold
 Their subjects' actions by their spies. 'Twere well
 To leave this spot at once. Maitreya, cast
 The fetters deep into this ancient well. (*His eyes throbbing.*)
 'Tis sad to miss a meeting with my love—
 But that such chance to-day at least is hopeless
 My left eye indicates; and without cause
 A sudden languor creeps into my heart.
 Let us leave this. (*Going.*) Ha, an evil omen!
 A heretic * approaches us. (*Stops.*) Yet—hold—
 Let him advance—we'll take another path. [*Exit.*

* A *Bauddha* mendicant or *Sramadaka.* Avoiding him is in harmony with the Brahmanical doctrine on this subject; at the same time, it is clear that the period of intolerance and persecution had not arrived, or he would not have so openly made his appearance in the presence of a Brahman.
 The *Sramanaka* is our old acquaintance the *Samvahaka,* see Act II.

END OF THE SEVENTH ACT.

ACT VIII.

SCENE THE SAME.

Enter the SRAMAŃAKA, *or Bauddha mendicant, with a wet garment in his hand.*

S'RAMAŃAKA (*sings*).

BE virtue, friends, your only store,
And restless appetite restrain,
Beat meditation's drum, and sore
Your watch against each sense maintain;
The thief that still in ambush lies,
To make devotion's wealth his prize.

Cast the five senses all away,
That triumph o'er the virtuous will;
The pride of self-importance slay,
And ignorance remorseless kill:
So shall you safe the body guard,
And Heaven shall be your last reward.

Why shave the head and mow the chin
Whilst bristling follies choke tho breast?
Apply the knife to parts within,
And heed not how deformed the rest:
The heart of pride and passion weed,
And then the man is pure indeed.

My cloth is heavy with the yet moist dye.* I will enter

---

* He has been staining it of a dull red, with the paste of an ochreous clay, commonly used for this purpose by *Sannyásins*, particularly now the *Sairas*.

this garden belonging to the Rájá's brother-in-law, and wash it in the pool, and then I shall proceed more lightly. (*Does so.*)

(*Behind.*) What, ho! you rascally Sramańaka, what are you doing there!

Sram. Alas, alas! here he is, Samsthánaka himself. He has been affronted by one mendicant, and whenever he meets another he sends him off with his nose slit like an ox. Where shall I fly to?—the lord *Buddha* be my refuge.

Enter SAMSTHÁNAKA *with the* VÍTA, *his sword drawn.*

Sams. Stop, you vile vagabond, or off I take that head of thine, as they snap off the top of a red radish in a dram-shop.*
(*Beats him.*)

Víta. Nay, nay, hold! beat not the poor wretch thus clad in the coloured garment of humility. This garden was intended by your excellency to be the seat of delight, and these trees were destined to afford shade and relief to the unsheltered; but now they are disappointed of their objects; they fail their promise, like the no longer hidden villainy of a scoundrel, and are only to be enjoyed at the risk of peril, like a new sovereignty disposed of before it is yet subdued.

Sram. Mercy, sir; be my protector, my saviour.

Sams. Hear him, the scoundrel, how he abuses me.

Víta. How so?

Sams. He calls me a *shaver*.†

---

* Where it is eaten as a relish to excite thirst and improve the flavour of the liquor.

† The original pun is *l'pásaka*, which means a worshipper or a barber. It was not possible to retain the sense and the pun also: as it is, the attempt to preserve anything like a quibble is so bad, that it is not attempted to follow the original in two more specimens of this sort of wit, resting on the words *dhampa*, meaning prosperous or an atheist, and *pwáya*, pious or a brick trough. The whole passage is this:—

" *Sra.* Sáadam, padídadu uhdáka.

" *Sak.* Bhávo bhávo, pekkha pekkha, akkodadi mam.

" *Víl.* Kim bravíti.

" *Sak.* U'hásaketti mam bhadádi; kim? Hagga ńáhide.

" *Víl.* Buddhopásaka! iti bhavantam stauti.

Vita. Not so, he entreats you humbly.

Sams. And what are you doing here?

Sram. I was about to cleanse my garment in this pond.

Sanís. Villain, was this superlative garden given to me by my sister's husband, the Rájá, for such a base purpose? Dogs drink here by day, and jackals by night: exalted in rank as I am, I do not bathe here, and shall you presume here to wash your foul and fetid rags;—but I shall make short work with you."

Vita. In that case I suspect he will not have long followed the profession.

Sams. How so?

Vita. Observe: his head shines as if it had only been lately shaven; and his garment has been so little worn that there are no scars† on his shoulder. The ochry dye has not yet fully stained the cloth, and the open web, yet fresh and flaccid, hangs loosely over his arms.

Sram. I do not deny it, worthy sir; it is true I have but lately adopted the profession of a beggar.

Sanís. And why so? why did you not become a beggar as soon as you were born, you scoundrel? (*Beats him.*)

Sram. Glory to Buddha.

Vita. Enough, enough! now let him go. (*To the Sram.*) Away with you.

Sanís. Stop, stop! I must first ask leave.

Vita. From whom?

Sams. My own mind.

Vita. Well, he is not gone.

" *Sak.* Thuna, *samanaká*, thuna.

" *Sru.* Tumam dhañño, tumam pasáé.

" *Sak.* Dhávo, dhaáée paádetti mam bhaáádí: kim? hagge *sálávake*, kamhláke kombhakále bá.

" *Vij.* Káddliamdiah! sanu dhanyas twam, padyas twam: iti bharantam stauti.

* *Tamam ekkapohíllam kalemi*,—I shall make you a man of one blow.

† Why they should be expected is very doubtful: the expression is *tálosya alpatayá cha chirorálfitáh skvadhe na játah tisak.*

Sams. My life, my heart, my chick, my child, shall this fellow go or stay? Very well, my mind says——
Vita. What!
Saṁs. He shall neither go, nor stay, nor move, nor breathe —let him fall down and be put to death.
Sram. Glory to Buddha! mercy, mercy!
Vita. Oh, let him go.
Saṁs. On one condition.
Vita. What is that?
Sams. He shall take all the clay of this pool out without muddying the water; or he shall make a pile of clean water and throw the mud aside.
Vita. Absurd! You might as well ask for skins of stone, and meat from trees. This world is sadly burthened with fools.

[*Sram. gesticulates imprecations.*

Sams. What does he mean?
Vita. He blesses you.
Sams. Speak my blessings.
Sram. Be as prosperous as you are pious.*
Saṁs. Begone! [*Exit Sram.*
Vita. Come, come, to other thoughts direct your mind;
    Look round the garden; mark these stately trees,
    Which duly, by the king's command attended,
    Put forth abundantly their fruits and flowers,
    And clasped by twining creepers, they resemble
    The manly husband and the tender wife.
Saṁs. The ground is quite a picture, strewed with many-tinted flowers; the trees are bowed down with blossoms; the graceful creepers completely surmount even their tops; and the monkeys are sporting about like so many jack-fruits.†
Vita. Here let us take our seat.
Saṁs. I am seated. And now, my good friend, trust me,

---

* This is an interpolation, as in the original he retires after repeating his apparent imprecation, to which no words are attached.
† The large fruit of the Artocarpus integrifolia.

I cannot help thinking of Vasantasená: she holds her place in my heart, and rankles like the abuse of a blackguard.

Vita. (*Aside.*) To little purpose are these thoughts indulged: So true it is—

The scorn of woman in ignoble breasts,
But adds fresh fuel to the scorching flame.
The manly heart disdain with scorn repays,
And soon subdues its unrequited passion.

Sams. What hour is it? That fellow Sthávaraka was ordered to be here early; what can be the reason he does not make his appearance? It is almost noon; I feel hungry, and it is impossible to think of walking at this time of day. The sun is now in mid-heaven, and looks as fierce as an angry ape; and the ground is as dry and shrivelled as *Gándhárí* looked when her hundred sons were slain.

Vita. 'Tis true: the cattle dozing in the shade

Let fall the unchamped fodder from their mouths;
The lively ape with slow and languid pace
Creeps to the pool to slake his parching thirst
In its now tepid waters; not a creature
Is seen upon the public road, nor braves
One solitary passenger the sun.
Perhaps the carriage from the beated track
Has turned aside, and waits a cooler hour.

Sams. Very likely, and I am left here to furnish a lodgment in my brains for the rays of the sun. The birds have all slunk into shelter amongst the branches, and passengers panting and breathing flame, are glad to mount the umbrella even in the shade. That fellow will not be here to-day; come let us amuse ourselves: I will give you a song.

(*He sings.*)

There, sir, what say you to that?

Vita. Say? That you are verily a *Gandharba.**

Sams. How should I fail being so; I make a practice of

---

* A chorister of *Swarga* or *Indra's* heaven.

taking asafœtida, cummin-seed, orris-root, treacle and ginger; my voice must necessarily be very *sweet.** I will give you another specimen. (*Sings.*)

There, what think you now?

Vita. That you are a very *Gandharba.*

Sams. I knew you would think so; but I take care to train myself suitably. I always feed upon meat presented to me by some of my slaves, and I have it fried in oil and ghee, and seasoned well with asafœtida and black pepper; that is your only diet for a sweet voice. Oh, that scoundrel, he will never arrive!

Vita. Have patience: he will soon be here. (*They retire.*)

Enter STHÁVARAKA *with the Car in which* VASANTASENÁ *is.*

Sthd. I am in a terrible fright; it is near noon; my master will be in a violent rage. Come up.

Vas. (*In the car.*) Alas! alas! that is not Vardhamána's voice. Who can it be? Whose vehicle is this? Has Chárudatta sent another car and servant to spare his own? Ha! my right eye throbs, my heart flutters, my sight is dim, everything forebodes misfortunes.

Sams. Master, the car is here.

Vita. How do you know?

Sams. Do you not hear a snorting like an old hog's?

Vita. You are right; here it is.

Sams. How, my good fellow, Stháváraka, are you come at last?

Sthd. Yes, sir.

Sams. And the car?

Sthd. Here it is, sir.

Sams. And the oxen?

Sthd. Here they are.

Sams. And yourself?

Sthd. We are all together, your honour.

---

* He is, in fact, punning or blundering upon *gandha*, fragrance, and *Gandharba*, a singer of heaven.

Sans. Then drive in.

Sthd. Which way, sir ?

Sams. Here, where the wall is broken.

Sthd. It is impossible, sir: it will kill the beasts, smash the car, and I shall get my neck broken into the bargain.

Sams. Do you recollect, sirrah, that I am the king's brother-in-law: be the cattle killed, I can buy others; let the car smash, I can have another made; and if you break your neck, I must hire another driver.

Sthd. That is very true, your honour ; the loss will be mine ; I shall not be able to replace myself.

Sams. I care not ; drive in here, over the broken walls.

Sthd. Very well, sir, here goes. Break the car, go to pieces you and your driver; others are to be had, and I must report your fate to your master. (*Drives.*) How, all safe ! There, sir, the carriage has come in.

Sams. You see what a lying rogue you are, and no mischief.

Sthd. Very true, sir.

Sams. Come, my friend, let us go to the car. You are my ever honoured teacher and master, precede : I know what is due to your dignity, ascend.

Vita. I comply.

Sams. Stop ! stop ! Did you make the carriage, pray ? I am the owner of it, and shall therefore get in the first.

Vita. I did as you desired.

Sams. Very possibly ; but you erred in not requesting me to precede.

Vita. Will your excellency be pleased to enter ?

Sams. That is right. I shall ascend. (*Getting up, returns hastily, and lays hold of the Vita in alarm.*) Oh dear! I am a lost man ; there's a thief or a she-devil in the carriage ! If a devil, we shall be robbed ; if a thief, we shall be devoured alive !

Vita. Fear not ; how should a she-devil get into a bullock carriage ? It was nothing but the shadow of Sthávarnka, I dare say, which, your eyes having been dazzled with the glare, you saw indistinctly, and mistook for a living figure.

Sams. My poor Sthávaraka, are you alive?

Sthd. I rather think so, your honour.

Sams. There certainly is a woman in the car,—look yourself. (*To the Vita.*)

Vita. A woman! ha, ha!
    Afraid to gaze upon the man of birth,
    Who prides himself on my companionship,
    They walk with downcast eyes, like shrinking cattle
    That hang their heads against the driving rain.

Vas. Alas, that odious wretch, the Rája's brother!
    What will become of me—unhappy girl!
    A luckless seed my coming hither sows
    In the parched soil of my disastrous fate.

Sams. That vile slave, not to have examined the carriage! —Come, master, look.

Vita. I am going.

Sams. Do jackals fly or crows run? Do men eat with their eyes and see with their teeth? So surely will I not stay here.

Vita. (*Looking in.*) How! can it be?
    What brings the doe into the tiger's den?
    Or does the cygnet fly the distant mate,
    Though bright as autumn's moon, to wed the crow?
    It is not well; or has your mother's will,
    On gain intent, compelled you to come hither
    To earn reluctant presents late despised?
    You are by nature false, your fickle tribe,
    I told you truly, ever are prepared
    To yield their blandishments to those they scorn.

Vas. Believe it not of me—I was deceived,
    Mistook the vehicle, and the fatal error
    Has brought me hither. Oh, befriend—protect me!

Vita. I will befriend you; banish every fear.

I will beguile this blockhead. (*Descends.*)
There is indeed a devil in the car.

Saṁs. Indeed! how happens it she has not run off with you? If a thief, how is it she has not eaten you up?

Vita. Never mind.
Hence to Ujjayin a line of groves affords
Unbroken shade; let us walk there, 'twere better.

Saṁs. How so?

Vita. 'Twill yield us healthy exercise, and spare
The jaded cattle.

Saṁs. So be it. Come, Sthávaraka, follow us with the carriage.—No, stop; I go on foot only before gods and Brahmans —I cannot walk along the road; I must get into the car, and then as I pass, the citizens will say to each other, There, that is he, his excellency the prince's most noble brother-in-law.

Vita. (*Apart.*) What is to be done? the case is critical,—
The remedy not obvious: yes, this were best.
(*Aloud to the prince.*) I did but jest. There is no female fiend. Vasantasená has come here to meet you.

Vas. Ah me!

Saṁs. Am I not, master, a fine fellow, another *Vâsudeva?*

Vita. Undoubtedly.

Saṁs. It is therefore that this unparalleled goddess waits upon me. I lately displeased her; I will now go and cast myself at her feet.

Vita. Well devised.

Saṁs. I go. (*Kneels to Vasantasená.*) Celestial Mother, listen to my prayers; behold me with those lotus eyes thus lowly at thy feet, and mark my hands uplifted thus to thy heavenly countenance. Forgive, most graceful nymph, the faults that love has urged me to commit, and accept me for thy servant and thy slave.

Vas. Away! your regard is my abhorrence. (*Spurns him with her foot.*)

Saṁs. (*Rising in great wrath.*) What! shall this head that

bows not to the gods, this head that my mother caressed, be
humbled to the ground, to be treated like a dead carcase by
the jackals in a thicket! What ho! Sthávaraka, where did
you pick up this woman?

Sthd. Why, sir, to tell you the truth, some village carts
blocked up the road near Chárudatta's garden; I got down to
clear the way, and in the meantime left the carriage at his
gate; I fancy she then came out of his house and ascended
the car, mistaking it for another.

Sams. A mistake! Oh, then, she did not come here to seek
me. Come down, madam, this carriage is mine. You come, I
suppose, to meet that beggar's brat, the son of a higgler,
and you take advantage of my cattle,—but turn out directly,
I say.

Vas. That which you make my blame I make my boast;
  As for the rest, whatever must be may be.

Sams. With these fair hands, armed with ten nails, and
dexterous in inflicting punishment, I drag you from the carriage by the hair of your head, as *Jatáyu** seized upon the
wife of *Báli*.†

Vita. Forbear, forbear, nor rudely thus invade .
  These graceful tresses. What destructive hand
  Would roughly rend the creeper from the tree,
  Or tear the blossom from the slender stem!
  Leave her to me, I'll bring her from the car.

(*Goes and hands Vasantasená down.*)

Sams. (*Aside.*) The wrath that her disdainful treatment
justly kindled is now more violent than ever: a blow! a kick!
to be spurned! I am resolved,—she dies. (*Aloud.*) Master, if
you have any relish for a mantle with a broad border and a

---

* *Jatáyu* is the name of a hero bird, the son of *Garuda* by *Syeni*: he
was slain by *Rávaña* in attempting to rescue *Sita* when carried off by that
demon.

† Here is a great confusion of persons; *Báli* carried off *Rumá*, the wife
of *Sugriva*.

hundred tassels, or have any curiosity to taste a bit of delicate flesh, now is your time.

Vita. What mean you?

Sams. Will you oblige me?

Vita. In anything not unreasonable.

Sams. There is no more flavour of unreasonableness than of she-devils in it.

Vita. Well, speak on.

Sams. Put Vasantasená to death.

Vita. (*Stopping his ears.*)
    Murder a young and unoffending female,
    Of courteous manners and unrivalled beauty,
    The pride of all *Ujjayin* ! Where shall I find,
    Believe you, a fit raft to waft my soul
    Safe o'er the river of futurity?

Sams. I will have one made for you. Come, come, what have you to fear? In this lowly place, who shall see you?

Vita. All nature—the surrounding realms of space ;
    The genii of these groves, the moon, the sun,
    The winds, the vault of heaven, the firm-set earth,
    Hell's awful ruler, and the conscious soul—
    These all bear witness to the good or ill
    That men perform, and these will see the deed.*

Sams. Throw a cloth over her then, and hide her.

Vita. Fool! you are crazed.

Sams. And you are an old good-for-nothing dastardly jackal. Very well, I shall find some one else. Sthávaraka shall do it. Here, Sthávaraka, my lad, I will give you gold bracelets.

Sthd. Thank your honour, I will wear them.

Sams. You shall have a gold seat.

Sthd. I will sit upon it.

Sams. You shall have every dainty dish from my table.

---

* This passage is in fact from Manu, with a slight deviation only in the order.

Sthá. I will eat it; never fear me.
Saṁs. You shall be head over all my slaves.
Sthá. I shall be a very great man.
Saṁs. But attend to what I order.
Sthá. Depend upon me, in everything that may be done.
Saṁs. It may be done well enough.
Sthá. Say on, sir.
Saṁs. Kill this Vasantasená.
Sthá. Excuse me, sir, I brought her here.
Saṁs. Why, you villain, am I not your master?
Sthá. You are, sir; my body is yours, but not my innocence: I dare not obey you.
Saṁs. Of whom are you, my servant, to be afraid?
Sthá. Futurity.
Saṁs. And who is Mr. Futurity, pray?
Sthá. The requiter of our good and evil deeds.
Saṁs. And what is the return for good?
Sthá. Wealth and power like your honour's.
Saṁs. And what for evil?
Sthá. Eating, as I do, the bread of slavery; I will not do, therefore, what ought not to be done.
Saṁs. You will not obey me? (*Beats him.*)
Sthá. Beat me if you will, kill me if you will, I cannot do what ought not to be done. Fate has already punished me with servitude for the misdeeds of a former life, and I will not incur the penalty of being born again a slave.
Vas. Oh, sir, protect me. (*To the Vita.*)
Vita. Come, come, be pacified. (*To the prince.*)

    Sthávaraka is right; revolving fate
    Has doomed him to a low and servile station,
    From which he wisely hopes a life of virtue
    Hereafter sets him free. Do you too think,
    Though degradation wait not close on crime,
    And many, obstinately foes to virtue,
    Suffer not here the punishment they merit,
    Yet destiny not blindly works. Though now

Her will gives servitude to him, to you
A master's sway; yet in a future being,
Your affluence may his portion be assigned,
And yours, to do submissively his bidding.

Sans. (Apart.) The old dastard, and this fool of a slave, are both afraid of futurity; but what shall I fear? I, who am the brother of a prince, and a man of courage as well as rank? *(To Sthávaraka.)* Begone, slave; retire into the garden, and wait apart.

Sthá. I obey, sir. *(To Vasantasená.)* Lady, fear not me. [*Exit.*

Sans. *(Tightening his girdle.)* Now, Vasantasená, die. *(Goes to seize her; the Vitá stops him.)*

Vitá. In my presence! *(Throws him down.)*

Sans. Ah, villain! would you kill your prince? *(Faints.)* Ah, you who have so long fed at my cost, do you now become my foe? *(Rising; apart.)* Let me think; this will do. I saw the old scoundrel give a signal. I must get him out of the way and then despatch her. *(Aloud.)* My good friend, how could you so mistake what I said? How could you suppose that I, born of so high a race,* should seriously purpose such an unworthy action? I merely used those menaces to terrify her into compliance.

Vitá. Believe me, sir, it is of little import
To boast of noble birth, unless accord
The manners with the rank:—ungrateful thorns
Are most offensive in a goodly soil.

Sans. The truth of the matter is, that Vasantasená is

---

* The term used to designate his family importance in this place, and again in the ninth act, is *Mallaka-pramáṇam*. *Mallaka* is said by the Commentator to mean a leaf used to wrap up anything, and that the Sakára intends to say *samudra*, the ocean; but this seems very gratuitous. *Mallaka*, as synonymous with *malla*, is a very common name amongst the princes of the Dekhin, and perhaps the Sakára may intend to compare his family to theirs. It might be thought not impossible that the author intended to express the Arabic term *Melek*, a king; but how or when did this word find its way to India?

bashful in your presence: leave us by ourselves a little. That fellow Sthávaraka, too, I am sure, intends to run away; go, bring him back, and I dare say when we are alone a little she will relent.

Vita. (*Apart.*) It may be true that, valiant in my presence,
 Vasantasená may continue still
 To drive this fool to madness by denial.
 Passion in privacy gains confidence.
 I will consent to leave them for a while.
 (*Aloud*). I shall retire and obey your orders.

Vas. (*Laying hold of his garment.*)
 Oh, leave me not! I have no hope but you.

Vita. You have no cause for terror. Hear me, sir:
 I leave Vasantasená as a pledge,
 And safe expect her from your hands again.

Sams. Be assured of it, she shall be so accepted.

Vita. In truth?

Sams. In truth.

Vita. (*Apart.*) He may deceive me. I'll at first retire;
 But so, that unobserved I may behold
 His acts, and satisfy me of his purpose.

Sams. He is gone, and now she dies. But hold:—perhaps he juggles with me, the sly old fox, and now lies watch to see what I am doing: he shall meet his match; the deceiver be deceived. (*He gathers flowers and decorates himself.*) Come, Vasantasená, child, why so pettish? come, come.

Vita. I see his love revives; I now may leave them. (*Departs.*)

Sams. I will give you gold, I will treat you tenderly, I will lay head and turban at your feet. Oh, if you still disdain me, and will not accept me as your slave, what have I to do longer with mankind?

Vas. Why should I hesitate? I spurn you;
 Nor can you tempt me, abject wretch, with gold.
 Though soiled the leaves, the bees fly not the lotus,
 Nor shall my heart prove traitor to the homage
 It pays to merit, though its lord be poor.

To love such excellence exalts my life,
And sheds a lustre on my humble lot.
And why should I forego it ? Can I leave
The mango's stately stem to twine around
The low and worthless *dhák* ?

Sams. What ! dare you compare the beggar Chárudatta to a mango-tree, and me to the *dhák*,* not even a *kimśuka* !* Is it thus you treat me and cherish the recollection of Chárudatta?

Vas. How can I cease to think of one who dwells for ever in my heart ?

Sams. We'll soon try that, and cut short your recollections and yourself together. Stop, you inamorata of a beggarly Brahman.

Vas. Delightful words ! proceed, you speak my praise.

Sams. Let him defend you if he can.

Vas. Defend me ! I were safe if he were here !

Sams. What ! is he *Śakra*, or the son of *Bali*—*Mahendra*, or the son of *Rambhá*—*Kálanemi*, or *Subhandu*—*Rudra* or the son of *Drona*—*Jaṭáyu*—*Chánakya*—*Dhundhumára* or *Triśanku* ? † If he were all these together, he could not aid you. As *Sítá* was slain by *Chánakya*, as *Draupadí* by *Jaṭáyu*, so art thou by me. (*Seizes her.*)

---

* They are both the same apparently ; but from the former growing on arid and concary soils it is stunted and mean, whilst the latter grows to a respectable tree.

† Several of these have been named before. *Śakra* is a name of *Indra*, the king of the gods : the son of *Bali* is *Angada*, a fierce monkey chief, one of Ráma's confederates. *Mahendra* is another name of Indra. The son of *Rambhá* is a personage of whom no notice has been found elsewhere, unless it be a mistake for the son of *Rádhá*, *Karna*. *Kálanemi* is a Daitya of some celebrity, and one of Rávana's attendants. *Subhandu* has not been identified. *Rudra* is a name of *Śiva*. The son of Drona is a celebrated hero in the *Mahábhárata* named *Aśwatthámas*. *Jaṭáyu* is a fabulous bird killed by *Rávana*. *Chánakya* is a statesman, the minister of *Chandragupta*. *Dhundhumára* is the name of a king of Oude of the Solar line, properly called *Kuvalayáśwa*, but termed *Dhundhumára* from slaying a demon named *Dhundhu* who annoyed the Saint *Uttanka*. *Triśanku* is a prince of the same family, elevated to heaven during his life by the sage *Viśwámitra*. All these persons occur in the Mahábhárata or Rámáyana.

Vas. Oh, my dear mother! Oh, my loved Chárudatta!
Too short and too imperfect are our loves—
Too soon I perish. I will cry for succour—
What! shall Vasantasená's voice be heard
Abroad? Oh, that were infamy! No more
But this. Bless, bless my Chárudatta.

Sams. Still do you repeat that name! Once more, now. (*Seizing her by the throat.*)

Vas. (*In a struggling tone.*) Bless my Chárudatta.

Sams. Die, harlot, die. (*Strangles her with his hands.*) 'Tis done, she is no more. This bundle of vice, this mansion of cruelty, has met her fate, instead of him whom she came in her love to meet. To what shall I compare the prowess of this arm! Destroyed in the fulness of her hopes, she has fallen like *Sítá* in the *Bhárata.* Deaf to my desires, she perishes in my resentment. The garden is empty; I may drag her away unperceived. My father and my mother, that *Draupadí*, as well as my brothers, may regret that they did not see the valiant actions of my mother's son.* The old jackal will be here again presently. I will withdraw and observe him.

Enter the Víta *and* Stihávaraka.

Víta. I have brought back Sthávaraka. Where is he? Here are foot-marks,—these are woman's!

Sams. (*Advances.*) Welcome, master: you are well returned, Sthávaraka.

Víta. Now render back my pledge.

Sams. What was that?

Víta. Vasantasená.

Sams. Oh, she is gone.

Víta. Whether?

Sams. After you.

Víta. She came not in that direction.

---

* This passage is in the original somewhat obscure. *Sutí roachída-bhádaka mamma piriá, maddaro, ki Doppadí, je ki pakkhadi kedimak varajídak puttaka kálattakak.*

Sams. Which way went you?
Vita. To the east.
Sams. Ah, that accounts for it; she turned off to the south.
Vita. I went south too.
Sams. Then, I suppose, she went north.
Vita. What mean you? I comprehend you not. Speak out.
Sams. I swear by your head and my feet,* that you may make yourself perfectly easy. Dismiss all alarm; I have killed her.
Vita. Killed her!
Sams. What! you do not believe me? Then look here, see this first proof of my prowess. (*Shows the body.*)
Vita. Alas, I die! (*Faints.*)
Sams. Hey-dey! is it all over with him?
Sthd. Revive, sir; it is I who am to blame: my inconsiderately bringing her hither has caused her death.
Vita. (*Reviving.*) Alas! Vasantasená,
 The stream of tenderness is now dried up,
 And beauty flies us for her native sphere.
 Adorned with every grace, of lovely aspect,
 Radiant with playfulness, alas! poor wench,
 River of gentle feeling, isle of mirth,
 And friendly refuge for all such as I am;
 Alas! love's richest store, a mart exhaustless
 Of exquisite delights, is here broke open.
 This crime will amply be avenged. A deed
 Done by such hands, in such a place committed,
 Will bring down infamy upon the state,
 And drive our guardian goddess from our city.
 Let me reflect;—this villain may involve
 Me in the crime—I will depart from hence.
      [*The prince lays hold of him.*
Detain me not; I have already been
Too long your follower and friend.

   * A very insulting oath.

THE TOY-CART.   139

Sans. Very likely, indeed. You have murdered Vasantasená, and seek to accuse me of the crime. Do you imagine I am without friends?

Vita. You are a wretch.

Sans. Come, come, I will give you money, a hundred *suvarnas*, clothes, a turban. The consequence of abuse is common to all men.

Vita. Keep your gifts.

Sthá. Shame! shame!

Sans. Ha, ha, ha! (*Laughing.*)

Vita. Restrain your mirth. Let there be hate between us.
  That friendship that confers alone disgrace
  Is not for me; it must no more unite us.
  I cast it from me, as a snapped
  And stringless bow.

Sans. Come, good master, be appeased. Let us go bathe.

Vita. Whilst you were free from crime you might exact
  My duty, but obedience to you now
  Would but proclaim myself alike unworthy.
  I cannot wait on guilt, nor, though I know
  My innocence, have courage to encounter
  Those speaking glances every female eye
  Will cast abhorrent upon one who holds
  Communion with a woman's murderer.
  Poor, poor Vasantasená! may thy virtues
  Win thee in after-life a happier portion;
  And may the days of shame, and death of violence
  That thou hast suffered in existence past,
  Ensure thee honoured birth, the world's regard,
  And wealth and happiness, in that to come. (*Going.*)

Sans. Where would you fly! In this, my garden, you have murdered a female; come along with me, and defend yourself before my brother-in-law. (*Seizes him.*)

Vita. Away, fool. (*Draws his sword.*)

Sans. (*Falls back.*) Oh, very well, if you are afraid, you may depart.

Vita. I am in danger here; yes, I will join Sarvilaka and Chandana, and with them seek the band that Árya has assembled. [*Exit.*

Saṃs. Go, fool, to death. Well, Sthávaraka, my lad, what think you of this business?

Sthá. That it is most horrible.

Saṃs. How, slave, do you condemn me? With all my heart, be it so. Here, take these. (*Gives him his ornaments.*) I make you a present of them, that when I am full dressed, you may be suitably equipped to attend me: it is my command.

Sthá. These are too costly,—what am I to do with them, sir?

Saṃs. Take them, take them, and away with you. Conduct the carriage to the porch of my palace, and there wait my coming.

Sthá. I obey, sir. [*Exit.*

Saṃs. My worthy preceptor has taken himself off in alarm. As to the slave, as soon as I return I will put him in confinement; so my secret is safe, and I may depart without apprehension. Hold! let me be sure,—is she dead, or must I kill her again? no, she is safe. I will cover the body with my mantle. Stop! it bears my name, and will discover me. Well thought of,—the wind has scattered about a quantity of dry leaves; I will cover her over with them. (*Collects the leaves and piles them over Vasantasená.*) Now to the court, where I will enter an accusation against Chárudatta of having murdered Vasantasená for her wealth. Ingeniously devised! Chárudatta will be ruined; the virtuous city cannot tolerate even the death of an animal.* Now to my work. (*Going.*) Here comes that rascally mendicant again, and by the very road I was about to take; he owes me a grudge for threatening to slit his nose, and should he see me here, he will out of revenge come forward and tax me with this murder. How shall I avoid him? I can leap the broken wall here. Thus I fly, as the monkey

---

* This may imply the wide diffusion of Bauddha tenets.

Mahendra leaped through heaven, over earth and hell, from Hanumat[*] Peak to Lanká. (*Jumps down.*)

Enter the SRAMAṆAKA *or Mendicant, as before.*

I have washed my mantle, and will hang it on these boughs to dry. No, here are a number of monkeys; I'll spread it on the ground. No, there is too much dust. Ha! yonder the wind has blown together a pile of dry leaves; that will answer exactly; I'll spread it upon them. (*Spreads his wrapper over Vasantasená and sits down.*) Glory to *Buddha!* (*Repeats the moral stanzas as above.*) But enough of this. I covet not the other world, until in this I may make some return for the lady Vasantasená's charity. On the day she liberated me from the gamester's clutches she made me her slave for ever. Holloa! something sighed amidst yon leaves! or perhaps it was only their crackling, scorched by the sun, and moistened by my damp garment. Bless me, they spread out like the wings of a bird. (*One of Vasantasená's hands appears.*) A woman's hand, as I live, with rich ornaments—and another; surely I have seen that hand before. It is, it is—it is the hand that once was stretched forth to save me. What should this mean? (*Throws off the wrapper and leaves, and sees Vasantasená.*) It is the lady Vasantasená; the devoted worshipper of *Buddha*. (*Vasantasená expresses by signs the want of water.*) She wants water: the pool is far away; what's to be done? Ha! my wet garment. (*Applies it to her face and mouth and fans her.*)

Vas. (*Reviving.*) Thanks, thanks, my friend; who art thou?

Sram. Do you not recollect me, lady? You once redeemed me with ten *suvarṇas*.

Vas. I remember *you*; aught else I have forgotten. I have suffered since.

Sram. How, lady?

Vas. As my fate deserved.

Sram. Rise, lady, rise; drag yourself to this tree: here,

---

[*] Hanumat is the monkey; Mahendra, the mountain.

hold by this creeper.* (*Bends it down to her; she lays hold of it and rises.*) In a neighbouring convent dwells a holy sister;† rest a while with her, lady, and recover your spirits: gently, lady, gently. (*They proceed.*) Stand aside, good friends, stand aside; make way for a young female and a poor beggar. It is my duty to restrain the hands and mouth, and keep the passions in subjection. What should such a man care for kingdoms? His is the world to come. [*Exit.*

* To a Bauddha ascetic female contact is unlawful. His observance of the prohibition, in spite of his gratitude and regard for Vasantasená, is a curious and characteristic delineation of the denaturalizing tendency of such institutions.

† The expression is *Edaśtiâ vihâre mamo dhammabhinís chiśladí.* Etasmin vihāre mama dharmabhaginī tishṭati. Convents for women are very characteristically Bauddha institutions: they did exist in the Burman empire till of late years, and are still to be met with in Nepaul and Tibet.

END OF THE EIGHTH ACT.

ACT IX.

THE HALL OF JUSTICE.

(Exterior and Interior.)

Enter OFFICER.

I AM commanded to prepare the benches in this hall for the judges. (*Arranges them.*) All is ready for their reception, the floor is swept, and the seats are placed, and I have only now to inform them all is ready. (*Going.*) Ha! here comes the king's brother-in-law, a worthless fellow; I will get out of his way. (*Retires.*)

Enter SANSTHÁNAKA, *splendidly dressed.*

I have bathed in limpid water and reposed in a shady grove, passing my time like a celestial chorister of elegant form, amidst an attendant train of lovely damsels, now tying my hair, then twisting it into a braid, then opening it in flowing tresses, and again gathering it into a graceful knot. Oh! I am a most accomplished and astonishing young prince, and yet I feel a vacancy, an interior chasm; such as is sought for by the fatal worm that works its darkling way through the human entrails. How shall I fill it up?—on whom shall I satiate my craving? Ha! I recollect; it is designed for the miserable Chárudatta. So be it. I will repair to the court, and cause an accusation to be registered against him, of the death of Vasantasená, asserting that he has robbed and murdered her. The court is open, I see. (*Enters.*) How! the seats are ready for the arrival of the judges. I shall wait their coming on this grass plot.

Doorkeeper. Here comes the Court; I must attend.

Enter the JUDGE, *with the* PROVOST *and* RECORDER * *and others.*

Crier. Hear, all men, the judge's commands.

Judge. Amidst the conflicting details of parties engaged in legal controversy, it is difficult for the judge to ascertain what is really in their hearts. Men accuse others of secret crimes, and even though the charge be disproved, they acknowledge not their fault, but, blinded by passion, persevere ; and whilst their friends conceal their errors, and their foes exaggerate them, the character of the prince is assailed. Reproach indeed is easy, discrimination of but rare occurrence, and the quality of a judge is readily the subject of censure. A judge should be learned, sagacious, eloquent, dispassionate, impartial; he should pronounce judgment only after due deliberation and inquiry ; he should be a guardian to the weak, a terror to the wicked ; his heart should covet nothing, his mind be intent on nothing but equity and truth, and he should keep aloof the anger of the king.

Provost and Rec. The character of your worship is as free from censure, as the moon is from the imputation of obscurity.

Judge. Officers, lead the way to the seat of judgment.

Off. As your worship commands. (*They sit.*)

Judge. Now go forth, and see who comes to demand justice.

Off. By command of his honour the judge, I ask, who waits to demand justice?

Sams. (*Advancing.*) Oh, oh! the judges are seated. I

---

* The *Sreshthis*, the chief of the merchants, and *Káyast'ha* or Scribe. From the way in which they interfere, they seem to sit as joint-assessors or commissioners with the judge. This is a curious, and, as far as yet known, a solitary picture of the practical administration of Hindu law under Hindu government. It is not exactly, perhaps, according to rule: the number, three or more, is correct. The judge may be either a Brahman, a Kshattriya, or a Vaisya, but the assessors should be Brahmans alone. Merchants, however, may be called in. The presence of the Káyast'ha, a man of mixed caste, as an assessor, is not in the books, although the Scribe is enumerated amongst the officers of the court.

demand justice; I, a man of rank, a *Vásudeva*, and brother-in-law of the Rája;—I have a plaint to enter.

Off. Have the goodness to wait a moment, your excellency, whilst I apprize the Court. (*Returns.*) So please your worship, the first plaintiff is his Majesty's brother-in-law.

Judge. The Rája's brother-in-law to proffer a plaint? An eclipse of the rising sun foreruns the downfall of some illustrious character: but there are other matters before us. Return and tell him his cause cannot come on to-day.

(*Officer returns to Samsthánaka.*)

Off. I am desired to inform your honour that your cause cannot be tried to-day.

Sams. How! not to-day? Then I shall apply to the King, my sister's husband. I shall apply to my sister, and to my mother, and have this judge dismissed, and another appointed immediately. (*Going.*)

Off. Stay one moment, your honour, and I will carry your message to the Court. (*Goes to the judge.*) Please your worship, his excellency is very angry; and declares if you do not try his suit to-day, he will complain to the royal family, and procure your worship's dismissal.

Judge. The blockhead has it in his power, it is true. Well, call him hither: his plaint shall be heard.

Off. (*To Sams.*) Will your excellency be pleased to enter; your plaint will be heard.

Sams. Oh, oh! first it could not be tried; now it will be heard; very well; the judges fear me: they will do what I desire. (*Enters.*) I am well pleased, gentlemen; you may therefore be so too, for it is in my hands to distribute or withhold satisfaction.

Judge. (*Apart.*) Very like the language of a complainant this! (*Aloud.*) Be seated.

Sams. Assuredly. This place is mine, and I shall sit where I please. (*To the Provost.*) I will sit here; no (*to the Recorder*), I will sit here; no, no (*puts his hands on the judge's head, and then sits down by his side*), I will even sit here.

Judge. Your excellency has a complaint?
Saṁs. To be sure I have.
Judge. Prefer it.
Saṁs. I will, in good time; but remember, I am born in a distinguished family. My father is the Rája's father-in-law; the Rája is my father's son-in-law; I am the Rája's brother; and the Rája is my sister's husband.
Judge. We know all this; but why dwell on family honours? Personal excellence is more important; there are always thorn-bushes in the fairest forests: declare therefore your suit.
Saṁs. This it is; but it involves no fault of mine. My noble brother-in-law, in his good pleasure, presented me, for my ease and recreation, the best of the royal gardens, the ancient *Pushpakaraṇḍaka*. It is my practice to visit it daily, and see it well swept and weeded, and kept in order; and having, as my wont, gone this day thither, what should I behold, but—I could scarcely believe my eyes—the dead body of a female!
Judge. Did you know the person?
Saṁs. Alas! too well. She was once our city's greatest pride. Her rich attire must have tempted some execrable wretch to beguile her into the lonely garden; and there, for the sake of her jewels, was the lovely Vasantasená strangled by his hands, not by me. (*Stops himself.*)
Judge. What neglect in the police! You heard the plaint, gentlemen; let it be recorded, including the words "not by me."
Rec. (*Writes it.*) It is done.
Saṁs. (*Apart.*) Vile carelessness! My heedlessness has plunged me into peril, like a man crossing a narrow bridge precipitately, who tumbles into the stream: it cannot now be helped. (*Aloud.*) Well, sagacious administrators of justice, you make a mighty fuss about a trifle. I was going to observe, not by me was the deed beheld. (*Puts his foot on the record, and wipes out the last part.*)

Judge. How, then, do you know the truth of what you have stated, that for the sake of her ornaments she was strangled by some person's hands?

Saṅs. I conclude so, for the neck was bare and swollen, and her dress rifled of its ornaments.

Prov. The case is likely enough.

Saṅs. (Apart.) Good; I am alive again.

Prov. Whom else do we require in this suit?

Judge. The case is twofold, and must be investigated both in relation to assertion and facts; the verbal investigation relates to plaintiff and respondent, that of facts depends upon the judge.

Prov. The cause then requires the evidence of Vasantasená's mother.

Judge. Undoubtedly. Officers, go and civilly call Vasantasená's mother into court.

Off. (Exit Officer, and returns with the old woman.) Come along, dame.

Moth. My daughter is gone to a friend's house. This old fellow comes and says to me: "Come along; his honour the judge has sent for you." I am ready to faint, and my heart flutters so.—Very well, sir, very well, sir, lead me to the court.

Off. Here we are;—enter. *(They enter.)*

Moth. Health and happiness to your worships!

Judge. You are welcome;—sit down. *(She sits.)*

Saṅs. Oh, old procuress, you are there, are you?

Judge. You are the mother of Vasantasená?

Moth. I am.

Judge. Where is your daughter?

Moth. At a friend's house.

Judge. The name of that friend?

Moth. (Apart.) Oh dear me, this is very awkward. *(Aloud.)* Surely, your worship, this is not a fit question for your worship to ask.

Judge. No hesitation;—the law asks the question.

Prov. and Rec. Speak out; the law asks the question; there is no impropriety in answering.

Moth. Why then, gentlemen, to say the truth, she is at the house of a very nice gentleman;—the son of Ságaradatta, grandson of the Provost Vinayadatta, whose own name is Chárudatta; he lives near the Exchange: my daughter is with him.

Sans. You hear, judges;—let this be registered. I accuse Chárudatta.

Prov. Chárudatta, her friend! he cannot be criminal.

Judge. The cause, however, requires his presence.

Prov. Certainly.

Judge. (*To the Scribe.*) Dhanadatta, write down that Vasantasená last went to Chárudatta's residence: this is the first step. Let me consider; how can Chárudatta be summoned hither? However, the law must be enforced. Officer, repair to Chárudatta, and say to him, the magistrate, with all due respect, requests to see him at his perfect convenience.

(*Officer goes out, and re-enters with Chárudatta.*)

Off. This way, sir.

Chár. The prince well knows my rank and character,
And yet thus calls me to his public court.
Haply he may have heard my car conveyed
The fugitive he feared beyond his reach,
Borne to his ear by some unfriendly spy.
Or haply—but away with fancies; soon
I learn the truth, arrived at the tribunal.

Off. This way, this way, sir.

Chár. What should this mean? his harshest note, yon crow
Responsive utters to his fellow's call,
With croak repeated. Ha! my left eye throbs;
What new misfortunes threaten?

Off. Proceed, sir, never fear.

Chár. Facing the sun, on yonder blighted tree,
The bird of evil augury is perched;
Ha! on my path, the black snake sleeping lies.

Roused from his slumber, he unfolds in wrath
His spiry length, and threatening beats the ground
With bulk inflated, as he turns on me
His angry eyes, and from between his fangs
Protrudes his hissing tongue. I slip, yet here
No plashy mire betrays my heedless feet.—
Still throbs my left eye, and my left arm trembles;
And still that bird in flight sinistral cries,
To warn me of impending ill. Yea, death—
Terrible death awaits me. Be it so—
It is not mine to murmur against destiny,
Nor doubt that righteous which the gods ordain.
Off. This is the court, sir, enter.
Chár. (*Entering and looking round.*)
    The prospect is but little pleasing.
The court looks like a sea;*—its councillors
Are deep engulphed in thought; its tossing waves
Are wrangling advocates; its brood of monsters
Are these wild animals—death's ministers—
Attorneys skim like wily snakes the surface—
Spies are the shell-fish cowering 'midst its weeds,
And vile informers, like the hovering curlew,
Hang fluttering o'er, then pounce upon their prey:
The beach, that should be justice, is unsafe,
Rough, rude, and broken by oppression's storms.
    [*As he advances he knocks his head against the door-frame.*
More inauspicious omens! they attend
Each step I take; fate multiplies its favours.

---

* That the translator may not be thought to have had an English rather than an Indian court in his eye, he enumerates the terms of the original for the different members of which it is said to consist. *Mantrina*, councillors; *Dútas*, the envoys or representatives of the parties; the wild animals, death's ministers, are *Nágas* and *Aswas*, elephants and horses employed to tread or tear condemned criminals to death; the *Chátras* are spies or runners; *Námednishas*, disguised emissaries or informers; and *Káyasthas* are scribes by profession, who discharge the duties of notaries and attorneys.

Judge. Chárudatta approaches. Observe him;—that face and form never gave shelter to causeless crime. Appearance is a test of character; and not only in man, but in elephants, horses and kine, the disposition never deviates from the perfect shape.*

Chár. Hail to the court; prosperity attend
 The delegated ministers of justice.

Judge. Sir, you are welcome; officer, bring a seat.

Off. It is here; be seated, sir. (*To Chárudatta; he sits.*)

Sams. So, Mr. Woman-killer, you are here: very decorous this, indeed, to treat such a fellow with so much civility; but never mind.

Judge. Worthy Chárudatta, allow me to ask if any intimacy or connexion has ever subsisted between you and this woman's daughter?

Chár. What woman?

Judge. This. (*Showing Vasantasená's mother.*)

Chár. (*Rising.*) Lady, I salute you.

Moth. Son, long may you live!† (*Apart.*) This is Chárudatta, then; really my daughter has made a good choice.

Judge. Tell us, Chárudatta, were you ever acquainted with that courtezan? (*Chárudatta ashamed, hesitates.*)

Sams. Ah! he pretends to be vastly modest, or very much alarmed; it is merely a pretext to evade confessing his vicious courses: but that he murdered the woman for her wealth, the prince shall soon make manifest.

Prov. Away with this hesitation, Chárudatta: there is a charge against you.

Chár. Well, sirs, what shall I say? What if she were
 A friend of mine? be youth accused, not habit.

Judge. Let me beg—no evasion, banish all reserve, speak the truth and act ingenuously: remember it is the law that calls upon you.

---

* This is literally translated, without any leaning to *Gall* or *Lavater.*
† Literally, long be my life: *chiroṃ me jīva.*

Chdr. First tell me who is my accuser?
Saṁs. I am—I.
Chdr. Thou! a mighty matter truly.
Saṁs. Indeed, you woman-killer! What! are you to murder such a woman as Vasantasená, and rob her of her jewels, and to think it will not be known?
Chdr. Thou art crazed.
Judge. Enough of this; declare the truth: was the courtezan your friend?
Chdr. She was, she was.
Judge. And where is Vasantasená now?
Chdr. Gone.
Prov. Gone! how, whither, and how attended?
Chdr. (*Apart.*) Shall I say she went privately? (*Aloud.*) She went to her own dwelling: what more can I say?
Saṁs. What more! Why, did you not accompany her to my princely garden; and did you not there, for the sake of her jewels, strangle her, with your own hands! How then can you say she is gone home?
Chdr. Foul calumniator.*

  No rain from heaven upon thy face descends,
  Dark as the jay's unmoistened wing in showers.
  These falsehoods parch thy lips, as wintry winds
  Despoil the shrivelled lotus of its beauty.

Judge. (*Apart.*) I see it were as easy to weigh *Himálaya*, [or] the ocean, or grasp the wind, as fix a stain on Chárudatta's reputation. (*Aloud.*) It cannot be, that this worthy man is guilty.
Saṁs. What have you to do with his defence?—let the case be tried.
Judge. Away, fool, is it not thus?—if you expound the *Vedas*† will not your tongue be cut out? if you gaze upon the mid-day sun, will you not lose your eye-sight? if you plunge

---

* The general sense of the passage is, "Your face is unwashed, dirty, foul with falsehood," a common oriental phrase here poetically expressed.

† Here we find the Brahminical notions enforced; such being the punishment of Śúdras who shall read and expound the *Vedas*.

your hand into flame, will it not be burnt? and think you that if you revile Chárudatta, the earth will not open and swallow you? This is Chárudatta—how can such a man have committed such a crime? He has exhausted in lavish munificence the ocean of his disregarded wealth, and is it possible that he, who was best among the best, and who has ever shown the most princely liberality, should have been guilty of a deed most hateful to a noble mind, for the sake of plunder?

Sans. I say again, it is not your province to undertake his defence; you are to try the cause.

Moth. I say the accusation is false. When in his distress my daughter intrusted a casket of jewels to his care, and it was stolen from him, even then he replaced it with a necklace of still greater value; and can he now, for the sake of wealth, have turned murderer? Oh, never! Alas! would that my daughter were here! (*Weeps.*)

Judge. Inform us, Chárudatta, how did she leave you—on foot or in a carriage?

Chár. I did not see her depart, and know not.

Enter VÍRAKA *in haste.*

Now go I to the court, to tell them how I have been maltreated, kicked, and abused for keeping a good look-out after the runaway. Hail to your worships!

Judge. Ha! here is Víraka, the captain of the watch: what brings you hither, Víraka?

Vír. Hear me, your honour. Whilst engaged last night in quest of Aryaka, who had broke loose, we stopped a covered carriage: the captain, Chandanaka, looked into it, and I was going to do so too, when he prevented me, pulled me back, and cuffed and kicked me. I beg your honours will take proper notice of this business.

Judge. We will. Whose was the carriage, do you know?

Vír. The driver said it belonged to this gentleman, Chárudatta; and that it carried Vasantasená to meet him in *Pushpakaraṇḍuka.*

Saṁs. You hear, sirs!

Judge. Truly this spotless moon is threatened by the demon of eclipse; the limpid stream is sullied by the falling of the banks. We will inquire into your complaint, Vîraka; in the meantime mount one of the messenger's horses at the gate; go to *Pushpakaraṇḍaka* with all speed, and bring us word whether the body of a murdered woman lies there.

Vír. I shall. (*Goes out, and presently returns.*) I have been to the garden, and have ascertained that a female body has been carried off by the beasts of prey.

Judge. How know you it was a female?

Vír. By the remains of the hair, and the marks of the hands and feet.

Judge. How difficult it is to discover the truth: the more one investigates, the greater is the perplexity. The points of law are sufficiently clear here, but the understanding still labours like a cow in a quagmire.*

Chár. (*Apart.*) When first the flower unfolds, as flock the bees
   To drink the honeyed dew, so mischiefs crowd
   The entrance opened by man's falling fortune.

Judge. Come, Chárudatta, speak the truth.

Chár. The wretch that sickens at another's merits,
   The mind, by passion blinded, bent to ruin
   The object of its malice, do not claim
   Reply, nor any heed to what they utter,
   Which from their very nature must be falsehood.
   For me—you know me—would I pluck a flower,
   I draw the tender creeper gently to me,
   Nor rudely rob it of its clustering beauty.
   How think you then?—could I with violent hands
   Tear from their lovely seat those jetty locks,
   More glossy than the black bee's wing, or how
   So wrong my nature, and betray my love,
   As with remorseless heart to blast in death
   The weeping charms that vainly sued for mercy!

* Rather an undignified simile for a judge.

Sans. I tell you, judges, you will be held as the defendant's friends and abettors, if you allow him longer to remain seated in your presence.

Judge. Officer, remove him from his seat. (*Officer obeys.*)

Chár. Ministers of justice, yet reflect. (*Sits on the ground.*)

Sans. (*Apart.*) Ha, ha! my deeds are now safely deposited on another's head; I will go and sit near Chárudatta. (*Does so.*) Come, Chárudatta, look at me: confess; say honestly, "I killed Vasantasená."

Chár. Vile wretch, away! Alas! my humble friend,
My good Maitreya, what will be thy grief
To hear of my disgrace! and thine, dear wife,
The daughter of a pure and pious race!
Alas! my boy, amidst thy youthful sports
How little think'st thou of thy father's shame!
Where can Maitreya tarry? I had sent him
To seek Vasantasená, and restore
The costly gems her lavish love bestowed
Upon my child—where can he thus delay!

Outside—Enter MAITREYA *with Vasantasená's jewels.*

I am to return these trinkets to Vasantasená; the child took them to his mother; I must restore them, and, on no account, consent to take them back again. Ha! Rebhila; how now Rebhila, what is the matter? You seem agitated, what has chanced? (*Listening.*) Hey! what say you, my dear friend? summoned to the court! this is very alarming. Let me think:—I must go to him, and see what it means; I can go to Vasantasená afterwards. Oh, here is the court. (*Enters.*) Salutation to your worships! where is my friend?

Judge. There.

Mait. My dear friend, all happiness——

Chár. Will be hereafter.

Mait. Patience.

Chár. That I have.

Mait. But why so downcast? what are you brought here for?

Chdr. I am a murderer—reckless of futurity—
    Repaying woman's tender love with blood—
    What else, let him declare.
Mait. What!
Chdr. (*Whispers him.*) Even so.
Mait. Who says so?
Chdr. (*To the Rája's brother-in-law.*)
    You miserable man, the instrument
    That destiny employs to work my fall.
Mait. Why not say she is gone home?
Chdr. It recks not what I say; my humble state
    Is not to be believed.
Mait. How, sirs! what is all this? Can he who has beautified our city with its chief ornaments, who has filled Ujjayin with gardens, and gates, and convents, and temples, and wells, and fountains,—can he, an utter reprobate, for the object of a few beggarly ornaments, have done such an iniquitous act? (*In anger.*) And you—you wretch, you king's brother-in-law, Saṅsthánaka,—you who stop at nothing, and are a stuffed vessel of everything offensive to mankind,—you monkey, tricked out with golden toys: say again before me, that my friend, who never plucked a flower roughly in his life, who never pulled more than one at a time, and always left the young buds untouched;—say that he has been guilty of a crime detestable in both worlds, and I will break thy head into a thousand pieces with this staff, as knotty and crooked as thy own heart.

Saṁs. Hear him, my masters. What has this crow-footpated hypocritical fellow to do with the cause between me and Chárudatta, that he is to break my head. Attempt it, if you dare, you hypocritical scoundrel. (*Mait. strikes him; a struggle ensues, in which Vasantasená's jewels fall from his girdle. Saṁsthánaka picks them up.*) See here, sirs! here,—here are the poor wench's jewels, for the sake of which yon villain murdered her.

    [*The judges hang down their heads.*

Chdr. (*To Mait.*) In an ill hour these jewels spring to light.
 Such is my fate, their fall will lead to mine.
Mait. Why not explain?
Chdr. The regal eye is feeble to discern
 The truth amidst perplexity and doubt.
 I can but urge—I have not done the deed,
 And poverty like mine must hope to gain
 Unwilling credence; shameful death awaits me.

Judge. Alas! Mars is obstructed and Jupiter obscured, and a new planet like a comet wanders in their orbits.

Prov. Come hither, lady (*to Vasantasena's mother*); look at this casket; was it your daughter's?

Moth. It is very like, but not the same.

Sams. Oh, you old baggage! your eyes tell one story and your tongue another.

Moth. Away, slanderer!

Prov. Be careful of what you say: is it your daughter's, or is it not?

Moth. Why, your worship, the skill of the workman makes it difficult to trust one's eyes; but this is not my daughter's.

Judge. Do you know those ornaments?

Moth. Have I not said? They may be different, though like: I cannot say more; they may be imitations made by some skilful artist.

Judge. It is true. Provost, examine them: they may be different, though like; the dexterity of the artists is no doubt very great, and they readily fabricate imitations of ornaments they have once seen, in such a manner, that the difference shall scarcely be discernible.

Prov. Are these ornaments your property, Chárudatta?

Chdr. They are not.

Prov. Whose then?

Chdr. This lady's daughter's.

Prov. How come they out of the owner's possession?

Chdr. She parted with them.

Prov. Consider, Chárudatta, you must speak the truth. Truth alone is internal satisfaction; not to declare the truth is a crime; the truth is readily told; seek not to conceal it by a lie.

Chdr. I do not know the ornaments; but this I know, they are now brought from my house.

Sarhs. You killed her in my garden first, and so obtained them; this prevarication is only to hide the truth.

Judge. Chárudatta, own the truth, or it must be my pleasure that heavy lashes fall upon that delicate frame.

Chdr. Sprung from a race incapable of crime,
I have not shamed my sires—if you confound
The innocent with the guilty, I must suffer.
(*Apart.*) If I have lost indeed Vasantasená,
Life is a burden to me. (*Aloud.*) What avails it
To proffer further plea? be it acknowledged.
I have abandoned virtue, and deserved
Abhorrence here and punishment hereafter.
Let me be called a murderer, or what else
It pleases him (*to Sarhs.*) to declare.

Sarhs. She is killed: say at once, *I* killed her.

Chdr. You have said.

Sarhs. You hear him: he confesses it; all doubt is removed by his own words: let him be punished. Poor Chárudatta!

Judge. Officer, obey the prince—secure the malefactor.

Moth. Yet, good gentlemen, hear me. I am sure the charge is false. If my dear daughter be slain, let him live, who is my life. Who are the parties in this cause? I make no complaint, and why then is he to be detained? Oh! set him at liberty.

Sarhs. Silence, you old fool! what have you to do with him?

Judge. Withdraw, lady. Officer, lead her forth.

Moth. My son, my dear son! (*Is forced out.*)

Sarhs. I have done the business worthy of myself, and shall now depart. [*Exit.*

Judge. Chárudatta, the business of proof it was ours to effect, the sentence rests with the prince. Officer, apprize the royal Pálaka, that the convicted culprit being a Brahman, he cannot according to Manu be put to death, but he may be banished the kingdom with his property untouched.

Off. I obey. (*Goes out and returns.*) I have been, and the king thus commands. Let the ornaments of Vasantasená be suspended to the neck of the criminal; let him be conducted by beat of drum to the southern cemetery, and there let him be impaled; that, by the severity of this punishment, men may be in future deterred from the commission of such atrocious acts.

Chár. Unjust and inconsiderate monarch.*

'Tis thus that evil councillors impel
The heedless prince into the scorching flames
Of fierce iniquity and foul disgrace;
And countless victims perish by the guilt
Of treacherous ministers, who thus involve
Both prince and people in promiscuous ruin!
My friend Maitreya, I bequeath to you
My helpless family; befriend my wife,
And be a second parent to my child.

Mait. Alas! when the root is destroyed, how can the tree remain?

Chár. Not so; a father lives beyond his death
And in his son survives; 'tis meet my boy
Enjoy that friendship which thou show'dst his sire.

Mait. You have ever been most dear to me, most excellent Chárudatta; I cannot cherish life deprived of you.

Chár. Bring my boy to me.

Mait. That shall be done.

---

* Possibly the political events described in this piece were not wholly matter of fiction, and Pálaka, leaning to the Bauddha doctrines, and disregarding Brahminical privileges, provoked the insurrection that is recorded in the drama.

Judge. Officer, lead him forth. Who waits there? Let the Chāndālas* be called. [*Exit with Court.*

Off. This way.

Chdr. Alas, my poor friend! †
  Had due investigation been allowed me,
  Or any test proposed—water or poison,
  The scales or scorching fire,‡ and I had failed
  The proof, then might the law have been fulfilled,
  And I deservedly received my doom.§
  But this will be avenged: and for the sentence
  That dooms a Brahman's death on the mere charge
  Of a malicious foe, the bitter portion
  That waits for thee, and all thy line, O king,
  Is hell. Proceed—I am prepared. [*Exeunt.*

---

* Whose caste makes them public executioners.

† The following lines are uttered *áside* or in the air, according to the original; that is, they are not spoken by any of the *dramatis personæ*. They are, however, so suitable to Chárudatta as to warrant a departure from the stage direction.

‡ The different modes of trial by ordeal.

§ Literally, the saw might have been applied to the body; *Krakachenā tartre dātavyam.*

END OF THE NINTH ACT.

ACT X.

The Road to the Place of Execution.

Enter Chárudatta with two Chándálas as Executioners.

1st Chd. Out* of the way, sirs! out of the way! room for Chárudatta. Adorned with the *kuravira*† garland, and attended by his dexterous executioners, he approaches his end like a lamp ill-fed with oil.

Chdr. Sepulchral blossoms decorate my limbs,
Covered with dust, and watered by my tears,
And round me harshly croak the carrion birds,
Impatient to enjoy their promised prey.

2d Chd. Out of the way, sirs! what do you stare at? a good man whose head is to be chopped off by the axe of destiny? a tree that gave shelter to gentle birds to be cut down? Come on, Chárudatta.

Chdr. Who can foresee the strange vicissitudes
Of man's sad destiny?—I little thought
That such a fate would e'er be my portion,
Nor could have credited I should live to be
Dragged like a beast to public sacrifice,
Stained with the ruddy sandal spots and smeared
With meal—a victim to the sable goddess.‡
Yet as I pass along, my fellow-citizens

---

* The Prákrit spoken by the Chándálas is exceedingly rude and difficult; the commentator is often evidently at fault, and furnishes very imperfect and unsatisfactory interpretations: several passages have been accordingly omitted, but none of any importance.

† Sweet-scented oleander, or rose bay. *Nerium odorum.*

‡ This is an addition of the commentator: the text implies that he is equipped as a victim, but does not say to what deity.

Console me with their tears, and execrate
The cruel sentence that awards my death.
Unable to preserve my life, they pray
That heaven await me, and reward my sufferings.

1st Chád. Stand out of the way—what crowd you to see? There are four things not to be looked at: *Indra* carried forth, the birth of a calf, the transit of a star, and the misfortune of a good man.* Look, brother Ahinta; the whole city is under sentence!—What! does the sky weep, or the thunderbolt fall without a cloud?

2d Chád. No, brother Goha, not so; the shower falls from yonder cloud of women; yet though all the people weep, yet such is the throng, that their tears cannot lay the dust.

Chár. From every window lovely faces shed
The kindly drops, and bathe me with their tears.

1st Chád. Here stop! strike the drum, and cry the sentence.
—Hear ye, hear ye! This is Chárudatta, son of Ságaradatta, son of Provost Vinayadatta, by whom the courtezan Vasantasená has been robbed and murdered; he has been convicted and condemned, and we are ordered by king Pálaka to put him to death: so will his Majesty ever punish those that commit such crimes as both worlds abhor.

---

* This passage is not clear; the expression is *Indu paródhiavate*, which seems to imply *Indrah pravdhyamánah*. The oldest commentary translates it *Pravardhamánas*, increasing, progressing; and supposes *Indra* put for his bow, the rainbow. It seems more probable, however, that the phrase alludes to some observance in honour of the deity which has fallen into disuse and is forgotten. Such, for example, as the *Sakradhwajotthána*, erection of a flag in honour of *Indra*, which, after being worshipped for some days, is directed to be removed privately at midnight, when all the people are asleep. (*Kálikà-Puráńa.*) The paraphernalia and circumstances of a public execution, according to Hindu fashions, are interestingly described here; the scantiness of the official attendance shows that the people were as easily managed then as at any subsequent period. The character of the executioner corresponds precisely with that of the Roman Carnifex; and, in like manner, the place of execution is the public cemetery, or place of burning the dead. The criminal is dressed as a victim with very classical decorations.

Chár. Dreadful reverse—to hear such wretches herald
My death, and blacken thus with lies my fame:
Not so, my sires—for them the frequent shout
Has filled the sacred temple, where the crowd
Of holy Brahmans to the gods proclaimed
The costly rite accomplished: and shall I,
Alas! Vasantasená, who have drunk
Thy nectared tones from lips whose ruby glow
Disgraced the coral, and displayed the charms
Of teeth more pearly than the moon's chaste light,
Profane my ears with such envenomed draughts
Of infamy whilst yet my soul is free!
   [*Puts his hands to his ears.*

1st Chdl. Stand apart there—make way!
Chár. My friends avoid me as I pass, and, hiding
Their faces with their raiment, turn away.
Whilst fortune smiles each stranger is a friend,
But friends are strangers in adversity.

1st Chds. The road is now tolerably clear,—bring along the culprit.

(*Behind.*) Father! father!
My friend! my friend!

Chár. My worthy friends, grant me this one indulgence.
1st Chds. What! will you take anything of us!*
Chár. Disdain not my request. Though basely born,
You are not cruel, and a gentle nature
Ranks you above your sovereign. I implore you,
By all your future hopes, oh once permit me
To view my son, ere I depart to death!

1st Chds. Let him come.—Men, stand back, and let the child approach: here, this way.

   Enter MAITREYA *with* ROHASENA.

Mait. Here we have him, boy, once more; your dear father, who is going to be murdered.

   * That is, how can a Brahman condescend to accept anything from a Chándála? There is some bitterness in the question.

Boy. Father! father!

Chár. Come hither, my dear child. (*Embraces him and takes his hands.*)

    These little hands will ill-suffice to sprinkle
    The last sad drops upon my funeral pyre.
    Scant will my spirit sip thy love, and then
    A long and painful thirst in heaven succeeds.
    What sad memorial shall I leave thee, boy,
    To speak to thee hereafter of thy father?
    This sacred string, whilst yet 'tis mine, I give thee.*
    The Brahman's proudest decoration, boy,
    Is not of gold nor gems; but this by which
    He ministers to sages and to gods.
    This grace my child when I shall be no more. (*Takes off his Brahmanical cord and puts it round his son's neck.*)

    1st *Chdd.* Come, you Chárudatta, come along.

    2d *Chdd.* More respect, my master; recollect, by night or day, in adversity or prosperity, fate holds its course, and puts men to trial. Come, sir; complaints are unavailing; and it is not to be expected that men will honour the moon when *Ráhu* has hold of him.

* The distinguishing mark of a man of the three superior classes is a cord worn over the left shoulder and under the right arm: it is imposed with much solemnity, and the investiture, with its accompanying formulæ, is considered to indicate the regeneration of the individual: whence his name *Dwija*, or twice-born. The rite is applicable to all the three superior castes, or the Brahman, Kshatriya, and Vaidya, to each of whom the term *Dwija* is appropriate; although, as the two latter are considered to be extinct, it now signifies the Brahman only. The cord of the Brahman should be made of cotton, that of the Kshatriya of a kind of grass, and that of the Vaidya of woollen thread. The investiture of the first should take place between the ages of five and sixteen; of the second, between six and twenty-two; and of the third, between eight and twenty-four. If delayed beyond the latter period the individual is considered degraded from his caste. An essential part of the ceremony is the communication of the *Gáyatrí* or holiest verse of the Vedas. It is communicable to all three, and is the following:—*Om*. Earth. Air. Heaven. Let us meditate on the supreme splendour of that divine Sun, who may illuminate our understanding.—*Om, bhúr bhuvah swah, tat savitur varenyam bhargo devasya dhímahi, dhiyo yo nah prachodayát.*

Roha. Where do you lead my father, vile Chándála?

Chdl. I go to death, my child; the fatal chaplet
  Of *Kararíra* hangs around my neck;
  The stake upon my shoulder rests,* my heart
  Is burdened with despair, as, like a victim
  Dressed for the sacrifice, I meet my fate.

1st Chdl. Hark ye, my boy: they who are born *Chdáddlas* are not the only ones; they who oppress the virtuous are *Chdáddlas* too.

Roha. Why, then, want to kill my father?

1st Chdl. The king orders us; it is his fault, not ours.

Roha. Take and kill me; let my father go.

1st Chdl. My brave little fellow, long life to you!

Chdr. (*Embracing him.*)
  This is the truest wealth; love equal smiles
  On poor and rich; the bosom's precious balm
  Is not the fragrant herb, nor costly unguent—
  But nature's breath, affection's holy perfume.

Mait. Come now, my good fellows, let my worthy friend escape: you only want a body,—mine is at your disposal.

Chdr. Forbear, forbear!

1st Chdl. Come on! stand off! what do you throng to see? a good man who has lost his all and fallen into despair, like a gold bucket whose rope breaks and it tumbles into the well.

2d Chdl. Here stop: beat the drum, and proclaim the sentence. (*As before.*)

Chdr. This is the heaviest pang of all; to think
  Such bitter fruit attends my closing life.
  And oh! what anguish, love, to hear the calumny,
  Thus noised abroad, that thou wast slain by me!
        [*Exeunt.*

---

* So condemned malefactors, according to the Roman code, bore their cross or gibbet to the place of execution.

SCENE II.—A ROOM IN THE PALACE.

STHÁVARAKA *discovered above, bound, listening to the drum and proclamation.*

How! the innocent Chárudatta to be executed, and I in chains still! I may be heard. What ho there! friends, hear me:—it was I, sinner that I am, who drove Vasantasená to the royal garden. There my master met us, and finding her deaf to his wishes, with his own hands strangled her. He is the murderer, not this worthy man.—They cannot hear me: I am too far off. Cannot I leap down?—it shall be so; better any chance than that Chárudatta should suffer. I can get out of this window and spring from the balcony: better I perish than Chárudatta, and if I die, heaven is my reward. (*Jumps down.*) I am not hurt, and fortunately my chain has snapped. Now, whence comes the cry of the Chándálas:—ha! yonder,—I will overtake them. What ho there, stop! [*Exit.*

SCENE III.

Enter CHÁRUDATTA *as before—to them* STHÁVARAKA.

Sthd. What ho, stop!

1st Chdl. Who calls to us to stop?

Sthd. Hear me; Chárudatta is innocent. I took Vasantasená to the garden, where my master strangled her with his own hands.

Chdr. Who comes rejoicing thus my latest hours,
To snatch me from the galling bonds of fate?
Like the full cloud, distent with friendly showers,
That timely hangs to save the dropping grain?
Heard you the words?—my fame again is clear.
My death I heeded not, I feared disgrace.
Death without shame is welcome as the babe
New-born. I perish now by hate
I ne'er provoked; by ignorance and malice—
I fall the mark of arrows dipped in venom,
And aimed at me by infamy and guilt.

1st Chád. Hark ye, Sthávaraka,—do you speak the truth?

Sthá. I do; and would have ere now proclaimed it: for fear of that I was chained, and shut up in one of the rooms of the palace.

Enter SAṀSTHÁNAKA (*above*).

I have had a most sumptuous regale in the palace here: rice, with acid sauce, and meat, and fish, and vegetables, and sweetmeats. What sounds were those I heard? The Chándála's voice, as harsh as a cracked bell, and the beat of the death-drum; the beggar Chárudatta is going to execution. The destruction of an enemy is a banquet to the heart. I have heard, too, that whoever looks upon the death of an adversary will never have bad eyes in his next birth. I will ascend the terrace of my palace and contemplate my triumph. (*Ascends.*) What a crowd has collected to see the execution of this miserable wretch! If so many flock to see him, what a concourse there would be to behold a great man like myself put to death! He is dressed like a young steer. They are taking him to the south. What brings them this way, and why ceases the noise? (*Looks into the chamber.*) Hey! where is the slave Sthávaraka? He has made his escape!—all my schemes will be ruined!—I must seek him. (*Descends.*)

Sthá. Here comes my master.

1st Chád. Out of the way there! make room! Here he comes, like a mad ox, butting with the sharp horn of arrogance.

Sam. Room, room here! My boy Sthávaraka, come you along with me.

Sthá. What, sir! are you not satisfied with having murdered Vasantasená, that you now endeavour to compass the death of the excellent Chárudatta?

Sam. I,—I,—a vessel of rich jewels, I murder a woman!

Crowd. Yes, yes, you murdered her; not Chárudatta.

Sam. Who says so?

Crowd. This honest man.

Sam. Sthávaraka, my servant. (*Apart.*) He is the only

witness of my guilt. I have ill-secured him. It shall be so.
(*Aloud.*) Hear ye, my masters: this is my slave; he is a thief,
and for theft I punished and confined him: he owes me a
grudge for this, and has made up this story to be revenged.
Confess (*to Síhdraraka*), is it not so? (*Approaches and in an
under-tone.*) Take this (*offers him a bracelet*); it is yours;—
recall your words.

Síhd. (*Takes the bracelet and holds it up.*) See here, my
friends, he bribes me, even now, to silence!

Sarhs. (*Snatches the bracelet.*) This is it; the very ornament
I punished him for stealing; look here, Chándálas: for pilfering
from my treasury, which was under his charge, I had him
whipped; if you doubt me, look at his back.

1st Chás. It is very true; and a scorched slave will set anything on fire.

Síhd. Alas! this is the curse of slavery, to be disbelieved
even when we speak the truth. Worthy Chárudatta, I can do
no more. (*Falls at his feet.*)

Chár. Rise, thou who feelest for a good man's fall,
And com'st a virtuous friend to the afflicted.
Grieve not thy cares are vain. Whilst destiny
Forbids my liberation, all attempts
Like thine will profit nothing.

1st Chás. As your honour has already chastised this slave,
you should let him go.

Sarhs. Come, come. What is this delay, why do you not
dispatch this fellow?

1st Chás. If you are in such haste, sir, you had better do it
yourself.

Roha. Kill me and let my father live.

Sarhs. Kill both; father and son perish together.

Chár. All answers to his wish. Return, my child,
Go to thy mother, and with her repair
To some asylum, where thy father's fate
Shall leave no stain on thee. My friend, conduct them
Hence without delay.

Mait. Think not, my dear friend, that I intend to survive you.

Chár. My good Maitreya, the vital spirit owes not
Obedience to our mortal will: beware
How you presume to cast that life away:
It is not thine to give or to abandon.

Mait. (*Apart.*) It may not be right, but I cannot bear to live when he is gone. I will go to the Brahman's wife, and then follow my friend. (*Aloud.*) Well, I obey; this task is easy. (*Falls at his feet, and rising, takes the child in his arms.*)

Saṃs. Holloa! did I not order you to put the boy to death along with his father? (*Chárudatta expresses alarm.*)

1st Chdś. We have no such orders from the Rájá—away, boy, away. (*Forces off Maitreya and Rohasena.*) This is the third station, beat the drum, and proclaim the sentence. (*As before.*)

Saṃs. (*Apart.*) The people seem to disbelieve the charge. (*Aloud.*) Why, Chárudatta, the townsmen doubt all this; be honest; say at once, "I killed Vasantasená." (*Chárudatta continues silent.*) Ho! Chańdála, this vile sinner is dumb; make him speak: lay your cane across his back.

2d Chdś. Speak, Chárudatta. (*Strikes him.*)

Chár. Strike! I fear not blows; in sorrow plunged,
Think you such lesser ills can shake my bosom?
Alone I feel the flame of men's reports,
The foul assertion that I slew my love.

Saṃs. Confess, confess!

Chár. My friends and fellow-citizens, ye know me.

Saṃs. She is murdered.

Chár. Be it so.

1st Chdś. Come; the execution is your duty.

2d Chdś. No; it is yours.

1st Chdś. Let us reckon. (*They count.**) Now, if it be my turn, I shall delay it as long as I can.

---

* They write or make marks or lines in various ways; such is the stage direction, but what is intended is not exactly known.

2d Chdt. Why?

1st Chdt. I will tell you:—my father, when about to depart to heaven, said to me, "Son, whenever you have a culprit to execute, proceed deliberately; never do your work in a hurry; for, perhaps, some worthy character may purchase the criminal's liberation; perhaps a son may be born to the Rája, and a general pardon be proclaimed; perhaps an elephant may break loose and the prisoner escape in the confusion; or, perhaps, a change of rulers may take place, and every one in bondage be set at large."

Saṁs. (*Apart.*) A change of rulers!

1st Chdt. Come, let us finish our reckoning.

Saṁs. Be quick, be quick! get rid of your prisoner. (*Retires.*)

1st Chdt. Worthy Chárudatta, we but discharge our duty; the king is culpable, not we, who must obey his orders: consider—have you anything to say?

Chár. If virtue yet prevail, may she who dwells
 Amongst the blest above, or breathes on earth,
 Clear my fair fame from the disastrous spots
 Unfriendly fate and man's accusing tongue
 Have fixed upon me—whither do you lead me?

1st Chdt. Behold the place, the southern cemetery, where criminals quickly get rid of life. See, where jackals feast upon one-half of the mangled body, whilst the other yet grins ghastly on the pointed stake!

Chár. Alas, my fate! (*Sits down.*)

Saṁs. I shall not go till I have seen his death. How—sitting!

1st Chdt. What! are you afraid, Chárudatta?

Chár. (*Rising.*) Of infamy I am, but not of death.

1st Chdt. Worthy sir, in heaven itself the sun and moon are not free from change and suffering: how should we, poor weak mortals, hope to escape them in this lower world: one man rises but to fall, another falls to rise again; and the vesture of the carcase is at one time laid aside, and at another resumed:

think of these things, and be firm. This is the fourth station: proclaim the sentence. (*Proclamation as before.*)

Enter the ŚRAMAŃAKA *and* VASANTASENÁ.

Sram. Bless me, what shall I do? Thus leading Vasantasená, am I acting conformably to the laws of my order? Lady, whither shall I conduct you?

Vas. To the house of Chárudatta, my good friend;
His sight will bring me back to life, as the bright moon
Revives the leaflets of the drooping flower.

Sram. Let us get into the high road: here it is. Hey! what noise is this?

Vas. And what a crowd is here!—inquire the cause;
For all Ujjayin is gathered on one spot,
And earth is off its balance with the load.*

1st Chdá. This is the last station: proclaim the sentence. (*Proclamation as before.*) Now, Chárudatta, forgive us; all will soon be over.

Chdr. The gods are mighty.

Sram. Lady! lady! they say here you have been murdered by Chárudatta, and they are therefore going to put him to death.

Vas. Unhappy wretch! that I should be the cause
Of so much danger to my Chárudatta.
Quick! lead me to him.

Sram. Quick, lady; worthy servant of *Buddha*, hasten to save Chárudatta. Room, good friends; make way.

Vas. Room! room! (*Pressing through the crowd.*)

1st Chdá. Remember, worthy Chárudatta, we but obey the king's commands; the sin is his, not ours.

Chdr. Enough! perform your office.

1st Chdá. (*Draws his sword.*) Stand straight, your face

* This is rather extravagant, but less so than Lucan's apprehension that Nero after his apotheosis might occasion a somewhat similar accident:
"Ætheris immensi partem si presseris unam,
Senties axis onus, librati ponderi coeli
Orbe tene media."

upwards, and one blow sends you to heaven. (*Chárudatta obeys, the Chándálas goes to strike, and drops his sword.*) How? I held the hilt firmly in my grasp! yet the sword, as unerring as a thunderbolt, has fallen on the ground! Chárudatta will escape; it is a sure sign. Goddess of the *Sahya* hills,* be pleased to hear me! If Chárudatta be yet set free, the greatest favour will be conferred upon the whole Chánḍála race.

2d *Chdá.* Come, let us do as we are ordered.

1st *Chdá.* Be it so. (*They are leading Chárudatta to the stake, when Vasantasená rushes through the crowd.*)

Vas. Forbear, forbear! in me behold the wretch
For whom he dies!

1st *Chdá.* Hey! who is this that with dishevelled locks and uplifted arms calls us to forbear?

Vas. Is it not true, dear, dearest Chárudatta? (*Throws herself on his bosom.*)

Sram. Is it not true, respected Chárudatta? (*Falls at his feet.*)

1st *Chdá.* Vasantasená! The innocent must not perish by our hands.

Sram. He lives! Chárudatta lives!

1st *Chdá.* May he live a hundred years!

Vas. I revive.

1st *Chdá.* Away! bear the news to the king; he is at the public place of sacrifice. (*Some go out.*)

Sams. (*Seeing Vasantasená.*) Alive still! Who has done this? I am not safe here, and must fly. [*Exit.*

1st *Chdá.* (*To the other.*) Hark ye, brother, we were ordered to put to death the murderer of Vasantasená: we had better therefore secure the Rája's brother-in-law.

2d *Chdá.* Agreed; let's follow him. [*Exeunt.*

Chár. Who thus, like showers to dying grain, has come
To snatch me from the uplifted sword and face
Of present death! Vasantasená,

* A form of *Durgá,* worshipped formerly in the *Vindhya* range, near Oujein.

Can this be she? or has another form
Like hers from heaven descended to my succour?
Am I awake, or do my senses wander—
Is my Vasantasená still alive?
Speeds she from spheres divine, in earthly charms
Arrayed again, to save the life she loved,
Or comes some goddess in her beauteous likeness?

Vas. (*Falls at his feet.*)
You see herself, the guilty cause that brought
This sad reverse upon thy honoured course.

Chár. (*Taking her up and looking at her.*)
My love, Vasantasená, is it thou?

Vas. That ill-starred wretch.

Chár. Vasantasená—can it—can it be?
And why these starting tears?—away with grief!
Didst thou not come, and like the wondrous power
That brings back life to its deserted source,[*]
Redeem triumphant from the grasp of death
This frame to be henceforward all thine own?
Such is the force of love omnipotent,
Who calls the very dead to life again!
Behold, my sweet, these emblems, that so late
Denoted shame and death, shall now proclaim
A different tale, and speak our nuptial joy—
This crimson vesture be the bridegroom's garb,
This garland be the bride's delightful present,
And this brisk drum shall change its mournful sounds
To cheerful tones of marriage celebration.

Vas. Ingenious ever is my lord's device.

Chár. Thy plotted death, dear girl, was my sad doing.
The Rája's brother has been long my foe;
And in his hate, which future doom will punish,
He sought, and partly worked his will, my fall.

Vas. Forbear, nor utter such ill-omened words.
By him, and him alone, my death was purposed.

[*] The mythological drug that restores the dead to life.

Chár. And who is this?
Vas. To him I owe my life:
His seasonable aid preserved me.
Chár. Who art thou, friend?
Sram. Your honour does not recollect me. I was employed as your personal servant: afterwards becoming connected with gamblers, and unfortunate, I should have been reduced to slavery, had not this lady redeemed me. I have since then adopted the life of a mendicant; and coming in my wanderings to the Rája's garden, was fortunately enabled to assist my former benefactress.

(*Behind.*) Victory to *Vrishabhaketu*,* the despoiler of *Daksha's* sacrifice!† glory to the six-faced scatterer of armies, the foe of *Krauncha*!‡ Victory to Áryaka, the subjugator of his adversaries, and triumphant monarch of the wide-spread, mountain-bannered earth!

Enter SARVILAKA.

This hand has slain the king, and on the throne
Of Pálaka ascends our valiant chief,
Resistless Áryaka, in haste anointed.
Now to obey his first commands, and raise
The worthy Chárudatta far above
Calamity and fear. All is achieved—

---

* The deity whose emblem is a bull—*Siva*.

† The *Prajápati* or patriarch *Daksha*, the son of *Brahmá*, married his daughter *Satí* to *Siva*, but disgusted with the son-in-law, omitted to invite him to a solemn sacrifice at which all the gods and sages were assembled. *Satí*, in a fit of vexation, threw herself into the sacrificial flame; and in revenge of this, as well as the affront offered him, *Siva* sent his attendant sprites, headed by *Virabhadra* to disturb the rite. This they easily performed; bruising and mutilating the gods themselves. The legend seems to have been a favourite in the south of India at the period when the caves of Elephanta and Ellora were excavated, being elaborately sculptured on their walls. It is told in the *Mahábhárata*, omitting the burning of *Satí*, which seems to be a Pauráńik addition.

‡ *Kárttikeya*, the Hindu Mars. *Krauncha* is one of the confederates of the demon *Táraka*, against whom *Kárttikeya* led the gods and triumphed.

Of valour and of conduct destitute
The foe has fallen—the citizens behold
Well pleased the change, and thus has noble daring
Wrested an empire from its ancient lords,
And won a sway as absolute on earth
As that which *Indra* proudly holds in heaven.
This is the spot;—he must be near at hand
By this assemblage of the people. Well begins
The reign of Áryaka, if his first cares
Reap the rich fruit of Chárudatta's life.
Give way, and let me pass; 'tis he!—he lives!—
Vasantasená too!—my monarch's wish
Is all accomplished. Long this generous Brahman
Has mourned his sullied brightness like the moon
That labours in eclipse, but now he bounds
Again to honour and to happiness,
Borne safely o'er a boundless sea of troubles
By firm affection's bark, and favouring fate.
How shall I, sinner as I am, approach
Such lofty merit; yet the honest purpose
Is everywhere a passport. Chárudatta,
Hail, most worthy sir!

[*Joins his hands and raises them to his forehead.*

Chár. Who thus addresses me?
Sar. In me behold
The plunderer, that desperate forced his way
By night into your mansion, and bore off
The pledge intrusted to your care: I come
To own my fault and throw me on your mercy.

Chár. Not so, my friend, you may demand my thanks.
(*Embraces him.*)
Sar. And further I inform you, that the king,
The unjust Pálaka, has fallen a victim,
Here in the place of sacrifice, to one
Who has avenged his wrongs and thine; to Áryaka,
Who ready homage pays to birth and virtue.

Chdr. How say you?

Sar. That the fugitive,
  Whom late your car conveyed in safety hence,
  Has now returned, and in the place of offering
  Slain Pálaka as a victim.

Chdr. I rejoice
  In his success—it was to you he owed
  Escape from his confinement.

Sar. But to you
  Escape from death; and to requite his debt
  He gives to your authority in Ujjayin,
  Along the *Vedd's** borders, *Kusávati*—
  A proof of his esteem and gratitude.

(*Without.*) Bring him along! bring him along! the Rája's villainous brother-in-law. (*Samsthánaka, his arms tied behind him, dragged on by the mob.*)

Sams. Alas, alas! how am I maltreated: bound and dragged along as if I were a restive ass, or a dog, or any brute beast. I am beset by the enemies of the state; whom can I fly to for protection?—yes, I will have recourse to him. (*Approaches Chárudatta.*) Preserve me. (*Falls at his feet.*)

Mob. Let him alone, Chárudatta; leave him to us; we'll dispatch him.

Sams. Oh, pray Chárudatta!—I am helpless, I have no hope but you.

Chdr. Banish your terror: they that sue for mercy
  Have nothing from their foes to dread.

Sar. Hence with the wretch!
  Drag him from Chárudatta. Worthy sir,
  Why spare this villain? Bind him, do you hear,
  And cast him to the dogs; saw him asunder;
  Or hoist him on the stake: dispatch, away.

---

* Neither Sir Charles Malet, nor Dr. Hunter, nor Sir J. Malcolm enable us to offer any account of this river or of *Kusávati*; we cannot therefore pretend to adjust their position. The river of Ujjayin is the *Siprá*; whether it is ever called the *Vedd* we have no knowledge.

Chár. Hold, hold! may I be heard?

Sar. Assuredly.

Saṁs. Most excellent Chárudatta, I have flown to you for refuge; oh, protect me! spare me now, I will never seek your harm any more.

Mob. Kill him, kill him! why should such a wretch be suffered to live? (*Vasantasena takes the garland off Chárudatta's neck, and throws it round Saṁsthánaka's.*)

Saṁs. Gentle daughter of a courtezan, have pity upon me: I will never kill you again, never, never!

Sar. Give your commands, sirs, that he may be removed, and how we shall dispose of him.

Chár. Will you obey in what I shall enjoin?

Sar. Be sure of it.

Chár. In truth?

Sar. In very truth.

Chár. Then for the prisoner——

Sar. Kill him.

Chár. Set him free.

Sar. Why so?

Chár. An humbled foe, who prostrate at your feet
Solicits quarter, must not feel your sword.

Sar. Admit the law, then give him to the dogs.

Chár. Not so!
His punishment be mercy.

Sar. You move my wonder, but shall be obeyed.
What is your pleasure?

Chár. Loose him, and let him go.

Sar. He is at liberty. (*Unties him.*)

Saṁs. Huzza! I am again alive.

(*Without.*) Alas, alas! the noble wife of Chárudatta, with her child vainly clinging to her raiment, seeks to enter the fatal fire, in spite of the entreaties of the weeping crowd.

Enter CHANDANAKA.

Sar. How now, Chandanaka, what has chanced?

Chan. Does not your excellency see yon crowd collected on

the south of the royal palace? There the wife of Chárudatta is about to commit herself to the flames; I delayed the deed by assuring her that Chárudatta was safe;—but who in the agonies of despair is susceptible of consolation or confidence?*

Chár. Alas! my love, what frantic thought is this!
Although thy widowed virtues might disdain
The abject earth, yet, when to heaven transported,
What happiness canst thou enjoy, whilst yet
The husband's presence fails his faithful bride. (*Faints.*)

Sar. Out on this folly! we should fly to save
The dame, and he is senseless—all conspires
To snatch from our exertions this reward.

Vas. Dear Chárudatta, rouse thy fainting soul;
Haste to preserve her; want not firmness now,
Or all is unavailing.

Chár. Where is she?
Speak love! where art thou?—answer to my call.

Chan. This way, this way! [*Exeunt.*

Scene—The WIFE *of* CHÁRUDATTA, ROHASENA *holding her garment,* MAITREYA *and* RADANIKÁ—*The fire kindled.*

Wife. Loose me, my child! oppose not my desires,
I cannot live and hear my lord defamed.

Roha. Hold! my dear mother; think of me your child;
How shall I learn to live, deprived of you?

---

* The ancient commentary, the MS. of which consulted was dated above two centuries ago, cites a verse, stating that from this speech to that of *Sarvilaka*, "You are fortunate in your friends," the whole is an interpolation, the work of *Nílakantha*, who considered that the author had not brought his characters together at the close with sufficient reason, and therefore devised the next scene. The cause assigned for the original defect seems rather an unaccountable one, "Through fear of sunrise;" but the phrase is a proverbial one, implying "finishing in a hurry." The passage is
"Yat súryodaya-bhayatah kavinochita-pátra-melanam na kṛitam,
Sundara-yuktibhir arachayad t-chandanokti Nílakaṇṭhas tat."
The style of the interpolation, although something different from that of the original, is ancient; and as the business and notions of the scene are genuinely Hindu, it has been retained in the translation.

Mait. Lady, forbear! your purpose is a crime:—our holy laws declare it sinful for a Brahman's wife to mount a separate pile.*

Wife. Better I sin than bear my husband's shame—
Remove my boy; he keeps me from the flames.

Rad. Nay, madam; I would rather give him help.

Mait. Excuse me: if you determine to perish, you must give me precedence; it is a Brahman's duty to consecrate a funeral fire.

Wife. What! neither listen to me! My dear child,
Remain to offer to your helpless parents
The sacred rites they claim from filial duty.
Alas! you know no more a father's care.

Chdr. (*Coming forward and takes his Child in his arms.*)
His father still will guard him.

Wife. His voice! his form!—it is my lord, my love!

Roha. My father holds me in his arms again! Now, mother, you are happy.

Chdr. (*Embraces his Wife.*)
My dearest love, what frenzy drove thy mind
To seek destruction whilst thy lord survived?
Whilst yet the sun rides bright along the sky
The lotus closes not its amorous leaves.

Wife. True, my loved lord; but then his glowing kisses
Give her glad consciousness her love is present.

Mait. And do these eyes really see my dear friend once more? The wonderful effect of a virtuous wife! Her purpose of entering the fire has reunited her with her lord. Long life to Chárudatta.

Chdr. My dear, my faithful friend. (*Embraces him.*)

Rad. Sir, I salute you. (*Falls at his feet.*)

Chdr. Rise, good Radanika. (*Puts his hand upon her shoulder.*)

Wife. (*To Vasantasena.*) Welcome, happy sister!

---

* This is still the law.

Vas. I now indeed am happy. (*They embrace.*)
Sar. You are fortunate in your friends.
Chdr. To you I owe them.*
Sar. Lady Vasantasená, with your worth
    The king is well acquainted, and requests
    To hold you as his kinswoman.
Vas. Sir, I am grateful. (*Sarvilaka throws a veil over her.*)†
Sar. What shall we do for this good mendicant?
Chdr. Speak, Sramanaka, your wishes.
Sram. To follow still the path I have selected,
    For all I see is full of care and change.
Chdr. Since such is his resolve, let him be made
    Chief of the monasteries of the *Bauddhas*.‡
Sar. It shall be so.
Sram. It likes me well.
Sar. Sthávaraka remains to be rewarded.
Chdr. Let him be made a free man;—slave no more.
    For these Chándálas let them be appointed
    Heads of their tribe; and to Chandanaka
    The power the Rája's brother-in-law abused
    To his own purposes, be now assigned.§
Sar. As you direct: is there ought else?—command.
Chdr. Nought but this.
    Since Aryaka enjoys the sovereign sway,
    And holds me as his friend;—since all my foes
    Are now destroyed, save one poor wretch released,
    To learn repentance for his former faults,

---

* The interpolation ends here.

† Marking thereby she is no longer a public character. The use of the veil in all oriental countries is well known, but its employment as in the text is a refinement upon its universal use. It seems, however, to have been understood as a type of the married condition by the early Christians, or as a sign of the subjection of woman to man. (See 1 Cor. xi. 10.) Amongst the Greeks the veil denoted a sacred and sacerdotal character.

‡ Literally, let him be made the master of the family (*Kulapati*) in the *Vihāras* throughout the land.

§ The post is that of *Dandapálaka*, chief of the police, or Kotwal.

Since my fair fame again is clear, and this
Dear girl, my wife, and all I cherish most,
Are mine once more, I have no further suit
That asks for your indulgence, and no wish
That is not gratified. Fate views the world
A scene of mutual and perpetual struggle,
And sports with life as if it were the wheel
That draws the limpid waters from the well.
For some are raised to affluence, some depressed
In want, and some are borne a while aloft,
And some hurled down to wretchedness and woe.
Then let us all thus limit our desires:
Full-uddered be the kine; the soil be fertile;
May copious showers descend, and balmy gales
Breathe health and happiness on all mankind;
From pain be every living creature free,
And reverence on the pious Brahman wait;
And may all monarchs, prosperous and just,
Humble their foes and guard the world in peace.

[*Exeunt omnes.*

REMARKS ON THE TOY-CART.

The preceding Drama cannot in equity be tried by laws with which the Author and his audience were unacquainted. If, therefore, it exceeds the limits of a play according to our approved models, we are not to consider it of disproportionate length; if it occasionally arranges the business of the stage after what we conceive an awkward fashion, we are not to pronounce it devoid altogether of theatrical ingenuity; and if it delineates manners repugnant to our social institutions, we are not to condemn them as unnatural or immoral. We must judge the composition after the rules laid down by Schlegel, and identify ourselves, as much as possible, with the people and the time to which it belongs.

Overlooking, then, those peculiarities which are clearly referable to age and country, it will probably be admitted, that the *Toy-Cart* possesses considerable dramatic merit. The action, if it want other unities, has the unity of interest; and proceeds with a regular, though diversified, march to its final development. The interest is rarely suspended, and in every case the apparent interruption is, with great ingenuity, made subservient to the common design. The connexion of the two plots is much better maintained than in the play we usually refer to as a happy specimen of such a combination:—the *Spanish Friar*. The deposition of Palaka is interwoven with the main story so intimately, that it could not be detached from it without injury, and yet it never becomes so prominent as to divert attention from that to which it is only an appendage.

There is considerable variety of character amongst the

inferior persons of the Drama, and the two Captains of the Watch, and the two Chāńḍālas, are plainly discriminated. The superior characters are less varied, but they are national portraitures, and offer some singular combinations: the tenderness and devotion of Vasantasenā seem little compatible with her profession, and the piety and gravity of Chárudatta still less so with his love. The master-piece of the play, however, is Samsthánaka, the Rája's brother-in-law. A character so utterly contemptible has perhaps been scarcely ever delineated: his vices are egregious; he is coldly and cruelly malicious, and yet he is so frivolous as scarcely to excite our indignation; anger were wasted on one so despicable; and without any feeling of compassion for his fate, we are quite disposed, when he is about to suffer the merited punishment of his crimes, to exclaim with Chárudatta, "Loose him, and let him go." He is an excellent example of a genus too common in every age in Asia, whose princes have been educated by sloth and servility, and have been ordinarily taught to cherish no principle but that of selfish gratification.

The music of Sanskrit composition must ever be inadequately represented by any other tongue; of the language of the play it is therefore unnecessary to speak. With regard to the sentiments and conceptions of the author, they have been rendered as faithfully as was practicable, and it will possibly be conceded that they are wanting neither in beauty nor in truth.

… VIKRAMA AND URVAŚÍ,

OR

THE HERO AND THE NYMPH.

A Drama,

TRANSLATED FROM THE ORIGINAL

SANSKRIT.

INTRODUCTION.

THE drama of VIKRAMA AND URVAŚÍ is one of the three plays attributed to KÁLIDÁSA, already advantageously known to the western world as the author of Śakuntalá. The introductory observation of the Manager in the prelude is our evidence to this effect; and it is corroborated by the correspondence of these two compositions, in many of their characteristic merits and defects. The subject of each is taken from heroic mythology, and a royal demigod and nymph of more than human mould are the hero and heroine of either; there is the same vivacity of description and tenderness of feeling in both; the like delicate beauty in the thoughts, and extreme elegance in the style. It may be difficult to decide to which the palm belongs; but the story of the present play is perhaps more skilfully woven, and the incidents rise out of each other more naturally than in Sakuntalá, while, on the other hand, there is perhaps no one personage in it so interesting as the heroine of that drama.

Although, however, there is no reason to doubt that this play is the work of the same hand as that translated by Sir William Jones, the concurrence does not throw any further light upon the date or history of the author. We can only infer, from the observance of the same chaste style of composition, and the absence of any forced construction or offensive conceits, that they are both the production of a period anterior to the reign of BHOJA, when his KÁLIDÁSA, a man of fancy and taste, could descend to write a whole poem, the *Nalodaya*, for instance, in a strain of verbal paltering and a succession of jingling sounds.

The richness of the *Prákŕit* in this play, both in structure and in its metrical code, is very remarkable. A very great portion, especially of the fourth act, is in this language; and in that act also a considerable variety of metre is introduced; it is clear, therefore, that this form of Sanskŕit must have been highly cultivated long before the play was written, and this might lead us to doubt whether the composition can bear so remote a date as the reign of VIKRAMÁDITYA (56 B.C.) It is yet rather uncertain whether the classical language of Hindu literature had at that time received so high a polish as appears in the present drama; and still less, therefore, could the descendants have been exquisitely refined, if the parent was comparatively rude. We can scarcely conceive that the cultivation of *Prákŕit* preceded that of Sanskŕit, when we advert to the principles on which the former seems to be evolved from the latter; but it must be confessed that the relation between Sanskŕit and *Prákŕit* has been hitherto very imperfectly investigated, and is yet far from being understood.

The mythological notions of the author, as inferrible from the benedictory stanzas opening all the three plays attributed to him, is rather adverse to a remote antiquity, as the worship of any individual deity as the Supreme Being, and with *Bhakti* or faith, appears to be an innovation in Hindu ritual and theology of a comparatively modern period. At the same time, the worship of *Śiva* undoubtedly prevailed in the Dekhin at the commencement of the Christian era, and VIKRAMÁDITYA the patron of KÁLIDÁSA, is traditionally represented as devoted to *Śiva* and his consort.

It may be thought some argument for the comparative antiquity of the present drama, that it tells the story of PURÚRAVAS very differently from the Puráñas, in several of which it may be found. We may suppose, therefore, that the play preceded those works; as, had it been subsequently composed, the poet would either spontaneously, or in deference to sacred authority, have adhered more closely to the Pauráñik legend. The difference in the Puráńas also indicates that corruption of taste, which we cannot hesitate regarding as the product of more modern and degenerate days.

The loves of PURÚRAVAS and URVAŚÍ are related in various Puráńas. The following is the story as it appears in the Vishńu Purāńa, in which and in the Padma,* it is more fully and connectedly detailed than perhaps in any other composition of the same class.

URVAŚÍ, the Apsaras, or one of the nymphs of heaven so named, having incurred the displeasure of MITRA and VARUŃA, was sentenced by them to become the consort of a mortal, and in consequence of this curse she became enamoured of the king PURÚRAVAS, the son of BUDHA and ILÁ. Forgetting her celestial duties, and foregoing the delights of Swarga, she introduced herself to the monarch, and her charms did not fail to make an impression on his heart. She was delicately and symmetrically formed, was graceful in her gestures, and fascinating in her manners; her voice was music, her countenance was dressed in smiles, and her beauty was such as might enchant the world: no wonder, therefore, that PURÚRAVAS was at once inspired with fervent love. Confiding in his rank and renown, the king did not hesitate to propose a matrimonial alliance to the nymph of heaven; she was nothing loth, but had not the power to comply, without previously exacting the bridegroom's consent to two conditions. PURÚ- RAVAS hesitated not to accede to the stipulations.

URVAŚÍ had with her two pet-rams, creatures of heavenly and illusive natures, and one of her conditions was, that the king should take these animals under his own charge, and guard against their being ever carried away by fraud or force. The other stipulation was, that the nymph was never to behold the person of the king divested of his raiment. On the ready

---

* It is the subject also of a work of some length in Telugu, called the Kavirāja-manoranjanam, or Purúravas-charitram, composed by Aryaya, the minister of a petty prince in the Dekhin, the Rája of Condavír. This story follows the Purāńas, but with some differences.

accession of PURÚRAVAS to these terms URVASÍ became his bride, and they dwelt together in the forest of *Chaitraratha*, near *Alaká*, the capital of *Kuvera*, for sixty-one years,* in perfect happiness and undiminished affection.

The absence of URVASÍ was very soon felt in the upper sphere, and the inhabitants of *Swarga* found their enjoyments stale and unprofitable, no longer heightened by the agreeable manners and entertaining society of the nymph. The whole body of *Apsarasas, Siddhas, Gandharbas*, and other tenants of Indra's heaven, regretted her loss, and determined to attempt her recovery as soon as the period of her exile, as denounced by the imprecation, should have expired. When this period arrived, they deputed some of the *Gandharbas* on the expedition, who undertook to bring about the violation of the terms on which the alliance of the king and the nymph depended. With this intent they entered the sleeping chamber of the monarch, and carried off one of the rams. The bleat of the animal woke URVASÍ, who echoed its cries with her lamentations, and aroused the prince. Apprehensive, however, of appearing before his bride undressed, PURÚRAVAS hesitated to pursue the thief, and thus incurred the angry reproaches of his spouse for his indifference to her loss. Presently the *Gandharbas* bore away the second ram, and the grief of URVASÍ was afresh excited; the king's indignation also could no longer be restrained, and, determined to pursue and punish the ravishers, he leaped naked out of bed, trusting that the darkness of night would screen him from the eye of his consort. This was what his enemies desired, and he was no sooner off the couch than a vivid flash of lightning revealed him to view, and put an end to his union with the nymph of *Swarga*. URVASÍ immediately disappeared, accompanying the *Gandharbas* to the halls of INDRA.

* This is, however, a mere moment in the extravagant duration of the life of *Purúravas* according to the *Puránas*: there is nothing of the kind in the play.

When PURÚRAVAS was conscious of his loss, his grief was so intense that it affected his intellects, and he long wandered frantic over the world in quest of his bride. After many years had elapsed he came to a lake in Kurukshetra, where he found several nymphs sporting on the bank; amongst them was URVASÍ. Recognizing her at once, he ran to her and with wild energy implored her return; the nymph, however, was no longer disposed, even if she had been permitted, to comply with his wishes, and was deaf to all his entreaties; and at last she succeeded in convincing him of the unreasonableness of his solicitations, and prevailed on him to resume his station, and the duties of a king, engaging on those terms to pay him an annual visit. PURÚRAVAS, however reluctantly, was compelled to submit, and returned sorrowfully but composed to his capital. His annual interviews with URVASÍ were punctually repeated, and the fruit of this intercourse was the birth of six sons,[*] A'YUS, DHÍMAT, AMÁVASU, VISWÁVASU, SATÁYUS, and SRUTÁYUS, who were the progenitors of the lunar race of kings.

The occasional interviews with his bride granted to PURÚRAVAS were far from satisfying his desires, and he still sighed for the permanent enjoyment of her society. The Gandharbas at last, pitying his distress, engaged to promote his reunion with the nymph, and sent the king a brazier charged with fire, with which they directed him to perform a sacrifice in the forest, to attain the gratification of all his wishes. The king repaired to the woods, but reflecting that he had quitted URVASÍ in order to celebrate this rite, giving up the substance for the shadow, he returned to seek the nymph, leaving the vessel of fire in the thicket. Not finding his consort, he again directed his steps to the forest, but there the brazier was gone, and on the spot where it had stood, a śamí[†] and aswattha[‡] tree

---

[*] All this part of the story, Urvasí's loss and recovery, and the birth of Áyus, are totally different in the play.

[†] Mimosa sama.   [‡] Religious fig.

had sprung up. After a little consideration PURÚRAVAS broke a branch from either tree, and carried them back to the palace, where, reciting the *Gáyatrí** and rubbing the sticks together, he generated fire with the friction: this primeval fire he divided into three portions, and with them he performed various sacrifices and oblations, until he obtained the rank of a *Gandharba*, and being elevated to the regions of *Swarga*, there enjoyed the constant society of his beloved URVAŚÍ.†

The latter circumstances of this legend seem to indicate the introduction of fire-worship into India by PURÚRAVAS, considered as a historical personage.‡ There may have been some old tradition to that effect, whence the *Paurdńik* writers derived the groundwork of their fable; but it is not noticed in the play, neither is any allusion made to it in the version of this story in another work in which it is found, the *Vrihat-Kathá*, which differs in many particulars from both the play and the *Puráńa*. The story there, however, is very concisely narrated, and the author has clearly taken merely the personages and course of the fable from what was currently known, and given his own colouring to the incidents. It adds, therefore, nothing to the history of the narrative, and may be either anterior or subsequent to the forms in which it is now presented to English readers. Another authority, however, the *Matsya-Puráńa*, tells the story more agreeably to the tenor of the drama, as follows:

"When a year had elapsed, the divine *Ilá* bore a son of surpassing splendour, arrayed in celestial raiment of a yellow colour, and richly decorated with heavenly gems. From his youth he was versed in regal duties, and was so skilled in the

---

* The holiest verse of the *Vedas*.

† The play makes no allusion to these incidents, closing with the appearance of the elder son, Áyus.

‡ The three fires are: the *gárhapatya*, or perpetual fire maintained by a householder; the *áharańíya*, or consecrated fire taken from the preceding and prepared for receiving oblations; and the *dakshińágni*, fire taken from either of the former and placed towards the south.

training of elephants that he taught the art, and acquired the appellation of *Gajasadhaka*. The gods being assembled at the mansion of her husband, *Vrihaspati*, to perform the rites due to his birth, inquired of *Tárá* whose son he was, and with much reluctance she acknowledged the royal *Soma* was his father. *Soma* therefore took the boy, and named him *Budha*, and gave him dominion on the earth, and inaugurated him supreme over the world. *Brahmá* and the rest conferred upon him the dignity of a planetary power, and then took their departure.

"The holy *Budha* begot by *Ilá* a son, who performed by his own might a hundred *aśwamedhas*. He was named PURÚRAVAS, and was revered by all worlds. He worshipped *Vishńu* on the peaks of Himálaya, and thence became the monarch of the sevenfold earth. KESIN and myriads of *Daityas* fell before his prowess, and URVASÍ, fascinated by his personal graces, became his bride.

"*Virtue*, *Wealth*, and *Desire*, once paid this monarch a visit, curious to ascertain which of them held the first place in his esteem. The king received them with respect, but paid to *Virtue* his profoundest homage. *Wealth* and *Desire* were offended by the preference shown to their companion. *Wealth* denounced a curse upon him, that Avarice should occasion his fall; and *Desire* declared that he should be separated from his bride, and on that account suffer distraction in the forest of Kumára on the Gandhamádana mountain; but *Virtue* declared he should enjoy a long and pious life, that his descendants should continue to multiply as long as the sun and moon endured, and should ever enjoy the dominion of the earth. After this the divinities disappeared.

"PURÚRAVAS was in the habit of paying a visit to *Indra* every day. Having ascended his car, accompanying the Sun in his southern course, he beheld on one occasion the demon KESIN seize and carry off the nymphs *Chitralekhá* and URVASÍ. The king attacked the demon, and destroyed him with the shaft of *Váyu*, by which he not only rescued the nymphs, but established *Indra* on his throne, which the demon had endangered. For this service *Indra* repaid the monarch with his friendship, and gave him additional power, splendour, and glory.

"Having invited the king to a festival, at which was represented the celebrated story of *Lakshmí's* election of a husband, the invention of BHARATA, INDRA commanded MENAKÁ, RAMBHÁ, and URVAŚÍ to perform their respective parts. URVAŚÍ, who represented *Lakshmí*, being engrossed by admiration of the king, forgot what she had to enact, and thereby incurred the high displeasure of the sage, who sentenced her to separation from the prince on earth, and condemned her to pine fifty-five years transformed to a vine, until restored to the regrets of PURÚRAVAS. URVAŚÍ having made the king her lord, resided with him, and after the term of the curse had expired bore him eight sons: *Áyus, Dhrítáyus, Ásádyus, Dhandyus, Dhrítimat, Vasu, Dirijátn,* and *Sátáyus,* all endowed with more than human power."

This story is evidently that of the play, although related less in detail, and with a few variations according to Paurániik taste; but it is clear that it is either derived from a common source with the narration of the drama, or which is not improbable, that it has borrowed from the latter its general complexion. The nature of the relation which exists between the fiction as it appears in the drama, and in the *Purána,* our readers will be able to appreciate for themselves after perusal of the former.

DRAMATIS PERSONÆ.

OF THE PRELUDE.

MANAGER. ACTOR.

OF THE PLAY.

MEN.

Pururavas.—King of *Pratishthána*.
Áyus.—The son of *Pururavas*.
Mánavaka.—The *Vidúshaka* and confidential companion of the King.
Chitraratha.—King of the *Gandharbas*, the attendants on *Indra*.
Nárada.—The divine sage, the son of *Brahmá*.
Chamberlain.
A Forester.
Palas. }
Gálava. } Two disciples of the sage *Bharata*.

WOMEN.

Urvasí.—An *Apsaras*, or nymph of *Indra's* heaven.
Chitralekhá.—Another nymph, her friend.
Sahajanyá. }
Rambhá. } Nymphs.*
Menaká. }

* According to the *Kásí-Khanda* there are thirty-five millions of these nymphs, but only one thousand and sixty are the principal. Of these, however, not more than five or six are the subject of Pauránik or poetical narrations, or *Urvasí, Menaká, Rambhá, Tillattamá,* and *Alambushá*. In their birth and denomination they offer some analogy to the goddess *Aphrodite:* like her they arose from the sea; and as her name is referred to aphros,

Auśinarī.—The queen of *Purūravas* and daughter of the king of *Kāśi* or *Benares.*
Nipuṇikā.—One of her attendants.

PERSONS SPOKEN OF.

Indra.—The chief of all the inferior deities, and sovereign of *Swarga* or Paradise.
Keśin.—A *Daitya* or Titan, an enemy of the gods.
Bharata.—A holy sage, the inventor of dramatic composition.
Guards.—Nymphs, &c.

Scene in the First Act, the Peaks of the *Himālaya*; in the second and third, the palace of *Purūravas* at *Pratiṣṭhāna*; in the fourth, the forest of *Akaluṣha*; and in the fifth again, at the palace.
TIME, Uncertain.

"foam or spray," so that of the *Apsarasas* is from *ap* "water" and *sarās* "who moves." Their origin is thus related in the first book of the *Rāmāyaṇa*:—

"Then from the agitated deep upsprang
The legion of *Apsarasas*, so named
That to the watery element they owed
Their being. Myriads were they born, and all
In vesture heavenly clad, and heavenly gems:
Yet more divine their native semblance, rich
With all the gifts of grace, and youth, and beauty.
A train innumerous followed: yet these fair
Nor God nor demon sought their wedded love:
Thus, *Rāghava*, they still remain—their charms
The common treasure of the host of heaven."

PRELUDE.

Enter the MANAGER.

MAY that *Śiva*[*] who is attainable by devotion and faith;[†] who is the sole male[‡] of the Vedánta,[§] spread through all space, to whom alone the name of Lord[||] is applicable, and who is sought with suppressed breath[¶] by those who covet final emancipation,[**] bestow upon you final felicity.

---

[*] The term used in the text is *Stháńu*, a name of Śiva, from *sthá* to stay or be, the existent or eternal.

[†] *Bhakti* faith, and *yoga* the practice of abstract meditation.

[‡] The *chapurusha*, the active instrument in creation.

[§] The theological or metaphysical portion of the Vedas.

[||] *Íswara*, which is derived from *iś*, to have power, or *aś*, to pervade: in the latter case the vowel is changed.

[¶] The exercise of *práńáyáma*, or breathing through either nostril alternately, and then closing both during the repetition mentally of certain formulæ.

[**] Inferior enjoyment in heaven is not an object of desire to the more enthusiastic of the Hindus, as it is but finite, and after its cessation the individual is born again in the world, and exposed to the calamities of a frail existence. The great aim of devotion is union with the supreme and universal spirit, in which case the soul no more assumes a perishable shape. The character of this benediction corresponds with that of *Śakuntalá* and the *Málavikágnimitra*, and all three indicate the author's belonging to that modification of the Hindú faith in which the abstract deism of the Vedánta is qualified by identifying the supreme, invisible, and inappreciable spirit with a delusive form, which was the person of *Rudra* or *Śiva*. It is of a more practical character, therefore, than pure *Vedántism*, and it is equally different from both the metaphysical and theistical *Sánkhya*. It is, in fact, the doctrine of the *Śaiva-Puráńas*. (See *As. Res.*, vol. xvii.) The Brahmans of the south and west are mostly of this sect; and whatever *Śankara-Swámin* may have taught, it is that of his descendants the *Daśnámi-Gosáins*. The sect is probably the oldest of all now existing in India.

100   THE HERO AND THE NYMPH.

Man. (*Looking off the stage.*) Ho! *Mánisha,*[*] come hither.

Enter ACTOR.

Act. Here am I, sir.

Man. Many assemblies have witnessed the compositions of former dramatic bards:[†] I therefore propose to exhibit one not hitherto represented, the drama[‡] of *Vikrama* and *Urvasi.*[§] Desire the company to be ready to do justice to their respective parts.

Act. I shall, sir.

Man. I have now only to request the audience that they will listen to this work of *Kálidása* with attention and kindness, in consideration of its subject and respect for the author.[||]

---

[*] A term by which it is proper to address one of the principal performers.

[†] *Kálidása* is therefore not the oldest dramatic writer.

[‡] The *Trotaka,* a drama in five, eight, or nine acts, the characters of which are mixed, or heavenly and human. See the Introduction, p. xxxi.

[§] Mr Lenz, in his very excellent edition and version of this play (Berlin, 1833), seems to think the title, *Urvasi-vikrama, Urvasia facturus,* would be preferable to that of *Vikramorvasi,* as the latter, if not a *Dwandwa* compound, is not capable of satisfactory translation, and if a *Dwandwa* compound, is not conformable to rule: the latter is matter of little moment with the poets; and that *Vikramorvasi* is the author's reading, appears from the text. The addition of *nama, Vikramorvasi nama trotakam,* makes no difference, as indeed the commentator shows, who entitles his comment, *Vikramorvasi-prakásiká,* the explanation of the *Vikrama* and *Urvasi.* With regard to the meaning of *Vikrama,* which is properly "heroism," it may be observed, that it is often used in a way where "king" or "hero" alone can be signified by it: thus *Vikramáditya* is as often called simply *Vikrama* as not. The traditions relating to him are termed the *Vikramacharitra;* the nine gems are said to be *ratnáni nava Vikramasya.* The word is applied also attributively, as *Dipakarńir (tá khyáto rájábhád rájya-vikramasá:* There was a king named Dipakarńi, the *Vikrama* of the realm. Here it might be thought equivalent to the Alexander or the Cæsar of his age, but it could not be so employed as a synonym of the Hindu Alexander himself, nor could it be so used in the universally-current (in India) title of the play. There can be no doubt, therefore, that by a poetic license *hero*ism is here put for hero, and the compound is of the *Dwandwa* class, in despite of the grammarians.

[||] The original may be so understood, although it is not quite clear.— *Pradayiahu dákshińyavatáń yadi vá sadvastu-purusha-bahumánat—dríshta*

(*Behind the Scenes.*)
Help, help ! if in the middle sky
A friend be found, to aid us fly !

Man. What sounds are these in the air, that like the plaintive bleat of lambs, break in upon my speech ? Was it the murmur of the bee or *Kôil's* distant song, or do the nymphs of heaven as they pass above warble their celestial strains ? Ah, no ! it is the cry of distress. The fair creation of the saint, the friend of *Nara*, Urvasí, has been carried off by a demon on her return from the halls of the sovereign of *Kailása*,* and her sisters are invoking some friendly power to their aid.

[*Exit.*

masobhir avahitaíh kriyám imám Kálidásaya. It is of little consequence, except that in the sense preferred it indicates the fame of the author to be established when this piece was written.

* *Kuvera*, the God of wealth, whose capital *Alaká* is supposed to be situated on mount *Kuvera*.

ACT I.

Scene First.

Part of the Himálaya Range of Mountains.

Enter in the Air a Troop of Apsarasas or Nymphs of Heaven.

Nymphs. Help, help! if any friend be nigh,
 To aid the daughters of the sky!

Enter Purúravas* *in a heavenly car, driven by his Charioteer.*

Pur. Suspend your cries; in me behold a friend,
 Purúravas, returning from the sphere
 Of the wide-glancing sun: command my aid,
 And tell me what you dread.

Rambhá. A demon's violence.

Pur. What violence presumes the fiend to offer?

Menaká. Great king, it thus has chanced: we measured back
 Our steps from an assembly of the gods

---

* *Purúravas is a king of high descent, being sprung by his mother Ilá from the sun, and his father Budha from the moon, being the grandson of the latter and great grandson of the former. His origin is ultimately derived from Brahmá, thus:*

Held in *Kuvera's** hall. Before us stepped
The graceful Urvasi, the nymph whose charms
Defeated Indra's stratagems† and shamed
The loveliness of *Sri*,‡ the brightest ornament
Of heaven: when on our path the haughty *Dánava*,
Kesin, the monarch of the golden city,§
Sprang fierce and bore the struggling nymph away.
Pur. Which path pursued the wretch?
Sahajanyá. 'Tis yonder.
Pur. Banish your fears;
I go to rescue and restore your friend.
Rambhá. The act is worthy of your high descent.
Pur. Where wait you my return?
Rambhá. Here, on this peak.
The towering *Hemakúta.*‖
Pur. (*To the Charioteer.*) Bend our course
To yonder point, and urge the rapid steeds
To swiftest flight. 'Tis done; before the car
Like volley'd dust the scattering clouds divide;
The whirling wheel deceives the dazzled eye,
And double round the axle seems to circle.
The waving chowrie on the steed's broad brow
Points backward, motionless as in a picture;
And backward streams the banner from the breeze
We meet—immovable.¶ We should outstrip

* The god of riches.
† See the note ‡ in page 201.
‡ The wife of *Vishńu*, goddess of prosperity and beauty.
§ *Hiráńyapura* is the name in the text.
‖ The golden or snowy peak.
¶ A very similar description, but less picturesque and just, occurs in the beginning of *Śakuntalá*, and the truth of it is rendered less striking by a loose translation. Sir William Jones translates Nishkampa-chámara-sikhá, "they tossed their manes," when it means "their manes and the chowries on their heads are unagitated," that is, they point against the wind without waving—a predicate much more indicative of a rapid advance against the breeze than the undulation of either. The chámara or chowrie, the white

The flight of *Vainaleya*,* and must surely
O'ertake the ravisher.   [*Exeunt.*
Rambhá. Now, sisters, on, and blithely seek
The golden mountain's glittering peak;
Secure the king extracts the dart
That rankles in each anxious heart.
Menaká. We need not fear.
Rambhá. Yet hard to quell,
The demon race.
Menaká. The brood of hell
Shall feel his prowess. Aid to bring
From mortal realms to *Swarga's* king—
He comes, and to his hand is given
Command o'er all the hosts of heaven.   [*They proceed.*
Rambhá. Joy, sisters, joy, the king advances;
High o'er yon ridgy rampart dances
The deer-emblazoned banner. See
The heavenly car rolls on;—'tis he.

Enter PURÚRAVAS *in his car slowly;* URVAŚÍ *in the car fainting,
supported by* CHITRALEKHÁ.

Chitral. Dear friend, revive.
Pur. Fair nymph, resume your courage.
Still wields the thunderer his bolt, and guards
The triple world from harm; the foes of heaven
Are put to flight:—why cherish this alarm
When its just cause is o'er? Unclose those lids—
The lotus opens when the night retires.
Chitral. Alas! her sighs alone declare her conscious.
Pur. Soft as the flower, the timid heart not soon
Foregoes its fears. The scarf that veils her bosom

---

bushy tail of the Tibet cow, fixed on a gold or ornamented shaft, rose from between the ears of the horse like the plume of the war horse of chivalry; the banner or banneret, with the device of the chief, rose at the back of the car; sometimes several little triangular flags were mounted on its sides.

* *Garuda*, the son of *Vinatá*.

Hides not its flutterings, and the panting breast
Seems as it felt the wreath of heavenly blossoms
Weigh too oppressively.
Chitral. Revive, my friend;
This weakness ill becomes a nymph of heaven.
Pur. Have patience; she recovers, though but faintly.
So gently steals the moon upon the night
Retiring tardily; so peeps the flame
Of evening fires through smoky wreaths; and thus,
The Ganges slowly clears her troubled wave,
Engulphs the ruin that the tumbling bank
Had hurled across her agitated course,
And flows a clear and stately stream again.*
Chitral. Awake, dear friend, the enemies of heaven
Are baffled in despair.
Urv. (*Reviving.*) By Indra's prowess.
Chitral. By prowess not inferior to *Mahendra's:*
By this most holy prince,† Purúravas.
Urv. (*Looking at Purúravas; then apart.*)
What thanks I owe the Dánava!
Pur. (*After looking at Urvasi; then apart.*) What marvel,
The nymph celestial blushed with humbled charms,
When, to rebuke their wantonness, the sage
Willed that this wondrous beauty should appear.
The creature of a sage!—it cannot be:
How could an aged anchoret,‡ grown old

---

* The idea in the last four lines is somewhat expanded, to convey more distinctly to European readers what one-fourth of their number would at once convey to those acquainted with the subject of the description. The original lines are exceedingly sweet and beautiful.

† He is always called a Rájarshi (Rája-Rishi or royal saint). In the classification of sages there are three orders; the Rájarshi, or kingly sage, such as JANAKA; the Brahmarshi, or Brahman sage, as VASISHTHA; and the Devarshi, or divine sage, as NÁRADA.

‡ *Nara* and *Náráyaṇa* were two saints, the sons of *Dharma* and *Ahinsá:* they devoted themselves to ascetic exercises which alarmed the gods, and

       In dull devotion, and to feeling dead,
       Conceive such matchless beauty—oh no! love
       Himself was her creator, whilst the moon
       Gave her his radiance, and the flowery spring
       Taught her to madden men and gods with passion.
Urv. Where are our friends?
Chitral. The king will lead us to them.
Pur. Trust me, they mourn your loss; nor is it strange
       That they, your friends, should miss you, when the
         eye
       In whose delighted path you once have moved
       Cannot but grieve to lose your lovely presence.
Urv. (*Apart*) Delightful words! they fall like drops of
         nectar.
       Nor wonder nectar from the moon should flow.
       (*Aloud.*) Not less my eagerness to see again
       The friends I love.
Pur. Behold them there! they keep
       Their anxious watch on *Hemakúta's* brow,
       And mark your coming, safe from the demon's grasp,
       Like the bright moon emerging from eclipse.
Chitral. Why do you gaze on me, dear friend?
Urv. The same delight and pain my eyes imbibe as—
Chitral. Whose?
Urv. My friends.

Indra sent *Káma* and *Vasanta*, or love and spring, with the nymphs of heaven to inflame the sages with passion, and thus end their penance. *Náráyana*, observing the gambols of the party, suspected their purpose. He invited them to approach, and treated them with so much civility, that they thought their object was attained. The sage, however, taking up a flowerstalk, placed it on his thigh, when a beautiful nymph appeared, the superiority of whose charms covered the nymphs of heaven with shame. *Náráyana* then told them to return to Indra, and bear him a proof he needed not the company of beauty, In the present he made him of the new-born nymph, who accompanied the *Apsarasas* to *Swarga*, and was called *Urvasí* from *úru* a thigh (*Vámana-Purána.*) The Commentator on the drama says, *Nara* and *Nárayana* were *Avatárus*, descents or incarnations of *Arjuna* and *Krishta*.

Rambhá. Attended by each brilliant star,
    Like *Chandra** in his radiant car,
    The king appears, and with him borne
    Behold our sister nymphs return.
Menaká. For both the boons our thanks be poured:
    The prince unharmed and friends restored.
Sahajanyá. Now, sister, see how hard to quell
    By mortal might the sons of hell.
Pur. To yonder lofty mountain guide the car.
    (*Apart*) Not vain our journey hitherward: 'tis much
    In the unsteady rolling of the chariot
    But for a moment to have touched the form
    Of this celestial nymph; the blissful contact
    Shoots ecstasy through every fibre. Here (*aloud*)
    Arrest our course. The maid's companion choir
    Press on to her embrace, like flowery vines,
    That bend to catch the beauty of the spring.
Chorus. Joy to the king. Propitious heaven
    Has victory to his prowess given.
Pur. Behold in these my triumph!
               [*Presenting Urvasí and Chitralekhá.*
Urv. My dear, dear sisters, little did I hope
    But late to feel once more this loved embrace.
               [*Embraces them.*
Chorus. May countless ages blest survey
    The mighty Purúravas' sway. [*A noise without.*
Charioteer. (*To the king.*)
    Sire, from the east the rushing sound is heard
    Of mighty chariots; yonder like clouds they roll
    Along the mountain cliffs; now there alights
    A chief in gorgeous raiment, like the blaze
    Of lightning playing on the towering precipice.
Nymphs. Our king, great *Chitraratha.*

---

* Like the moon with the two stars of *Vishkhá*, one of the lunar asterisms containing two stars.

Enter CHITRARATHA, *the king of the Gandharbas* (attended).*

Chitrar. Illustrious victor, friend of Indra, hail!
Pur. King of the heavenly quiristers, receive
    The welcome of a friend.† What brings you hither?
Chitrar. When Indra learnt from Nárada the rape
    Of this fair damsel by the *Daitya*, Kesin,
    He bade me gather the *Gandharba* train
    And hasten to her rescue. I obeyed;
    But ere we marched, news of your triumph came
    And stopped our progress. For your friendly aid
    I bear you now our monarch's thanks, and more—
    His wish to see you in the heavenly courts
    Your worth has opened to your welcome visit.
    This service is most dear to him. The nymph
    Is now your boon—first given by *Nárdyaśa*
    To grace the halls of *Swarga*—now redeemed
    From hands profane by your resistless valour.
Pur. You rate the deed too high. Not mine the glory,
    But his, the Thunderer's, from whom derived
    The strength of those who conquer in his cause.
    The very echo of the lion's roar,
    As through the rocky rifts it spreads and deepens,
    Appals the mighty elephant.
Chitrar. 'Tis well.
    This modesty becomes your worth. Humility
    Is ever found the ornament of valour.
Pur. Excuse me to the monarch. Other claims
    Demand my distant presence; lead the nymph
    Back to the king.
Chitrar. Your will shall be obeyed.

---

* The *Gandharbas* are the male attendants and choristers in the courts of *Siva, Indra*, and *Kuvera*.

† The stage direction here is, "They shake hands:" "*Parasparam hastau spriśatah.*"

Urv. (*Apart to Chitralekhá.*)
Speak for me, my dear friend; my lips refuse
To bid adieu to my protector.—Speak.
Chitral. (*To the king.*)
Illustrious sir, my friend commands me ask
Your leave to carry back with her to heaven,
As one she dearly cherishes, your fame.
Pur. Farewell!—I trust ere long to meet again.

The GANDHARBAS *and* APSARASAS *ascend;* URVAŚÍ *loiters and pretends to be stopped.*

Urv. A moment pause! (*To Chitralekhá.*) Dear girl, this straggling vine
Has caught my garland—help me to get loose.
Chitral. No easy task, I fear—you seem entangled
Too fast to be set free: but come what may,
Depend upon my friendship.
Urv. Thanks, thanks,
Be mindful of your promise.
[*Chitralekhá employed in disengaging her.*
Pur. A thousand thanks, dear plant, to whose kind aid
I owe another instant, and behold,
But for a moment and imperfectly,
Those half-averted charms.
Charioteer. Come, royal sir,
Let us depart. The demon foes are hurled
Deep in the ocean wave—just punishment
For their rebellion against *Swarga's* king.
Now let the shaft, whose headlong force resembles
The blast of fate, sleep in its wonted quiver,
As cowers the snake within his gloomy covert.
[*They mount.*
Pur. Ascend the car.
Urv. Ah! me; ah! when again
Shall I behold my brave deliverer!
[*Departs with Chitralekhá and the nymphs.*

Pur. (*Looking after her.*)
What idle dreams does frantic love suggest!
What arduous tasks inspire! The beauteous nymph
Bears off my heart in triumph through the path
Her sire* immortal treads: so flies the swan
Through the mid air, charged with its precious spoil,
The milky nectar of the lotus stem.
[*Exit in his car.*

* Náradyada or Vishnu, according to the commentator.

END OF THE FIRST ACT.

ACT II.

THE GARDEN OF THE PALACE OF PURÚRAVAS AT
PRAYÁGA (*Allahabad*).*

Enter MÁNAVAKA, *the Vidúshaka*.

IT is mighty inconvenient this, for a Brahman like myself, one so much sought after and subject to such frequent invitation, to be burthened with the king's secret! Going so much into company as I do, I shall never be able to set a guard upon my tongue. I must be prudent, and will stay here by myself in this retired temple, until my royal friend comes forth from the council chamber. (*Sits down and covers his face with his hands.*)

Enter NIPUNIKÁ, *an Attendant on the Queen*.

The daughter of the king of Kásí † is quite sure, that since the king returned from the regions of the sun, he is no longer the same; he must have left his heart behind him,—what else can be the reason? I must try and find it out: if that crafty Brahman be in the secret, I shall easily get at it. A secret can rest no longer in his breast than morning dew upon the grass. Where can he be?—eh!—yes, there he sits deep in thought,

---

* It is also in other places called Pratishṭhána, and is described as at the confluence of the Yamuná and Ganges on the bank of the latter: it should seem, therefore, so late as the composition of this drama the ancient city still stood opposite to its present site. The ruins, according to Hamilton, are still to be seen at Jhusi on the left bank of the Ganges. (*Hamilton's Genealogies of the Hindus.*) Allahabad or Prayága was a holy place, having been the seat of *Bharadwája's* hermitage; but it never was a city until Akbar made it one.

† The ancient name of Benares, which is recognisable in the Cassida of Ptolemy.

like a monkey in a picture. Now to attack him, that is all I have to do. Árya* Mánavaka, I salute you!

Mán. Prosperity attend you. (*Apart.*) The king's secret is bursting forth at the mere sight of that hussy Nipuńiká. (*Aloud.*) Well, Nipuńiká, how is it you leave your music-practice† for the garden?

Nip. The queen has sent me to pay you a visit, sir.

Mán. And what may be her Majesty's commands?

Nip. She bids me say that she has ever esteemed you as her good friend, and that it is, therefore, with some surprise she finds you utterly indifferent to her present anxiety.

Mán. Why, what's the matter? Has my royal friend done anything to displease her?

Nip. Oh, that is not the point! My mistress knows the cause of his melancholy well enough; nay more, he let out the secret himself, and, in a fit of absence, addressed the queen by the very name of his new love.

Mán. (*Apart.*) Indeed! Oh, if his Majesty cannot keep his own secrets, why should I be plagued with them? (*Aloud.*) Why, what the deuce, Nipuńiká, did he call the queen?—Urvaśí!

Nip. And, pray, who is Urvaśí?

Mán. The nymph, the *Apsaras.* Ever since the king saw her, he has been out of his senses; he not only neglects her grace, but annoys me and spoils my dinner.

Nip. (*Apart.*) So, so; I have settled that matter, as I expected. (*Aloud.*) Well, I must return to the queen. What am I to say to her?

Mán. Tell her I am weary of attempting to cure my friend, the king, of this idle fancy of his. The only remedy is the sight of her lotus countenance.

Nip. You may depend upon me. [*Exit.*

The Warder. (*Without.*)

All hail to the monarch who toils through the day,

---

* A term of respect.

† *Sangíta-vidhára* for *Sangíta-vyápára*; practice of music, singing, and dancing.

To shed o'er his subjects the light of his sway,
As travels unceasing the sun in his sphere
To chase from the universe darkness and fear.
The lord of lone splendour an instant suspends
His course at mid-noon ere he westward descends;
And brief are the moments our young monarch knows,
Devoted to pleasure or paid to repose.*

Mid. (Listening.) Ha! my royal friend has arisen from his seat, and is coming hither; I will await him.

---

* Frequent occasion will occur to notice the *Vaitálika*, a sort of poetical warder or bard, who announces fixed periods of the day, as dawn and evening, &c., in measured lines, and occasionally pours forth strains arising from any incidental occurrence. He here announces the arrival of the sixth hour or watch of the day, about two or three o'clock, in which alone he says the king can follow his own inclination. It appears, indeed, that the royal station was by no means a sinecure. The *Agni-Purána* lays down rules for the apportioning of the regal day; but the same are more fully detailed in the last story of the *Dasa-Kumára*, upon the authority of *Chánakya*, the celebrated minister of Chandragupta, who is always cited as the author of the *Níti*, or Institutes of Government. From the *Dasa-Kumára* it appears that the day and night was each divided into eight portions, corresponding accordingly to one hour and a half, and they are thus disposed of: Day—first portion, the king being dressed is to audit his accounts; second, he is to pronounce judgement in suits appealed to him; third, he is to breakfast; fourth, he is to receive and make presents; fifth, to discuss political questions with his ministers and councillors; sixth, he is, as stated in the drama, his own master; seventh, he is to review the troops; eighth, he holds a military council. Night—first portion, the king is to receive the reports of his spies and envoys; second, he sups or dines; third, he retires to rest after the perusal of some sacred work; the fourth and fifth portions, or three hours, are allowed for sleep; in the sixth, he must rise and purify himself; in the seventh, he holds a private consultation with his ministers, and furnishes the officers of government with instructions; and the eighth is appropriated to the *Purohita* or priest, the Brahman and religious ceremonies, after which the business of the day is resumed. The author of the play has conformed to this distribution; bringing Purúravas from council at the sixth portion of the day. The precise hour depends upon the period of the year, the different portions being reckoned from sunrise. We may infer that the poet intends this to be about two P.M., as at the end of the act he makes the king describe the time as being past noon, when the heat is most oppressive; the sixth watch accordingly begins in the drama about one o'clock.

VOL. I.   O

Enter PURÚRAVAS.

Pur. One glance sufficed; the unerring shaft of love
Laid bare the path, and gave a ready access
To that celestial nymph, to seat herself
Throned in my heart.

Mád. (*To himself.*) Ah! that is exactly what the poor daughter of Káśirája complains of.

Pur. (*To the Vidúshaka.*) You have kept my secret safe?

Mád. (*Apart.*) That baggage must have betrayed me! Why else should he ask the question?

Pur. (*Alarmed.*) How, you are silent!

Mád. Don't be alarmed; the fact is, that my tongue is so accustomed to the restraint I have put upon it, that I cannot answer off-hand even your inquiries.

Pur. 'Tis well! Now then for recreation—
What shall we do?

Mád. Pay a visit to the kitchen.

Pur. With what intent?

Mád. Why, the very sight of the savoury dishes in course of preparation will be sufficient to dissipate all melancholy ideas.

Pur. With you it may, for what you covet there
You may obtain; what my desires affect
Is hopeless! Where should I then seek diversion?

Mád. May I ask if the person of your Highness was not beheld by the lady Urvasí?

Pur. What then?

Mád. Why, then, I should think her not quite so uncomeatable.

Pur. The fit compeer of beauty such as hers
Must needs be more than human.

Mád. What you say only adds to my surprise. What signifies madam Urvasí's unrivalled beauty? Am I not equally without a peer, in ugliness?

Pur. Words cannot paint her every excellence.
Hear her, Mádavaka, described in brief.

Mdá. I am all attention.

Pur. Her loveliness yields splendour to her ornaments,
　　Her purity gives fragrance to her perfumes;
　　All the similitudes that poets use
　　To picture beauty, it were gross flattery
　　To them, to name with her surpassing charms.

Mdá. This is mighty well! but in the will-o'-the-wisp* fancy for such superhuman excellence, I should think your Majesty had taken the *chátaka*† for your model. Where, please you, shall we go?

Pur. To melancholy moods the only solace
　　Is solitude;—go onwards to the grove.

Mdá. (*Apart.*) What absurdity! (*Aloud.*) This way, sir; here is the boundary of the grove, and the southern wind‡ advances with due civility to meet you.

Pur. He comes to teach me, as he amorous sports
　　Amongst the blossoms of the *mádhaví*§
　　And dances frolic with the *kunda*‖ flowers,
　　With all the impassioned fervour of desire
　　And graceful ingenuity of love—
　　I mark in him my pictured sentiments.

Mdá. The only likeness I see is your mutual perseverance. But here we are; please you to enter?

Pur. Precede! I fear my coming hither vain,
　　Nor yield these shades relief to my affliction—
　　Though with intent to gain tranquillity,
　　I seek these paths of solitude and peace;
　　I feel like one contending with the stream,
　　And still borne backwards by the current's force.

Mdá. Why entertain such feelings?

---

* Literally, being desirous of the waters of the mirage.

† A bird said to drink no water but rain.

‡ During the hot weather the prevailing breeze in Hindustan is from the south.

§ A creeper with white flowers.　　‖ A kind of jasmine.

Pur. How avoid them?
  What I affect is of no light attainment:
  The very thought presumption, and now love,
  The five-armed god,* whose shafts already pierce me,
  Call to his aid these passion-breathing blossoms,
  The mango's fragrant flowers and pallid leaves,
  Light wafted round us by the southern breeze.
Mál. Away with despondence! Be assured that in a little time *Ananga*† will be your friend, and help you to obtain your desires.
Pur. I take your words as ominous.
Mál. But now let your Highness notice the beauty of this garden, heralding, as it were, the presence of the spring.
Pur. I mark it well. In the *kuravaka*,
  Behold the painted fingers of the fair
  Red-tinted on the tip and edged with ebony;
  Here the *asoka* puts forth nascent buds
  Just bursting into flowers, and here the mango
  Is brown with blossoms, on whose tender crusts
  Scant lies the fragrant down; methinks I see
  The pride of spring on either hand attended
  By budding infancy and flowering youth.
Mál. The bower of jasmines yonder, with its slab of black marble, is studded thick with blossoms, and the bees crowd about them in heaps; it invites your Majesty to repose.
                              [*They enter the arbour.*
Pur. As you please.
Mál. Now, seated in this shade, you may dissipate your cares by contemplating the elegant plants around us.
Pur. How should I learn composure? As my eye

* The Hindu Cupid is armed with a bow strung with bees and five arrows, each tipped with a flower, and exercising peculiar influence on the heart.

† Love, the unembodied deity; having been once destroyed by *Siva*, burnt to ashes by the fire of his eye, in resentment of *Kama's* aiming his darts at him.

Rests on the towering trees, and from their tops
Sees the lithe creeper wave, I call to mind
The graces that surpass its pendulous elegance.
Come, rouse your wit, and friendship may inspire
Some capable expedient to secure me
The object of my wishes.

Mán. Well, I will turn the matter over in my mind; but you must not disturb my cogitations by your sighs.

Pur. (*Feeling his eyes twinkle.*)
The moon-faced maid is far beyond my reach;
Then, why should love impart such flattering tokens?
They teach my mind to feel as if enjoyed
The present bliss, hope scarcely dares imagine.
         (*They retire.*)

   Enter URVASÍ *and* CHITRALEKHÁ *in the air.*

Chitral. Tell me, dear girl, your purpose: whither go we?
Urv. Nay, tell me first, do you recall the promise
You made me jestingly upon the brow
Of *Hemakúta*, when your friendly hand
Detached my vesture from entangling thorns?
If it be still within your recollection,
You need not ask me whither we proceed.
Chitral. You seek the moon of monarchs, Purúravas.
Urv. Right, girl; though ill it argue of my modesty.
Chitral. Whom have you sent the envoy of your coming?
Urv. None, but my heart; that has long gone before me.
Chitral. But first consider.
Urv. Love impels me; how can I delay?
Chitral. I have no more to offer.
Urv. Assist me with your counsel, which way best
We may proceed, to meet with no impediment.
Chitral. There is no fear; the all-wise preceptor*
Of the immortals has imparted to you

  * *Vríhaspati*, the planet Jupiter and teacher of the gods.

The spell that renders you invincible,
And mightier than the mightiest foe of heaven.*

Urv. My heart is confident, and yet my fears
Will sometimes bid me doubt.

Chitral. Behold where meet
Gangá and *Yamuná* / in the bright mirror
Of the broad waves, the palace of the king,
The crest-borne gem of *Pratishṭhána* views
Complacently its own reflected glory.

Urv. The scene in truth might tempt us to believe
The fields of heaven were here in prospect spread—
But where to find its lord, the pitying friend
Of all the helpless children of misfortune!

Chitral. Let us alight and hide us in this garden,

---

* In a former note on this passage some doubt was expressed as to its purport, the text being read "Abaridḍam ńâma, siṁha-baṅdhaniṁ vijjam," explained by the commentator, "Aparjitáṁ nâma sikhábaṅdhaniṁ vidyâm," the crest-binding science named the invincible. The term *aparájitá* occurs in "*Sikunṭolá* ; abaṅdiḍá nâma suramahansi ;" rendered by the late M. Chézy, "Cet amulette d'une nature toute divine, et célèbre sous le nom de l'invincible (*apanridjitá*)," and he has proposed to read the similar passage in this place, Siṁha-baṅdhaṁ-vidyá, which he translates, "un talisman nommé *apanritji*, capable d'enchaîner les lions." Mr. Lenz, following his authority, reads here, Siṁidha-baṅdhâni vidyá, "Leonem domandorum scientia." I am afraid that both are wrong. *Sikhá* is the explanation given by the commentator. The Prákrit representative of this is *sikhá*, as it occurs in the Calcutta edition, the dental being substituted for the palatal sibilant, by the rule in Vararuchi's Grammar Sashoh sah, as *śiśa* for *siśi*, and *h* for *kh*, by the rule *Kha-gha ṣha-ḍha-bhâm hah ; as suhaṁ* for *sukhaṁ :* so a little farther on we have *sikhi-bhavaṁa-bhidaṁ* for *sikhá-bharaṇa-bhidam*. Again, the word could not be *Siṁha* if it were even intended for the same Sanskrit word signifying a lion. It would be *siho*, the *anuswára* being rejected, and the vowel made long, as in *sakhi siho* for *sikhya-siṁha*, according to the rule, *siṁha-jihvayośicha*, ex. for *sihhah, siho ; jiárá, jihá*. The only correction needed, therefore, was the elision of the *anuswára* reading, instead of *siṁhá, sikhá*, the Prákrit form of *sikhá*, as it occurs in the comment. Taming lions, as the faculty of a superhuman being, would need neither talisman nor drug, and the binding of the crest or braid of hair is an act of much more mystical importance in Hindu estimation : apparently the power is merely that of becoming invisible.

Whose groves may vie with Indra's, till we learn
Some news of him we seek.
Yonder I view him! [*They descend.*
He waits thy coming to display his beauty
With undiminished brightness, like the moon,
That newly risen, expects a while his bride
The soft moonlight, ere he put forth his radiance.

Urv. More graceful seems he than when first he met
My gaze.

Chitral. No doubt; come, let us approach.

Urv. No, hold a moment! let us conceal ourselves
In veiling mist,* and lurking thus unseen
About the arbour, we may overhear
What thoughts he utters in this solitude,
Communing with one only friend.

[*They become invisible to the king and the Vidushaka.*

Vid. I have it; difficult as it is, I have hit upon a plan for securing you an interview with your charmer.

Urv. (*Behind.*) How! who! what female is so blest to be
The object of his anxious thoughts?

Chitral. Employ
Your meditation to discover her.

Urv. I fear too soon to know what may befall.

Vid. Did your Majesty hear me observe I had devised an expedient?

Pur. Say on; what is it?

Vid. This it is: let your Majesty cherish a comfortable nap; your union will then be effected by your dreams; or

---

* Being visible to the audience and invisible to individuals on the stage is a contrivance familiar to the plays of various people, especially our own, as the Ghost of Hamlet, that of Banquo, Ariel in the Tempest, and Angelo in the Virgin Martyr, who repeatedly enters invisible. The wardrobe of some of our old Comedians comprised a robe to walk invisible, which Gifford supposes was a dress of light gauzy texture. Something of the kind is used here apparently, as the stage directions are "covered with a veil," and "throwing aside the veil."

delineate a portrait of the lady Urvasí, and recreate your
imagination by gazing on her picture.
Urv. Be of good cheer, my heart!
Pur. I fear me both impracticable.
  How can I hope to taste repose that dreams
  Might give me Urvasí, while fierce the shaft
  Of Káma* rankles in my breast! And vain
  The task her blooming graces to portray;
  The tears of hopeless love at every line
  Would fill my eyes, and hide her beauties from me.
Chitral. You hear?
Urv. I do,—yet scarcely yet confide.
Mád. Ah well! my ingenuity extends no farther.
Pur. Cold and relentless; little does she know,
  Or knowing, little heeds my fond despair.
  Yet cannot I reproach the archer god,
  Although, by giving to my hope such aim,
  He tortures me with barren, wild desires.
Chitral. What say you now?
Urv. I grieve that he should deem me
  Cold and unfeeling. I cannot now appear
  Before I make these charges some reply:
  I'll make a *bhúrja* leaf,† and will inscribe
  My thoughts on it, and cast it in his way.
    [*She writes upon the leaf and lets it fall near the*
          Vidúshaka, who picks it up.
Mád. Holla! what is here, the slough of a snake dropped
upon me to eat me up?
Pur. It is no snake-skin, but a leaf and something written
on it.
Mád. No doubt the lady Urvasí, unperceived, has over-
heard your lamentations, and sends this billet to console you.

* The Hindu Cupid.
† A kind of birch, the leaf of which is used as paper in some parts of
Upper India, as that of the palm is in the Peninsula.

Pur. Hope dawns upon my passion. (*Reads the leaf.*)
Your guess was right.

Mdd. Oblige me, then, by letting me hear what is written.

Urv. Indeed! sir, you are curious.

Pur. (*Reads.*)
"Thou wrong'st me, lord, to think I do not feel
Alike the pains that o'er thy bosom steal.
The breeze that softly floats through heavenly bowers,
Reclined upon my couch of coral flowers,
Sheds not on me its cool reviving breath,
But blows the hot and scorching gale of death:
O'er all my form the fevered venom flies,
And each bright hud beneath me droops and dies."

Mdd. I hope you are pleased. You have now as much cause for rapture, as I should consider it to be civilly asked to dinner when I felt hungry.

Pur. How say you! cause for rapture! This dear leaf
Conveys indeed assurance most delightful:
Yet still I sigh to interchange our thoughts,
Met face to face, and eye encountering eye.

Urv. Our sentiments accord.

Pur. The drops that steal
Fast from my tremulous fingers may efface
These characters traced by her tender hand:
Take you the leaf, and as a sacred trust
With care preserve it.

Mdd. Phoo! what matters it now? Since, by the assenting sentiments of the lady Urvasi, your desire has borne flowers, will it not bear fruit?

Urv. Now, Chitralekha, whilst I summon courage
To issue into view, do you appear,
And give the monarch notice of my purpose.

Chitral. I shall obey. (*Becomes visible.*) Hail, to the king!

Pur. Fair damsel, you are welcome; yet forgive me,
The less, your lovely friend comes not along:

The sacred streams before us show less stately
Until they flow in unison.

Chitral. Royal sir,
The cloud precedes the lightning.

Pur. Where is Urvasi?
You are inseparable.

Chitral. She salutes the king,
And makes this her request.

Pur. Say, her command.

Chitral. Once, by the enemy of the gods assailed
And captive made, your valiant arm redeemed her.
Again in peril, she applies to you,
And claims your guardian shield against a foe
More formidable still, from *Madana*,*
Whom you have armed against her.

Pur. You tell me, gentle nymph, your fair friend pines
With amorous passion; but you do not see
The ardour that consumes this heart for her.
Alike our glowing flame: then quickly aid
Our union to cement, as close combines
Iron with iron,† when each fiery bar
With equal radiance glows.

Chitral. Appear, my friend!
The potent deity with like relentlessness
Afflicts the prince, and now to you I call
The herald of his sufferings.

Urr. Faithless friend,
Thus to desert me!

Chitral. It will soon be seen
Which merits best the title of deserter;
But now, be present.

Urv. (*Appearing.*) Triumph to the king!

Pur. The wish is victory.

---

* Another name of *Kāma* or Cupid.
† The art of welding iron was, therefore, known to the Hindús.

THE HERO AND THE NYMPH.

When from the sovereign of the gods transferred
By lips celestial to a mortal monarch.*
        [*Takes her hand and leads her to a seat.*
Má. Fair lady, I am the Brahman of the king, and his
friend, and so may claim some notice. (*Urvasí bows to him
smiling.*) Prosperity attend you.
                    A MESSENGER *of the Gods in the air.*
Mess. Ho, Chitralekhá! Urvasí, repair
Swift to the palace of the Lord of air ;
There your appointed duties to fulfil,
And give expression to the wondrous skill
Of Bharata, your master.† To the dome
Divine, the world's protecting rulers‡ come,

---

* That is, the customary wish with which Indra is addressed, when applied by you to a mortal, is in fact a boon to that effect. The words are, *Jeadu jaadu mahárdśa,* " May the great prince conquer."

† *Bharata* is the supposed inventor of dramatic composition.

‡ The *Lokapálas,* or guardians of the world, are sometimes confounded with the deities presiding over the different cardinal points ; but this is not quite correct, and they are more properly the divinities who were appointed by *Brahmá* upon the creation of the world, to act as rulers over the different kinds of created things. The list occurs in several *Puráńas ;* but the following is from the *Mahábhárata,* the *Harivanśa* portion.

Indra, sovereign of the three *Lokas,* or earth and the regions above and below.

Soma—of sacrifices, ascetic rites, the lunar and solar asterisms, Brahmans, and healing herbs.

Daksha—of the *Prajápatis,* the patriarchs or first-created and progenitors of mankind.

Varuńa—of the waters.

Vaiśvánara—of the *Pitrís* or manes.

Váyu—of the *Gandharbas,* of unembodied element, of time and sound.

Mahádeva—of the *Mitris,* of the spirits of ill, of kine, of portents and planets, of infirmities and diseases, and of ghosts.

Vaiśravana—of the *Yakshas, Rakshasas, Guhyakas,* of wealth and of all precious gems.

Sesha—of the entire serpent race.

Váruki—of the *Nágas* or ophite tribes of *Pátála.*

Takshaka, younger brother of the *Adityas*—of snakes.

Parjanya—of oceans, rivers, clouds, and rains.

Chitraratha—of the *Gandharbas.*

220   THE HERO AND THE NYMPH.

Eager to view the scene that genius fires,
That passion animates, and truth inspires.

Kámadeva—of the *Apsarasas*.
Nandi, the bull of *Siva*—of all quadrupeds.
Hiranyáksha and *Hiranyakasipu*—of the *Daityas*.
Viprachitti—of the *Dánavas*.
Mahákála—of the *Ganas* or *Siva's* attendants.
Vritra—of the children of *Andyusha*, the wife of *Twashtri*.
Ráhu—the son of *Sinhiká*—of evil portents and prodigies.
Sanémisara—of the divisions of time, from the twinkling of an eye to the period of an age.
Suparna—of birds of prey.
Garuda—of the winged race.
Aruna—the brother of *Garuda*, was made by Indra ruler in the East.
Yama, the son of *Áditya*—in the South.
The son of *Kasyapa*, *Amburdja*—in the West.
Pingala, the son of *Pulastya*—in the North.

Having thus nominated the presiding spirits, various *Lokas* or districts were created by *Swayambhú*, as brilliant as the sun or fire, radiant as lightning, or chastely beaming as the moon, of various colours, movable at will, many hundreds of *yojanas* in extent, the fit abodes of the pious, exempt from sin and pain. Those Brahmans whose merit shines conspicuous are elevated to these regions, those who practise piety and worship devoutly, who are upright and benevolent, free from cupidity and cherishers of the poor.

Having thus distributed his sons, *Brahmá* departed to his own dwelling *Pushkara*. The deities rambled through the districts, and engaged in the charges respectively assigned them, being all cherished by *Mahendra*. The gods, with Indra at their head, as placed by *Swayambhú*, discharging their guardian duties obtained fame and heaven, and receiving their share of sacrifices enjoyed prosperity and happiness.

Some of the early sections of the *Kási-khanda* of the *Skanda-Purána*, or from the 9th to the 23d, contain a description of the several *Lokas*, the cities or spheres of the different divinities, as they are traversed by *Sivasárman* on his way from earth to the region of *Siva*. He passes in this route the *Lokas* of the nymphs, of the sun, of *Indra*, *Agni*, *Nirriti*, *Varuna*, *Váyu*, *Kuvera*, of the *Ganas*, or attendants of *Siva*, of *Soma*, of the lunar asterisms, of *Budha*, *Sukra*, *Bhauma*, *Guru*, and *Sani*, or the planets Mercury, Venus, Mars, Jupiter, and Saturn, of the seven *Rishis*, of *Dhruva*, the *Lokas*, called *Maharloka*, *Janaloka*, and *Tapoloka*, and that called *Satyaloka*, the abode of *Brahmá*, and *Vaikuntha* and *Kailása*, or the regions severally of *Vishnu* and *Siva*. This disposition of the spheres, however, has evidently received a peculiar colouring from the Pauránik cosmography, and the sectarial bias of the *Skanda-Purána*.

Chitral. Hear you, my friend ! be speedy in your parting.
Urv. I cannot speak.
Chitral. My friend, great prince, requests
Permission to depart. She owes obedience
To heaven's high king, and dreads lest her delay
Incur his wrath.
Pur. Not mine to interrupt
The tasks your mighty Lord assigns. Farewell !
Do not forget me !
[*Urvasi and Chitralekhá depart.*
Pur. (*To the Vidúshaka.*) She disappears ! What else deserves my gaze !
Mds. Why, perhaps, this. (*Looking for the bhúrja leaf.*) (*Apart.*) Bless me, I have been so fascinated myself by the smiles of the lady Urvasi, that the leaf with her billet upon it has unconsciously slipped out of my hands.
Pur. You were about to speak.
Mds. Yes, I was going to say, do not lose your fortitude. The nymph is firmly attached to you, and her going hence will not relax the attachment.
Pur. Of that I feel assured. The sighs that heaved
Her panting bosom as she hence departed,
Exhaled her heart, and lodged it in my bosom,
Free to dispose of it, although her person
Be forced to wait upon a master's will.*
Mds. (*Apart.*) I am all in a flutter lest he should ask me for that abominable leaf.
Pur. What shall console my eyes ! Give me the leaf.
Mds. The leaf ! dear me, it is not here !—it was a leaf of heaven, and must have gone after Urvasi.
Pur. Heedless blockhead !

---

* Rowe is less daring, although in the *Rival Queens* he makes Alexander say something of this kind :
"*Alex.* (*To Statira.*) My fluttering heart, tumultuous with its bliss, would leap into thy bosom."

Mda. Let us search for it. Here, here!
  [*They search for the leaf and retire.*
Enter in the foreground, AUṢĪNARĪ, *the* QUEEN, *with* NIPUṆIKĀ *and Attendants.*
Auṣ. You saw his Highness, you are sure, Nipuṇikā,
  Entering the arbour with Máńavaka.
Nip. Why should your Majesty doubt my report?
Auṣ. Well, let us seek him then, and unobserved,
  Amidst these shades we may detect the truth.
  But what is yon that meets us like a shred
  Of some rent garment, floating on the wind?
Nip. A *bhojpatra* leaf;—there seem to be some marks like letters upon it; it is caught by your Grace's anklet. (*Picks it up.*) Will it please you read it?
Auṣ. Glance o'er its tenor, and if not unfit
  To meet our ear, peruse what there is written.
Nip. It looks like a memorial verse. Eh, no! now it strikes me, they must be lines addressed by Urvaśī to the king; this is some carelessness, now, of that blockhead Máńavaka.
Auṣ. Read, I shall conceive its purport.
Nip. (*Reads the lines as above.*)
Auṣ. Enough!—proceed; and with this evidence
  We shall confound our nymph-enamoured swain.
They go round the arbour, the KING *and* MÁŃAVAKA *advance.*
Mda. Eh! is not that the leaf yonder on the mount, just on the edge of the garden?
Pur. Breeze of the south, the friend of love and spring,
  Though from the flower you steal the fragrant down
  To scatter perfume, yet why plunder me
  Of those dear characters, her own fair hand,
  In proof of her affection, traced! Thou knowest,
  The lonely lover that in absence pines
  Lives on such fond memorials.
Mda. No, I was mistaken; I was deceived by the tawny hue of the peacock's tail.

Pur. I am every way unhappy.

　　　AUŚÍNARÍ *and her train advance.*

Auś. Nay, my good lord,
　　I pray you be consoled, if, as I deem,
　　The loss of this occasion your distress.
　　　　　　　　　　[*Offering the leaf.*

Pur. (*Apart.*) The queen! (*Aloud.*) Madam, you are welcome.

Auś. You do not think me so.

Pur. (*To the Vidúshaka apart.*) What is to be done?

Vid. I don't know: what excuse can a freebooter offer when he is taken in the fact?

Pur. This is no time to jest. (*Aloud.*) Believe me, madam,
　　This leaf was not the object of my search,
　　Nor cause of my anxiety.

Auś. Excuse me,
　　If I suspect that your denial seeks
　　But to conceal the truth.

Vid. Your grace had better order dinner: that will be the most effectual remedy for his Majesty's bile.

Auś. You hear, Nipunika, this most sage counsellor;
　　And how he would remove his friend's distress.

Vid. Why not, madam? Is not everybody put into good humour by a hearty meal?

Pur. Peace, blockhead! you but heighten my offence.

Auś. Not yours the offence, my lord: 'tis mine, who tarry
　　Here, where my presence is not wished; 'tis soon
　　Removed.　　　　　　　　　[*Going.*

Pur. Yet stay, I own myself to blame,—
　　Curb your resentment, that alone convicts me:
　　When monarchs are incensed it cannot be
　　But that their slaves are guilty. [*Falls at her feet.*

Auś. Think me not
　　So light of purpose, as to be beguiled
　　By such assumed respect. You make, my lord,
　　An awkward penitent: I cannot trust you.

Nip. Come, madam, come!

(*The queen repels the king, and exit.*)

Mds. Her Majesty has gone off in a hurry, like a river in the rains. You may rise. (*To the king, who has continued prostrate.*)

Pur. I might have spared myself the pains.
　　A woman is clear-sighted, and mere words
　　Touch not her heart. Passion must give them credit.
　　The lapidary, master of his craft,
　　With cold indifference eyes the spurious gem.

Mds. You care very little about this, I suppose; the eye that is dazzled with light cannot bear the lamp.

Pur. Not so. 'Tis true that Urvasí engrosses
　　My heart, but Kásíraja's daughter claims
　　My deference; less indeed, that her contempt
　　Disdains my protestations, and this scorn
　　Will justify requital.

Mds. Well, let us have done with her Majesty, and think a little of a famished Brahman. It is high time to bathe and eat.

Pur. 'Tis past mid day. Exhausted by the heat,
　　The peacock plunges in the scanty pool
　　That feeds the tall tree's root: the drowsy bee
　　Sleeps in the hollow chamber of the lotus
　　Darkened with closing petals: on the brink
　　Of the now tepid lake the wild duck lurks
　　Amongst the sedgy shade; and even here,
　　The parrot from his wiry bower complains,
　　And calls for water to allay his thirst.　　[*Exeunt.*

END OF THE SECOND ACT.

ACT III.

Scene I.—The Hermitage of Bharata.

Enter Gálava* *and* Pailava,† *two of his disciples.*

Gál. Well, friend Pailava, what news? Whilst you were at *Mahendra's* palace with the Sage, I have been obliged to

---

* *Gálava* was a saint of some note, and is the hero of a long legend in the *Udyoga-Parvan* of the *Mahábhárata.* He there appears as the pupil of *Viśvámitra.* At the expiration of his studies he importuned his master to tell him what present he should make him. *Viśvámitra,* being out of humour, at last desired him to bring him eight hundred horses, each of a white colour, with one black ear. *Gálava* in his distress applied to *Garuda,* who was his particular friend, and with him repaired to *Yayáti,* king of *Pratishthána.* *Yayáti,* being unable to comply with the sage's wish, presented him his daughter *Mádhaví,* whom *Gálava* gave in marriage successively to *Haryaśwa,* king of Ayodhyá, *Divodása,* king of Káśí, *Uśínara,* king of Bhoja, and received from each, upon the birth of a son by her, two hundred of the steeds he was in quest of. These horses were originally a thousand in number. The saint *Richíka,* having demanded the daughter of *Gádhi,* sovereign of Kányakubja, as his wife, that prince, to evade the match, being afraid to decline it, required the steeds in question as a present in return. *Richíka* obtained them from the god of ocean, *Varuna,* and transferred them to his father-in-law, by whose descendants six hundred were sold to different princes, and the rest given away to the Brahmans. *Gálava,* having procured the horses which were in possession of the kings, took them and the damsel, still by virtue of a boon a virgin, and presented them together to *Viśvámitra.* The sage received them and begot a son by her, *Ashtaka,* to whom he resigned his hermitage and his stud, and retired to the woods: the place was thence called *Ashtakapura.* The lady after this was reconducted by *Gálava* to her father, and he, in imitation of his preceptor, spent the rest of his days in solitary devotion.

† *Paila* is the name of a *Rishi,* by whom the *Rig-Veda* was arranged and subdivided into two portions. It is not certain that he is intended in this place by the name *Pailava,* although not unlikely.

VOL. I.

stay at home to look after the holy fire. Were the immortals pleased with the specimen of our master's skill?

Pail. How could they choose but be pleased?—there was eloquence and melody for them. The drama was *Lakshmí's choice of a lord;*[*] the nymph Urvaśí quite lost herself in the impassioned passages.

Gdl. There is something not quite right implied in your applause.

Pail. Very true, for unluckily Urvaśí stumbled in her part.

Gdl. How so?

Pail. You shall hear. Urvaśí played *Lakshmí;* Menaká was *Váruńí.* The latter says:—

> *Lakshmí,* the mighty powers that rule the spheres
> Are all assembled: at their head appears
> The blooming *Kêśava.* Confess, to whom
> Inclines your heart?

Her reply should have been—To *Purushottama;* but instead of that—To *Purúravas,* escaped her lips.

Gdl. The intellectual faculties are but the slaves of destiny. Was not the Sage much displeased?

Pail. He immediately denounced a curse on her, but she found favour with *Mahendra.*

Gdl. How so?

Pail. The sentence of the Sage was, that as she had forgotten her part, so should she lose her divine knowledge. But when the performance was over, Indra observing her, as she stood apart, ashamed and disconsolate, called her to him.

---

[*] Or the *Lakshmí-Swayamvara.* It was common in the Hindu society of former times for princesses and women of rank to select a husband for themselves. The candidates for the hand of the lady were invited to her father's house, and after previous festivities for some days, were collected in a hall, round which the damsel passed and selected her future lord, by throwing a garland round his neck: the marriage rite was then celebrated as usual. The custom is the subject of much pleasing poetic description in the *Mahábhárata,* the *Naishadha,* and other works. A translation of the *Samyamvara of Draupadí* from the former is published in the *Calcutta Quarterly Magazine* for September 1825.

The mortal who engrossed her thoughts, he said, had been his friend in the hour of peril; he had aided him in conflict with the enemies of the gods, and was entitled to his acknowledgment. She must accordingly repair to the monarch, and remain with him till he beholds the offspring she shall bear him.

Gál. This was like *Mahendra*; he knows all hearts.

Pail. Come, come! we have been chattering here till it is almost the time when our preceptor performs his ablutions. Come, we have no time to lose; let us attend him.

[*Exeunt.*

Scene II.—Part of the Gardens of the Palace.

Enter the Chamberlain.

As long as life is vigorous, man endures labour for the sake of procuring wealth; when farther advanced in age, his toils are lightened by the participation of his children; but for me, my strength is daily undermined and my body exhausted by this servitude. Waiting on women is the devil. I am now to find the king, and tell him that her Majesty, having dismissed all anger and resentments, is desirous of paying her homage to him this evening, for the completion of the vow in which she has engaged.* The close of the day is agreeable enough here in the palace. The peacocks nod upon their perches and the doves flock to the turret tops, scarcely distinguishable from the incense that flows through the lattices of the lofty chambers. The venerable servants of the inner apartment are all busily engaged in propitiatory rites, and substituting lamps for the offering of flowers that decorated the holy shrines throughout the day. Ah! here comes the prince, attended by the damsel train with flambeaux in their delicate hands: he moves like a mountain, around whose stately

---

* Obligations self-imposed are in constant practice amongst the Hindus. In this case, the queen has engaged to forego her ornaments and to hold a rigid fast until the moon enters a certain asterism.

skirts the slender *karnikára* spreads its brilliant blossoms. I will wait him here.

Enter PURÚRAVAS *and the* VIDÚSHAKA, *with female attendants* * *carrying torches.*

So ends the day; the anxious cares of state
Have left no interval for private sorrow,
But how to pass the night: its dreary length
Affords no promise of relief.

Chamberlain. (*Advances.*) Glory to the king! So please your Grace, her Majesty expresses a wish to be honoured with your presence on the terrace of the pavilion of gems, to witness from it the entrance of the moon into the asterism Rohiṇí.

Pur. Go, my good friend, apprise her Majesty
She may dispose of us. [*Exit Chamberlain.*
What object, think you, that the queen, in truth,
Proposes by the vow she has assumed?

Vid. I suppose she repents of her pettishness, and wishes to be friends with you again. This is but an excuse to bring you to her presence, when she may efface the recollection of the indignity with which she treated you.

Pur. 'Tis very likely. Prudent wives full soon
Repent the scorn that urged them to repel
An humbled husband, and are glad to seek
Some fair pretext to win his love again—
We will indulge her Grace. On to the chamber.

Vid. 'Tis here. Ascend these steps of crystal, smooth shining as the waters of the Ganges. The pavilion of gems is particularly lovely when evening sets in. (*They ascend.*) The moon is just about to rise; the east is tinged with red.

---

* This might be supposed a copy of Mohammedan manners, but it is not necessarily so, having been the practice of the Hindus before the Christian era; for the king's person, when within the palace, used to be attended by women, his guards and other troops being stationed without the gates. Thus Strabo: "Regis corpus mulieres curant, ex quoque de parentibus emptæ, qui regem custodiunt, et reliquus exercitus manent extra portas." IV. 15.

Pur. 'Tis even so: illumined by the rays
Of his yet unseen orb, the evening glooms
On either hand retire, and in the midst
The horizon glows, like a fair face that smiles
Betwixt the jetty curls on either brow
In clusters pendulous. I could gaze for ever!

Mài. Ho! here he comes, the king of the Brahmans, as beautiful as a ball of almonds and sugar.

Pur. Oh, base similitude! Your thoughts, my friend,
Have rarely nobler prompter than your stomach.
    [*Carries his hands to his forehead, and bows to the moon now risen.*
Hail, glorious lord of night! whose tempered fires
Are gleaned from solar fountains, but to yield
The virtuous fruit eternal, as they light
The flame of holy sacrifice, whose stores
Ambrosial serve but to regale the gods
And the immortal fathers of mankind—
All hail to thee! whose rising ray dispels
The glooms of eve, and whose pale crescent crowns
The glorious diadem of *Mahádera.**

Mài. Enough, sir; your grandfather bids you, by me his interpreter, sit, that he may repose himself.

Pur. (*Makes the Vidúshaka sit, and then seats himself.*)
The splendour of the moon is light enough:
Remove the torches and command my train
Retire to rest.

---

* The first of these specifications refers to the astronomical facts of the moon's deriving its light from the sun, and by its positions forming the days of the lunar month, on which particular ceremonies are to be observed. In the latter case it is supposed to move in the *Manḍala*, the sphere or orbit of the sun, and when in conjunction, as at the new moon or *Amávásyá*, funeral obsequies are especially to be celebrated. According to mythological notions also, the moon is the grand receptacle and storehouse of *amṛita* or ambrosia, which it supplies during the fortnight of its wane to the gods, and on the last day to the *Pitris* or deified progenitors. As personified, the moon is the father of *Budha* and grandfather of *Pururavas*, as already shown. The half-moon, as frequently noticed, is worn by *Siva* upon his forehead.

All. As you command. [*Withdraws with the torch-bearers.*
Pur. I think we may not yet expect the queen:
 And now we are alone, I would impart
 My thoughts.
Mâd. Out with them; there is no appearance of her yet; and it is well to keep up your spirits with hope.
Pur. You counsel well. In truth, my fond desire
 Becomes more fervid as enjoyment seems
 Remote, and fresh impediments obstruct
 My happiness—like an impetuous torrent,
 That, checked by adverse rocks, a while delays
 Its course, till high with chafing waters swollen,
 It rushes past with aggravated fury.
Mâd. There is one thing to be said: notwithstanding your anxiety has made you something thinner, it has rather improved than impaired your personal appearance. I argue from this that a meeting with the nymph is not very distant.
Pur. My right arm by its glad pulsation soothes
 My grief, like you, with hope-inspiring words.
Mâd. A Brahman's words, be assured, are never uttered in vain.

Enter above in a heavenly car URVASÍ *and* CHITRALEKHÁ : URVASÍ *in a purple dress with pearl ornaments.**

Urv. Now, my dear girl,
 What say you ? Do these purple robes become me,
 Thus trimmed with pearls ?
Chitral. I cannot think of words
 To speak my admiration—only this,
 Would I were Purúravas.
Urv. My dear friend,
 I feel my strength desert me ; bring him quickly,
 Or quickly lead me to his royal palace.

---

* The text is, *Abhisáriká-veśi*, in the garb of a woman who goes to meet her lover. The specification of the translation is from Urvasí's first speech: the term is *níla*, which means dark-blue or black, most ordinarily the former.

Chitral. We are there. Behold it,
   White gleaming in the moon-light, whilst below
   The *Yamuná's* blue waters wash its foot;
   Like the snow-tufted summits of *Kailása,*
   Rising in radiance from their hoary base.
   Advance.
Urv. One moment—exercise the power
   Of meditative vision. Where is the king,
   The master of my heart, and what employs him?
Chitral. (*Apart.*) I will rouse her fears.
   I see him: in a fit solitude he waits
   Impatiently the coming of the bride.
                    [*Urvasí expresses despair.*
   How, silly wench! what else would you desire
   Should be his occupation?
Urv. Ah, my friend,
   My fluttering heart is easily alarmed.
Chitral. In the pavilion of bright gems awaits
   The king, his trusty friend alone attends him,
   Let us thither.
Urv. Proceed.
                    [*They descend and leave the car.*
Pur. As spreads the moon its lustre, so my love
   Grows with advancing night.
Urv. Ah me! I fear
   Even yet to trust. Let us remain invisible,
   And overhear their conference, till doubt
   Be all dispersed.
Chitral. Be it as you will.
Mán. The rays of the moon are charged with ambrosia; do you find no benefit from them?
Pur. Small is their power, or that of aught, to mitigate
   The pangs of love. Soft beds of fragrant flowers,
   Sandal's cool unguent, strings of gelid pearl,
   And these mild tempered rays, exhaust on me
   In vain their virtue; nothing can allay

The fever of my heart. She, she alone,
The goddess I adore, or secret converse,
That ever speaks of her, can yield me rest.
These limbs that pressed her side, when on we drove
Through fields of ether, are still warm with life;
All else a lifeless load that burthens earth.

Urv. I need no more concealment. [*She advances hastily.*
Woe is me;
He deigns not to regard me.

Chitral. In your haste
You have forgotten to put off the veil
That screens you from his sight.

(*Behind.*) This way, your Grace.
[*All listen; Urvasí throws herself into the arms of Chitralekhá.*

Mád. The queen is here! we had better be mute.
Pur. Assume the resemblance of indifference.
Urv. What shall we do?
Chitral. Remain invisible.
Not long her purposed stay: by her attire
She holds some sacred vow.

Enter the QUEEN, *with attendants bearing offerings; the Queen is dressed in white; flowers are her only ornaments.*

Queen. This union with the constellation yields
New brilliance to the lord of Rohiní.*

All. Such effect attends your Grace's encounter with his Majesty.

Mád. (*To Purúravas.*) She comes, I imagine, to offer her benedictions; or under the resemblance of a solemn vow, she wishes to obliterate the recollection of the indignity with which she lately repelled your advances. Well, I think her Majesty looks very charming to-day.

Pur. In truth she pleases me. Thus chastely robed
In modest white, her clustering tresses decked

* The moon.

With sacred flowers alone,* her haughty mien
Exchanged for meek devotion; thus arrayed
She moves with heightened charms.
Queen. (*Advancing.*) Hail to the king!
All. Hail to the king!
Pur. Madam, you are welcome. [*Leads her to a seat.*
Urv. (*Behind.*) She merits to be called divine;† the bride
Of heaven's great king‡ boasts not surpassing dignity.
Chitral. Your commendations speak you free from envy.
Queen. My gracious lord, I would perform a rite
Of which you are the object, and must beg you
Bear with the inconvenience that my presence
May for brief time occasion you.
Pur. You do me wrong;
Your presence is a favour.
Vid. May such inconvenience often befall me as to pronounce a benediction on like occasions.
Pur. (*To the queen.*) How call you your observance?
Nip. (*On the queen's turning to her.*) The conciliation of regard.§
Pur. Is it even so? Yet, trust me, it is needless
To wear this tender form, as slight and delicate
As the lithe lotus stem, with rude austerity.
In me behold your slave, whom to propitiate
Claims not your care; your favour is his happiness.
Urv. (*Smiling scornfully.*) He pays her mighty deference.
Chitral. So he should—
When the heart strays, the tongue is most profuse
Of bland professions to the slighted wife.
Queen. Not vain my vow, since it already wins me
My lord's complacent speech.

---

* Or with the blossoms of the holy *Dúrva* grass.
† *Devi*, or goddess, is one of the titles appropriate to the state of queen.
‡ *Sachí*, the wife of Indra.
§ *Pia-ppasádaka.*

Mdá. Enough said on both sides; these civilities require no further reply.

Queen. Come, girls, the offerings, that I may present them
To the bright deity, whose rays diffuse
Intenser lustre on these splendid walls.

All. Here are the perfumes, madam, here the flowers.

[*Gives them, and the queen goes through the usual form of presenting the Arghya or oblation of fruits, perfumes, flowers, &c.*

Queen. These cakes present Mánavaka, and these
Give to the chamberlain.

[*The attendant takes a tray of sweetmeats first to the Vidúshaka and then to the Kanchukin.*

Mdá. Prosperity attend your Highness; may your fast prove fortunate.

Chamberlain. Prosperity to the queen!

Queen. Now, with your Grace's leave, I pay you homage.

[*Presents oblations to the king, bows, and falls at his feet, then rises.*

Resplendent pair who o'er the night preside,
Lord of the Deer-borne* banneret, and thou
His favourite, Rohiní†—hear and attest
The sacred promise that I make my husband.

---

* The car of the moon is decorated with a small flag on which a deer is represented.

† *Chandra*, or the moon, is fabled to have been married to the twenty-seven daughters of the patriarch *Daksha*, or *Aswiní* and the rest, who are in fact personifications of the Lunar Asterisms. His favourite amongst them was *Rohiní*, to whom he so wholly devoted himself as to neglect the rest. They complained to their father, and *Daksha* repeatedly interposed, till finding his remonstrances vain, he denounced a curse upon his son-in-law, in consequence of which he remained childless and became affected by consumption. The wives of *Chandra* having interceded on his behalf with their father, *Daksha* modified an imprecation which he could not recall, and pronounced that the decay should be periodical only, not permanent, and that it should alternate with periods of recovery. Hence the successive wane and increase of the moon. (*Padma Purána, Swarga Khadda,* Sec. II.) *Rohiní* in astronomy is the fourth lunar mansion, containing five stars, the principal of which is Aldebaran.

Whatever nymph attract my lord's regard,
And share with him the mutual bonds of love,
I henceforth treat with kindness and complacency.

Urv. Oh, my dear friend, how much these words assuage
The apprehensions of my heart.

Chitral. She is a lady
Of an exalted spirit, and a wife
Of duty most exemplary. You now
May rest assured, nothing will more impede
Your union with your love.

Mdd. (*Apart to Purúravas.*) The culprit that escapes before
his hand is cut off, determines never to run such a risk again.
(*Aloud.*) What, then, is his Majesty indifferent to your
Grace?

Queen. Wise sir, how think you? To promote his happiness
I have resigned my own. Does such a purpose
Prove him no longer dear to me?

Pur. I am not what you doubt me; but the power
Abides with you : do with me as you will.
Give me to whom you please, or if you please
Retain me still your slave.

Queen. Do what you list.
My vow is plighted—nor in vain the rite,
If it afford you satisfaction. Come,
Hence, girls, 'tis time we take our leave.

Pur. Not so :
So soon to leave me is no mark of favour.

Queen. You must excuse me, I may not forego
The duties I have solemnly incurred.

[*Exit with train.*

Urv. Why, girl, I doubt the Rájá still affects
His queen. So be it ; it is now too late
For me to hope my heart can be reclaimed

Chitral. Away with doubt ; you have no need to fear.

Pur. Is the queen far removed ?

Mdd. You may say whatever you wish, safely enough.

You are fairly given over by her, like a sick man by his
physician.

Pur. I fear I am, by faithless Urvaśí.
  Would she were here; and that the gentle music
  Of her rich anklets murmured in my ears;
  Or that her lotus hands, as with light step
  She stole behind me, spread a tender veil
  Before my eyes; that in this shady bower
  She deigned descend spontaneous, or drawn hither
  With welcome violence by some fair friend,—
  Ha! the lovely daughter of Náráyaśa!
    [*Urvaśí has advanced behind the king and covers his
    eyes with her hands.*

Vid. How knows your Grace?

Pur. It must be Urvaśí,—
  No other hand could shoot such ecstasy
  Through this emaciate frame. The solar ray
  Wakes not the night's fair blossom—that alone
  Expands when conscious of the moon's dear presence.

Urv. (*Appearing.*) Joy to the king!

Pur. All hail, bright nymph of heaven!
                                [*Leads her to a seat.*

Chitral. (*Advancing.*) Be the king blest!

Pur. I feel I am already.

Urv. The queen, my friend, has just presented me
  This pious prince, and therefore I approach
  His person, as the object of my love.
  You cannot say I claimed a part in him
  Before the right was granted me.

Mis. What! were you here ever since sunset?

Pur. I have no purpose to dispute the claim.
  But let me ask, if such assent were needed,
  Who was it that first granted you permission
  To rob me of my heart.

Chitral. My friend, I know,
  Can proffer no reply—then let this be.

Now grant me my request; I must depart
To minister to Súrya at the term
Of the spring festival: till my return
Be careful that this nymph have never cause
To mourn the heaven she has resigned for thee.

Mád. Heaven, indeed! why should she ever think of such a place?—a place where they neither eat, nor drink, nor close their eyes even for a twinkle.*

Pur. The heaven of *Indra* is the eternal source
Of joy ineffable: it cannot be
The cares of Purúravas should efface
The memory of immortal bliss—
Yet, nymph, of this be confident, my soul
Shall know no other sovereign than your friend.

Chitral. 'Tis all I ask: be happy, Urvasí,
And bid me now adieu!

Urv. (*Embracing her.*) Forget me not.

---

* The gods are supposed to be exempt from the momentary elevation and depression of the upper eyelid, to which mortals are subject, and to look with a firm unintermitted gaze. Hence a deity is termed *Animisha* and *Animeshá*, one whose eyes do not twinkle. Various allusions to this attribute occur in poetry. When *Indra* visits *Sítá* to encourage her, he assumes at her request the mark of divinity—he treads the air, and suspends the motion of the eyelids (*Rámáyańa*). When *Agni*, *Varuńa*, and *Indra*, all assume the form of *Nala* at the marriage of *Damayantí*, she distinguishes her mortal lover by the twinkling of his eyes, whilst the gods are *stabdha-lochana*, fixed-eyed (*Mahábhárata*, *Nalopákhyána*). And when the *Aswini-Kumáras* practise the same trick upon the bride of *Chyavana*, she recognises her husband by this amongst other indications (*Padma-Puráńa*). The notion is the more deserving of attention, as it is one of those coincidences with classical mythology which can scarcely be accidental. *Heliodorus* says: "The gods may be known by the eyes looking with a fixed regard, and never closing the eyelids;" and he cites Homer in proof of it. An instance from the Iliad which he has not noticed, may be cited perhaps as an additional confirmation, and the *marble eyes* of Venus, by which Helen knew the goddess, and which the commentators and translators seem to be much perplexed with, are probably the *stabdha-lochana*, the fixed eyes, of the Hindus, full, and unveiled even for an instant, like the eyes of a marble statue.

Chitral. That I should rather beg of you, thus blest
With one the only object of your wishes.
[*Bows to the king, and exit.*

Mdd. Fate is propitious and crowns your Majesty's desires.

Pur. 'Tis true, I reach the height of my ambition.
The haughty canopy that spreads its shade
Of universal empire o'er the world;
The footstool of dominion, set with gems,
Torn from the glittering brows of prostrate kings,
Are in my mind less glorious than to lie
At Urvasi's fair feet and do her bidding.

Urv. I have not words to speak my gratitude.

Pur. Now I behold thee thus! how changed is all
The current of my feelings—these mild rays,
Cool, vivifying, gleam; the shafts of *Madana*
Are now most welcome—all that was but late
Harsh and distasteful to me, now appears
Delightful by your presence.

Urv. I lament,
I caused my lord to suffer pain so long.

Pur. Nay, say not so! the joy that follows grief
Gains richer zest from agony foregone.
The traveller who faint pursues his track
In the fierce day, alone can tell how sweet
The grateful shelter of the friendly tree.

Mdd. The moon is high; it were as well to go in.

Pur. Conduct the way: and, dearest, may the hours
With thee be still prolonged, as when, without thee,
They tardy brought the day.
[*Exeunt into the pavilion.*

END OF THE THIRD ACT.

ACT IV.[*]

Scene—The Forest of Akalusha on the skirts of Gandhamádana, one of the mountainous barriers of Meru.

Strains without.[†]

Soft voices low sound in the sky,
Where the nymphs a companion deplore,

---

[*] This act is without a parallel in any of the dramas yet met with. It is almost entirely in *Prákrit*, and the *Prákrit* is arranged not only in metrical forms peculiar to that language, but according to particular musical rhythm, as intended to be sung. Again, there are stage directions for the measure to which certain gesticulations are to be performed, so that it partakes both of the operatic and melo-dramatic character. The names of the airs and measures are not current in the present day, nor known to the Pandits; the explanations of them in the "*Tiká*," or "Commentary on the Drama," are quoted usually from *Bharata*, whose rules no longer exist in a collective form. The manuscript, however, being full of errors, little assistance has been derived in this respect from the annotator; but his definitions of the airs seem to be extracted chiefly from the *Sangita-Ratnákara*, from which authority it appears that this subject has yet been very insufficiently investigated, as the modifications of the six *Rágas* amounted to two hundred and sixty-four, with the whole of which we are yet unacquainted. *Soma* enumerates, according to Sir William Jones, nine hundred and sixty variations. A. R. III. 71.

In the former edition an attempt was made to explain in the notes the meaning of the terms employed in the text to indicate varieties of metre, melody, and gesticulation; but the subject is scarcely appropriate to a translation, and would more fitly accompany the Sanskrit text. It has therefore, for the most part, been now omitted; and those who take an interest in it will find as much illustration as it perhaps admits, in the notes of the Calcutta edition of the text, and in the elaborate dissertation of Mr. Lenz in his edition of the same.

[†] The expression is *Akshiptiká*, and as a musical term implies, *Air*, the adaptation of notes, or their names to poetical rhythm. *Bharata* adds, as cited by the commentator, it serves to introduce characters on the stage.

And lament, as together they fly,
The friend they encounter no more.
So, sad and melodious awakes
The plaint of the swan o'er the stream,
Where the red lotus blossoms, as breaks
On the wave, the day's orient beam.

Enter CHITRALEKHÁ *and* SAHAJANYÁ.

Chitral. (*Looking up.*)
The swans along the stream that sail
A fond companion's loss bewail—
With murmuring songs they soothe their grief,
Or find from tender tears, relief.

Sah. Now, Chitralekhá, what has chanced to cloud
Your countenance; it indicates your heart
Is ill at ease; what causes your distress?
Tell me, that I may share and soothe your sorrow.

Chitral. It is not all unknown to you. Engaged
Amidst our band in paying wonted service
To the all-seeing Sun, I have not shared
The vernal sports, my Urvasí away.

Sah. This we all know, and know your mutual love.

Chitral. Whilst dwelling on her memory, anxious to learn
Some tidings of her, I employed my power
Of bringing absent objects to my view;
And by this art I learn what much alarms me.

Sah. Say on.

Chitral. The king, by Urvasí's persuasions,
Resigned of late the reins of rule, and sought
With her the groves of *Gandhamádana.**

---

* The *Gandhamádana* mountain is one of the four boundary mountains enclosing the central region of the world, called *Ilávrita*, in which the golden mountain of the gods, or *Meru*, is situated. The *Puránas* are rather at variance as to its position. According to the *Váyu* it lies on the West, connecting *Níla* and *Nishadha*, the North and South ranges. The *Vishńu-Puráńa* places it on the South, the Western mountain being there called *Vipula*. It has, however, a *Gandhamádana* to the West amongst

Sah. Amid such lovely scenes, the amorous pair
Would most enjoy each other's company.
What followed?
Chitral. Whilst wandering pleasantly along the brink
Of the *Mandákiní*, a nymph of air,
Who gambolled on its sandy shore, attracted
The monarch's momentary glance—and this
Aroused the jealous wrath of Urvasí.
Sah. Ungenerous girl! although it proves her love,
Yet destiny is mightier.
Chitral. Thus incensed,
My friend disdainfully repelled her lord;
In sooth, her mind was darkened by the curse
The Sage erewhile denounced; and troubled thus,
She heedlessly forgot the law that bars
All female access from the hateful groves
Of *Kártttikeya.* Trespassing the bounds
Proscribed, she suffers now the penalty
Of her transgression, and to a slender vine
Transformed, there pines till time shall set her
free.
Sah. How vain the hope to shun the will of fate!
What other cause could interrupt a love
So fervent.—Where is now the king?
Chitral. He roams,
Frantic with sorrow, through the wood, in search
Of his lost bride, nor night nor day desists
From the sad quest. These rising clouds that teach
Passion to pious sages, augur ill

---

he projecting branches or filaments of *Meru*. The *Bhágavata* places it on the East of *Meru*. The *Mahábhárata* agrees with the *Váyu-Purána*. The *Padma-Purána* is at variance with itself, and places it in one passage on the West, and in another describes it as on the East. According to this *Purána*, *Kuvera* resides on it with the *Apsarasas*, *Gandharbas*, and *Rákshasas*. The *Sítá*, alighting on its top, thence descends to the *Bhadráśwa-varsha*, and flows to the Eastern Sea.

VOL. I.

For his alleviation—I much fear
There is but little hope of remedy—
    [*Repeats the first stanza,* "*The swans along the stream
        that sail,*" *&c.*

Sah. But think you there is no expedient then
To re-unite these lovers?

Chitral. There is but one.
    The sacred gem that owes its ruby glow
    To the bright tint of *Gaurí's** sacred feet,
    Alone effects their union.

Sah. Let us hope it—
    Their delicate forms endure not agony,
    Violent and protracted, and the gods
    Can surely never purpose such a pair
    Should wholly perish—they will soon devise
    Some means of their relief—to their high power
    We leave them.—Come. The glorious sun reveals
    His countenance; let us depart and pay
    Our wonted adorations. (*Sings.*)

    Amidst the lake, where the lotus shining,
        Its flowers unfolds to the sunny beam,
    The swan, for her lost companion pining,
        Swims sad and slow o'er the lonely stream.
                        [*Exeunt.*

ANOTHER PART OF THE FOREST.

(*Strains without.*) †

AIR.

The lord of the elephant train
    Now wanders afar from his mate,

---

* *Durgá* or *Párvatí*, the bride of *Siva.*

† Or in the text the *Pravésaka* the Introducer—either a person on the stage or near it, who occasionally interposes to let the audience know who is coming when none of the characters perform that duty: the annunciation is in the same metre as the first, the *Akshipiki*.

And franticly comes, to complain
To the woods of his desolate state.
Distraction his vigour consumes,
As he plunges amidst the dark bowers,
While o'er his vast bulk sweetly blooms
The garland of wild forest flowers.

Enter PURŪRAVAS *hastily, looking up to the heavens, his dress disordered, and his general appearance indicative of insanity.*

Hold, treacherous fiend, suspend thy flight, forbear—
Ah! whither wouldst thou bear my beauteous bride?
And now his arrows sting me—thick as hail
From yonder peak whose sharp top pierces heaven,
They shower upon me.
[*Rushes forward as to the attack—then pauses and looks upwards.*]

AIR.

The lonely cygnet breasts the flood,
Without his mate, in mournful mood;
His ruffled plumage drooping lies,
And trickling tears suffuse his eyes.

It is no demon—but a friendly cloud;
No hostile quiver—but the bow of Indra:
The cooling rain-drops fall, not barbèd shafts,
And I mistake the lightning for my love.
[*Faints—then revives, and rising.*]

AIR.

I madly thought a fiend conveyed
Away from me my fawn-eyed maid:
'Twas but a cloud that rained above
With the young lightning for its love.

Where can she bend her steps—or is she here
Invisible, in anger? If she seek
The skies, her love for me will soon revive.
Once mine again, not all the demon host

That brave the gods, should force her from my arms.
Alas! no more my gaze delighted dwells
Upon her loveliness—How sad the chance!
Fate heaps calamities with diligent malice
On those whom once misfortune has assailed.
Hence have I lost my love, when genial airs
And overshadowing clouds, veiling the day,
Had shed intenser rapture on her presence.

AIR.

Ye clouds whose ceaseless torrents shed
   New glories through the gloomy air,
   A while your angry showers forbear,
Nor burst upon this humbled head—
   Give me to find my love, and then fulfil
   Your wrath—Content, I bow me to your will.

Away with this humility—the wise
Call kings the lords of time—I will assert
My power, and bid the seasons stay their course.

AIR.

The tree of heaven invites the breeze,
   And all its countless blossoms glow;
   They dance upon the gale; the bees
     With sweets inebriate, murmuring low,
Soft music lend, and gushes strong
The *kóil's* deep thick warbling song.

No, I will not arrest the march of time,
For all around behold my state apparelled—
The clouds expand my canopy—their lightnings
Gleam as its glittering fringe. Rich chowries wave
Of many-coloured hues from flowering trees.
The shrieking peafowl, clamorous in their joy,
Are the loud heralds of a sovereign's honours;
And those bright torrents, flashing o'er the brows
Of the tall mountains, are the wealthy streams,
Poured forth profuse from tributary realms.

Fie on it! what have I to do with pomp
And kingly pride? my sole sad business here
To thread the woods in search of my beloved.

Air.

The monarch of the woods
  With slow desponding gait
Wanders through vales and floods,
  And rocks and forest bowers,
  Gemmed with new springing flowers,
And mourns heart-broken for his absent mate.

Ah me! whatever I behold but aggravates
My woe. These bright and pendulous flowers,
Surcharged with dew, resemble those dear eyes
Glistening with starting tears. How shall I learn
If she have passed this way? The yielding soil,
Softened by showers, perchance may have retained
The delicate impression of her feet,
And show some vestige of their ruby tincture.*
Where in this lonely thicket may I hope
To gain some tidings of her? Yon proud bird,
Perched on the jutting crag, that stately stands
With neck outstretched and spreading tail, to tell
His raptures to the clouds, haply may give
Some kind intelligence.

Air.

The royal elephant, the dread
  Of all his rival foes,
With downcast eye and tardy tread,
  Through tangled thickets goes;
  To solitary grief a prey,
  His loved companion far away.

* The soles being stained with the red juice of the *Mehndi*.

AIR.

I will speak to this peacock—Oh tell,
  If, free on the wing as you soar,
In forest, or meadow, or dell,
  You have seen the loved nymph I deplore—
You will know her, the fairest of damsels fair,
By her large soft eye, and her graceful air.

                  [*Advancing to the bird, and bowing.*

Bird of the dark-blue throat and eye of jet,
Oh tell me, have you seen the lovely face
Of my fair bride, lost in this dreary wilderness?
Her charms deserve your gaze. How! no reply?
He answers not, but beats a measure. How!
What means this merry mood? Oh yes, I know
The cause. He now may boast his plumage
Without a peer, nor shame to show his glories
Before the floating tresses of my Urvaśí.
I leave him, nor will waste a thought on one
Who feels no pity for another's woes.

                          [*Proceeds—Music.*

Yonder, amidst the thick and shady branches
Of the broad *jambu*, cowers the *kśil*—faint
Her flame of passion in the hotter breath
Of noon. She of the birds is wisest famed—
I will address her.

AIR.

Majestic as sails the mighty cloud
  Along the dusky air,
The elephant cometh hither to shroud
  In the thickets his despair.
From his heart all hope of delight is riven,
  And his eyes with tears o'erflow,
As he roams the shades, where the sons of heaven
  Descend to sport below.

AIR.

Say, nursling of a stranger nest,*
  Say, hast thou chanced my love to see,
Amidst these gardens of the blest,
  Wandering at liberty,
Or warbling with a voice divine
Melodious strains more sweet than thine?
                              [*Approaches, and kneels.*

Sweet bird—whom lovers deem Love's messenger,†
Skilled to direct the god's envenomed shafts
And tame the proudest heart; oh, hither guide
My lovely fugitive, or lead my steps
To where she strays.
                [*Turns to his left, and as if replying.*
            Why did she leave
One so devoted to her will? In wrath
She left me, but the cause of anger lives not
In my imagination; the fond tyranny
That women exercise o'er those who love them
Brooks not the slightest show of disregard.
How now! the bird has flown. 'Tis ever thus—
All coldly listen to another's sorrows.
Unheeding my affliction, lo, she speeds,
Intent on joy expected, to yon tree,
To banquet on the luscious juice the *jambu* ‡
From its now ripe and roseate fruit distils.
Like my beloved, the bird of tuneful song
Deserts me. Let her go—I can forgive her.
                                    [*Proceeds.*
Ha!—on my right—amidst the wood I hear

---

* The *kóil*, like the cuckoo, is said to leave its eggs in the nests of other birds.

† Because the *kóil's* song is especially heard at the season of spring, the friend of love.

‡ The rose-apple, so denominated from its odour: it is, however, the *mahríjambu* that is mentioned in the text.

A tinkling melody. 'Tis the sweet chime
My fair one's anklets echo to her footsteps.

AIR.

Through the woods the stately elephant strays,
    And his glances despair express;
On his limbs the enfeebling malady preys,
    And his steps are slow with distress;
In his eyes the starting tear-drops swell,
As his thoughts on his lost companion dwell.

Alas! the gathering of the clouds deceives
The swan, who hails rejoicingly the time
For periodic flight to *Mánasa*.
I hear his song of gladness, not the sound
Of tinkling anklets. Ere yet the troop begins
Its distant march I will address the chief.
Ho! Monarch of the tribes that breast the stream,
Forbear a while your course: forego the provender
Of lotus stems, not needed yet, and hear
My suit—redeem me from despair—impart
Some tidings of my love; 'tis worthier far
To render kindly offices to others
Than meanly labour for a selfish good.
Though bent on *Mánasa*, he gazes on me,
As if to own he had beheld my love.
Why seek to veil the truth? If my beloved
Was never seen by thee as graceful straying
Along the flowery borders of the lake,
Then whence this elegant gait?—'Tis hers—and thou
Hast stolen it from her, in whose every step
Love sports—thy walk betrays thee; own thy crime,
And lead me quickly to her. (*Laughs.*) Nay, he fears
Our royal power—the plunderer flies the king.
                    [*Proceeds—Music.*

THE HERO AND THE NYMPH.

Yonder I see the *chakwa** with his mate;
Of him I will inquire.

AIR.

In groves of tall trees with bright blossoms blooming,
And vocal with many sweet murmured tones,
The lord of the herd, whom grief is consuming,
Distracted, the loss of his mate bemoans.

AIR. *After a pause.*

Ah no, he replies, I taste, on the wing,
The joys of the cool returning spring,
And as each feather thrills with delight,
I mark not the fair that meet my sight.

Yet tell me—hast thou seen her? Know'st thou not
Who asks thy answer? The great king of day
And monarch of the night are my progenitors:
Their grandson I, and by their own free choice,
The lord of Urvaśí and of the earth.
How—silent! Thou might'st measure my affliction
By what thou feelest; all the air resounds
With thy incessant plaints, if, but a moment,
Thy fair companion nestling hides in sport
Amongst the lotus leaves, and flies thy view.
Alas! to one whom fate has cursed like me,
Nought is propitious; I will ask no more.

[Proceeds—Music.

How beautiful the lotus!—it arrests
My path and bids me gaze on it—the bees
Murmur amidst its petals—like the lip
Of my beloved it glows, when that has been
Somewhat too rudely sipped by mine, and sweetly
Protests against such violence—I will woo
This honey-rifler to become my friend.

[Advances.

---

* The *Chakravāka* or *Ruddy* goose: the birds are supposed to be separated through the night.

AIR.

Unheeding the cygnet at first,
    His beak in the nectar of passion dips;
But fiercer and fiercer his thirst—
    As deeper he sips.
Say, plunderer of the honeyed dew, hast thou
Beheld the nymph whose large and languid eye
Voluptuous rolls, as if it swam with wine?
And yet methinks 'tis idle to inquire;
For had he tasted her delicious breath,
He now would scorn the lotus. I will hence.

                                           [*Proceeds.*

Beneath the shade of yon *kadamba* tree
The royal elephant reclines, and with him
His tender mate. I will approach—yet hold,
From his companion he accepts the bough
Her trunk has snapped from the balm-breathing tree,
Now rich with teeming shoots and juicy fragrance.
                                     [*Advances, then pauses.*
He crushes it! I may proceed.

AIR.

King of the forest, whose sports have felled
    The stateliest trees, the thicket's pride;
Oh, say, in these shades hast thou beheld,
    More bright than the moon, my wandering bride?
                                 [*Advancing a few paces.*
Chief of the mighty herd, say, hast thou seen
My love—like the young moon her delicate frame,
And with eternal youth her beauties glow;
Her voice is music—her long tresses wear
The jasmine's* golden hue. Hadst thou afar

---

* *Yathibi-hrvala-keli*, having hair brown as the yellow *jasmine*, golden or auburn,—a very strange idea for a Hindu. It is said that in the west of India such hair is sometimes seen, but the prejudice in favour of ebon locks is so strong that it is considered a morbid affection of the hair, and the women dye and conceal it.

Beheld her charms, they must have fixed thy gaze.
Ha, he replies ! That kind assenting roar
Conveys some intimation—oh repeat
The sound—consider that we should befriend
Each other, bound by various common ties.
Thou art the sovereign of the forest ; me
They term the king of men. Thy bounty sheds
Thy frontal fragrance on the air ; my wealth
On all is showered profuse. Amongst the bands
Of lovely nymphs, obedient to my will,
One only Urvasí commands my love ;
As thou hast chosen this, thy favourite,
From all the herd. Thus far our fates accord ;
And never be the pangs of separation,
Such as distract my bosom, known to thee ;
Propitious be thy fortunes. Friend, farewell.
[*Proceeds.*
What have we here ! Deep in the mountain's breast
A yawning chasm appears : such shades are ever
Haunts of the nymphs of air and earth. Perchance
My Urvasí now lurks within the grotto
In cool seclusion—I will enter. All
Is utter darkness. Would the lightning's flash
Now blaze to guide me—no, the cloud disdains,
Such is my fate perverse, to shed for me
Its many-channelled radiance. Be it so.
I will retire—but first the rock address.

AIR.

With horny hoofs and a resolute breast
  The boar through the thicket stalks ;
He ploughs up the ground, as he plies his quest
  In the forest's gloomiest walks.

Say, mountain, whose expansive slope confines
The forest verge, oh tell me, hast thou seen
A nymph as beauteous as the bride of love,

Mounting with slender frame thy steep ascent,
Or wearied resting in thy crowning woods?
How—no reply! remote he hears me not—
I will approach him nearer.

AIR.

From thy crystal summits the glistening springs
  Rush down the flowery sides,
And the spirit of heaven delightedly sings,
  As among thy peaks he hides.
Say, mountain so favoured, have the feet
Of my fair one pressed this calm retreat?

Now, by my hopes, he answers! he has seen her—
Where is she?—say. Alas! again deceived—
Alone I hear the echo of my words,
As round the cavern's hollow mouth they roll
And multiplied return. Ah, Urvasi! *(Faints.)*

            [*Recovers, and sits as exhausted.*
Fatigue has overcome me. I will rest
Upon the borders of this mountain torrent,
And gather vigour from the breeze that gleans
Refreshing coolness from its gelid waves.
Whilst gazing on the stream, whose now swollen waters
Yet turbid flow, what strange imaginings
Possess my soul and fill it with delight!
The rippling wave is like her arching brow;
The fluttering line of storks, her timid tongue;
The foamy spray, her white loose-floating vest;
And this meandering course the current tracks,
Her undulating gait; all these recall
My soon-offended love—I must appease her.

AIR.

Be not relentless, dearest,
  Nor wroth with me for ever.
I mark where thou appearest
  A fair and mountain river.

Like *Gangá* proud thou showest,
 From heavenly regions springing;
Around thee, as thou flowest,
 The birds their course are winging.

The timid deer confiding,
 Thy flowery borders throng;
And bees, their store providing,
 Pour forth enraptured song.

AIR.

In the lowering east the king of the deep
 Expects his coming bride;
His limbs are the clouds that darkly sweep
 The skirts of the heaving tide;
And his tossing arms are the tumbling waves,
Where the gale o'er the heaving billows raves.

With rapture he dances, the lord of the main,
 And proud in his state appears;
His steps are pursued by the monster train,
 The deep sea darkness rears;
And the curlew, the swan, and glistening shell,
And the lotus, the monarch's glory swell.

The bellowing surges his fame resound,
 And dash at the gates of heaven;
The sea with the sky they threat to confound,
 But back with shame are driven;
For now the young rains are armed for their right,
And their prowess arrests old Ocean's might.*
            [*Approaches, and bows.*

O nymph adored, what crime have I committed,
That thus you fly from one so wholly yours,
Who now implores your pity, and with terror

---

* This and the preceding verse are much expanded in the translation, in order to express their meaning; the first being very brief, and the second both brief and obscure.

Anticipates your loss! Relent—return—
This is not Urvasi. She would not quit me
Even for the Ocean King. What's to be done?
Fortune crowns those who yield not to despair—
I'll back to where my love first disappeared.
Yonder the black deer couchant lies; of him
I will inquire. O antelope, behold,
The royal elephant *Airdrata*,*
Scorched by the pangs of solitude, explores,
In search of his lost mate, the groves of *Nandana*;†
Whose close-embowering walks are resonant
With the glad *kòil's* song, as pleased he sips
The juicy nectar of the clustering blossoms.
How! he averts his gaze, as he disdained
To hear my suit! Ah, no!—he anxious marks
His doe approach him—tardily she comes,
Her frolic fawn impeding her advance.

AIR.

A nymph of heaven has left her sphere
To make a heavenly region here,
  And treads this sacred ground;
Her slender waist, her swelling hips,
Her languid eye, her ruby lips,
  With youth unfading crowned.
Oh tell me, through the tangled maze,
If wandering she has met thy gaze,
  Deer of the soft black eye,
Ere yet beneath the yawning brink
Of sorrow's gulph, immersed I sink?
  Befriend me, or I die—

                                                  [*Advances.*
Lord of the bounding herds, say, hast thou seen
My fair, whose large and languid eye resembles
That of thy tender mate? He heeds me not,

---

* The elephant of *Indra*.   † The garden of *Indra*.

But springs to meet his doe. Be happy both,
Though fate still adverse frowns on my desires.
                                    [*Proceeds, and pauses.*
How now !—what stream of ruddy radiance breaks
Through the cleft rock ? No flame could have survived
The fast descending torrents; 'tis perchance
Some sanguine fragment of the lion's feast.
No—'tis a gem—more roseate than the blush
Of the *asoka* blossom, and the sun
Would grasp it with his beams—it pleases me,
And I will make it mine.

            AIR.

    With tearful eye and dejected gaze,
        Despairing his love to meet,
    All lonely the royal elephant strays
        Through the forest's still retreat.

Why should I take the jewel ? She whose brow,
Bound with *Manddra* fillet, best had worn
The costly gem is far—far from me—why
Should I distain the ruby with my tears ?
                    [*Going—a voice in the air.*
    Take up the gem, my son; its radiant red
    The feet of *Hema's* holy daughter shed *
    And wondrous virtue gave. Let it adorn
    Thy hand, and thou wilt shortly cease to mourn
    Thy absent bride—once more by this restored
    To bless her sorrowing and lamented lord.
Pur. What voice is this ! Descends some friendly sage
    In pity of my griefs, or in some deer
    Disguised, directs me thus ? Seer, I obey
    And thank thy holy counsel. Gem divine,
    Restore me to my love, and I will bear thee

---

* *Gauri* or *Parvati*; the stone is fabled to have received its colour and virtues from contact with the soles of her feet stained with the red of the Mehndi (*Lawsonia inermis*).

High on my diadem, and hold thee ever
As dear as Iswara his crescent moon.

[*Takes the gem and proceeds, then pauses.*

What means this strange emotion, as I gaze
Upon this vine? No blossoms deck its boughs;
Nipped by the falling rains, like briny tears,
That wash the ruddy freshness from the lips,
The buds have perished, and the mournful shrub
All unadorned appears to pine in absence;
No bees regale her with their songs; silent
And sad, she lonely shows the image
Of my repentant love, who now laments
Her causeless indignation. I will press
The melancholy likeness to my heart.

AIR.

Vine of the wilderness, behold
    A lone heart-broken wretch in me,
Who dreams in his embrace to fold
    His love, as wild he clings to thee.
And might relenting fate restore
    To these fond arms the nymph I mourn,
I'd bear her hence, and never more
    To these forbidden haunts return.

[*Goes to embrace the creeper, which is transformed to Urvasi.**

What can this mean! through every fibre spreads
The conscious touch of Urvasi—yet all
I deemed her charms deceived me—let me wake
And realise the vision or dispel it.
'Tis no deceit—'Tis she—my best beloved. [*Faints.*

Urv. (*In tears.*) Revive, my lord.
Pur. (*Reviving.*) Thy loss, dear love, has plunged my sinking
    spirit

---

* Or, "enters as it were in its very place," *Tatah pravisati tatsthana eva Urvasi.*

Deep into dreariest gloom ; but now thy sight
Arrests my soul, and calls me back to bliss.

Urv. I knew not of your woe, myself deprived
Of conscious being.

Pur. How ! What mean you ? Speak !

Urv. I will explain ; but let me first implore
Forgiveness, that my causeless wrath has wrought
So sad a change in you.

Pur. Enough, enough ;
You mine once more, all else is quite forgotten,
And every thought is ecstasy. But come,
Say how you cheered your time, your lord away ?
For me—

AIR.*

I have sued to the starry-plumed bird,
   And the kóil of love-breathing song ;
To the lord of the elephant herd,
   And the bee as he murmured along ;
To the swan, and the loud waterfall,
   To the chakwa, the rock, and the roe :
In thy search have I sued to them all,
   But none of them lightened my woe.

Urv. To me, all news of my lamented lord
Came but in fond imaginings.

Pur. How thus ?

Urv. In ancient days, the warrior god adopted
A cœnobite's observance ; and for this,
Retiring to the woods that stud the vale
Of *Gandhamáddana*, then called *Akalusha*,
He framed this law—

Pur. What law ? Proceed !

Urv. The female that should rashly pass the bounds
Proscribed, and penetrate the forest shades,

* *Charchort.*

VOL. I.   R

Should instant metamorphose undergo,
And to a twining shrub should be transformed,
Alone from such sad change to be redeemed
By the celestial gem, whose ruby glow
Is gleaned from *Gauri's* foot. This law I broke.
Bewildered by the sage's imprecation,
I thoughtless plunged into the thicket's glooms
Shunned ever by the gods, and in a vine
My form and faculties a while were lost.

Pur. 'Tis all explained. No ordinary cause
I knew detained thee from me: thee, whose fears
Brooked not my momentary separation,
Even in thy dreams. The virtue of the gem,
As thou hast said, this day effects our meeting.
Behold it here!

Urv. The ruby of reunion:
This holy gem restores me to my nature.
   [*Takes it and puts it respectfully to her forehead.*

Pur. A moment thus: let me behold thy brow,
Irradiated by this heavenly jewel,
Like the red lotus ere its buds expand.

Urv. The king delights to flatter me; but now
Let us return to *Pratishthána*. Long
The city mourns its absent lord, and I,
The cause of his departure, shall incur
The angry censures of the people. Come,
How will it please you travel?

Pur. Yonder cloud
Shall be our downy car, to waft us swift
And lightly on our way; the lightnings wave
Its glittering banners, and the bow of Indra
Hangs as its over-arching canopy
Of variegated and resplendent hues.

AIR.

The ardent swan his mate recovers,
  And all his spirit is delight:
With her aloft in air he hovers,
  And homeward wings his joyous flight.

                    [*Exeunt on the cloud—Music.*

END OF THE FOURTH ACT.

ACT V.

THE PALACE OF PURÚRAVAS.

Enter MÁNAVAKA.

At last, thank the fates, the king has returned with Madam Urvasí from the groves of *Nandana*, the pleasant gardens of the Gods. My friend is once more attentive to his royal duties and the cares of state; yet he seems out of spirits. What should be the cause ? Except the want of children, he has nothing to grieve for. This is a bustling day. The king and his queen have just performed their royal ablutions where the *Yamuná* and the Ganges meet : he must be at his toilet by this time, and by joining him I shall secure a share of the flowers and perfumes prepared for him.

(*Noise behind.*) The ruby ! the ruby ! A hawk, taking it for a piece of flesh, has borne away the ruby of reunion which had been taken out of its red palm-leaf case, and was being carried to the king for him to wear while absent from the nymph !

Mán. Here's a pretty piece of work ! the jewel my friend so highly prized. Ho, here he comes, not yet attired. I will keep aloof.

Enter PURÚRAVAS *in haste, followed by the* CHAMBERLAIN, *a* HUNTER,[*] *and attendants.*

Pur. Where is the winged thief that rashly courts
  His own destruction, and presumes to violate
  The dwelling of his sovereign ?

---

[*] The *Vidúshaka*, in some copies *Richaka*, explained a *Kiráta* a forester. The *Kirátas*, the mountaineers and savage tribes of India, were known to the ancients as the *Cirrhadæ* on the Coromandel coast. They appear to have been independent, but were tributary to the Hindu kings, or perhaps only rendered personal service.

Hunter. Yonder he goes, the golden chain of the jewel hanging from his beak.

Pur. I see him! As he rapid flies around
In airy rings, the whirling chain appears
To hem him in a fiery circle.
What's to be done?

Mdá. (*Advancing.*) Punish him, to be sure; put the culprit to death.

Pur. Bring me my bow.

[*A female attendant* * *goes out and returns with a bow and arrows, which she gives to the king.*]

'Tis now too late—he flies
Far to the south, beyond the arrow's reach.
Red as *aśoka* flowers, the precious gem
Graces the sky; with sullen fires it glows
Like angry Mars, burning at intervals
Through the thick clouds that overhang the night.
My good *Tillarya* (*to the Chamberlain*), give command, the bird
Be tracked, and followed to his perch.

Cham. The king shall be obeyed.   [*Exit.*†

Mdá. Now please you sit; the thief will not be able to escape your power.

---

* A *Yavaní*, which is rather inexplicable. The Mohammedan princes had guards of African women in their harems, and the presence of female attendants in those of the Hindú sovereigns has also been adverted to; but the term *Yavana* has been applied by the later Hindús to the Mohammedans; and it is not likely that either Persian or Arabian women ever found their way into the inner apartments of Hindú princes, as personal attendants or guards. If, as has been supposed, *Yavanas* formerly implied Greeks, it is equally impossible that Greek women should have fulfilled such an office, as few could have found their way to India, or even to Bactria; and those would have been, it may be supposed, too highly valued by their countrymen to have been suffered to act as slaves to barbarians. Perhaps Tartarian or Bactrian women may be intended.

† There is evidently much more art in the conduct of the business in this place than in the Toy Cart. The Chamberlain would there have been sent out, and would have returned immediately, in all probability, instead of any dialogue filling up the interval.

Pur. (Sits.) Were it an ordinary gem, its loss
    Would move me not; but to lose this would vex
      me;
    To it I owe reunion with my love.
Mis. Well, there is this comfort, as you have the lady, you are no longer in need of the jewel.

    Enter the CHAMBERLAIN, *with an arrow and the jewel.*

Cham. Victory to your Grace! The bird, condemned by your Majesty's decree, has fallen, pierced by this shaft; the ruby is recovered. It has been cleansed with water; please you say to whom it shall be intrusted.
Pur. Ho, Forester! replace the gem
    Safe in its casket.
Hunter. As your Majesty commands.
                               [Exit the Kirâta or Forester.
Pur. Know you to whom the shaft belongs?
Cham. There is a name inscribed upon it, your Grace, but my eye-sight cannot distinguish the characters.
Pur. Let me see them.
       [Takes the arrow, and expresses wonder and delight.
Cham. With your Grace's leave I will now attend to other duties.   *[Exit.*
Mis. What does your Majesty study so intently?
Pur. Listen—"The arrow of the all-subduing Áyus,
    The son of Urvaśí and Purúravas."
Mis. Joy to your Grace! Fate has crowned your wishes.
Pur. How should this be? But for the interval
    Of the Naimisha* sacrificial rite,
    My Urvaśí has always been with me.
    I do recall, indeed, a transient period,
    When her soft cheek was paler than the leaf

---

* The *Naimishya* sacrifice is the great sacrifice performed at the *Naimisha* forest by the assembled sages, which lasted twelve years according to the *Mahábhárata*, a thousand according to the *Bhágavata*.

Cold-nipped and shrivelled, and her eloquent eye
Betrayed unwonted lassitude; aught else
I never noted.

Mdd. Oh, you must not suppose that the nymphs of heaven manage these matters like those of earth. No, no; they have the power to counteract all such appearances.

Pur. It may be so. Yet why this mystery?
Why keep from me all knowledge of my child?

Mdd. Oh, there 's no accounting for the fancies of celestial spirits.

Enter CHAMBERLAIN.

Cham. So please your Majesty, a saintly dame and a young lad from the hermitage of *Chyavana* * solicit admittance.

Pur. Let them enter—quick!

---

* *Chyavana* is the son of *Bhrigu*, the son of *Brahmá*, by his wife *Puloma*. A *Rákshasa*, or fiend, attempting to carry off *Puloma*, the child was prematurely born, whence his name, from *chyu*, to fall from. Upon his birth his splendour was such as to reduce the insulter of his mother to ashes (*Mahábhárata Ádi-Parva, Puloma-Adhyáya*). The sage having adopted a life of ascetic devotion, was so immersed in abstraction that he became completely covered with the nests of white ants. *Sukanyá*, the daughter of king *Saryáti*, wandering in the forest, observed what she thought two lights in an ant-hill, and thrust in two blades of *kusa* grass, which when withdrawn were followed by a flow of blood. Much alarmed, the princess repaired to her father and related what had happened. The king, conjecturing the truth, immediately went to the spot to deprecate the wrath of the *Rishi*, and pacified him by giving him the damsel in marriage. After being married some time, the *Aswini-Kumáras* passing by *Chyavana's* residence conferred upon him youth and beauty, in requital of which boons he gave them a share in the *soma* juice offered at sacrifices to the gods. The gods, with *Indra* at their head, opposed this grant, and *Indra* lifted up his hand to strike *Chyavana* dead with his thunderbolt, when the sage paralysed his arm. To appal the gods he created the demon *Mada*, intoxication personified, in terror of whom and of the power of the saint, the gods acceded to the participation of the *Aswini Kumáras* in divine honours. *Indra* was restored to the use of his arm, and *Mada* was divided and distributed amongst dice, women, and wine—*Bhavishyat-Purána*, and the *Dána-dharma* section of the *Mahábhárata*.

Enter a TÁPASÍ *or Female Ascetic, and a Boy with a bow in his hand.*

Mds. Observe him, sir. That warrior lad must be the owner of the arrow; he is your perfect image.

Pur. May it prove so! My imperfect sight
Is dimmed with tears; my heart is overcome
With tenderness, and strong emotions crowd
My agitated mind; on all my limbs
A sudden tremor seizes. How I long
To clasp him to my bosom!

Cham. Here pause, most reverend lady.

Pur. (*Bowing.*) Hail, holy dame!

Táp. May fortune ever wait
The glorious line of Soma! (*Apart.*) Now, methinks,
The king has inward intimation given him
I bring him here his son. (*Aloud.*) Boy, pay your homage.

[*Áyus bows.*

Pur. May your years be many!

Áyus. (*Apart.*) If I dared listen to my heart, I should
Believe this were my father, I his son;
For what affection else would give a charm
To the endearments and embrace of age?

Pur. What brings thee to our presence, saintly dame?

Táp. Let the king hear. This princely youth, the son
Of Urvasí, was for some cause confided,
Without your knowledge, to my secret care.
The ceremonies of his martial birth
The pious Chyavana has duly ministered,
Taught him the knowledge fitted to his station,
And lastly trained his growing youth to arms!"

---

* The original has *dhanurvidyá*, archery, which is always put for military science in general. That archery, however, was the predominant branch of the art among the Hindus, is evident from this use of the term, and from all descriptive accounts of heroic education. Ráma, his sons, the Pándavas, Áyus, and all other princes, are represented in the *Rámáyańa*, *Mahábhárata*,

But now my charge expires, for an act
This day achieved, unfits him to remain
An inmate of the peaceful hermitage.

Pur. What act?

Tap. Whilst on his mission with the *Rishi's* sons,
To gather fuel, flowers, and holy grass
From the adjacent woods, he aimed a shaft
Against a hawk, now perched upon a tree
With his fresh prey, and took his felon life.
This deed of blood excludes him from our haunts,
And by the sage's orders I conduct him
Again to Urvasí. I would see the queen.

Pur. Be seated, and meanwhile, Tálavya,
Apprise our queen, that we would see her here.
                                            [*Exit Chamberlain.*
Come hither, boy. As the moon's silver ray
Affects the lunar gem, his presence sheds
Spontaneous joy, and through each fibre darts
The consciousness that I behold my son.

Tap. Obey your sire.

[*The Prince advances and prostrates himself. Purúravas raises and embraces him, and places him on the footstool of his throne.*]

Pur. Salute your father's friend. Boy, fear not.

Mid. What should he fear? he has seen baboons enough in the hermitage.

Ayus. (*Smiling.*) Accept my homage, sir.

Mid. Fortune attend you ever!

    Enter URVASÍ, *preceded by the* CHAMBERLAIN.

Cham. This way, your Grace.

Urv. (*Seeing Ayus.*) What youth is this, who, in the royal presence,

and all poems and plays, as making archery a principal part of their education, furnishing a remarkable analogy, in this respect, to the practice of the ancient Persians and Scythians.

Armed with the bow and quiver, honoured sits
Upon the golden footstool, whilst the king
Is fondly playing with his twisted tresses!
Ha! *Satyavati* too! it is my son;
His growth outstrips my memory.

Par. Behold your mother, boy: her gaze intent
Is fixed upon you, and her heaving bosom
Has rent its veiling scarf.

Tdp. Haste to embrace her.

[*Ayus rises and goes to his Mother, who embraces him,
then, after a pause,*

Urv. Hail, holy mother!

Tdp. Ever may you know
Your lord's affection!

Ayus. Mother, accept my salutations.

Urv. (*Kisses him.*) My dear boy,
Be long your father's happiness and pride.
(*Advances.*) Glory to the king!

Par. To the matron, honour!

[*Hands Urvasi to a seat with him on the throne.*

Be seated all. [*They sit.*

Tdp. The princely youth is perfectly accomplished
In all the science that becomes his rank,
And is of years and strength to bear the load
Of martial mail. Unfitted to the thoughts
And duties of the tranquil hermitage,
I yield him, therefore, in the royal presence,
Back to his mother's arms.

Urv. And I receive him
Most willingly: for it is no longer meet
He should disturb the quiet of devotion.
When he is satiate with his father's sight
He may revisit you; till then, farewell.

Par. And bear my reverence to the holy sage.

Ayus. Will you not take me with you, *Satyavati*?

Tdp. No, my dear child: the labours of the student
Are all performed; 'tis time you enter now
On loftier duties,*
Ayus. Well, if it must be so,
Farewell; but send me here my favourite peacock.
Tdp. I will; and boy, remember that you heed
Your father ever. Peace be unto all! [*Exit.*
Pur. Thus blessed, my love, with thee and with my son,
I envy not the happiness of Indra.†
Urv. Ah, me! [*Weeps violently.*
Pur. What means this sudden grief!
Why, when I contemplate with ecstasy
The proud perpetuation of my race,
Should these dear drops in swift succession spread
A pearly fillet on thy heaving bosom!
Urv. Alas, my lord! the name of *Swarga's* king
Brings to my memory a dread decree
By him denounced, which, happy in the sight
Of this loved boy, I had a while forgotten.
When for your love I gladly left the courts
Of heaven, the monarch thus declared his will:—
" Go, and be happy with the prince, my friend;
But when he views the son that thou shalt bear him,
Then hitherward direct thy prompt return."
'Twas fear of this that bade me keep concealed
My infant's birth, and instant I conveyed him
To *Chyavana's* retreat, entrusting him
To yonder pious dame to be instructed;
Such my pretext, in our most sacred lore.
The fated term expires, and to console
His father for my loss, he is restored.—
I may no longer tarry.

* Or literally, " You enter now the second order, that of the householder."
† Or, " I think myself, like *Indra* with *Pavlomi* (his bride) and *Jayanta* (his son)."

Pur. Adverse fate
    Is still intent to mar my perfect joy.
    Scarce have I known the blessing of a son,
    When my fair bride is snatched from my embrace.
    The tree that languished in the summer's blaze,
    Puts forth reviving, as young rain descends,
    Its leafy shoots, when lo! the lightning bursts
    Fierce on its top and fells it to the ground.
Mdd. I see nothing left for this but to abandon the throne, assume the coat of bark, and betake yourself to the forests.*
Urv. But what remains for me, my task on earth
    Fulfilled? Once gone, the king will soon forget me.
Pur. Dearest, not so. It is no grateful task
    To tear our memory from those we love.
    But we must bow to power supreme; do you
    Obey your lord; for me, I will resign
    My throne to this our son, and with the deer
    Will henceforth mourn amidst the lonely woods.
Ayus. Excuse me, sire; my years are all unfit
    For such a burthen; one so long upheld
    By such exalted merits.
Pur. Fear it not.
    The elephant cub † soon tames the forest herds;
    The snake scarce hatched concocts the deadly poison;
    Kings are in boyhood monarchs, and endowed
    With powers inborn to rule the race of man:
    Nature, not age, gives fitness. (*To the Chamberlain.*)
        Tálavya, bid
    Our ministers and priests be all prepared
    For this our son's inauguration—speed!

---

* Such appears to have been a common practice with the princes of India, when satiate with years and power, or disgusted with the world.

† The young *gandhagaja* soon subdues other elephants, is the expression in the original. They are said to fly the odour of some particular excretion, whence the name of the animal.

Cham. I obey.
  [*Exit sorrowfully, and all on the scene express grief.*
Pur. What sudden splendour breaks! whence are these
    flashes
  Of lightning in a cloudless sky?
Urv. 'Tis Nárada.
Pur. His braided curls are of a golden dye;
  His sacred cord, bright as the silver moon;
  Around his neck are strings of heavenly pearl;
  Like a celestial tree with glittering stem
  He moves. Prepare we to receive him.
Urv. Here,
  This offering of respect, gathered in haste,
  Present the sage.
              [*Gives the king some flowers.*

    NÁRADA *descends.*

Nár. Triumph attend
  The brave defender of this middle sphere!
Pur. (*Presenting the oblation.*) Reverence to the sage!
Urv. Accept my homage.   [*Bows.*
Nár. Never be wife and husband disunited.
Pur. (*Apart.*) Oh, might this be! (*Aloud.*) Advance, my son,
    and pay
  Your adoration to the holy seer.
Ayus. Áyus, the son of Urvasí, presumes
  To pay you homage.   [*Bows to Nárada.*
Nár. May your days be many! King, attend:
  The mighty Indra, to whom all is known,
  By me thus intimates his high commands:—
  Forego your purpose of ascetic sorrow.
  The sages, to whose wisdom past and future
  Are as the present, have foretold at hand
  Hostilities in heaven, and the gods will need
  Your prowess: then relinquish not your arms

And Urvasí shall be* through life united
With thee in holy bonds.
Urv. These happy words
Extract a barbed arrow from my bosom.
Pur. Whatever Indra wills I shall obey.
Nár. 'Tis wisely said : he will not be unthankful.
The fiery element sustains the sun ;
The sun returns his rays to nourish fire.
[*Looking upwards.*
Rambhá, appear, and bring the holy wave
Consigned by Indra to your charge, to consecrate
The prince's elevation to the throne,
As partner of the empire.†
[*Rambhá and other nymphs descend with a golden vase containing the water of the heavenly Ganges, a throne and other paraphernalia, which they arrange.*
Ram. All is prepared.
Nár. Prince, to your seat.
[*Náradu leads Ayus to the throne of Inauguration, takes the golden ewer from Rambhá, and pours water on the head of the prince.*
Rambhá, complete the rite.
[*Rambhá and the Apsarasas perform the rest of the ceremony.*]‡
Ram. Now, prince, salute your parents and the sage.
[*As Ayus bows to them respectively, they reply.*
Nár. Unvarying fortune wait upon thy reign !
Pur. My son, sustain the honour of your lineage.
Urv. My son, be still obedient to thy sire.
[*Chorus of bards without.*

* This is a very material variation in the story as told in the play and in the *Puráńas*: the passage *Tena sa imám sastrem manyastaryam ; iyaṁ cha Urvasí pdraddyus tárat mhadharmachárídí bhavishyati.*

† As Yayanitja, young king or Cæsar.

‡ The stage directions in the original are not more explicit, and the comment is silent.

Glory, all glory, on Áyus attending,
 Still in the son may the father we trace;
Justice and valour together extending
 The sway of his sceptre and fame of his race.
Son of the monarch the universe filling,
 Son of the God of the mist-shedding night,
Son of the sage,* whom the great Brahmá willing,
 Called with creation to life and to light.

Second Chorus.

Now bright o'er the regions the glories are gleaming,
 The sceptre and sway of the father have won,
And brighter than ever the radiance is streaming,
 Enhanced and confirmed by the fame of the son.
So Gangá descends from the peaks of the mountain
 That shine with the light of unperishing snows,
And mighty, meandering far from their fountain,
 In the breast of the ocean the waters repose.

Ram. (*To Urvasi.*) No ordinary fate, dear sister, blesses you
 With such a son and lord.

Urv. I own my happiness.
 Come, my dear child, and offer to the queen,
 Your elder mother, filial homage.

Pur. Hold,
 One moment; we will presently together.

N'dr. The splendours of your son's inauguration
 Bring to my memory the glorious time
 When *Mahásena* † was anointed chief
 Of all the heavenly hosts.

---

* Or the son of Purúravas, the son of Budha, the son of Chandra or the moon, the son of the sage Atri, one of the will-engendered sons of the creator Brahmá.

† Kártikeya, the son of Siva, who shortly after his birth was appointed general of the armies of heaven, against the Daityas or Titans under Táraka.

Pur. To you I owe
Such honour.
Nár. Is there ought else Indra can do
To serve his friend?
Pur. To hold me in esteem
Is all I covet. Yet haply may this chance :—
May learning and prosperity oppose
No more each other, as their wont, as foes,
But in a friendly bond together twined,
Ensure the real welfare of mankind.*

[*Exeunt omnes.*

---

* A singular but characteristic concluding benediction. One copy adds a stanza desiderative of universal prosperity, but it does not occur in another. It may be here observed that the translation has been made from two copies of the text and one of the comment, all of them full of blunders. The sense has therefore often been made out conjecturally.

REMARKS

ON

THE HERO AND THE NYMPH.

IF it was necessary to peruse the preceding drama with a liberal allowance for national peculiarities, it is equally requisite, in the present instance, to adapt our faith to the national creed, and to recognize, for poetical and dramatic purposes, the creations of the mythology of the Hindus.

In this respect, however, no very violent demand is made upon our imagination, as we have none of the monstrous extravagancies of the system forced upon our credulity. The intercourse of heroes and of goddesses is the familiar theme of our youthful studies, and the transformation of Urvaśí into a vine is not without abundant parallels in the metamorphoses of Ovid. The personages and situations of the superhuman portion of the drama are both elegant and picturesque; and the grouping of the nymphs upon the peaks of the Himálaya, or the descent of Nárada through the fields of ether, might be represented with as much beauty as facility by the machinery of the theatres of Europe.

There is also a peculiarity in the mythos of this drama, which identifies it with the dramatic compositions of antiquity. Trivial as the incidents may appear, unimportant as may be the loves of the hero and the heroine, both persons and events are subject to an awful control, whose interference invests them with a dignity superior to their natural level. Fate is the ruling principle of the narrative; and the monarch and the nymph, and the sovereign of the gods himself, are portrayed as subject to the inscrutable and inevitable decrees of destiny.

The simplicity of the story does not admit of much display of character, but the timid constancy of Urvasí is not unhappily contrasted with the irresolute haughtiness of the queen. The poet, too, has shown himself not unacquainted with the springs of human feelings, and his observations on the relations of the sexes in domestic life are equally shrewd and just.

The chief charm of this piece, however, is its poetry. The story, the situations, and the characters are all highly imaginative, and nothing, if partiality for his work does not mislead the translator, can surpass the beauty and justice of many of the thoughts. To select one as an example were to disparage a number of other passages, and they may be left to the critical acumen and taste of the reader.

UTTARA-RÁMA-CHARITRA,

OR

CONTINUATION OF THE HISTORY OF RÁMA.

A Drama,

TRANSLATED FROM THE ORIGINAL

SANSKRIT.

INTRODUCTION.

The Uttara-Rāma-Charitra, or continuation of the history of Rāma, is one of the three dramas attributed to Bhavabhúti, and the internal evidence of the composition fully corroborates the traditional appropriation. The style is equally vigorous and harmonious as that of the *Málatí* and *Mádhava*; several of the sentiments found in that play recur in this; and the general character of the two dramas, notwithstanding the difference of their subjects, offers many analogies. We have the same picturesque description and natural pathos in both.

The subject of the Uttara-Rāma-Charitra is, as the name implies, a continuation of the history of Rāma, the prince of Ayodhyá, and comprises the events that occurred subsequent to the war which constitutes the subject of the *Rámáyana*. It is taken from the last or supplementary section of that poem, one of the two principal poetical works of the Hindus not wholly mythological, and which have some pretensions to be included in the Epic class. It is, however, more correctly speaking, a continuation of a play by the same author, the *Víra-Ráma-Charitra*, in which the martial exploits of Rāma, as described in the *Rámáyana*, are dramatised. The date at which the *Uttara-Ráma-Charitra* was composed cannot be deduced, with certainty, from anything that occurs in the course of the play. It offers nothing, however, that is incompatible with the period at which the author is said to have flourished, or the eighth century, as will be noticed in the introduction to *Málatí* and *Mádhava*. The style is classical, and although elaborate, is not deformed by extravagant refinement. The thoughts are pure and undisgraced by conceits; and altogether the composition belongs to the era of good taste in Hindu writing, although in an advanced period, and upon the eve of its decline. But the most decided evidence of an early date is furnished by the allusions to the *Vedas*, and to some parts of the Hindu ritual which are not now familiarly known, and which there is reason to think have long fallen into disuse. The condition of the Hindu religion must have been very different, when this drama was composed, from any under which it has been observable for some centuries past.

The story of RÁMA has been communicated to European readers so fully in the writings of Jones, Wilford, Maurice, Ward, and Faber, as well as in the *Hindu Pantheon* of Moor, and in the translation of the two first books of the *Rámáyaṇa*, by the Rev. Messrs. Carey and Marshman, of Serampore, as well as probably by this time in the translation of the whole poem by A. W. Schlegel, that the events which precede the action of the following drama will be familiar to many of those who may peruse it. In order, however, to render it intelligible to those to whom the story may be unknown, a brief recapitulation of the previous adventures of its hero may not be superfluous. The author himself has not thought a preparation of this kind unnecessary even for a Hindu audience, as he has introduced, with some ingenuity, a summary sketch of the leading incidents of RÁMA'S earlier career. A reference to the notes accompanying that part of the drama will more fully explain the circumstances there alluded to, and supply some particulars of RÁMA'S adventures, not comprised in the following brief narrative.

The deities of the Hindu Pantheon by no means enjoy undisturbed possession of divinity, and they are obliged to contend for their own supremacy, or for the protection of the world, with various formidable races known as *Asuras*, *Daityas*, *Dánavas*, and *Rákshasas*, or different orders of Titanic and gigantic beings of superhuman strength and vitality, who, from the earliest periods,

Extruere montes ad sidera summa parabant,
Et magnum bello solicitare Jovem.

Of these, the *Rákshasas* bear the least of a celestial character, and belong to the malignant creations of ancient and modern fable, who to gigantic strength and stature unite particular hostility to man, and an appetite for human flesh. In the poetical mythology of the Hindus they are descended from BRAHMÁ through one of his will-born progeny, the sage and saint PULASTYA; but their numbers are every day augmented by the addition of the disembodied spirits of wicked men, condemned to this form for a season, in punishment of their crimes; and the class also comprehends sundry deformed and hideous bands, who are especially attached to the service of the god of wealth, and are supposed to keep watch over his treasures.

The first and most celebrated of the posterity of PULASTYA were RÁVAŃA and his brethren—
——propago
Contemtrix superum, sævæque avidissima cædis,
Et violenta.

The half brother of KUVERA the god of wealth, RÁVAŃA, a *Rákshasa* with ten heads, dispossessed that deity of his capital *Lanká*, in which he seated himself, and thence spread terror, not only over the world, but throughout the heavens, compelling many of the subordinate divinities to perform the menial functions of his palace. To terminate these violences and alarms, VISHŃU was obliged to come down to earth, where he was born as RÁMA or RÁMACHANDRA, the eldest son of DAŚARATHA, a prince of the Solar dynasty and sovereign of *Ayodhyá* or *Oude*, by his wife KAUŚALYÁ. Other portions of the same deity animated the sons of DAŚARATHA, by his other wives, KAIKEYÍ and SUMITRÁ, the former of whom gave birth to BHARATA, and the latter to LAKSHMAŃA and ŚATRUGHNA. A number of the minor deities and the attendant spirits of heaven likewise assumed terrestrial shapes, and in the form of apes and bears became the warriors and allies of RÁMA.

Whilst yet a lad, the services of RÁMA were solicited by the sage VIŚWÁMITRA to repel and slay the fiends, by whom the religious rites of himself and other pious individuals were interrupted. RÁMA accordingly accompanied him, destroyed the *Rákshasí* or female fiend TÁRAKÁ, and slew or chased other evil genii from the residence of the sages. On this occasion VIŚWÁMITRA transferred to RÁMA and his descendants the command of the celestial weapons, or the power to wield the elements in war.

After these exploits, VIŚWÁMITRA conducted RÁMA to *Mithilá*, the kingdom of JANAKA, whose daughter SÍTÁ, now marriageable, was to reward the prowess of the prince who should bend a bow, given to an ancestor of the monarch of *Mithilá* by the god SIVA. RÁMA alone succeeded in the attempt, and snapped the bow asunder. The indignity thus offered to his tutelary divinity aroused the wrath of PARAŚURÁMA, a previous incarnation of VISHŃU, still upon earth, who, coming to *Mithilá* to defy and exterminate RÁMACHANDRA, was foiled by his junior, and obliged to return, humbled and in peace, to the retirement whence he had hastened on hearing of the bow's being broken. RÁMA received the recompense of his vigour in the hand of SÍTÁ; and at the same time URMILÁ her sister, and MÁNDAVÍ and SRUTAKÍRTTI, her cousins, were married to the other three sons of DAŚARATHA.

When RÁMA approached to years of maturity, his father, by the advice of his ministers, and according to the wishes of his people, proposed to associate him in the government as *Yuvarájá*, young king, or Cæsar: a delegation of authority that seems to have been constant under the old political system of the Hindus, and traces of which have been preserved to the present day, in the petty Hindu states to the east of Bengal. Domestic intrigue, however, forced DAŚARATHA to forego his purpose, and to change the elevation of RÁMA into exile. His second wife, KAIKEYÍ, instigated by the counsels of a female attendant, insisted upon the king's fulfilment of a promise which he had formerly made, and which, like the pledge of the gods of *Olympus*, was not to be recalled, whatever mischief might ensue. DAŚARATHA, when formerly wounded dangerously in battle, was preserved by the cares of KAIKEYÍ; in acknowledgment of which service he offered her two boons whenever she should demand them. These she now claimed,—the installation of her son BHARATA, and the banishment of RÁMA for fourteen years, and DAŚARATHA was forced to comply, although upon the departure of his son he expired with grief. BHARATA refused to accept the succession to the throne, and hastened after RÁMA to bring him back to the capital; but that prince, in veneration of his father's memory, determined to fulfil his injunction, notwithstanding his decease; and leaving BHARATA regent during his absence, repaired to the forests of Southern India, accompanied by his wife, and LAKSHMAŃA his brother.

Conformably to current traditions, and the evidence of names assigned to different places in the peninsula, RÁMA passed from *Ayodhyá* to the south-west, and first established himself near the sources of the *Godávarí* in the *Daśdaka* forest. On his journey, and during his residence in the thickets, he encountered and discomfited various members of the RÁKSHASA tribe, and amongst others maltreated SÚRPAŚANKÁ, the sister of RÁVAŃA, requiting the tender sentiments with which he inspired her by cutting off her nose and ears. She first applied to her brothers, KHARA and DÚSHAŃA, who guarded the forests with numerous bands of RÁKSHASAS, to avenge her; but when they were slain in the quarrel by the sons of DAŚARATHA, she carried her complaints to RÁVAŃA in *Lanká*, and instigated him to resent the injuries that had been inflicted on her person, especially by inspiring him with a passion for SÍTÁ. In order to effect his purpose RÁVAŃA repaired to *Panchdvatí*, the residence of RÁMA, with MÁRÍCHA, the son of TÁRAKÁ, who, transforming himself into a deer, beguiled RÁMA from his cottage in chase of the supposed animal. LAKSHMAŃA, by desire of SÍTÁ, going to look for his brother, she was left alone, on which RÁVAŃA, approaching her as an old mendicant, then discarded his disguise, and carried her off. On his way he was at first stopped by

JAṬÁYU, a mythological being, a chief of the winged tribes, and a friend of DAŚARATHA, who was speedily overcome and left mortally wounded, and RÁVAŇA effected his retreat to Lanká without further opposition.

On returning to his cottage and searching for his missing bride, RÁMA discovered the wounded JAṬÁYU, and before he expired, learned from him who was the ravisher of SÍTÁ, but not his residence; in quest of which, he plunged into the forests in the central part of the peninsula, and by the advice of a headless monster, whom he slew, repaired to the mountain *Rishyamúka* at the sources of the *Pampá* river, where SUGRÍVA, the monarch of the monkeys, held his court. On arriving at this spot, he found the monkey monarchy distracted by intestine divisions, and SUGRÍVA deprived of his wife and shorn of his authority by his brother BÁLI. RÁMA having formed an alliance with SUGRÍVA, engaged and killed BÁLI, and restored to his associate the supreme sovereignty over the baboons, and the capital *Kishkindhyá*. SUGRÍVA, in acknowledgment of this service, dispatched his principal monkeys in all directions to discover SÍTÁ, in which search HANUMAT was successful. The party he accompanied, headed by ANGADA, the son of BÁLI, proceeded southward to the sea, where they encountered SAMPÁTI the brother of JAṬÁYU, by whom they were apprised of the site of *Lanká* and the detention of SÍTÁ there by its ten-headed king. HANUMAT undertook to seek her there; and jumping across the arm of the sea, obtained access to the palace where SÍTÁ was confined, and an interview with that princess. Having thus ascertained the place of her existence, HANUMAT, after setting *Lanká* on fire, returned to RÁMA, and conveyed to him the information which he had been sent out to procure.

On receipt of this intelligence, RÁMA, accompanied by SUGRÍVA and an innumerable host of his monkey subjects, advanced to the point of the peninsula opposite to the northern extremity of Ceylon, where a passage across the channel by which that island is separated from the Coromandel coast was accomplished, by casting rocks and mountains into the sea, and thus constructing a bridge, the vestiges of which are said to be still visible in the reef of rocks which render the Straits of Manar impassable to vessels of burthen. At this point, RÁMA was joined by VIBHISHAŃA, the brother of RÁVAŃA, who having in vain counselled the restitution of SÍTÁ, and incurred by his advice the displeasure of the sovereign of Lanká, deserted his cause and went over to the enemy.

Having crossed the sea and encamped in the vicinity of the capital of RÁVAŃA, the baboon army was encountered by the monstrous bands in the service of Lanká, and a variety of engagements ensued, which, although attended by the occasional discomfiture of the assailants, ended in the utter defeat of the RÁKSHASAS, and the death of RÁVAŃA by the hands of RÁMA. Upon his fall SÍTÁ was recovered; but before being readmitted to her husband's embraces, she was compelled to vindicate her purity by undergoing the ordeal of fire. Having passed unhurt through the blazing pile, and being further justified by the oral testimony of BRAHMÁ and other gods, as well as the spirit of DAŚARATHA, her father-in-law, she was once more united to RÁMA, who, installing VIBHISHAŃA in the kingdom of Lanká, over which he is supposed still to reign, returned to Ayodhyá, where BHARATA gladly restored the sovereignty to his brother.

The incidents that immediately followed the return of RÁMA to his capital form the subject of the drama, and therefore require no notice in this place. The catastrophe is, however, differently brought about in the RÁMÁYAŃA and Raghuvanśa, a poetical account of RÁMA and his race, and closes in a different manner. RÁMA discovers his sons in consequence of their recital of the RÁMÁYAŃA at his sacrifice, and SÍTÁ, upon her innocence being recognised by the people, is suddenly carried off by the goddess of the earth, and disappears for ever. This dénouement is very judiciously altered to her reunion with her sons and husband, in the play. RÁMA died soon after the disappearance of SÍTÁ, and divided his kingdom between his sons; but KUŚA, being the elder, and having established his capital at *Ayodhyá*, is regarded as the continuer of the line of RAGHU. The *Kachwáha Rájpúts* affect to derive their descent from KUŚA, whilst another *Rájpút* tribe, the *Baldkuja*, regard LAVA as the founder of their race.

DRAMATIS PERSONÆ

MEN.

Ráma.—King of *Ayodhyá*.
Kuśa, } his twin sons.
Lava,
Lakshmaña.—The brother of *Ráma*.
Chandraketu.—The son of *Lakshmaña*.
Válmíki.—A holy sage, the author of the *Rámáyaña*, and preceptor of *Kuśa* and *Lava*.
Janaka.—The father of *Sítá*, formerly king of *Mithilá*, now leading an ascetic life.
Sambúka.—An ascetic killed by *Ráma*, but appearing in his spiritual character.
Ashídrakva.—An ascetic.
Sumantra.—The charioteer of *Chandraketu*.
Durmukha.—An emissary employed by *Ráma*.
Saudhátaki, } two of *Válmíki's* pupils.
Bháduáyana,
A *Vidyádhara.*—A male spirit of air.

WOMEN.

Sítá.—The wife of *Ráma*.
Arundhatí.—A pious dame, the wife of the sage *Vasishtha* and guardian of *Sítá*.
Átreyí.—A pious dame, the wife of the sage *Atri*.
Kauśalyá.—The aged mother of *Ráma*.
Vásantí.—The guardian spirit of the forest of *Janasthána*.
Tamasá.—A river goddess.
Muralá.—The same.
A *Vidyádharí.*—A female spirit of air.

CHARACTERS IN THE SCENE IN THE LAST ACT.

Gangá.—The goddess of the Ganges.
Pṛithiví.—The goddess of the earth.
        Celestial spirits, guards, pupils, &c.

THE SCENE of the first Act is in the Palace of *Ráma* at *Ayodhyá*; of the second, in the forest of *Janasthána* along the *Godávarí*; in the rest of the piece it lies in the vicinity of *Válmíki's* hermitage at *Bithúr* on the Ganges.

An interval of twelve years occurs between the first Act and the remainder of the play. The time of each Act is that of representation.

PRELUDE.

Enter MANAGER.

Man. I praise the foot of the illustrious *Bharabhúti.*[*] We present this our salutation to the celebrated bards of old, and thus we obtain the divine goddess of eloquence,[†] who is a portion of the Supreme Spirit.

This being the festival of the glorious *Kálapriya-Nátha*,[‡] I apprise you, sirs, that we purpose representing the *Uttara-Ráma-Charitra*, the composition of *Bharabhúti*, entitled *Srí-Kantha*, of the race of *Kasyapa*, and assimilated to an equality with *Brahmá* by the favour of *Saraswatí*.[§] I act a native of *Ayodhyá*,[||] and a stranger approaches——

This is the season of the inauguration of the renowned Ráma,

---

[*] The first sentence in this introductory benediction, *Sri-karintja-Bharabhúti-charmádni nausmi*, is not noticed by the commentator, and has been omitted in the Calcutta edition of the text, in consequence, no doubt, of its being considered, as it evidently is, the work of a different hand. The rest of the passage is of a peculiar character, but is probably part of the original composition.

[†] Or, literally, "We acquire divine ambrosial speech."

[‡] The *Málatí* and *Mádhava* was composed for a similar festival.

[§] The goddess of eloquence and wife of *Brahmá*; the allusions to *Bharabhúti*'s family decent are explained in the *Málatí* and *Mádhava*.

[||] *Ayodhyá* is the original of the name now given to a whole province or kingdom, *Awadh* or *Oude*. It was formerly confined to the capital, the kingdom bearing the designation of *Kósala*. It was for many years the sovereignty of the princes of the Solar line. The remains of the ancient city are still to be seen at the town of Oude, situated on the banks of the Ghagra, seventy-nine miles from Lucknow and adjoining Fyzabad.

the threatening meteor of the race of *Pulastya*;* and the drum of rejoicing sounds unweariedly by night and day. But what should this mean; why are the public places to-day so silent and unfrequented?

Enter ACTOR.

Act. The monkey chiefs,† and friendly fiends, and all the warriors in alliance with the prince in the war of Lanká, have

---

* Intending especially the giant king of *Lanká*, *Rávaña*, and his brothers destroyed in the war with *Ráma*. *Rávaña* was the son of the sage *Vísravas*, by *Nikashá*, the daughter of *Sumáli*, a demon, who, observing the splendour of *Kuvera*, a son of the sage by his wife *Iravini*, directed his daughter to propitiate the sage, that she also might have children by him. Having succeeded in obtaining the good graces of *Vísravas*, *Nikashá* had by him *Rávaña*, *Kumbhakarña*, and *Vibhíshaña*, and a daughter, *Súrpañakhá*.

Rávaña was engendered after the performance of a sacrifice with fire, in consequence of which he was born of an uncouth appearance, with ten heads and twenty arms. *Vísravas*, his father, was the son of *Pulastya*, one of the will-begotten sons of *Brahmá*. Although, therefore, a holy sage, he is often alluded to as the progenitor of the *Rákshasas*, of which race *Rávaña* and his brethren were such distinguished members (*Uttara-Rámáyaña* and *Padma Purana*). The *Bhágavata* agrees nearly with them, but names the mother of the *Rákshasas*, *Khumbhínasí*.

A very different legend is given in the *Vana-Parvan*, of the *Mahábhárata*. *Pulastya*, the son of *Brahmá*, begot *Kuvera*, who, by paying great attention to his grandfather, was made by him immortal, and appointed the god of wealth. His capital was *Lanká*, and the *Rákshasas* were his guards. His carrying favour with *Brahmá* incensed his father, and *Pulastya* assumed the form of a holy sage, named *Vísravas*. To propitiate this wrathful manifestation of his father was *Kuvera's* next object, and with this view he gave him three *Rákshasís* as handmaids, *Pushpotkatá*, *Ráká*, and *Málini*. By the first *Vísravas* had *Kumbhakarña* and *Rávaña*; by the second, *Khara*, and a daughter, *Súrpañakhá*; and by *Málini*, *Vibhíshaña*.—We have a different account again in the *Linga-Purana* (ch. 63). *Pulastya* had by *Iravilá*, the daughter of *Tṛiṇavinda*, a son named *Vísravas*, who had four wives: *Devavarñiní*, the daughter of *Vṛihaspati*; *Pushpotkatá*, and *Ráká* (or *Vákâ*), the daughters of the demon *Mályavat*, and *Nikashá*, the daughter of the demon *Sumáli*. By the first he had *Kuvera*, or *Vaisravaña*; by the second, *Mahodara*, *Prahasta*, *Mahápáráva*, and *Khara*, and *Karáñansí*, a daughter; by the third he had *Triṣiras*, *Dushaña*, and *Vidyujjihwa*, and *Śyámiká*, a daughter; and by the last, or *Nikashá*, the virtuous *Vibhíshaña*.

† *Ráma* was accompanied on his return to *Ayodhyá* by *Vibhíshaña*, the brother and successor of *Rávaña*, and by the monkey chiefs, *Sugríva*, *Anga-*

been dismissed to their several homes, as have the holy sages, assembled from various realms, whose reception has been hitherto the occasion of perpetual festivity.

Rama. True: and the mothers of *Rághava*,* under the guidance of Vasishtha,† and preceded by Arundhatí,‡ have departed to the dwelling of their son-in-law.

Act. I am a stranger here, you know; inform me who is this son-in-law?

Mana. The late king *Dasaratha*§ had a daughter named *Sántá*, whom he gave to king *Lomapáda* to adopt, and whom *Rishyasringa*‖ the son of *Vibhándaka*, espoused.¶ He now holds the ceremony of the twelve years' sacrifice,** and the elders have gone to assist at its celebration, leaving with his

---

da. and *Hanumat.* They assisted at his coronation, and then returned to their dwellings in the *Dekhin* and *Lanká.*

* Or *Ráma.* The term is a patronymic, implying his being a descendant of *Raghu.* His mothers are the widows of his father *Daśaratha:* *Kauśalyá*, the mother of *Ráma*; *Sumitrá*, the mother of *Lakshmaṇa* and the youngest son, *Satrughna*; and *Kaikeyí*, the mother of the third son, *Bharata.*

† The family priest of *Ráma*'s race, the son of *Brahmá* in one birth, and of *Mitra* and *Varuṇa*, or the sun and the sea, in another.

‡ Arundhatí is the wife of Vasishtha.

§ *Daśaratha*, the son of *Aja* and father of *Ráma*, was a distinguished prince of the Solar dynasty. Buchanan supposes him to have lived in the fifteenth century before the Christian era.

‖ *Rishyaśringa*, the *deer-horned*, was born of a doe, and had a small horn on his forehead; whence his name.

¶ These circumstances are all narrated in the *Rámáyaṇa* at length.— Book 1, sections viii. ix. x. *Lomapáda* was king of Anga.

** This number offers some analogy to the visits of the gods to Ethiopia's blameless race; when

"Twelve days the powers indulged the genial rite."

Macrobius, however, would read this twelve hours, or the interval between sun-set and sun rise, when Jove, as that planet, is below the horizon. It is true, the original leaves him at liberty to propose such a reading, as neither days nor hours are specified in this place. The return of the deities, however, is more specific.

Twelve *days* were passed, and now the dawning light
The gods had summoned to the Olympian height.

The same critic conceives, also, that some allusion may be made to the

permission, the daughter of Janaka* at the capital. But come, time wears; let us go meet our friends at the palace, as was appointed.

Act. But tell me, in your opinion, has the title of *Most Pure* been very judiciously granted by the king to his bride ?

Muna. Mind your own affairs; why talk upon improper subjects ? Men are ever evil disposed towards the purity of words and women.

Act. Most maliciously true: especially as the calumnies insinuated against *Vaidehi*,† in consequence of her residence in the dwelling of the *Rákshasa*, were refuted by her passing the fiery ordeal.‡

signs of the zodiac.—(Sat. 1. xxiii. Somn. Scipion. lib. 2.) The number has very possibly some secret import, astronomical or mythological, both amongst the Hindus and Greeks.

* *Janaka* was king of Mithila, and a man of great piety and learning. He was the reputed father of Sítá, the wife of Ráma, having found her an infant in the earth, upon ploughing it for a sacrifice.

† Sítá bears the patronymic *Vaidehi* as the daughter of the king of *Videha*.

‡ After the recovery of Sítá from *Rávana*, Ráma welcomed her coldly, and after intimating some suspicions unfavourable to her chastity, refused to receive her: on which Sítá determined to commit herself to the test of fire. Having entered the fire prepared for this purpose in the presence of the gods and of *Dasaratha*, the deceased father of Ráma, it proved innocuous, and *Agni*, its deity, restored Ráma his bride unhurt, and declared her purified by the ordeal she had undergone. *Dasaratha* also bore testimony to Sítá's virtue, and Ráma's doubts being thus dissipated, he joyfully received his bride (*Uttara-Rámáyana*.) According to the *Brahma-Vaivarta-Purána*, Sítá herself was not carried off by *Rávana*, her shadow or *chháyá* being substituted by *Agni* for her substance. It was this semblance, also, that entered the fire, in order to give *Agni* an opportunity of restoring the original to Ráma. The *Padma-Purána* (*Pátála Khanda*) dispenses with the ordeal, but brings forward *Agni*, *Váyu*, *Varuna*, *Brahmá*, and *Dasaratha* to swear to Sítá's innocence; *Brahmá* farther consoles Ráma by declaring it was necessary Sítá should have been carried off by *Rávana*, as his rape of a virtuous woman was the only cause of destruction to which he was subject, agreeably to the curse denounced upon him by *Nala-Kuvera*, and the previous boon conferred upon him by *Brahmá*. In the *Uttara-Khanda* of the same *Purána*, she enters into the fire, as in the other authorities.

Man. Yet, should such reports as are still current reach the king, they will cause him great distress.

Ad. The sages and the gods will provide for the best. Where is his Majesty? (*Listening.*) Oh, I hear Janaka, his father-in-law, has just left him to return to his own kingdom; and the king has quitted his seat of justice to repair to the inner apartments to console the queen.

[*Exeunt.*

ACT I.

Scene 1.—The Palace.

Ráma *and* Sítá *discovered.*

Droop not, dear Sítá; our respected friends
Have parted from us with no less reluctance
Than we have felt, but duty must be done.
To loftier claims must self-indulgence yield;
And they who venerate their household fire
Must bear the task such sacred charge imposes.*

Sítá. I know the truth of this, my dearest lord;
But still to separate from our nearest friends
And cherished kindred, cannot choose but grieve us.

Ráma. True, love—
But these, the sorrows of a feeling heart,
Are the sad portion of man's social life:
And, fearing them, the sage abandons all,
To quell desire, in solitary woods.

Enter Attendant.

Att. Rámabhadra! (*Checking himself.*) Mahárája!
Ráma. (*Smiling.*) My worthy friend: I better love to hear
The name of Rámabhadra, from the mouths
Of those who were my father's followers.†
What is your message?
Att. Ashtávakra waits,
From Rishyasringa's hermitage.
Sítá. What should delay his entrance?

---

* The maintenance of a perpetual fire implies also the observance of all the occasions on which sacrifices with fire are offered, and all those duties which a householder is enjoined.

† The mode here adopted of delineating Ráma's kindly disposition is very Shakespearian.

Enter the Ascetic ASHTÁVAKRA.*

Ash. Health and peace to both!
Ráma. Respect await you, venerable sir!
    Be seated.
Sítá. I salute you with respect;
    And hold me highly honoured to receive
    The pious kinsman of my sainted sister.
Ráma. No cares disturb my brother's holy peace,
    Nor my respected sister's!
Sítá. Dwell we ever in their recollection?
Ash. Assuredly. They are well. Lady, to you
    The sage Vasishtha thus addresses him.
    Thy mother is the all-sustaining earth;
    Thy father is a king of no less fame
    Than the primeval patriarchs; thy lord
    Draws his proud lineage from the king of day,

---

* *Ashtávakra* is the hero of a curious legend in the *Mahábhárata*. *Kahoda*, his father, was the pupil of *Uddálaka* and married his preceptor's daughter. He was so much addicted to study that he rather neglected his bride when far advanced in her pregnancy, and was rebuked for his conduct by his son yet unborn. The father indignantly pronounced that he should be born crooked, in punishment of his impertinence, and hence his name *Ashta*, eight (limbs), and *Vakra*, curved. *Kahoda* went to the great sacrifice of Janaka, king of *Mithilá*, soon after the birth of his son. To that festival came a seeming *Bauddha* sage, who, overcoming all his competitors in argument, had them thrown into the river. *Kahoda* venturing to encounter him suffered this fate. When Ashtávakra was in his twelfth year he first heard of his father's mischance, and to revenge it, set off for the yet unfinished sacrifice, it being one of those already noticed as of twelve years' duration. Although young in age, the saint was mature in wisdom, and overcame his father's conqueror. When he insisted on his being thrown into the river, the supposed disputant declared himself to be the son of *Varuńa*, the god of the same waters, who had commenced a similar sacrifice with that of Janaka, at the same time, and to secure the attendance of learned *Brahmans*, had adopted the expedient of sending his son to defeat them in disputation, and give them a subsequent ducking. The object being effected, they were dismissed with honour, and the parties separated mutually content. Ashtávakra, by his father's instructions, bathed in the *Samangá* river, and by so doing was rendered perfectly straight. (*Mahábhárata, Vana-Parva.*)—He was married to the daughter of the sage *Vadánya.*—(*Dána-Dharma.*)

And his illustrious house have ever owned
Our spiritual guidance. What alone remains?
That from thee spring an offspring to inherit
The conjoint honours of each glorious race?

Ráma. I thank the sage. In this imperfect world,
Man's tardy speech lags after things foregone;
But with the saints, the thoughts their lips express,
Precede, and presage sure, events to come.

Ash. Arundhatí and all the holy dames,
And Sántá, bid thee well consider this:
Now there is hope of heirs, what must be done
Must be effected speedily.

Ráma. Declare it:
What must be done?

Ash. This *Rishyasringa* tells me to impart.
Thou, queen,* art not ungentle. This, my son,
Is destined to secure thy happiness;
And I shall see thee bearing on thy lap
A smiling progeny.

Ráma. So may it be!
Is there aught else Vasishṭha's wish ordains?

Ash. Attend.
The holy sacrifice absorbs our care,
And you, my son, are young in years and power.
Remember therefore that a king's true wealth,
His real glory, is his people's welfare.

Ráma. So *Maitrávaruṇi* † has ever taught us:
And I am ready, pity, pleasure, love,
Nay, even Sítá, to resign, content,
If it be needful for the general good.

Sítá. In this my lord does honour to his race.

Ráma. Who waits? Attend upon the sage.

Ash. (*Rises and circumambulates them.*)
Behold the prince. [*Exit.*

---

* Or in the text *kalhoruparidá*, in reference to her protracted pregnancy.
† A name of Vasishṭha, the son of *Mitra* and *Varuṇa*.

Enter LAKSHMANA.

Laksh. Glory to Ráma!
  Come, my most noble brother, on these walls
  Behold a skilful artist has portrayed
  Your story, as he learnt the tale from me.
Ráma. You have the skill
  To dissipate our queen's uneasiness.
  How far proceeds the tale, good brother?
Laksh. To where the queen
  Was purified by flame.
Ráma. Most pure by birth,
  She needed not the consecrated wave,
  Nor sacred fire, to sanctify her nature.
Laksh. Daughter of sacrifice, respected Sítá,
  Secure of a devotion that will cease
  With life alone, forgive me.
Ráma. The base herd
  Of men may censure rank and worth unheeded
  But their foul calumnies do not deserve
  By thee to be repeated. The flower that breathes
  With nature's fragrance, on the brow should blossom,
  Nor with contempt be trampled on the ground.*
Sítá. Come, let us see these paintings.
  [*They rise and Exeunt.*

SCENE II.—THE GARDEN OF THE PALACE, WITH A PAVILION.
  Enter LAKSHMANA, SÍTÁ, *and* RÁMA.

Laksh. Behold the picture! †

* This idea occurs in *Málati* and *Mádhava*.

† A long scroll in compartments, apparently fixed against a wall. Such pictures being panoramic representations of holy places usually, are still not uncommon, whilst the *Mahábhárata* and *Rámáyańa*, in illuminated and embellished portable scrolls, are very frequent. It is not uncommon, also, in the Western Provinces, to meet with a kind of fresco painting upon the walls of gardens, or enclosures of tanks, representing mythological or historical subjects.

Mítá. What are these that crowd
Around my lord, and seem to hymn his praises?
Lakṣh. They are the heavenly arms, that *Viśwámitra*,*
The holy sage from *Kuśa* sprung, the friend
Of all mankind, obtained from great *Kriśáśwa*,†

---

* *Viśwámitra* was born a prince in the Lunar dynasty. According to the *Rámáyaṇa* he was the fourth from *Prajápati*, but the *Bhágavata* makes him the fifteenth from *Brahmá*. They agree in calling him the son of *Gádhi*, who, according to the first, was the son of *Kuśanábha*, and according to the second, the son of *Kuśámba*. *Viśwámitra* was sovereign of Kanoj, and engaged in war with the sage *Vasishṭha* for the possession of the all-bestowing cow. In this contest, the cow produced all sorts of forces, particularly *Mlechchhas*, or barbarians, by whose aid *Vasishṭha* overcame his adversary. There can be little doubt that this legend is an allegorical account of a real transaction, and that by the cow we are to understand India, or the most valuable portion of it, for the sovereignty of which either two princes or two tribes, the *Bráhmans* and *Kshattriyas*, contended. One of the parties calling to their aid the barbarians, the Persians, and not impossibly the Greeks, triumphed by their means. *Viśwámitra* was born a sage, in consequence of his mother partaking of some charmed food prepared by the *Muni Richíka* for his wife, her daughter. After observing the superior might of the *Bráhmans*, he engaged in a course of austerities, to rise from the martial order in which he was born to that of the sacerdotal, and ultimately compelled *Brahmá* to grant him that elevation. (*Rámáyaṇa*, I. Sect. 41 52, *Mahábhárata*, Ádi-Parvan, *Bhágavata*, ix. 15, &c.)

† Two sovereigns of the name of *Kriśáśwa* are traceable, one a king of *Ayodhyá*, the other of *Viśálá*. The position of the former in the Solar genealogy stands thus in Buchanan's authorities:

Bhágavata.	Vaṃśa-Latá.	Hari-Vaṃśa.
Nikumbha	Nikumbha	Nikumbha
Varhadáśwa	Varhadáśwa	Sanghatáśwa
Kriśáśwa	Kriśáśwa	Kriśáśwa
Senajit	Yuvanáśwa	Prasenajit
Yuvanáśwa		Yuvanáśwa

But the *Vishṇu-Puráṇa* goes from *Nikumbha* to *Prasenajit* at once, omitting the two intermediate princes.

Kriśáśwa, the sovereign of *Viśálá*, is the son of *Sahyama* and father of *Somadatta*, according to the *Bhágavata* and *Vaṃśa-Latá*. Buchanan is mistaken in supposing the former interposes a *Sahadeva* between him and *Sahyama*. *Devajit* or *Devaka* is the son of *Sahyama*, with *Kriśáśwa* or his brother. The mistake arises from considering *saha*, with, as part of the

And gave them to the prince to wage the fight
With that malignant demon *Táraká*.*
Kúśa. Pay reverence, Sítá, to the arms divine.
The ancient sages and the gods themselves
By penance for a thousand years endured,
Obtained the sight of these celestial arms,
Radiant and holy, for the wars of heaven.†

name. The text has, *Saṁyamád dris Kriddwák saha-Drumjaḥ*: explained by the comment, *Drvajma* or *Devakena sahitaḥ*.

Buchanan places the *Ayodhyá* prince in the eighteenth century before Christ, and the sovereign of *Vidáká* in the fourteenth; the latter is, therefore, made subsequent to Ráma, who is supposed by him to have flourished in the fifteenth.

Neither of these persons, however, appears to be the *Kŕisíśwa* of the text, who is more probably a sage. One so named, a *Muni* or *Devarshi*, is said to have married two of the daughters of *Daksha, Jayá* and *Vijayá*, according to the *Rámáyana*, but *Archi* and *Dhishaná* in the *Bhágavata*. He is also said to have been a writer on dramatic representation: whence an actor or a dancer is termed in the *Amara-Kosha*, *Kŕisáswin*. Nothing further of him has been ascertained.

* A female fiend, the daughter of the *Yaksha Suketu*, and wife of the *Daitya Sunda*. She was changed into the form of a *Rákshasí*, after the death of her husband, by the curse of the sage *Agastya*. Having devastated the flourishing districts of *Malaja* and *Karusha*, and obstructing the sacrifices of the sages, *Viśwámitra* applied to Ráma for aid, and her destruction was his first exploit. (*Rámáyana*, 1. Sec. 23-25.)

† These weapons are of a very unintelligible character. Some of them are occasionally wielded as missiles, but in general they appear to be mystical powers exercised by the individual: such as those of paralyzing an enemy, or locking his senses fast in sleep, or bringing down storm and rain and fire from heaven. In the usual strain of the Hindu mythology, they are supposed to assume celestial shapes, endowed with human faculties, and in this capacity are alluded to in the text. The list of them, one hundred, is given in the first book of the *Rámáyana*, and there also they are described as embodied, and address Ráma, saying "Command us, Oh, *Rághava* of mighty arm—Here we are, Oh, chief of men, command us; what shall we do for thee?" The son of *Raghu* replied: "Depart all of you, and in time of necessity when called to mind, render me assistance." They then circumambulated Ráma, and having said, So be it, received his permission to depart, and went whence they came." The *Rámáyana* calls them also the sons of *Kŕisáswa* and the sons of *Jayá* and *Vijayá*, the daughters of *Prajápati*. (*Rámáyana*, 1. Sec. 20, 28, and 42.)

Sítá. (*Bowing.*) Receive my adoration.—
Ráma. They will aid
  Thy children.
Sítá. I am grateful.
Laksh. There, the scene
  Is changed to Mithilá.*
Sítá. Yes, I see my lord.
  Dark as the deep blue lotus is his hue,
  And strength and grace in every limb appear.
  Paternal looks dwell wondering on his face,
  Lovely with graceful curls, whilst high disdain
  Swells every feature, as with force divine,
  He snaps asunder the celestial bow.†
Laksh. See where your sire and the holy son
  Of *Gautama*, the priest of Janaka,‡
  Welcome Vasishṭha and the rest who now
  Become their kin!
Ráma. No wonder; for the alliance that united
  Raghu with Janaka, could to none
  Be else than pleasing, and where *Viśwámitra*
  Himself was donor and receiver.
Sítá. A solemn scene, where gifts of kine secure
  Auspicious destiny, and four bright youths
  Are knit in marriage bonds with four fair maids.§

---

* The country north of the Ganges, between the *Gandaki* and *Kosi* rivers, comprehending the modern provinces of *Purniya* and *Tirhút*. The remains of the capital founded by Janaka, and thence termed *Janakpur*, are still to be seen, according to Buchanan, on the northern frontier; at the *Janickpoer* of the maps.

† This bow originally belonged to *Siva*, who wielded it victoriously against the other gods at *Daksha's* sacrifice, but without success, against *Vishńu*, on which he gave it to *Devaráta*, one of Janaka's ancestors, subsequent to whom it remained in the family. Like the bow of *Ulysses*, it was employed by Janaka to ascertain the strength of the candidates for his daughter's hand, none of whom were able to bend it; but it was broken with ease by *Ráma.* (*Rámáyańa*, I. Sec. 52, 53, and 62.)

‡ *Satánanda*, the son of *Gautama* and *Ahalyá*, and family priest of the king of *Mithilá*.

§ The sons of *Daśaratha* were *Ráma*, *Lakshmańa*, *Bharata*, and *Sa-*

I recognise you all;—and there—and then,
Am I.

Ráma. The season, too, is there recalled,
When the sage son of *Gautama,* thy hand,
With golden bands begirt, as if it were
The festival embodied, placed in mine.

Laksh. Behold the princess, and this is *Mándavi—*
This *Srutakírtti—*

Sítá. And the fourth—

Laksh. Why ask me?
You know that this is *Úrmilá.*
But here direct your eye—'tis *Bhárgava.**

Sítá. His look alarms me.

Ráma. Reverence to the saint.

Laksh. You should observe him well; for he, by Ráma—

Ráma. (*Interrupting.*)
Much else remains that more deserves attention.

Sítá. This modesty full well becomes my lord.

Laksh. Here we are in *Ayodhyá.*

Ráma. Ah! too well,
Too well does memory bring back the time,
When yet an honoured sire was alive,
Whilst yet a mother's love watched o'er our being;

---

trughna. At the time that Sítá was married to the former, the other daughter of Janaka, *Úrmilá,* was given to Lakshmaña, and the two other brothers were married to *Mándavi* and *Srutakírtti,* the daughters of *Kusadhwaja,* the sovereign of *Sankásya,* or, according to the *Agni Puráña,* of *Káśi* or Benares, and brother of Janaka.

* The descendant of *Bhrigu, Paraśuráma,* who was an incarnation of *Vishńu* for the destruction of the *Kshattriyas.* He was the son of *Jamadagni* the son of *Ríchíka,* the son of *Bhrigu* according to some, and grandson according to others. Being a disciple of *Siva,* he was highly incensed at the presumption of *Rámachandra,* and intercepted him on his return, to punish him for breaking the bow of that deity. He was compelled, however, to acknowledge the superiority of the younger warrior; and after deprecating his anger, retired to a life of devotion on mount *Mahendra.*—(*Rámáyańa,* l. 72.) In the *Mahábhárata,* Ráma shoots arrows at him, and strikes him senseless.

When all was joy. Ah, me! those days are gone.
But here behold—see how the youthful bride,
Fair Sítá, wins maternal admiration:
Her smiling countenance resplendent shines
With youth and loveliness; her lips disclose
Teeth white as *jasmine* buds; her silky curls,
Luxuriant shade her cheeks, and every limb
Of slightest texture moves with natural grace,
Like moonbeams gliding through the yielding air.

Laksh. Here is the wretched *Manthará.**

Ráma. (*Turning away.*)

Look here, love!—see the groves of *Śringavera*,†
Where from the monarch of the forest tribes
We met a friendly welcome.

Laksh. (*Apart.*) He avoids
The conduct of his step-dame. ‡

Sítá. And now behold assumed,
The braid of penance. §

Laksh. Yes: the task severe,
The elders of our race their state deposed,
In favour of their progeny adopted, ||
Was here by youth sustained; and opening life,
Content to languish in the forest's gloom.

---

* The confidential attendant of *Kaikyí*, the second wife of *Daśaratha*, by whose instigations that princess opposed Ráma's accession to the throne, and insisted on his exile.

† *Śringavera* was a city on the north bank of the Ganges (or more properly a village, as the country on both sides of the Ganges was here a forest), inhabited by *Nishádas* or wild tribes, of whom *Guha* was the chief, by whose assistance Ráma, Lakshmaña, and Sítá were ferried over to the south bank of the Ganges, a day's march above its junction with the Jumna.

‡ Of *Kaikyí*.

§ The *Jatá*, or matted hair, assumed by Ráma and Lakshmaña on dismissing the royal chariot at the village of *Śringavera*, to indicate their entering upon a forest or ascetic life.—(Rám. ii. 10.)

|| It appears to have been customary for the ancient princes of the Hindus, when enfeebled by years, to transfer the crown to the successor and retire to a hermitage.

Sítá. Behold—the pure and sacred *Bhágírathí.**

Ráma. Goddess benign, who o'er the race of *Raghu*
Thy guardian care extendest, I salute thee!
Thy downward path *Bhagírath's* prayers propell'd,
And thy pure waves redeem'd his ancestry,
Reduced to ashes by the wrath of *Kapila*,
As through the bowels of the earth they sought
The steed escaped from *Sagara's* sacrifice.†
Deign, heavenly mother, to bestow thy care
On this thy daughter, and with emulous love,
Like chaste Arundhati, her days defend.

Laksh. See, *Bharadwája's* ‡ hermitage, the road

---

* The Ganges, so named from having been brought down to earth by the devotions of king *Bhagíratha*.

† *Sagara*, purposing to perform an *Aswamedha*, or sacrifice of a horse, set, as an essential part of the ceremony, the horse at liberty, who was carried off by one of the serpents of *Pátála*. The king directed his sons, by his wife *Sumati*, sixty thousand in number, to recover the steed. Their efforts, though unavailing, were enough to alarm the gods and demons, and to ensure their own destruction. After penetrating deep towards the subterraneous regions, they came upon the horse grazing near *Kapila*, an incarnation of *Vishńu* as a sage, whom the sons of *Sagara* challenged as the thief of the horse. *Kapila*, incensed, reduced them all to ashes with a blast from his nostrils. *Ansumat*, the son of *Asamanjas*, the son of *Sagara*, by his other wife, *Kesiní*, afterwards discovered the reliques of his uncles, and learned from *Garuda*, also their uncle, that the waters of the Ganges were necessary to procure them admission to heaven. Neither *Sagara* nor his successors, *Ansumat* and *Dilípa*, were able to effect the descent of Gangá, this being reserved for the son and successor of the latter, *Bhagíratha*. The austerities of this prince successively propitiating *Brahmá*, *Umá*, and *Mahádeva*, the Ganges was, by their power, compelled to flow over the earth, following *Bhagíratha* to the sea, and thence to *Pátála*, where the ashes of his ancestors were laved by its waters. The Ganges was called *Bhágírathí*, in honour of the king, and the ocean termed *Ságara*, in commemoration of *Sagara* and his sons.—(Ráma, I. 35.)

‡ The accounts of this individual are rather obscure, but he was a Muni and expounder of the *Vedas*. In some places he is called the son of *Vríhaspati*, and in the *Harivansa* is said to have been adopted by *Bharata* as king of *Pratishthána*. In the *Rámáyana* he appears as a sage residing at *Prayága*, or Allahabad, where a temple dedicated to him still exists. In the *Mahá-*

302　　　　　UTTARA-RÁMA-CHARITRA.

   To *Chitrakúta*,* and the sable tree
   That shades *Kálindí's* † borders.
Sítá. Does my lord
   Recall these scenes to memory?
Ráma. Could it be,
   That I should ever cease to recollect them?
   I see you now, as on my breast reclined
   And in my arms sustained, that delicate frame,
   Exhausted with the long and weary way,
   Sinks in o'erpowering slumber.
Laksh. Behold *Virádha*, ‡ who denies admission
   To *Vindhya's* § thickets.

---

bhárata he is described as residing at Haridwár, and the father of *Drona*, the military preceptor of the *Pándava* and *Kaurava* princes. He is also the parent of *Arundhatí*, the wife of *Vasishtha*.

* A mountain not far from the south bank of the Jumna, Ráma's first residence in his exile, and, according to the *Rámáyana*, at that time the seat of *Válmíki's* hermitage. Many temples and establishments of *Vaishnava* ascetics exist at this spot, now called *Chitrakote*, and it is at different seasons a place of great resort.

† The *Kálindí* is the Jumna river, the daughter of *Kalinda*, a name of the sun. The tree should be the imperishable *Ber* tree, which has long been famed at *Allahabad*, and which is still represented by a withered stem in the care of *Pátálapurí*, underground, but it should appear from the text that it grew in daylight, and the play probably preceded the construction of the cavern. There was, no doubt, a very ancient and venerable fig tree at Allahabad, perhaps for some centuries, for it is alluded to in various vocabularies as *Medini*, &c.; it is also described in the *Kásikhanda*, and *Kúrma-Purána*. The first notice, however, is in the *Rámáyana* (B. II. Sect. 41 and 42); Ráma, with his wife and brother resting under the shade of it after crossing the Jumna; so that not only was the tree in the open air, but it was on the opposite side of the river to that on which it is now traditionally venerated.

‡ A demon of formidable size and aspect, the son of *Kála* and *Satahrndá*, residing in *Dandakáranya*, and encountered by Ráma on his leaving the hermitage of Atri. Having seized Sítá, and threatened to devour the princes, he was attacked by them and slain by Ráma.—(*Rámáyana*, B. III. Sect. 7, 8.)

§ The Vindhya mountains extend across Central India, and throw out branches behind Agra and Delhi to the north, and on the south to the extremity of the Peninsula.

Sítá. He is too horrible.

Mark where my lord collects the broad palm leaves,
And weaves a shade to screen me from the sun,
As to the forests of the south we travel.

Ráma. We come to where, amidst the southern forests,
By mountain brooks the holy sages dwell,
And here they spread their simple stores,* and cheer
The stranger guest with hospitable right.

Laksh. Amidst the thicket tall *Prasravaṇa*
Rears its dark brow, eternally with clouds
Invested, from whose watery stores, assembled
Within the echoing caverns, fair *Godávarí*
Bursts forth, and down the mountain wends her way
Through gloomy shades and thick entangling woods.

Ráma. Recall'st thou, love, our humble happy dwelling
Upon the borders of the shining stream,
Where every hour, in fond endearments wrapped,
Or in sweet interchange of thought engaged,
We lived in transport, not a wish beyond
Each other, reckless of the flight of time?

Laksh. See *Panchavatí* † next, and here behold
The demon *Súrpaṇakhá*. ‡

Sítá. Ha, my dear lord,
Behold! (*As if alarmed.*)

Ráma. How now! afraid of separation?
'Tis but a picture, love.

Sítá. I cannot chuse,
But suffer terror at so vile a presence.

---

* Or, dress a handful of the *nívára* or wild rice.

† The forest along the Godávarí.

‡ The sister of *Rávaṇa*, a female fiend of hideous form and sanguinary propensities. Having seen Ráma on the banks of the Godávarí, she offered herself as a bride to him, and on his refusal to Lakshmaña; but both rejecting her advances, she attempted to destroy Sítá, on which Lakshmaña by his brother's commands cut off her nose and ears. She fled to her brothers *Khara* and *Dúshaṇa*, and incited them to revenge her.—(*Rámay.* B. III. Sect. 23, 24.)

Ráma. The sad events that Janasthána * witnessed
  Are once more present here.
Laksh. And here again,
  The anguish which the craft of wicked fiends
  And violence inflicted is renewed,
  And the rude stone and adamantine rock
  Dissolve in gentle pity, as they witness
  The prince's sorrows in the lonely forest.
Sítá. Alas! that the delight of Raghu's race
  For me should thus have suffered.
Laksh. Let us avert our thoughts
  To subjects more auspicious. Here, observe
  Displayed the valour of the great *Jatáyu*,
  The ancient monarch of the winged tribes,
  Of days coeval with a *Manu's* reign,
  From *Kasyapa* descended.† Here, extend
  The forests of the west, where from the gloom
  The headless sprite‡ our devious path arrested.

---

* According to the comment, this place in the present age is called *Nasik*, situated on the Godávarí, not far from the Western Ghats, and a place of pilgrimage.

† *Jatáyu*, a bird of divine nature and descent and preternatural longevity, the son of *Garuda*, the son of *Kasyapa*. He was the friend of *Dasaratha*, and on one occasion saved his life. That prince having gone to the ecliptic to rescue *Rohini* from the hands of *Sani*, his carriage was consumed by a glance from the eye of the latter. *Dasaratha* falling was caught and sustained by *Jatáyu* on his expanded wings. When *Sítá* was carried off by *Rávaná*, *Jatáyu* attempted to stop him, but was slain by the *Rákshasa*.

‡ This *Kabandha* or headless monster is possibly the original of the anthropophagi of the East, and the "men whose heads do grow beneath their shoulders." He is described as vast as a mountain, of a sable hue, without legs; but with arms a league long, a formidable mouth in his belly, and a single eye of vast dimensions in his breast. He seized with his long arms both Ráma and Lakshmana with an intention to devour them, but the princes extricated themselves by cutting off his arms. The monster then inquiring who they were, and being informed of their names and lineage, rejoiced in his mutilation as the means of freeing him from a form to which he had been metamorphosed from that of a handsome *Dhanava*, the grand son of *Danu*, one of the wives of *Kasyapa*, in consequence of the impre-

The mountain *Rishyamuku** see, and here
The dwelling of *Matanga*.†—This, the dame ‡
Whose life of penance now obtained reward.
Here are the sources of the *Pampá*,§ where
The grief of Ráma broke beyond restraint,
And fast descending tears at intervals
Concealed from view the beauties of the scene.‖
Here mark the son of air, the monkey chief,
Of strength resistless and wide-wasting wrath.
The guardian of the world—the firm ally
Of *Raghu's* race—illustrious *Hanumat*.

cation of a *Rishi* named *Sthúlasiras* as a punishment for his frightening the ascetics by assuming hideous shapes. The effects of the curse were produced by his defying *Indra*, who in the contest struck off his head and legs with his thunderbolt, but could not kill him, as he had obtained the boon of longevity from *Brahmá*. The appearance of Ráma was the term of his transformation, and his body being burnt by his desire, he recovered his original shape and returned to *Swarga*, previously directing Ráma to seek the residence of *Sugríva*. (*Rámáyana*, III. 82, 83, 81.)

* This mountain, and the scenes in its vicinity alluded to, are said to be known by the same appellations in the neighbourhood of *Anagundi*, a part of the Dekhin, the maps of which are disgracefully defective. The mountain itself was the residence of the deposed monarch of the monkeys, *Sugríva*. It comprised, of course, the whole of the tract about the sources of the *Pampá*; but in the *Rámáyana*, Ráma passes them before he comes to the dwelling of the monkey chief.

† On the ascent to the mountain occurs the forest of *Matanga*, or the *Meghaprabha* wood, in which the trees never wither and the flowers never fade. The saint and his disciples had long disappeared; but his hermitage had remained inaccessible to noxious or inimical beings, and the cooking utensils left by him, awaited, in perfect order, the arrival of Ráma, being destined for his accommodation.

‡ A *Sarari*, or female forester, named *Sravaná*, who had attended on *Matanga's* disciples, and whose ascension to *Swarga* was to be the reward of her acting as guide to Ráma.

§ A river rising in the *Rishyamuka* mountain, and flowing into the *Tungabhadra*, below *Anagundi*.

‖ Not, however, before expatiating upon them at great length, at least in the *Rámáyana*, *Áranyakánda*, last section. The MSS. from which the translation was made differ here in many respects from the Calcutta edition.

Rāma. Reverence and glory to our hero friend!
  Here let us pause, for every scene suggests
  Heart-rending recollections.
Laksh. But a moment—
  Regard the deeds incredible the hands
  Of monkey warriors in their rage achieve.
  Here view our triumph*—Now we close the scene.†
Sítá. My dearest lord, this picture has inspired
  A foolish fancy;—may I give it utterance?
Rāma. Fear not to speak it, love.
Sítá. I long once more to wander through the shades ‡
  Of the brown woods, and plunge amidst the wave
  Of *Bhágírathí's* cool translucent stream.
Rāma. Lakshmaña!
Laksh. I understand you, and will order forth
  The easy rolling car without delay;
  As such desires the learned have declared
  Should speedily be gratified.§   [*Exit.*
Sítá. But you will sure be with me, my good lord?
Rāma. Cruel! what need to ask your Ráma this?
  Come, let us enter this pavilion, love.
Sítá. Most willingly; unusual lassitude
  Creeps o'er my frame and woos me to repose.
Rāma. Recline on me, thy couch, and around my neck
  Throw those dear arms, the lovely, living band
  Of moon-gems melting in the lunar ray,
  As weariness the pearly drops exhales.—

---

* The death of *Rávaṇa* and defeat of his troops, with the capture of *Lanká*.

† A few exclamatory sentences are henceforward omitted, and the description of the picture is compressed.

‡ Sítá's exposure required her own concurrence, which the desire she has just intimated affords. It is also ominous of what is to follow.

§ The term *dohada* usually signifies the desire of a pregnant woman, or longing, to which the Hindus attach equal importance as did the nations of Europe.

What can this mean? a sudden transport glows
In every nerve, shedding such strange emotion;
I know not whether it be pain or pleasure,
If poison parch my veins, or I have quaffed
The maddening wine-cup. Can such magic, hid
In this fair touch, thus overcome my nature?

Sítá. It is thy constant love; no charms of mine.

Ráma. Thy tender voice revives life's languid blossom;
And whilst its sound subdues each softening sense,
It comes like heavenly nectar on the ear,
And pours its balmy medicine on the soul.

Sítá. Dear flatterer, cease; here let us taste repose.

[*Looking round.*

Ráma. What seeks my Sítá? Be these arms thy pillow.
Thine, ever since the nuptial knot united us,
Thine, in the days of infancy and youth,
In lonely thickets and in princely palaces,
Thine ever—thine alone.

Sítá. True—true—my ever kind and cherished lord.

[*Sleeps.*

Ráma. Her latest waking words are words of love,
And nought of her but is most dear to me.
Her presence is ambrosia to my sight;
Her contact, fragrant sandal; her fond arms,
Twined round my neck, are a far richer clasp
Than costliest gems; and in my house she reigns
The guardian goddess of my fame and fortune.
Oh! I could never bear again to lose her.

Enter ATTENDANT.

Att. My lord, there waits—

Ráma. Who?

Att. Your personal attendant, Durmukha.

Ráma. He brings me word of what reports are spread
Amongst the citizens. Go, bid him enter.

[*Exit* ATTENDANT.

Enter DURMUKHA.*

Dur. (*To himself.*) How can I venture to communicate
  The idle calumnies the giddy people
  Invent against the queen?—No matter;
  Unhappy that I am, it is my duty.
Sítá. (*In her sleep.*) Where art thou, dearest Ráma?
Ráma. She dreams that I have left her; or the view
  Of our portrayed adventures has disturbed
  Her gentle slumbers. Ah! how blest is he
  Who ever dwells in long confirmed affection,
  Alike in pleasure or in pain, whose heart
  Reposes tranquilly in every fortune,
  And on whose waning, as his budding life,
  Love constant waits. Oh! how can fate be won
  To grant such happiness?
Dur. Hail to the king!
Ráma. What hast thou to report?
Dur. The people are ill pleased; the general cry
  Is, Rámabhadra disregards his subjects.
Ráma. What reason have they thus to think of me?
  Declare what fault they charge me with.
Dur. 'Tis thus they talk. [*Whispers.*
Ráma. Shame on the vile traducer who assails
  Domestic happiness! No common means
  Redeem'd *Vaidehí* from the former scourge
  Of foul calumnious tongues; yet scandal foams,
  Like a mad hound, with still o'erflowing venom.
  What's to be done? Alas! what choice remains!
  The general good must be preferred. To that
  My father sacrificed his son—his life—
  And I must do my duty. Now it chances
  As by the sage *Vasishtha* 'twas foretold,
  My noble ancestors, the lofty race
  That boast the sun their sire, have bequeathed

---

* The *kanchukin*, or chamberlain; an old Bráhman is the fittest person.
† Sic.

A spotless reputation to my keeping;
And how shall I deserve the glorious charge
If calumny attach to aught that's mine?
Daughter of sacrifice! Fair child of earth!
Glory of Janaka's exalted race!
The loved of sages and their sainted dames!
Casket of Ráma's being! Cheering light
Of the dark forest-dwelling! Utterer
Of tender eloquence! Alas! what cause
Has rendered destiny thy ruthless foe?
All thy good deeds, distorted, turn to ill;
All thy munificence awards thee shame;
And whilst thou art about to give the world
A worthy lord, that world, ingrate, condemns
Thee to a widowed, solitary home.
Durmukha, go, bid Lakshmaña attend
To lead the queen to exile.

Dur. How so, my lord! must she, whose spotless fame
The flame has evidenced, in whom there live
The hopes of *Raghu's* line, be banished hence,
To please a thankless and malignant people?

Ráma. Nay, blame them not. No lack of love or honour
Towards the royal house, but adverse destiny
Instils these thoughts. And who, that witnessed not
The wondrous test of purity, could credit
Such marvels in a distant region wrought?
Go, then, and do our bidding.

Dur. Alas, poor queen! [*Exit.*

Ráma. Cruel task! I have become a savage.
The wife whose every hour since infancy
To me has been devoted, and whom all
Beloved by me have tenderly caressed,
I ruthlessly and fraudulent consign,
Like a domestic bird, to certain death.
Wretch that I am! why shall my touch impure
Pollute these charms? Hold me not thus—let loose

Your tender grasp, dear Sítá, from a man
Whom every crime degrades. You think you cling
Around the sandal's fragrant trunk, and clasp
The baleful poison-tree—let go—thus—thus.
    [*Detaches himself and rises.*
What now is life?—a barren load; the world?—
A dreary, arid, solitary wild.
Where can I hope for comfort? Sense was given me
Only to make me conscious of affliction,
And firmly bound in an unyielding frame.
Departed sires! prophets and sages! all
Whom I have loved and honoured!* and all ye
Who have shown honour and regard for Ráma!
Celestial flame! auspicious parent, Earth!
To whom amongst ye dare I raise my voice?
What name may I invoke, nor wrong its sanctity?
Will ye not shrink from my solicitation
As from an outcast's touch; from me, who chase
My wife, the honour of my house, away,
And doom *Kathorngarbhá*† to despair,
Like a dread offering to infernal fiends?
    [*Bows down to Sítá's feet.*
Adored *Vaidehí!* for the last, last time,
Thy lovely feet exalt the head of Ráma.
(*Without.*) Help! help for the Bráhman tribe!‡
Ráma. How now!

    Enter MESSENGER.

Mess. The assembled sages on the *Yamuná's* bank,
Disturbed amidst their ritual by *Lavaka,* §
The demon, fly to Ráma for protection.

* The original specifies the individuals.
† Sítá.
‡ The term is *abrahmanyam*. *Abrahmanyam* implying the absence of
protection to the Bráhmans, and their incurring some distress.
§ The son of the *Asura Madhu,* by *Kumbhínasí* the daughter of *Virarus*
and sister of *Rávana.* He inherited from his father a trident, presented by

Rāma. Still this profane intrusion! I will send
  Śatrughna* to chastise this impious son
  Of *Kumbhīnasī.* [*Going, looks back.*
  Alas! my queen, what will become of thee?
  Goddess divine! all-bearing Earth! protect
  This, thine own daughter, at the solemn rite,
  By thee brought forth,—the only stay of Janaka,
  The sole remaining hope of *Raghu's* race.
    [*Exit.*
Sitá. (*Waking.*) Oh, my loved husband! Ah! deceived
  By evil dreams I call on him. How! gone!
  Left me alone! asleep! well, well;
  I will be very angry with thee, Ráma.
  I will henceforth be mistress of myself;
  Suppress my foolish fondness, and will learn
  Henceforth to chide thee. Who attends! How now!

Enter DURMUKHA.

Dur. Prince Lakshmaña requests you will be pleased
  To come and mount his chariot.
Sítá. I will come.
  But gently, my good friend; the pleasing load
  I bear, retards my steps. Accept my homage,
  Gods of the race of *Raghu* and of Janaka,
  Feet of my honoured lord, and all
  Propitious saints, and ancestors revered.
    [*Exeunt.*

Sire to *Madhu*, the holder of which was invincible. *Śatrughna* subdued and slew him, by surprising him without his weapon. *Lavaṇa* was sovereign of *Mathurá*, to the government of which his conqueror succeeded. *Mathurá* was previously called *Madhuvana*, or *Madhupuri*, the grove or city of the demon *Madhu.*

* The youngest of his brothers.

END OF THE FIRST ACT.

ACT II.*

Scene—Janasthána Forest.

Enter Átreyí,† a female ascetic.
I see the genius of these groves approach.
She bears her flowery tribute.‡

*Enter Vásantí, the Dryad of Janasthána, with flowers,
which she presents.*

Vás. Hail, holy dame! thy presence brings §
Delight to all our groves and springs:
Thy blessing and thy prayers be mine;
These fountains and these bowers are thine.
Here, in the tall tree's shade repose,
Where cool the limpid current flows,
And feast upon the blameless root,
Or pluck the overhanging fruit,—
The fitting fare of those who dwell
In silent grove, and hermit cell,—
And consecrate the calm retreat
With pious thoughts and converse sweet.

Átr. (*Takes the present.*)
Kindness of heart and gentleness of speech,
Modest demeanour, innocence of thought,

---

* An interval of twelve years has elapsed since the first Act.

† The wife of the sage *Atri*, more usually termed *Anasúyá*, the daughter of *Kardama Rishi*.

‡ She comes with an *arghya*, a present indicative of respect to a superior. It matters not of what it consists; and in this case is appropriately of flowers.

§ The conversation of mythological personages is so little attractive in general, that I have attempted to give it relief in this drama by a lighter measure, at the expense sometimes, perhaps, of close fidelity.

Unsullied nature, and devout associates,—
These are the charms and mystic powers of virtue,
And, with sincerity united, hallow
The grossness of existence. [*Sits.*

Vds. Tell me, venerable dame,
Who thou art, and what thy name?

Atr. Behold in me the wife of *Atri.**

Vds. Tell me, partner of the seer,
What thy holy purpose here?

Atr. Amidst these forests dwells the great *Agastya*,†
And many other holy teachers here
With him reside: from them I come to learn
The holy *Vedas*, having lately left
The lessons of Válmíki.‡

Vds. Yet wise, *Prachetas*'§ son, his mind
The deepest, darkest, truths can find,
And on him other sages wait,
Familiar with the laws of fate,
The books of *Brahm* were there made clear—
Why then this weary journey here?

Atr. I'll tell thee, spirit: in Válmíki's bower

---

* One of the will-born sons of *Brahmá*, and progenitor of the moon.

† Agastya was the son of *Mitra* and *Varuña* conjointly, and born in a water-jar along with *Vasishtha*. Having commanded the *Vindhya* mountain to lie prostrate till his return, he repaired to the South of India, to *Kolapur*, where he continued to reside, and appears to have been mainly instrumental in introducing the Hindu religion into the Peninsula.

‡ The author of the *Rámáyaña*, settled at *Chitrakúta* at the time of Ráma's exile, but at this time at *Hitásr*.

§ Válmíki was the son of *Varuña*, the regent of the water, one of whose names is *Prachetas*. According to the *Adhyátma-Rámáyaña*, the sage, although a Bráhman by birth, associated in his youth with foresters and robbers. Attacking on one occasion the seven *Rishis*, they expostulated with him successfully, and taught him the *mantra* of Ráma reversed, or *Mára, Mára*, in the inaudible repetition of which he remained immovable for thousands of years, so that when the sages returned to the same spot, they found him still there, converted into a *valmika*, or ant-hill, by the nests of the termites, whence his name of Válmíki.

What causes were there of delay and hindrance
To interrupt the weighty task.   Attend.
Borne by some deity, two infant children,
Of more than common natures, at the hermitage
Arrived, and from their holy studies whiled
The gravest sages—nay, the very animals
Confessed the same surprising fascination.

Vas. Their names!

Atr. Kuśa and Lava were the names assigned
By their celestial guardian; and in proof
They were not of mere mortal race, they brought
Along with them the arms of heavenly fabric.
The sage received them; and with care paternal
Válmíki rears them. In their earliest years,
Except the sacred *Vedas*, they were taught
All sciences, and chief the use of arms;
But when they saw ten summers, he invested them,
After the kingly fashion, with the cord,*
And placed the Holy Scriptures in their hands.
Such is their aptness, they have far excelled
The oldest scholars, whose less active intellects
Toil after them in vain. The mind, alike
Vigorous or weak, is capable of culture,
But still bears fruit according to its nature.
'Tis not the teacher's skill that rears the scholar:
The sparkling gem gives back the glorious radiance
It drinks from other light, but the dull earth
Absorbs the blaze, and yields no gleam again.

Vas. 'Tis justly urged, and this compels
Thy feet to seek our saintly cells.

Atr. Another cause disturbed our pious studies—

---

* A thread worn by the three first orders of the Hindus over the left shoulder and under the right arm. It is imposed with much solemnity, as part of the ceremony of regeneration, whence the three castes are termed *Dwijas*, or twice-born. The thread of the military class is made of flax, and should be put on between the ages of ten and twenty-two.

The sage Valmíki in his noontide walk,
Along the *Tamasá*,* beheld a fowler
Strike to the ground one of a gentle pair
Of birds, that murmured love upon the bank.
Filled with affliction at the piteous sight,
The sage gave utterance to his wrath, and prompted
By the inspiring goddess,† thus proclaimed
His thoughts in unpremeditated verse:
" Hope not, barbarian, length of days to know,
Whose hand could deal so merciless a blow,
One of a harmless pair could thus destroy,
Consigned to death amidst the thoughts of joy."‡

Vds. 'Twas genius spoke, and first on earth
A heaven-descended art had birth.

Atr. The verse was scarcely uttered, when lo! *Brahmá*
Appeared before the sage, and thus addressed him:
" Thy spirit is awakened—now thou feelest
The present god, whose soul is eloquence.
Complete thy task—declare thy lofty strain,
The deeds of Ráma to the listening world.
This day, the new-born ray of heavenly knowledge
Breaks on thy sight, first poet amongst men."
This said, he disappeared. The sage obeyed,
And, first of mortals, sang, in measured strains,
The inspiration of the god who rules
O'er eloquence, the glorious deeds of Ráma.

Vds. To all the world the sacred tongue
Of gods and *Veds* shall hence belong.§

Atr. 'Tis true; and thus on our retired studies

---

* A small river near *Chitrakote*, commonly called the *Tonse*.

† *Saraswati* or *Vání*, the goddess of speech and eloquence.

‡ The original here inserts the stanza of the *Rámáyańa* (I. 2. 18), which is there also stated to be the first *śloka*, or stanza, ever composed.

§ The literal expression is, *hanta, panditah samsatrah*—Alas! the world is learned.

Profane intrusion may be apprehended.
Enough! I now have rested. Friendly spirit,
Show me the way to great *Agastya's* dwelling.

Vás. The road through *Panchavati* leads;
And here across the stream proceeds.

Átr. The clear *Godávari*—yonder extends
Prasravana, whose high tops touch the clouds;
This is the sacred forest, *Janasthána*,
And thou, if I mistake not, art Vásantí.

Vás. You speak my name.

Átr. These scenes suggest most painful recollections.
My poor child Jánakí, 'twas here thy fate
Once placed thee, and I think I see thee still,
Although, alas! thy name is all that 's left
Of one who was so dear to me.

Vás. How, say you! Does aught ill attend
The fortunes of my dearest friend?

Átr. Not evil fortune only—evil fame. [*Whispers.*

Vás. Alas, alas! relentless fate,
Is there no limit to thy hate? [*Faints.*

Átr. Revive, my child; be comforted.

Vás. Such, gentle Sítá, beauteous queen,
Thy destiny hath ever been.
Ah, Ráma! but I will not chide—
Declare, Átreyí, what beside
Befell my hopeless friend, conveyed
By Lakshmaña to forest shade?

Átr. It is not known.

Vás. But where, oh! where
Was then Vasishťha's guardian care?
Where was Arundhatí divine,
And all the chiefs of *Raghu's* line?
The ancient queens? were all content
To mark, unmoved, such sad event?

Átr. The elders of the race had all repaired
To *Rishyasringa's* hermitage—but late,

The twelve years' rite is finally effected.
They quit the hermit; but Arundhatí
Returns not to Ayodhyá whilst deprived
Of Sítá, and with her the queens agree.
'Twas, therefore, by *Vasishtha* counselled, they
Should for a while be tenants of those groves,
Where wise Válmíki and his pupils dwell.
Vás. And what doth Ráma?
Átr. He prepares
An *Aswamedh** ——
Vás. What female shares
The solemn rite? I fear him wed
To some new queen.
Átr. 'Tis idly said;—
A golden image of his cherished Sítá
The sacrifice partakes.
Vás. 'Tis well
He holds his faith; yet who can tell
Men's hearts? the purest comprehend
Such contradictions, and can blend
The force to bear, the power to feel,
The tender bud and tempered steel.
Átr. Already the pure steed, o'er whom the charms
By *Vishwadeva* spoken are pronounced,
Is loosed to roam at will: his guards attend
According to the ritual. By the son
Of Lakshmaña, the noble Chandraketu,
Arrayed in mail, and with bright weapons armed,
From heavenly arsenals, the bands are led—
Scarce went they forth, when lo! a Bráhman brought
His son's dead body to the palace gate,
And called for succour to the Bráhman tribe.
Reflecting, when unseasonable death
Afflicts his people, that the monarch's faults

* The solemn sacrifice of a horse.

Must be the cause, full sorely Ráma grieved;
When to console him came a voice from heaven
Commanding him go forth and seek S'ambúka:
One of an outcast origin, engaged
In pious penance: he must fall by Ráma,
And then the Bráhman's son will live again.
This heard, the king assumed his arms, ascended
His car celestial, and he traverses
Even now the realms in quest of this ascetic.

Vás. Speed, Ráma, speed! the foe inhales
In these deep shades the healthful gales,
His only sustenance: but now,
Thy coming terminates his vow;
And thy blest steps shall spread around
New glories on this sainted ground!

Atr. Come, friendly spirit, haste we hence!

Vás. I lead. The sun, with glow intense,
Shoots through the sky, and drives to shade
The silent songsters of the glade.
Alone, amidst the loftiest boughs,
The dove repeats her tender vows;
Or wild fowl cry, as pleased they mark,
Their insect prey amid the bark.
By tangling branches overhead
A cooling gloom beneath is spread,
Where rests the elephant, reclining
Against the ancient trunk, or twining
His tusk around the branchy bower;
He scatters round a leafy shower
Of flowery buds, that falling seem
An offering to the sacred stream,
Whose crystal waters placid flow
Along the verdant shore below.

[*Exeunt.*

Enter RÁMA *in his car, with his sword drawn.*

Hand, thou hast done thy duty, and let fall

The sword of vengeance on the *Śúdra's* head,
To grant existence to the Bráhman's son.
This act was worthy him of whom thou'rt part.
Not such thy deed, when thrusting Sítá forth
To bear her burthen to the lonely woods.*

Enter SAMBÚKA † *as a celestial spirit.*

Sam. Glory to Ráma! death's terrific king,
Awed by thy prowess, renders back to life
The Bráhman's son: the youth is with his sire.
To thee Sambúka reverently bows,
For 'tis to thee he owes his present glories.
The death that is inflicted by the pious
Is but a passport to felicity.

Ráma. I joy in both events.
Long may you live a tenant of those realms
To which your penances have raised you; where
The pure and unimpassioned sages dwell,
And taste the bliss that recompenses virtue!

Sam. Not to my penance, but to thy benevolence
I owe this exaltation; yet I wrong
The force of my devotions, which have brought thee
In quest of such an abject worm as I.
Thou shouldst be sought out by the world, its great
And powerful defence; yet thou hast deigned
To quit Ayodhyá for the *Dańdak* forest,
And hither bend thy steps in search of me.

Ráma. And is this *Dańdaka*? do I once more
Behold the vast, the venerable shades,
Awful and dark with aged trees, and echoing
With roaring torrents from surrounding hills,
The haunt of pious seers, and holy pilgrims?

---

* The construction of the original is something different, and Ráma, according to the stage direction, striking at nothing, is lauded by unseen panegyrists. "This act is worthy of Ráma! now may the Bráhman's son revive."

† Having been killed by divine hands, he of course obtained deification.

Sum. This is the scene of thy triumphant prowess,
    Where countless demons fell beneath thy sword,*
    Hence *Janasthána's* timid denizens
    Pass their calm days in undisturbed devotion.
Ráma. Lies *Janasthána* here?
Sum. Towards the south,
    It skirts these thickets, through whose spacious bounds
    Wander at will the monsters of the wild.
    Fierce o'er the mountain stalks the ravenous tiger,
    Or lurks in gloomy caves; through the thick grass
    Curls the vast serpent, on whose painted back
    The cricket chirps, and with the drops that dew
    The scales allays his thirst. Silence profound
    Enwraps the forest, save where babbling springs
    Gush from the rock, or where the echoing hills
    Give back the tiger's roar, or where the boughs
    Burst into crackling flame, and wide extends
    The blaze the dragon's fiery breath has kindled.
Ráma. I recognise the scene, and all the past
    Rises to recollection. These drear shades
    Appalled not *Sitá,* well content to brave
    The forest gloom with *Ráma* at her side.
    Such was her wondrous love, that cheerfully
    She trod the wild. What wealth need man desire,
    Who in the fond companion of his life,
    Has one that shares his sorrows, and disperses
    All anxious care with exquisite delight?
Sum. Dismiss such melancholy thoughts. Observe
    The peafowl's glorious plumage, as he lights
    Beneath yon copse—behold, through tufted grass,
    Where come the trooping deer, bounding to covert,
    Nor fear the gaze of man; there cooling fall
    The sparkling torrents; as they flash beneath
    The overhanging willows, or the boughs

* Or in the text 14,000 *Rákshases,* besides the three principal, *Khara, Dúshana,* and *Triśiras.*

Laden with fruit declining to the stream,
And vocal with innumerable choristers.
The she-bear growls along the flowery brink,
And from the incense-bearing tree, the elephant
Snaps the light branch, and all its gum exudes,
And breathes rich perfume through the balmy air.
I quit thee, lord, to visit, with thy leave,
Ere I ascend to heaven, *Agastya's* cell.

Ráma. Bo thy path propitious!

[*Exit* SAMDÚKA.

'Twas here that long and happily I dwelt,
Ere other duties, and the cares of empire
Disturbed my tranquil joys. But such our lot—
Each various station has its proper claim.
The hermit's calm suits not the rank of king,
Nor kingly state the peaceful hermitage.
Scenes of repose, with lavish nature graced,
Haunts undisturbed of timid birds and deer,
Streams decorated with th' untrodden fringe
Of flowery blossoms and luxuriant creepers,
I know ye well. Yon distant wavy ridge,
Like a faint line of low-descending clouds,
Defines *Prasravan*, whose lofty crest
Was once the vulture king, *Jatáyu's*, seat;
And from whose sides precipitously falls
The broad *Godávarí*. At the hill foot,
And on the margin of the stately wood,
Among dark trees, upon whose branches, bowed
Into the shining stream beneath, the birds
Sang sweet and oft, our leafy cottage stood.
And here is *Panchavatí*, long the witness
Of our contented stay, and the abode
Of Sítá's dearest friend, the fair Vásantí,
The kindly genius of these ancient shades.
Alas, how changed my fortune! Sad I pine
In lonely widowhood—affliction sheds

A deadly venom through my veins—despair,
Like a barbed arrow shot into my heart,
There sticks, and rankles in its cureless wound.
Let me beguile the hour, and try to lose
The memory of my sufferings, as I gaze
Once more on these dear scenes. Yet even they
Are not unchanged: where once the river flowed
A verdant bank extends; and where the trees,
Close wove, denied admittance to the day,
An open champaign bares its breast to heaven.
Scarce could I deem the spot the same; but still
The mighty landmarks tower aloft, and round
The same tall mountains mingle with the skies.
How may I dare to look upon these woods
Alone, without my love, with whom my days
Were once within their confines pass'd in peace
And happy converse in our humble dwelling!
Let me not think of this.

Sum. (*Returning.*) All hail to Ráma!
The seer *Agastya*, when he heard from me
Your presence in these wilds, thus speaks his wishes.
The tender *Lopámudrá** and the saints
Who share our hermitage, will think it happiness
If, from thy heavenly car alighting, thou
Wilt for short season visit us. Then come,
Ere thou resume thy journey to Ayodhyá.

Ráma. Be it done.

---

* *Agastya* having seen his ancestors suspended by their heels in a pit, was told by them that they could only be extricated from their position by his begetting a son. In order to obtain a wife for this purpose, he made a girl of the most graceful parts of the animals of the forest, and gave her, without his privacy, to the king of *Vidarbán*, to be his daughter. She was named *Lopámudrá* from the distinctive beauties (*mudra*) of animals, as the eyes of deer, &c., being subjected to loss (*lopa*) in her superior charms. When marriageable, *Agastya* demanded her of her father, and, although sorely against his will, the king was obliged to consent to her becoming the wife of the sage. (*Mahábhárata, Vana-Parvan.*)

Bear with me, *Panchavati*, that obeying
The pleasure of the sage, I still presume
To trespass on thy confines.

Sum. Here lies our path. Yonder is tall *Krounchdval*,
Amidst the dark glens of whose wooded sides
The raven silent flits, and hoots the owl,
And whines through whistling caves the shrilly breeze:
And countless pea-fowl, with discordant shrieks,
Chase into sapless trunks and time-worn trees
The frightened snakes. Far to the south extends
The lofty range of hills, whose towering peaks
Are diademed with clouds; whose central caverns
Roar loud with mighty waters, as from the earth
The springs of the *Godávarí* burst forth;
And at whose base the sacred conflux blends,
In one broad stream, the loud, encountering torrents.

END OF THE SECOND ACT.

ACT III.

THE DAŃḍAKA FOREST CONTINUES.

Enter TAMASÁ *and* MURALÁ, *two river goddesses.*

Tam. How now, sister, whither bent?
Mur. By the holy matron sent,
    Lopámudrá, charge of care
    To Godávarí I bear.
Thus the matron bids me say:—
Ráma still through many a day,
Though exterior calmness screen
His sorrow, deeply mourns his queen;
And his declining form declares
The anguish that his bosom tears;
For soonest shall the soft heart perish
That loves a secret grief to cherish,
As gourds with coat of clay encased
Earliest into ripeness haste.
Brooding o'er his bosom's woes,
Ráma now desponding goes
Through the forest confines, where
Every object wakes despair.
Fond, he lingers on each spot,
Speaking of a happier lot,
When delightedly he strayed
With his Sítá through the shade.
Happiness for ever flown,
Now he weeps, and weeps alone;
And such sad despairing mood,
Nursed by gloom and solitude,
May to fierce distraction grow,
And the firmest mind o'erthrow.

>   Lest such hapless chance befall
>   Thou his sinking sense recall.
>   Moistened by thy gelid spray,
>   Cooling breezes round him play;
>   Balmy with the lotus bloom,
>   Shed the breeze its soft perfume:
>   So thy friendship shall dispense
>   Freshness on each fading sense.
>
> *Tam.* 'Tis kindly done; but mightier art
>   To-day performs its surer part.
>
> *Mur.* What art?
>
> *Tam.* Attend: 'tis not unknown,
>   When Sítá, helpless and alone,
>   Left by Lakshmaṅa, deplored
>   Her hapless fate and cruel lord;
>   The sudden throes of nature came
>   Distracting o'er her tender frame,
>   And, wild with agony, she gave
>   Her beauties into Gangá's wave.
>
> *Mur.* 'Tis true; and in the moment bore
>   Two lovely boys, whom to the shore,
>   Beneath the wave, the realms of shade,
>   The goddess of the stream conveyed:
>   And there with earth's great goddess, tended
>   With pious pains, till time had ended
>   The first and fond maternal care;
>   When Gangá took the nursling pair
>   To wise Válmíki's hermitage,
>   And gave them to the assenting sage.
>   Now, grown in strength and sense, appears
>   Each youth beyond his childish years,
>   Worthy his high imperial line,
>   The holy sage and nurse divine.
>
> *Tam.* And now, throughout the regions flies
>   The fame, the fierce ascetic dies,

　　　　In *Janasthana's* drear domain
　　　　By *Ramabhadra's* falchion slain;
　　　　And Gangá from *Sarayú* hears
　　　　The news, and *Lopamudra's* fears
　　　　For Ráma; and she hither speeds,
　　　　Pretending some domestic rite
　　　　That Sítá must fulfil, and leads
　　　　The princess to her husband's sight.
Mur. 'Twas wisely thought.　Amidst affairs
　　　　Of empire, Ráma's private cares
　　　　Are scattered—but whilst thus he wends,
　　　　And grief alone his steps attends,
　　　　He feels his loss: but what device
　　　　To Ráma shall his queen entice?
Tam. 'Tis thus contrived: The queen of floods
　　　　Sends Sítá to these ancient woods
　　　　To gather flowers, and with them pay
　　　　Devotion to the god of day,
　　　　From whose bright loins the glorious race
　　　　Of *Raghu* their high lineage trace.
　　　　And homage, therefore, should be done
　　　　This day, to their great sire, the sun,
　　　　For that the lucky knot* has told
　　　　Twelve years their rapid course have rolled
　　　　Since, from the daughter of the earth,
　　　　Kuśa and Lava drew their birth.
　　　　Go forth, exclaimed the queen, my child,
　　　　Nor fear to tread the lonely wild:
　　　　For by my power a veiling cloud
　　　　Thy presence in these groves shall shroud
　　　　From spirits who o'er the wood preside,
　　　　And more from mortal eyes shall hide.

---

* The *Mangala-granthi*, literally rendered in the text. The expression alludes to the practice still in use amongst the Hindus, of making a knot every year of a person's life in the string or thread which is wound round the paper scroll on which the calculations of his nativity are inscribed.

By her command, too, I attend,
Her tender pupil to defend
From aught of harm, and hence am found
To-day upon this holy ground.
Mur. To *Lopahanded* I depart,
The blissful tidings to impart.
But who comes here!
Tam. 'Tis Sítá; mark,
How lovely, through her tresses dark
And floating loose, her face appears,
Though pale and wan, and wet with tears.
She moves along like Tenderness
Invested with a mortal dress;
Or, like embodied Grief, she shines,
That sad o'er love in absence pines.
Mur. Bowed down by sorrow, see, she droops,
Like the soft lotus as it stoops
Its head, when some rude hand has broken
The slender stem. Those sighs betoken
A labouring heart, and withering care
With wasteful hand is busy there;
For every limb more fragile shows,—
So, when the sun of autumn glows,
The tender leaflet languid lies,
Shrinks in the scorching blaze, and dies.
[*Exit* MURALÁ.
Enter SÍTÁ (*as described*) *with flowers.*
Sítá. 'Tis very strange! Methought I heard the voice
Of my dear friend Vásantí once again.
(*Voices in the wood.*) The elephant is Sítá's, whom the queen
With her own tender hands is wont to feed:
And now he perishes—as to the stream
He with his mate repairs, a monstrous elephant,
Wild from the woods, approaches to assail him.
Sítá. Ah, my dear lord!—haste, haste thee to preserve
My favourite, my child, from death—the view

  Of these familiar scenes suggests to me
  Phrases alike familiar once—but now—
  Ah me!—my husband—   [*Faints.*
    Re-enter TAMASÁ.

Tam. Revive, my child.   [*Recovering her.*
Ráma. (*Without.*) Here, guider of the car—here stay our course.
Sítá. What voice was that? oh, it comes o'er my soul,
  Like the low muttering of the thundercloud,
  That promises refreshing dews to earth,
  And calls me back to life!
Tam. What means this rapture?
  Why such delight from inarticulate sounds,
  Like the fond peahen at the muttered thunder?
Sítá. Sounds inarticulate, saidst thou?
  To my enraptured ear it seemed
  My dear lost lord had uttered the blest sounds.
Tam. It may be: for 'tis noised amongst mankind,
  The subjugation of the ascetic *Sudra*
  Conducts the hero to this ancient forest.
Sítá. Thus pays he faithfully the lofty dues
  Exacted by his station.—But he comes—
  Do I again behold him?—Yes, 'tis he!
  His gait declares him; but how pale and thin,
  Like the fast waning moon in morning skies!
  Oh, support me! [*Throws herself into the arms of Tamasá.*
Ráma. (*Rushing in.*)* Goddess adored!
  Celestial daughter of Vidéha's kings! [*Falls fainting.*
Sítá. Ah me, ill-fated! See, his lotus eyes
  Close at the sight of me! His deep distress
  O'ermasters every sense! Oh save him! save him!
          [*To Tamasá.*

---

* In the original, Ráma is supposed to fall behind the scenes, and Sítá goes out to him, when they are again discovered, or, in the language of the text, Enter Ráma fainted. Several speeches also, ruinous of the otherwise good stage effect, are omitted.

Tam. Dismiss your terrors—you can best restore him:
That gentle hand can bring him back to life.
Sítá. Say'st thou—
  (*Kneels, takes one of Ráma's hands in one of hers, and applies the other to his forehead.*)
'Tis so—his spirits are recovering.
Ráma. What should this mean? the heavenly balm that wakes
The dead to life is poured into my heart;
Or from the moon ambrosial dews descend,
Drop on my soul, and rouse me to existence.
Such is the power that well-known touch possesses
To change insensibility to life,
And cheer the chill of dark despair with hope.
Sítá. (*Withdrawing.*) Oh! this is too much for me.
Ráma. Why! was it not
My Sítá that restored me?
Sítá. Ah, my lord now seeks me.
Ráma. I will search.
Sítá. (*To Tamasá.*) I must not meet
His gaze uncalled. My lord will be displeased
That I approach him thus unbid.
Tam. Fear not;
By *Bhagavati's* powerful will enshrined,
You walk, unseen, e'en by the sylvan deities.
Ráma. Sítá! loved Sítá!—No, she is not here.
Where art thou flown—or was it but a dream?
Oft has my fancy anxiously explored
My Jánakí's retreat, and now, illusively,
It finds her in these shades.*
(*Behind.*) Help! help!
Or Sítá's elephant will be destroyed.
Ráma. My Sítá's favourite! Who dares molest
The animal she loved?   [*Rises, and is going.*

---

* A few speeches that follow are here omitted; and several subsequent passages have been also left out, as injurious to the interest of the scene.

Enter VÁSANTÍ.

Vás. The pride of *Raghu* in these honoured groves—
Hail, prince!

Sítá. My friend Vásantí.

Ráma. Do I see
My Sítá's dearest friend!

Vás. The same; but speed
To save the elephant. Cross the *Godávarí*,
Where Sítá's name gives virtue to the ford,
Leaving *Jatáyu's* mountain on the right.

Sítá. Alas, *Jatáyu!*
The forest is a waste deprived of thee!

Ráma. How many recollections do these names
Sadly recall!

Vás. No more delay; quick, follow me!

[*Exeunt* VÁSANTÍ *and* RÁMA.

Sítá. Tell me, dearest Tamasá, cannot, in sooth,
The wood nymphs see me?

Tam. Why should you doubt?
The might of Gangá far exceeds the power
Of every deity.

Sítá. Then let us follow
My lord and my dear friend. [*Exeunt.*

THE BANKS OF THE GODÁVARÍ.

Enter RÁMA *and* VÁSANTÍ, *and afterwards* SÍTÁ *and* TAMASÁ.

Ráma. Glory to *Godávarí!*

Vás. Now, prince, secure
The victory to him, whom as a child
Thy princess fondly cherished.

Ráma. Live and conquer!

Vás. 'Tis even thus—he triumphs o'er his foe.

Ráma. Fate, Sítá, has obeyed thee, and the elephant,
Whose sportive frolic pilfered from thine ears,

With trunk as flexile as the lotus fibres,
Their fragrant pendants, now in earliest youth
Defies the mighty monarch of the woods.
Nor less his tenderness than prowess. Mark
The arts he practises to gain the favour
Of his loved mate, as he imbibes the wave
Perfumed with lotus buds, and with his trunk
Sprinkles the fragrant dews upon her form,
Or rears the broad leaf of the lotus high
Above her head, to screen her from the sun.

Sítá. Well pleased, my Tamasá, I view this child
Of my affections; but, alas! the sight
Recalls the memory of far dearer sons.
How fare my boys?

Tam. In him you may behold them—
Such strength and courage as are his, are theirs.

Sítá. Ah me, unhappy! not alone condemned
To separation from my lord, but doomed
To live divided from my children!

Tam. Fate has so willed it.

Sítá. How have I deserved
A doom so harsh—what sins have I committed,
That the sweet faces of my lovely boys,
Shaded with curling locks and bright with smiles,
Where the red lips the budding teeth display,
Should never know the kisses of a father?

Tam. If fate be gracious, they may know them yet.

Sítá. As they recur to memory, my bosom
Swells with a mother's passion, and their sire
Full in my gaze, I seem once more to live
Blest amongst mortals.

Tam. Truly it is said,
The love that children waken is the bond
That binds their parents strongest to their faith;
And even when the wedded pair are held
By fond affection, still there needs this tie

          To make their happiness complete and lasting.*

Vás. Be seated, prince. Here in this plantain grove
    Behold the marble which in happier days
    Supported thee and Sítá. Here she sat,
    And from her hands gave fodder to the deer
    That boldly crowded round their gentle mistress.

Ráma. I cannot bear to look upon it.   [*Weeps.*

Vás. (*Aside.*) Oh, that my lovely friend could now behold
    The altered state of her once beauteous lord,
    His manly form, whose graces, ever new,
    Were once the grateful objects of her sight,
    Now shrunk and withered, and by ceaseless grief
    Now pale and haggard his once blooming cheeks.

(*Aloud.*) Put forth your brightest fruits and flowers, ye trees
    Ye breezes, breathe the perfume of the lotus;
    And ye soft choristers, pour all your voices
    In sweet continuous song, for Ráma comes;
    Once more he visits his erst-loved domains.

Ráma. Here let us rest awhile.

Vás. Permit me ask,
    How fares the prince, brave Lakshmańa?

Ráma. (*Not hearing her, apart.*)
    'Twas in these scenes
    The gentle *Maithilí* delighted fed
    The innocent animals confiding round her.
    Where'er I turn, sad recollections rise,
    And my hard heart resolves itself in dew.

Vás. The *Mahárája* does not speak of Lakshmańa.

Ráma. (*Apart.*) Her cold respectful manner, and her voice
    With starting tears, broken and indistinct,
    I comprehend; she knows the tale: (*To her.*) The prince
    Is well.   [*Weeps.*

---

* A few speeches of the dialogue are here, and in some following passages, omitted, merely to compress a scene which, being devoid of action, is extended to a disproportionate length in the original, especially as the speeches of Sítá and Tamasí sometimes suspend the conversation of Ráma and Vásantí through an inconvenient interval.

Vás. Then why these tears?
Sítá. Vásantí, this is cruel:
My lord demands respect from all, and most
From those who love me.
Vás. How hadst thou the heart
To drive that gentle being from thee? Once
She was thy love, thy other, dearer life,
Light of thine eyes, and nectar of thy soul—
How can such deed be credited of Ráma?
Ráma. The world compelled it.
Vás. Why?
Ráma. I know no cause.
Vás. Obdurate man, to heed the world's reports
Alone, nor reck the scorn that waits the cruel!
Hast thou forgotten what disastrous fate
Befell the fawn-eyed Sítá, when she dwelt
Before in lonely woods? What then occurred
May make thee tremble for what since has chanced.
Ráma. What horrible suggestions! Yes, I see
My Sítá once again the spoil of fiends.
In vain her slender form and lovely looks
Demand compassion; vainly do those eyes
Roll wild with terror, fearful as the glance
Unsteady of the yearling fawn, and vain
The tender burden that she graceful bears,
To move the savages to pity. Where,
O where, abandoned Sítá, art thou now?
Sítá. Alas! he weeps aloud.
Tam. 'Tis better thus
To give our sorrows way. Sufferers should speak
Their griefs. The bursting heart that overflows
In words obtains relief; the swelling lake
Is not imperilled, when its rising waters
Find ready passage through their wonted channel.*

---

* *Lit.* "By those who are in sorrow their sorrows should be uttered, as the heart in the agitation of grief is upheld by words." The sen-

Mark *Rámabhadra*—little cause has he
To thank mankind; yet, faithful to his duty,
He labours for their good, who oft have been
The source of ill to him, though still affliction
Unceasing for thy loss preys on his life,
As scorching summers parch the fragile flower.
He knows no pleasures, nor partakes the joys
Of social converse,—'tis to him relief
To-day to give a vent to sighs and tears.

Ráma. Alas!
Affliction rends my heart, and yet it breaks not:
Sorrow unnerves my frame, but leaves me conscious;
Though fires internal burn, they not consume me;
And fate, that tortures, yet forbears my life.
Ah, people of *Ayodhyá!* ye refused
Your queen a home amongst ye, and remorseless
Drove her to wander in the lonely wilds.
Be satisfied. The memory of the virtues
I loved so long now overpowers my strength,
And I too, homeless, melt away in tears.

Vás. Nay, nay, my lord, be firm.

Ráma. Be firm, Vásantí!
Alas! the twelve long years the world has been
Deprived of Sítá, have to me been nothing.
I have not lived: there has not been a Ráma.
Yet still I have endured—though sharp the pain
As if a burning brand or venomed sting
Were lodged within my breast—I have endured it.
But now the firmness of my heart is broken,

---

timent is familiar to the dramas of Shakespeare. Thus, in *Richard the Third:—*

"*Eliz.* Why should calamity be full of words?
"*Duch. of York.* Let them have scope, though what they do impart
Help nothing else, yet do they ease the heart."

And in *Macbeth:—*

"Give sorrow words; the grief that does not speak
Whispers the o'erfraught heart, and makes it break."

As round me rise so many sad memorials
To call my Sítá once again to view.
In vain I struggle with my inward passion,
And check the growing sorrows that distract me.
The anguish of my mind will force expression
More vehement, because so long repressed.
The rushing river, for a while impeded,
First saps the barrier, and at length its current
Impetuous sweeps the opposing sands away.

Vás. (*Aside.*) He is much moved; I will divert his thoughts
To other objects. Look around you, prince,
And mark the scenes that Janasthána offers.
Behold the spot, where in yon shady bower
Of twining creepers wove, you often sate,
To watch, impatient, Sítá's homeward course
From the *Goddvari's* pure stream; and she,
Who coming marked remote your fond anxiety,
As fearful of rebuke for long delay,
Bowed sportively her head, and with closed palms,
Touched her fair front to deprecate your anger.

Sítá. Cruel Vásantí! this is unmerciful,
Thus with heart-piercing shafts, incessantly
To wound the bosom of my lord and mine.

Ráma. Relentless Jánakí, where'er I gaze
I view thy charms—in vain, for thou art pitiless.
My heart is bursting—all my vigour flies me.
The world is a wide desert; I am burnt
With inward fires—deep, deep, in thickest gloom
My soul is plunged, and all is night around me.
  [*Faints.*

Sítá. Alas! his senses fail him; as his thoughts
Revert to me, unhappy, his existence,
The hope of all, is thus again endangered.

Tam. Fear not, your hand revives him.
  [*Sítá acts as before.*

Vás. He recovers.

Ráma. Once more, ambrosia,
   Spread o'er each limb by that celestial hand,
   Restores my parting spirit, and converts
   My sorrows to ineffable delight.
   Joy, joy, Vásantí, thou wilt share my joy!
Vás. Whence is this transport?
Ráma. Sítá, she is found!
Vás. Where?
Ráma. Here—before us—dost thou not see her?
Vás. Why mock my sorrows? why thus rend a heart
   Already broken by my Sítá's loss?
Ráma. I mock thee not; I could not be deceived.
   Too well I know the touch of that dear hand,
   The marriage rite first placed in mine; even now,
   Cool as the snow-drift to my fevered palm,
   And soft as jasmine buds I grasp it—here—
      [*By a sudden effort he catches hold of Sítá's hand.*
Sítá. Alas! I yield.   [*Struggling.*
Ráma. Vásantí, it is real!
   This rapture is too much; it quite unmans me;
   'Tis no delusion; touch, and be convinced.
Vás. Alas! he raves.   [*Sítá gets away.*
Ráma. 'Tis gone again! I feared it.
   From my cold touch the cool palm shrinks; my grasp,
   Trembling, ill held the tremulous prisoner,
   And it has slipped away. What! no where! Speak,
   Pitiless *Vaidehí!*
Sítá. I am rightly called,
   To mark this agony and live.
Ráma. Oh, where—
   Where art thou, dearest? Hear my call! appear!
   Be not unmerciful! oh, fly me not!
   'Tis strange; it must be phantasy, or else
   Vásantí would have seen her. Do I dream?
   Does Ráma sleep? or doth the mighty power
   That framed the universe, and oft delights

To spread delusion, fabricate a phantom,
To cheat me of my senses?

Sid. Nay, loved Ráma,
'Tis I who play a phantom, and deceive thee.

Ráma. My friend Vásantí, those who love me still,
Can gather little pleasure from my presence;
Why should I longer cause thy tears to flow?
Forgive me; let me hence.

Sítá. (*To Tamasá.*) Again I lose him.

Tam. Yield not to despair. Seek we the feet
Of *Bhagavatí*, to perfect the rites,
That will for Kuśa and for Lava win
Auspicious days to come.

Sítá. Oh, let me look,
A little moment longer, on a form
I never, never, may behold again!

Ráma. I go to finish, now, my *Aśwamedha*.
I have my bride.

Sítá. What is it that I hear?

Ráma. The image of my Sítá,
Wrought of pure gold, will grace the festival.*

Sítá. Thou art, indeed, the son of *Daśaratha!*
My past affliction all is now effaced;
Thrice happy she whom my loved lord reveres,
Who glads his heart, and is the hope of nations.

Tam. You speak your own eulogium, love.

Sítá. Forgive me. (*Seems ashamed.*)
You must despise this weakness.

Tam. Let us depart.

---

* Thus in the *Alcestis* of *Euripides*, *Admetus*, in order to console himself for the loss of his spouse, declares that—

> "By the hand of skilful artists framed,
> Her image shall be placed upon my couch."

The spirit with which Ráma has the image of Sítá formed is much more worthy of a hero and king. In all his conduct, indeed, he is vastly superior to *Admetus*; and in the delineation of a situation in some respects similar, the Hindu poet is equally superior to the Grecian.

Sítá. I follow you.

Tam. But with averted eye,
　Casting its languid looks, not to the path
　The feet should tread; the painful effort strives,
　In vain, to overcome the strong attraction.

Sítá. I bow me to the feet of my dear lord,
　The source of every blessing.　　　　[*Fainting.*

Tam. Be of courage.

Sítá. Alas! how short an instant to behold
　The bright moon gleaming through contending clouds.

Tam. How manifold the forms affection takes,
　And yet is one unchanged! as water, seen
　In bubbles, eddies, billows, is the same
　Unaltered element.

Ráma. (*In his car, to the Charioteer.*)
　This way direct my rapid car.

All. (*Addressing mutually each other.*)
　May holy mother Earth,
　The empress of the floods, with all the spirits
　Of forests and of streams, the bard inspired,
　The sage *Vasishtha*, and his pious dame,
　Protect your path, and guide you unto happiness!

END OF THE THIRD ACT.

ACT IV.

THE HERMITAGE OF VÁLMÍKI.

Enter SAUDHÁTAKI *and* BHÁNDÁYANA, *two Ascetic disciples.*

Bhád. Behold, Saudhátaki, our humble dwelling!
  Válmíki's holy hermitage assumes
  The face of preparation; he expects
  Unwonted guests to-day; the wild deer feed
  Upon unusual fragments, and the air
  Is filled with savoury odours.*

Sau. There must be
  Some wondrous cause, to make our grey-beards lay
  Their lectures by to-day.

Bhád. There is a cause,
  And that of no mean import.

Sau. Tell me, I pray you,
  What venerable ox may we expect
  To visit us?

Bhád. For shame! refrain from jests:
  The great *Vasishtha* hither brings the queens
  Of *Dasaratha*, with Arundhatí,
  From *Rishyasringa* to our master's dwelling.

Sau. *Vasishtha* is it?

Bhád. The same.

Sau. I crave his pardon. I had thought, at least,
  It was a wolf or tiger we should look for.

Bhád. How so?

---

* The text deals more in particulars. The deer is said to drink the scum of the water in which the ordinary sort of rice, as well as wild rice, has been boiled, and the air is charged with the smell of ghee, boiled rice, and vegetables, mixed with the fruit of the jujube, in the course of culinary preparation.

Suv. Why else was there provided
  The fatted calf for his regale?
Bhâs. Why, know you not,
  The *Vedas*, which enshrine our holy law,
  Direct the householder shall offer those
  Who in the law are skilled, the honied meal,
  And with it flesh of ox, or calf, or goat,
  And the like treatment shall the householder
  Receive from *Brâhmans* learned in the *Vedas*?†

---

* He quotes the text *Samdhio madhuparkâ*, a rather extraordinary liberty in such a place.

† Some texts of Manu would seem to authorise the eating of animal food at all seasons, observing merely the preliminary ceremony of offering a portion of it to the gods or manes, like the heroes of Homer, with whom a sacrifice is only the prelude to a feast. Thus,

"Having bought flesh himself, or obtained it by aid of another, he who eats it, after worshipping the gods or manes, commits no sin."—(*Manu*, v. 32.)

"He who eats animals which may be eaten, is not defiled by the daily practice of the act: for animals which may be eaten and those who eat them were alike created by *Brahmâ*" (v. 30). He admits, also, that animal food has been used by ancient sages, even as nourishment, without regard to sacrificial consecration. "Deer and birds were killed by *Brâhmans* for sacrifice; also for the nutriment of dependants, as was formerly done by *Agastya*" (v. 22). However, *Manu* prohibits the expenditure of life for the gratification of the appetite, and restricts the use of animal food to the *Madhuparka* sacrifice and offerings to the manes and to the gods. "*Manu* has declared that animals may be killed in offerings to the gods in sacrifice and the *Madhuparka*, but not on any other occasion" (v. 41). The *Madhuparka* here implies the respectful reception of a guest, which included the presentation of a mixture of curds and honey (*madhu*, honey, and *parka*, aspersion). This is the ceremony alluded to in the text; and, agreeably to the law of *Manu*, meat was added to the offerings, comformably to the text: "Let him offer to a *Brâhmaṇa*, versed in the *Vedas*, a large ox or goat."—(*Mitak.* p. 48.) Mr Colebrooke observes, that "It seems to have been anciently the custom to slay a cow on this occasion, and the guest was therefore called a *goghna* or cow-killer."—(*As. Res.* vii. 289.) Flesh was also distributed on public occasions, when *Brâhmaṇas* were assembled. Thus, *Yudhishthira*, on taking possession of the splendid hall of audience constructed for him by *Maya Dânava*, fed many thousand *Brâhmaṇas* with all sorts of viands, including the flesh of bears and deer. The great repugnance to animal diet that now exists amongst the Hindus in some provinces must have been of comparatively

Sau. You must mistake.

Bhdd. How so !

Sau. Admit the meal of flesh
 Was for *Vasishtha* dress'd ; why was it not
 Alike provided for the royal sage !
 To Janaka were curds and honey given ;
 No flesh.

Bhdá. 'Tis true ; for though the sages use
 To eat of flesh, yet Janaka foregoes
 The practice. Sorrowing for his daughter's fate,
 He leads an anchoret's abstemious life,
 And in the woods of *Chandradwip* has spent
 Long years of solitude and self-denial.

Sau. What brings him here ?

Bhdá. To see the sage Válmíki ; and Kausalyá
 Is summoned by Arundhatí to meet
 Her ancient friend *Vaideha*.

Sau. Let us leave
 These elders to themselves, and join the youth,
 Who make the utmost of their holiday.

Bhdá. Agreed.

modern origin. We may be satisfied from the above, that the *Brahmadas* seldom wanted excuses for partaking of it, and the other castes were not likely to be more scrupulous. In fact, the *Kshattriyas* were especially authorised to use it, and never hesitated to avail themselves of the permission. Thus Ráma, in his peregrinations, is described by Válmíki as catching, killing, and cooking the dinner of his spouse and himself :—

   Their thirst allayed, the princes ply the chase,
   And a fat stag soon falls beneath their arrows.
   A fire they kindle next, and dress their prize ;
   Then, offering to the gods and manes made,
   With Sítá they the social banquet share.
        —(*Rámáyana*, b. ii. sec. 40.)

The *Mahábhárata*, however, has in some places a leaning to the opposite doctrine, and in the *Dána dharma* section, Bhíshma expatiates to Yudhishthira at considerable length upon the merit of abstaining from animal food, placing charitness of life amongst the first of virtues, a doctrine adopted apparently, or at least more rigidly professed, in order to compete upon an equal footing with the *Bauddhas* and *Jainas*.

See from the dwelling of Válmíki comes
The royal sage, and rests beneath the tree
That shades the cell. A deep and ceaseless sorrow
Preys on his heart, like a destroying fire,
That, lighted in the trunk of some tall tree,
Consumes unseen its sap. Let us withdraw.

[Exeunt.

Enter JANAKA.

My anguish, like a sharp-toothed saw, corrodes
Incessantly my heart. Whene'er I think
Upon my child, my sorrows freshly flow,
Like the continuous current of a river.
How hard it is, that neither age nor grief,
Nor penances austere, release my spirit
From this consuming frame—nor dare I loose
The vital spark myself, for deepest hell,
Where the sun never shines, awaits the wretch
Who lifts his hands against his own existence.
By recollection every hour renewed,
In spite of fleeting years, my griefs survive.
Daughter of sacrifice, alas! my Sítá,
That such should be the sad vicissitude
Thou shouldst have suffered, that it shames thy sire
To weep thy destiny as he could wish.
My child, my child! to memory still recur
Thy infant charms, thy lotus countenance,
Chequer'd with smiles and tears, where starting teeth
Like young buds shone, and thy sweet childish prattle
Tripping in utterance. Earth, mighty goddess,
Whose glory fire, and holy sages witness,
And *Gangá*, and the god of *Raghu's* race,
The sun, why cruel hast thou sought the death
Of thine own daughter? She to whom thou gavest,
As eloquence to wisdom, birth, and ever
Wast worshipped by her as her guardian deity.

Arundhatí approaches; with her comes
The queen of *Dasratha*, my dear friend
Kauśalyá. Who shall put his trust in life?
Once in the royal mansion did she shine
The goddess of prosperity—I shame her
By such comparison—yet, now, she bows
To tyrant destiny, and pines in anguish.
Why should I heed my sufferings, when I mark
The sad reverse she feels? alas! her sight,
That once was bliss, is now as painful to me
As brine to a raw wound.

Enter KAUŚALYÁ, ARUNDHATÍ, *and* ATTENDANT.

Arun. You must comply. The sage commands you come
To meet the king; he is already here.
Why this reluctance, lady?

Atten. Be advised.
Arouse your firmness, madam, and obey
The orders of the sage *Vasishtha*.*

Kau. I obey.
Yet hard the task to face mine ancient friend.
His grief and mine are one, and mine already
O'erpowers my heart—its fibres must give way.

Arun. Such pain is unavoidable; the griefs
Man feels, when absent from a faithful friend,
Renew at his encounter, and again
Extend, and deepen through a thousand channels.

Kau. Alas! how can I meet his gaze, deprived
Of his beloved child?

Arun. Think, you behold
In him a venerable relative,
To whom the great preceptor of his race,†

---

* The attendant has one or two speeches more, which are omitted in the translation.

† *Yájnavalkya*, a sage and legislator, and teacher of one portion of the *Yajur Veda*.

The sacred knowledge of the *Vedas* gave.

Kau. I see in him a royal sage, the friend
Of an illustrious sovereign, and the sire
Of her I called my daughter. Ah! I dream
Of other days and joys, that destiny
Has now, alas, unsparingly destroyed.

Jan. All hail! Arundhatí, to whom the earth
At twilight bends its waving head in homage:
Whom the three worlds revere, and who enjoyest
The love of him, of sages first and best,
Who lives the source exhaustless of pure light.

Arun. May light supreme illume thee—may the sun
That shines eternal hallow thee!*

Jan. My friend,
How fares the noble mother of the king?

Kau. Alas! [*Faints.*

Jan. What's this?

Arun. Your sight too well recalls
Her lord, her children, and the long past days
Of happiness, now gone—the fond remembrance
O'ercomes her strength—the matron's heart is still
As soft and delicate as the tender flower.

Jan. Alas! that I should be the cause of suffering
To one I have not seen so long, the wife
Of my still cherished friend—united with me
In closest bonds—dear as my heart, my peace,
Dear as my person, or my life itself,
The present fruit and object of my being,
Or whatsoever else were dearest to me.

---

* The salutation and reply are both very curious. The first is a little unintelligible, but both are precisely in the spirit of the *Gáyatrí*, or sacred verse of the *Vedas*, and indicate a system very different from the common Hindu polytheism. The text of Janaka's speech is corrupt, but *Arundhati's* reply is, *paramá jyotis te prabhátám, ayam tedám pundits darah puro rájá ya esha tapati :—* May supreme light enlighten thee, may this divine light who glows, purify thee.

And is not this his wife ! and can I give
Her pain, that does not equally afflict
My friend ?—for she was ever one with him
In joy and sorrow. Fate is here alone
To blame : then let me, as I think of him,
Forbear to agonise her sinking heart.

Kau. Where art thou, dearest Jánakí ? Methinks
I still behold thy graceful limbs, as light
As lunar rays, and mark thy lotus face,
Budding with playful smiles, and shedding pride
And fortune on thy marriage celebration,
As the delighted monarch called thee child,
And bade thee sit upon his knee, and termed thee
The pride of *Raghu's* loftiest hope, the bond
Of Janaka's exalted house, and his.

Jan. Imperial *Dasaratha*, every way
Within my heart thy memory is secured.
Fathers in social life but rarely prize
Their daughters, and confine their fond regard
To those who wed them ; but not thus didst thou,
For SÍTÁ ever was to thee a daughter,
And cherished as thy child ; but thou art gone,
And the dear seed of our alliance blighted.
Fie upon life ! the world is now a hell.

Kau. My child, my Jánakí ! in vain I mourn thee ;
Nor will my life, enfeebled by despair,
Yet bound in chains of adamant, release me.

Arun. Take comfort, princess ; give your tears some respite,
Recall the words your pious teacher uttered,
Who prophesied at *Rishyasringa's* dwelling,
The dews of happiness would yet descend,
And cheer the last days of your closing life.

Kau. I have no relish, now, for worldly happiness.

Arun. You cannot doubt the seer's prophetic sight.
Trust me, what he hath said will surely be :
Whate'er is uttered by the holy *Bráhman*,

          Who is the light divine made manifest,
          Must come to pass—the blessing which invoked
          Propitious *Lakshmí* to the nuptial rite,
          Was not unmeaning, nor pronounced in vain.
                                    [*A noise behind.*

Jan. The boys amidst their sports.
Kau. Little suffices to the joys of youth. (*Looks out.*)
          But who is yonder—strong, and light, and active?
          He bears the noble port of *Rámabhadra*:
          Who should this be, that he so charms my sight?
Arun. (*Apart.*) This must be one that *Bhágirathí* named
          To me in secrecy; which should it be,
          Kuśa or Lava?—we will ascertain.
Jan. In sooth, he bears a strong similitude:
          His parted locks, dark as the lotus leaf,
          Denote the warrior tribe, and 'mongst his fellows
          He shows a proud pre-eminence. It seems
          That Ráma once more has become a boy—
          Who is this youth that thus delights our sight?
Arun. Some *Kshattriya* lad, who here awhile pursues
          His sacred studies.
Jan. You have rightly judged
          His birth: for see, on either shoulder hangs
          The martial quiver, and the feathery shafts
          Blend with his curling locks: below his breast,
          Slight tinctured with the sacrificial ashes,
          The deer-skin wraps his body; with the zone
          Of *Murvá* bound, the madder-tinted garb
          Descending vests his limbs; the sacred rosary
          Begirts his wrist, and in one hand he bears
          The *pipal* staff, the other grasps the bow.*
          Arundhatí, whence comes he?

---

* These insignia of the military student are according to *Manu*, with the addition of the ashes of the fuel used in sacrifice, and the bracelet or rosary of the seeds of the elæocarpus, which are not indispensable accompani-

Arun. You forget;
   I came here but to-day.
Jan. (*To the attendant.*) My worthy friend,
   Go to Válmíki, and of him inquire
   Who is this boy: and tell the boy himself,
   Some aged persons wish to talk with him.
Atten. As you command. [*Exit.*
Kau. What think you?—will he come?
Arun. What busy fancies has his sight suggested?
   Dismiss them; they are idle.
Kau. He hears our messenger respectfully;
   Dismisses him, and hither comes the youth.
Jan. The natural graces of expanding youth,
   Though lost to fools, familiar to the wise,
   Shed not the virtue that in him resides.
   As he advances, he attracts my mind,
   Firm though it be, as sways the slender rod
   Of magnet force the ponderous mass of iron.

           Enter LAVA.

Lava. To talk with me; and yet I know them not.
   How am I to address them—ignorant
   What claims their birth, or tribe, or name may give them
   To my respect? yet, to the aged, this
   At least is due. (*Approaches.*) Conceive the brow of Lava
   Is bent to do you reverence.
Arun. and Jan. Long life await you!
Kau. Long be thy days, my child!
Arun. Come hither, child. (*Embraces him; then apart.*)
   This dear embrace, so long delayed,
   Fulfils at length my every wish.
Kau. Come hither, youth. (*Embraces him.*)
   He is, indeed, most like,

---

ments, and indicate a bias to the *Saiva* faith. The *pipal* staff is a staff made of the wood of the *pipal* or holy fig-tree. The *tuna* of *muncu* is a girdle fastened over one hip and hanging loosely over the other, made of the fibres of a kind of creeper, *Sansvieria zeylanica.*

Not only in his stature, nor in hue
As jetty as the sable leaves that float
Upon the stream, nor in his mellow voice,
Deep as the wild duck's cry when gathering pleased
The fibres of the lotus stalk; but most
His firm flesh is like Ráma's to the touch,
Hard as the seed-cup of the water-lily;
Then in his countenance—there well I see—
Dost thou not note it? (*To Janaka.*) Look attentively—
The features of my daughter, beauteous Sítá.

Jan. I mark it well.

Kau. My heart misgives me: hast thou a mother, child,
Or lives thy father in thy recollection?

Lava. Neither.

Kau. Whose art thou?

Lava. Wise Válmíki's.

Kau. Say on.

Lava. I know no more.

(*Behind.*) Warriors take heed, 'tis Chandraketu's order,
That none disturb the holy hermitage.

Arun. The prince is here; he leads the martial escort
That guards the consecrated steed; haply
We may behold him; this is fortunate.

Kau. The son of Lakshmaña commands—those sounds
Descend like drops of nectar in my ears.

Lava. Reverend sir, who is this Chandraketu?

Tam. Hast thou ever heard, brave youth,
Of Ráma and of Lakshmaña?

Lava. The heroes
Of the *Rámáyaña*?

Jan. The same.

Lava. How, should I not know it?

Jan. The son of Lakshmaña is Chandraketu.

Lava. The son of Úrmilá: the grandson thus
Of *Mithilá's* pious king.

Arun. He knows the history.

Jan. Since you are so well skilled in this, dear boy,
   Tell us what other offspring had the sons
   Of *Dasaratha?*
Lava. So much of the tale
   Is not yet taught us.
Jan. Is it not composed?
Lava. It is, but not imparted; save a portion
   For *Bharata*, the master of the drama,
   To be performed, prepared, and, by the Sage
   Himself, transcribed for an especial purpose.
Jan. What purpose?
Lava. To be taught by *Bharata*
   To the *Apsarasas*.*
Jan. All this excites our curiosity.
Lava. Our reverend master
   Is much engaged in this, and has despatched
   His pupils with his work. Along with them,
   Their guide and guard, in arms my brother went.
Kau. Hast thou a brother, child?
Lava. I have; his name is *Kusa.*
Kau. Is he the elder?
Lava. In that his birth had just the start of mine.
Jan. Twin brethren are you then?
Lava. Grave sir, we are.
Jan. Tell us how far the tale of Ráma comes.
Lava. To Lakshmaña's return, when he had left
   The delicate Sítá in the pains of travail,
   Amidst the lonely woods, deserted thus,
   To still the foul aspersions of the people.
Kau. Alas, my lovely child! that such a change,
   The cruel work of destiny, should fall
   Upon thy tender frame—and thou alone!
Jan. Poor helpless queen!
   Disgrace, the forest terrors, and the pains

---
* The nymphs and actresses of *Indra's* paradise.

Of child-birth, all at once assail thy life;
The fiends impure close round their fated prey.
No refuge in thy fears. I cannot cease
To recollect thy sufferings.

Lava. Dame, who are these? *(To Arundhatí.)**

Arun. Janaka and Kausalyá.

Jan. Shame on the thankless race that wronged thy fame,
And Ráma's haste to listen to their calumnies.
The cruel blow that has o'erwhelmed my child
Arouses all my soul, and tempts my wrath
To deal with arms, or direr imprecations,
Destruction on my Sítá's persecutors.

Kau. Preserve us, dame, appease the royal sage.

Arun. Such expiation still must be performed
By all whom public calumny assails.
Remember Ráma is thy son: he claims
Thy love; the helpless people, too, demand
A king's compassion.

Jan. I indulge no hate
To either; Ráma ever is my son;
And for the citizens, I call to mind
Women and children, men infirm with years,
And sacred *Brahmans* form the varied throng.

Enter PUPILS.

Pup. The horse, the horse!—so often in the *Vedas*
Read of—unseen, comes living in our sight.

Lava. The horse, the horse!—the mighty beast of war—
The beast of sacrifice. How looks he? tell me.

Pup. With four firm hoofs he spurns the ground: erect
He bears his arching neck; behind he lashes
His flowing tail, and scatters wide the grain.—
But whilst we chatter here he bounds away,
Come and behold.   [*Lay hold of Lava.*

---

* The stage direction here is expressed with German precision. *Lava*
surveys them with respectful and painful curiosity.

Lava. Elders, they drag me from you. [*Exeunt.*
Arun. Follow your pleasure.
Kau. Let us accompany him;
  I live but in his sight.
Arun. His speed defies
  Our tardy steps; we cannot keep in view
  So fleet a runner.

Enter ATTENDANT.

Mess. I have seen Válmíki,
  And to your questions thus replies the sage:—
  That which is fit for you to know, in time
  Shall be made known.
Jan. His answer is mysterious.
  Come, matron and my friend; seek we, ourselves,
  The venerable sage.
        [*Exeunt.*

ANOTHER PART OF THE GROVE.

Enter LAVA and the PUPILS.

Pup. See, prince, is it not wonderful!
Lava. I see,
  And recognise the *Aśwamedhik* steed.
Pup. How know you him?
Lava. Have you not read
  The section that describes him? See, the guards
  In mail arrayed, with spears and maces armed,
  A hundred each, attend upon his course.
  If you believe me not, go ask of them.
Pup. Ho! Soldier! tell, why is this steed so guarded?
Lava. (*Apart.*) The *Aśwamedha* is the glorious rite
  Of all subduing monarchs; 'tis the mark
  Of high pretension, and inflicts discredit
  On every other of the warrior race.

Guard. The horse! brave youths. Upon the banner look,
   And listen to the herald's cry: the steed
   Is his who triumphed o'er the ten-necked fiend,
   The only hero of the seven-fold world.
Lava. This is unbearable.
Pup. The prince is wise. What is it that he talks of?
Lava. Is earth deserted by the *Kshattriya* tribe,
   That such proud vaunts are hazarded?
Guard. Compared
   With our great prince, who can be called a *Kshattriya*?
Lava. Babblers! If there be such, they are, and know
   No fear. Enough; away with idle words.
   I, even I, will hurl that banner down,
   Though guarded by your arrows. Hear me, friends
   And fellows of my sports, drive off the horse
   With clods of turf, and let him scamper hence
   To gambol with the deer.
                      [*The boys run off.*

Enter a SOLDIER.

How now, imp of mischief, what would you do?
Away; a line of ruthless troops advance
To punish such mad pranks. The prince, with bow
Prepared, but gazing on yon lovely forest,
Awhile perceives you not; then haste away,
And hide yourselves amidst those clustering trees.

The Boys return.

(*To Lava.*) 'Tis done, as you desired.
The soldiers raise their bows, and point their shafts
Against you, and the hermitage is still
Remote. Fly; fly with the speed of deer.
                            [*Run off.*
Lava. Let the shafts fall, and the wide yawning bow
   Expand its monstrous jaws, bristling with teeth

Innumerous and vast, round which the string
Laps like a tongue, impatient to distend
Its mighty stomach with its prey, and roaring
Loud as the clang of thunder-clashing clouds.

[*Exeunt.*

END OF THE FOURTH ACT.

ACT V.

Behind.

Ho, soldiers! haste, or we are put to shame!
See, hither speeds the prince: his charioteer
Urges the fiery steeds: Sumantra whirls
The lash, and on they bound, whilst o'er the head
Of Chandraketu his red banner floats
Loose to the breezes.

Enter CHANDRAKETU *in his Car, driven by* SUMANTRA.

Chan. What marvel's this, Sumantra, what brave hero
Thus from his ceaseless-sounding bowstring rains
A shower of countless shafts upon our host?
Like a bright crest upon the brow of battle
The warrior shines, and as the mantling glow
Of scorn and anger kindles on his cheeks,
He wears a more than human loveliness.
Strange, that a lad, the son of some recluse
Or holy sage, should with such desperate valour
Singly defy a multitude of foes,
As if he was a scion yet unknown
Of *Raghu's* stock. With wonder I behold
His fiery darts that roar along the sky,
Like some wild elephant that cries with anguish,
When on his front the cleaving falchion falls.

Sum. Like thine his person; and his lofty bearing
Defies both gods and demons. As I gaze on him,
I call to memory Ráma, when, in youth,
He aimed his arrows at the host impure
That harassed *Kuśika's* exalted son.

Chan. I feel abashed when I observe his prowess.
Unmoved he stands, though round him madly rages

The storm of battle—through the murky air,
With clouds of dust obscured, the whirling sword
Flashes like lightning—rattle the rushing cars,
With jangling bells harsh pealing; onward roll
Like thunder-clouds the ponderous elephants,
Dark-laden with the tempest of the war.
He shouts defiance, and his clanging bow
Is heard above the rattling drums, more loud
And more reiterated than the din
Which mountain bowers reverberate to the roar
Of the wild elephant. The hero heaps
The earth with trunkless, tossing heads, as offerings
To satisfy the hungry king of death.

Sum. (*Apart.*) I dread to bring these daring youths together.
Should Chandraketu fall—and yet his birth
Demands the danger—if *Ikshwáku's* heir
Be wanting in the hour of peril, where
Shall man expect protection?

Chan. On every side the cowards yield. Oh, shame!
Sum. Prince, we are now within the hero's hail.
Chan. What name has by the heralds been proclaimed?
Sum. Lava.
Chan. Lava! Hero, hear!
Forbear these foes unworthy. Here am I.
On me exhaust thy daring, as on thee
My prowess longs to satisfy its craving.

Sum. He hears you, prince, and for a nobler enemy
Suspends pursuit: e'en so the lion's cub
Foregoes the flying elephant herd, and turns
To brave the falling thunderbolt.

Enter LAVA.

Lava. Hail, valiant prince! your words proclaim you worthy
Your lofty lineage, and of my encounter.
See, I obey your call! ——— (*Voice without.*)

What! do the slaves, once scattered from the field,
Return to seek the fight, and bar my way?
Though louder were their shouts than ocean's roar,
When o'er the wreck of worlds the blasts of fate
Drive his tumultuous waves, their clamours yield
Fresh fuel to my wrath, whose rising fires
More uncontrollable and fiercely glow,
Than the dread flames deep caverned in the earth,
And fed with splintered rocks.

Chan. Regard them not.
Esteem me as thy friend, for I admire
Thy merits; and consider thou as thine
Whate'er to me belongs. Thine are these troops,
And should not move thy anger; be thy prowess
Tried by the test of mine, and mine alone.

Lara. (*Turning back.*) This is indeed an honour, to receive
Such high encomium for this royal youth,
The bravest of the children of the sun.
Why measure him with these? Yet can I bear
These clamorous menaces, that from the crowd
Defy me? no; I thus efface my shame.

[*Rushes out.*

Chan. Behold him, where he speeds: with high disdain
He draws his bow against the crowds in front,
Whilst others press his rear. So central gleams
The bow of *Indra*, 'midst divided clouds,
Tossed in dissevered masses by the gale.
Ho! warriors, hear me: shall we thus be shamed
By such unequal fight?—shall valiant men
Attack a slender youth?—shall plaited mail
Oppose the deer-skin?—and the rattling car,
And horse, and elephant, combine to crush
A single foeman, as on foot he braves ye?

Lara. (*Returning.*) He pities me. Indeed, this waste of time
Shall cease. With heavenly arms I fight,

And they no more impede me.
[*Stands in the attitude of meditation.**]

Chan. What is this?
The shouts are stilled.

Lava. Now for a nobler foe.

Sum. This is no common deed: the youth must wield
Celestial weapons.

Chan. It is true; for see,
In fearful change that equal pains the eye,
Alternate gloom to flashing lightning yields.
How like a painted army stands our host,
As the resistless charm subdues their senses;
And now along the sky dark vapours float
In masses, ponderous as the peaks of *Vindhya*,
And blackness gathered from the depths of hell;
Like molten brass, red sullen flames by fits
Glow through the gloom, and loud the breeze awakes,
As 'twere the wind of final dissolution.

Sum. Whence could he gain such power?

Chan. From whom,
But his great master, wise *Prachetas'* son?

Sum. Not his the gifts: *Krisásva's* progeny
By him on *Viswámitra* were bestowed,
And he to Ráma gave them.

Chan. Yet, perchance,
Others, who equally the light of truth
Within themselves possess, may of themselves
Obtain possession of the self-same powers.

Sum. Enough! Be on your guard; he comes.

Chan. and Lava. (*Together.*) 'Tis strange:
Some hidden cause my heart with rapture fills
At sight of this fair youth. Is it the hope
Of future converse—is it his lofty worth—

---

* This is a specimen of the use of the heavenly arms of which mention was made in the First Act. The weapon here employed is the *Jrimbhaka*, or that which causes drowsiness; its influence is the result of *dhyána* or meditation.

Is it the fond transmission of regard
Felt in a former being—or does some tie
Of kindred undiscovered wake delight?

Sum. From various sympathies affection springs
In living beings. Oft the world's report,
The aspect of the stars, the eye's caprice,
Engenders love ere merit wins regard.
The sudden friend exacts no pledged requital;
For pure attachment is a bond sufficient
To knit two hearts together.

(*Looking at Lava, then aside.*)
Can it be!
Ah no! fate in the germ destroyed
The lovely plant. The parent stem cut down,
What flower shall blossom more?

Chan. I quit the car.

Sum. Why so?

Chan. To pay my homage to this valiant youth,
And do a soldier's duty. To assail
At such advantage one who fights on foot
The god of arms* forbids.

Sum. (*Apart.*) What shall I do?
The prince's will is worthy of his race,
And must not be opposed. Yet—can I bear
To witness such a conflict?

Chan. What will you say,
When men shall ask my father's honoured friend,
If Chandraketu did his duty?

Sum. Right.
War is the *Kshattriya's* duty, and thy race
Has never shrunk from contest: then proceed,
And shew thee worthy thy illustrious sires.†

---

* The *Sastra-devatá*, literally rendered in the text; but the Hindu Pantheon recognises no such personage, except *Kártikeya* is intended. Perhaps merely the authorities or inspired teachers of the military art are intended.

† Several speeches of little interest are here omitted.

Lava. What mingled feelings rise as I approach him!
    Dear to the night-flower as the rising moon,
    His presence offers rapture to my sight;
    But, as I grasp the heavy-clanging bow,
    I feel my ardour for the fight revive,
    And all my soul on fire.
Chan. (*Descending from the car, and bowing to Sumantra.*)
    Accept, my friend,
    The lowly reverence of Chandraketu,
    Born of a race that boasts the Sun their sire.
Sum. May your great sire defend the sons he loves
    In the dread hour of battle; may *Varáha*,*
    All mighty and eternal, grant you fame,
    And victory, and virtue, till you equal
    The founder of your house;† may the great sage,
    Your race's guardian, aid you; may the gods
    Of air, and fire, and heaven, and may *Suparṇa*‡
    And *Vishńu's* self, infuse into thy heart
    Their own celestial daring. Be the clang
    Of Ráma's bowstring and of Lakshmaṇa's
    The charm of potency to win thee victory.
Lava. Prince, you well become
    The glittering car; this courtesy exceeds—
Chan. Do you, then, mount
    An equal chariot.
Lava. (*To Sumantra.*) Honoured sir, persuade
    The prince to keep his seat.
Sum. So you assent
    To Chandraketu's wishes.
Lava. That would I do
    Most cheerfully; but we are foresters,
    The untaught tenants of the wood, and want
    The princely skill to guide the car of battle.

---

* The Incarnation of *Vishńu* as a boar.
† *Kakutstha*, the son of *Bhagíratha* and father of *Raghu*.
‡ *Garuda*, the monarch of the birds.

Sum. It is more strange that you so well are skilled
  In dignity and courtesy. Trust me, youth,
  Could *Rámabhadra* but behold thee thus,
  His heart would melt with tenderness towards thee.
Lava. His fame has reached me, and I honour him;
  And though I have presumptuously disturbed
  The royal sacrifice, yet not the less
  I feel deep reverence for the pious chief.
  His vaunting followers alone provoked me,
  To wipe away the infamy they heaped
  On all the *Kshattriya* tribe.
Chan. Is it so hard
  To own a sire's pre-eminence?
Lava. Not so:
  But knows the prince the duties of a soldier?
Sum. You do not know the mighty *Rámachandra*.
  Then speak not of him; you may boast, 'tis true,
  You mastered feeble hearts like those in fight;
  But when a foe like *Jámadagnya** bends
  Beneath your arm, then you may vaunt your prowess.
Lava. A mighty triumph, truly! Is it not granted
  A *Bráhman's* weapons are his words, and when
  He wields a warrior's arms, his inexperience
  Bears them inert? To conquer such a champion—
  And such was *Jámadagnya*—is, methinks,
  But scanty matter for a hero's praise.
Chan. Enough, enough! what hero, heavenly-born,
  Descends on earth to hold in disesteem
  The son of *Bhrigu*, and who disregards
  The might resistless that restored security
  To all the universe?†

* The son of *Jamadagni, Parasuráma.*

† He destroyed the *Kshattriya* or military race, except, it is said in some accounts, those in the solar line. Other statements aver that he exterminated all except some of the females who were married to *Brahmans*, and thus continued the warrior tribe. As, however, many princes of both the solar and lunar dynasties are long subsequent to *Parasuráma*, we must under-

Lam. (*In an ironical tone.*) I know the deeds
  Of *Raghupati.* Long may he enjoy
  His well-earned honours ; long may listening worlds
  Admire the tale of his heroic exploits.
  Still, glory wait upon the overthrow
  Of a weak woman ; the advance that showed
  No sign of fear when *Khara* felt his valour ;
  And the bold scheme that conquered *Indrajit.**
Chan. Injurious youth, thy pride indeed is vast.
Lava. Away, great prince, I do not heed thy frown.
Sum. They burst with rage, and every limb is shook
  With furious passion ; glows each sanguine eye
  Like the red lotus ; the discoloured cheek,
  And agitated brow are like the moon

---

stand his extermination of the *Kshattriyas* with a certain reservation. This is evidently necessary from the ordinary tenor of the story, which represents him as exterminating them twenty-one times : a succession of destructive feats he could scarcely have achieved, unless he "seven times thrice slew the slain."

* The destruction of *Tárakí,* the disturber of the sacrifices of *Viswámitra,* is related in the first book of the *Rámáyana,* and the death of a woman is forbidden to a soldier. The backwardness of Ráma, or as it is described in the original, the three steps that were not in advance, does not so occur in the ordinary copies of the *Rámáyana,* and the passage may have undergone some modification, as derogatory to the hero. Nothing about Ráma's retiring three paces has been met with in that part of the *Rámáyana* which describes the death of *Khara* in the *Áranya-Kánda* ; but it is admitted that Ráma felt alarm upon the approach of a mace hurled at him by the *Rákshasa* : "Seeing that weapon, like the mace of death, approaching, the prince was alarmed, considering that its flight could not be equalled or opposed by common arrows, the mace of the demon being of celestial origin." The attack upon *Indrajit,* which proved fatal to him, was the result of *Vibhíshana's* advice, who was aware of a prophecy announced by *Brahmá,* that whoever should interrupt by force of arms a certain sacrifice commenced by that chieftain, would prove his destroyer. *Indrajit* was engaged in the rite, when, by the recommendation of *Vibhíshana,* Lakshmana and a party of Ráma's host were sent to attack the *Rákshasa,* who guarded him. The latter were routed. *Indrajit* abandoned the unfinished ceremony to come to their rescue, and was ultimately slain by Lakshmana ; the exploit, therefore, added little to the glory of Ráma, as he took no part in the conflict, and as its result was predestined.

Stained with strange spots, or, like the water-lily,
When o'er its ruffled leaves the black bee spreads
His fluttering wings.

Lava and *Chan.* (*Together.*) Hence to the field of fight.

[*Exeunt.*

END OF THE FIFTH ACT.

ACT VI.

Enter a VIDYÁDHARA *and* VIDYÁDHARÍ (*a Male and Female Spirit of Air*) *in their Car.*

M. Sp. A fearful fight: less fierce the blows
When gods and Titans meet as foes.
See, love, what bright achievements grace
The warriors of the solar race.
Strained to each breast the bow is bent,
The shaft unintermitted sent;
The jangling bells incessant ring,
And frequent twangs the rattling string.
Whilst an alarum, long and loud,
Is sounded by yon thunder-cloud,
Inflated by supernal power,
In honour of such battle hour.
Quick, on each youthful champion's head,
A shower of heavenly blossoms shed,
Culled from the nectar-breathing tree
Of youth and immortality.

F. Sp. But what is this? o'er all the sky
The sudden streaks of lightning fly.

M. Sp. 'Tis *Mahádeva's* eye of flame
That opens on this battle game;
And from between the awful lashes,
Terrific in its glory, flashes
Such sparks, as scattered from the sun
On *Twashtri's** whirling circle spun.

---

* *Twashtri,* the artist of the gods, the same with *Viswakarman,* the father-in-law of *Súrya.* When *Sanjná,* unable to endure the splendours of her lord, fled from his embraces, the sun had recourse to her father, who, in order to temper his fierceness, put the planet on the grindstone and took off the edge of his rays.

Ah, no! I see the fiery blaze*—
'Tis Chandraketu's arm displays;
Around his car, with bannerot,
And spears, and waving chowries set,
The fatal radiance rapid dances,
And on the chieftain's armour glances.
The warrior glows with yellow light,
The car is pale with ashen white—
'Tis all in flame—the god of fire
Puts forth his dread resistless ire,
And crackling, sparkling, roaring, strong,
His lambent furies curl along.
Now with the force of falling thunder
They rive the firmest rocks asunder.
The air is parching, love; beneath
My sheltering robe more coolly breathe,
And let us to a distance haste.

F. Sp. No further need; the peril's past;
The scorching vapour glows no more,
The clouds distil their gelid store,
And pond'rous through the ether float,
As murky as the peafowl's throat,
Save where along their skirts entwine
The lightnings, like a wavy vine.

M. Sp. The shafts of *Varuna* † arrest
In Lava's hand the fiery pest;
Yet still in vain; for now the wind,
From every quarter unconfined,
Comes sweeping forth, as 'twould displace
The world from off its solid base;
And swift along the lowering sky
The clouds before its fury fly:
And nature shakes, as if the gloom

---

* The *Agneya* weapon, one of celestial armoury, or the weapon of fire.
† The deity of water, which element is wielded in the conflict.

Were Time's profound and yawning tomb,
Devouring all; or fatal slumber
Were now preparing to encumber
The movements of the world, and close
Nárdyaś's senses in repose,
That, lost in him, the things of earth
Should cease awhile to issue forth.
'Twas wisely done, with *Váyu's* * force
To stem the torrent's gathering course,
And chase the clouds on Nature's breast,
Whence first they sprang, again to rest.

F. Sp. But who is this, that from his car
Alights to intercept the war,
And with his gentle speech controls
The fury of these daring souls?

M. Sp. 'Tis *Raghupati;* † he has slain
The fierce ascetic, and again
He seeks his realm. His voice they hear,
And cast aside the sword and spear:
Lava is calm; and lowly bends
The prince, as the great chief descends.
May fate conclude, as now begun,
This meeting of the sire and son.   [*Exeunt.*

Enter RÁMA, LAVA, *and* CHANDRAKETU.

Ráma. Come, Chandraketu, to my breast, and cool
With thy embrace the fervour of my heart.

Chan. Receive my humblest homage.

Ráma. Fate, assuredly,
That gives thee power to wield celestial arms,
Auspicious smiles upon thy course.

Chan. My sire,
In this does fortune smile, that I have found

---

* The deity of wind, the element opposed to that of water.
† The lord, or chief, of the house of *Raghu*—Ráma.

            A friend in this brave youth : may *Raghu's* lord
            Behold him with the same complacent eye
            He turns on me.
Rāma. This is indeed a presence
            Of loftiest promise, active and robust,
            As made a soldier's duty to fulfil,
            To guard religion, and protect mankind.
            Nor is there vigour only ; lighter graces
            Are there concentred, and apparent virtues,
            As if each excellence the world admires
            Assumed a visible and human form.
Lava. (*Apart.*) Is this the mighty chief, the friend of virtue,
            The stay and trust of men, the comforter,
            The living shape of worth—embodied excellence?
            His sight subdues me—all my enmity
            At once subsides—a new and strong affection
            Grows in my bosom—all my pride is gone,
            And shame o'ercomes me. First of the first is he—
            As holiest shrines have oft a holier still.
Rāma. 'Tis strange a single glance should soothe my sorrow
            And fill my breast with passionate regard!
            What should the cause be? for, without a cause,
            How should affection ever be engendered?
            When no exterior motives can be traced,
            Some secret spring must influence the heart.
            Such are the sympathies that nature prompts,
            When to the rising sun the flower expands,
            And melts the moon-gem in the lunar ray.*
Lava. Instruct me, prince, who is this glorious chief?
Chan. The elder of our house.

---

* The doctrine of sympathies was once very familiar to the philosophy of Europe. The moonstone, sunstone, and ironstone are three gems, according to the Hindus, the properties of which are analogous to the nature of the objects whence they are named. The latter is the magnet, the other two are fanciful : but probably the idea of them is derived from some natural substance.

Lava. How, *Raghunátha!*
  Blest be the hour that I behold this deity.
  (*Advances and bows down to the feet of Ráma.*)
  Accept the veneration, prince, of Lava,
  The lowly scholar of *Prachétas'* son.
Ráma. Arise, brave youth, forego this prostrate homage,
  And find an equal welcome in my arms.
                                    [*Embraces him.*
Lava. I merit not such graciousness; the less
  That blind presumption led me here in enmity.
  Forgive, my sire, the foolishness of Lava.
Ráma. What faults require forgiveness for my son?
Chan. Those of his native valour; for disdaining
  The proud pretensions of the guards who followed
  The sacrificial steed, he has displayed
  Himself a hero.
Ráma. It was bravely done,
  And like a *Kshattriya.* The true warrior brooks not
  The vain assumptions of superior glory:
  Fierce as the sun may dart his rays, he finds
  The sunstone give them back in fiercer fire.
Chan. His brave disdain approves my friend a *Kshattriya*;
  But more—he wields no common arms; observe,
  Our troops are motionless, struck thus by him.
Ráma. (*To Lava.*) My son, undo the charm; and, Chandraketu,
  Go forth and range them in array again,
  And soothe their disappointed valour.
Chan. I obey.   [*Exit.*
Lava. (*After meditating.*) The weapon is withdrawn.
Ráma. My son, these arms
  Are of celestial origin; their use,
  A mystery. The gods themselves obtained them
  By ages of devotion, and the *Rishis*
  Of primal days and powers supernal, saw them,
  Self-radiant and endowed with wondrous virtue.
  The holy texts that should enforce their service

The great *Krikhlwa* taught * to *Viśwámitra*,
Through countless centuries his pious pupil;
And I from him received the sacred weapons,
Bound to attend for ever on my race.
Then tell me, Lava, by what potent means,
Whence, and from whom, didst thou obtain these arms?

Lava. Of themselves, uncalled, unsought-for, did they come
To me and to my brother.

Ráma. Thy brother?

Chan. We are twin.

Ráma. Where is he?

Kuśa (behind).

What say you, Lava is engaged alone
With Chandraketu's train? Then shall to-day
The pride of empire set in ignominy,
The towering crest of *Kshattriya* shall be humbled.

Ráma. Whom have we here? of deepest jet his hue,
And at his voice each hair upon my body
Starts up erect, like flowers that lift their heads
When hollow murmurs tell the coming storm.

Lava. 'Tis even he, my elder brother, Kuśa,
Returned from *Bharata's* abode.

Ráma. My son,
Invite him hither.

Lava. I obey; behold him!

Enter Kuśa.

This bow, whose string emits such vivid radiance
As gleams from heavenly arms, is fit for combat
With any of the mighty chiefs that trace
Their royal lineage, through the high descent
Of *Manu, Vaivaswata*, from the sun,

---

* Literally, "he declared to *Viśwámitra* the *Upanishad* containing the *Mantra*." It is clear, therefore, that by the use of these weapons, we are to understand the employment of charms, and the command over the elements, with which we are familiar in the magic of all countries.

Although of prowess to protect the gods
And tame the fiercest of the foes of heaven.
Ráma. What lofty daring does this youth display!
What brave defiance sparkles in his eye!
He seems to hold confederated worlds
As grass to trample on; he shakes the earth
With his proud tread; and though of tender years,
He shows of mountain stature. Is he mortal,
Or is it the spirit of valour that assumes
A mortal form?
Lava. Glory to your arms!
Kuśa. Rather to thine;
How now! I hear glad news—what's this?—war! war!
Lava. Restrain this swelling port, and hither come
With due humility.
Kuśa. Why so?
Lava. The godlike lord
Of *Raghu's* lineage deigns to give you welcome.
Kuśa. The godlike hero of our master's verse,
The guardian of the universal world?
Lava. The same.
Kuśa. How may I dare approach such majesty?
His presence awes me." Justly has the bard
That sings his deeds entitled him divine.
Great sire, the scholar of *Prachetas*, Kuśa,
Bows thus in veneration.

   [*To Ráma.*

Ráma. Rise, my child,
And yield me thy embrace. (*Embraces him.*) It is
   most strange:
Alike from either of these youths, the touch
Spreads rapture through my frame; from every pore
The dews, affection-born, distil, as if

* A few short speeches of no importance are omitted.

  External consciousness were manifest;
  And as my heart dissolves with ecstasy,
  My form in waves of nectar seem to float.
Lava. Please you, sire,
  To rest beneath the shelter of this tree.
  The sun is high, and on my father's brow
  Darts fiercely.
Ráma. As you will. (*They sit under a tree.*)
  (*Apart.*) In every look and act, these youths display
  The majesty that would become an empire.
  Upon their forms has nature set the signs,
  Like rays of light within a costly gem,
  Or drops of nectar on a lovely lotus,
  That indicate such glorious destiny,
  As should alone to *Raghu's* sons pertain.
  Dark as the dove's blue neck is their deep hue;—
  Such shoulders has the monarch of the herd;—
  Their dauntless looks are like the angry lion's;—
  And, like the deep-toned music of the drum
  Of holy sacrifice, each mellow voice.
  I see in each my own similitude;
  And not alone my likeness, but in much
  They wear the lovely semblance of my Sítá.
  The lotus countenance of Jánakí
  Is even now before me;—such those teeth
  Of pearly whiteness;—such the pouting lip,
  The taper ear, and such the expressive eye,
  Although 'tis tempered with a manly fierceness.
  Their dwelling in these groves, the very same
  Where Sítá was abandoned, and so like—
  And then the heavenly weapons, self-presented,
  That, as the sages say, would never quit
  Our line without due cause—my queen's condition,
  Borthened with promised joys—these thoughts distract
  My heart, and fill my soul with hope and terror.

How can I learn the truth?—how ask these youths
The history of their birth?

Lava. What should this be? the countenance that sheds
Delight on all is now suffused with tears,
Like the bright lotus stained with drops of dew.

Kuśa. Remember, brother, of his queen bereft
The mighty Ráma cannot choose but sorrow.
Torn from the heart beloved, the world becomes
A dreary waste, and this sad separation
Is doomed to know no term. How could you utter
Such simple doubts, who know the song of Ráma!

Ráma. I am afraid to ask them. Let me hush
These fancies—my emotion has excited
Their notice and their pity—let me be firm.
Have you perused, my sons, Válmíki's verse?
I fain would hear something of his description
Of the bright glories of the solar race.

Kuśa. We have perused the poem. I retain
Some passages; please you, I will repeat them.

Ráma. Let me hear them.

Kuśa. "She formed for love; and Ráma's tender breast
To love, the prince was now supremely blest;
Nor less her lord did Sítá's thoughts inspire,
And mutual passion crowned each heart's desire."

Ráma. I cannot check my tears—so true this strain.
Alas! the uses of the world are now
Stale and unprofitable—a disordered chaos,
Involved in care, and closed by separation.
Where is the happiness on which our hopes
May rest with confidence? where is the worth
That mutually delights? where is that firm
And lasting union of two loving hearts,
Inseparably one in joy and sorrow?
Life ever blooms, but error ever blights it.
Blest be the verse that calls again to mind
The least of all the thousand excellences

That time, the foe of memory, would rob me of.
I see my Sítá now—when budding youth,
Expanded day by day into the bloom
Of woman, and when full-blown beauty joined
With ardent passion to subdue my heart,
And animate my every thought with love.
'Tis past,—how wonderful!

[*Sinks into meditation.*

Lava. How lost in thought he seems! not even a sigh
Steals forth, a sign of life: so silent lies
Some sacred statue in its holy shrine.*

(*Behind.*) The sages of the hermitage—the queen
Of *Daśaratha*, and Arundhatí,
Alarmed to hear the violence the youths
Have offered to the steed, are coming hither;
Yet slow their progress—age retards their flight,
Their limbs are tardy though their minds are fleet.

Ráma. What! are Arundhatí and Janaka,
Vasishṭha, and my honoured mother, here!

[*Rising and looking out.*

Yes, I behold the monarch; like a thunderbolt
His sight affects me: with the holy priests
Who joined our hands; with so much to recall
The hopes that all have perished; thus to meet him,
And not to fall into a thousand fragments!
What task remains for Ráma to perform!

(*Behind.*) Alas! the unexpected sight of Ráma
O'ercomes the aged king; and now the queen,
Hastening to aid her ancient friend, beholds
Her son and senseless falls.

Ráma. Revive, my sire!
My dearest mother! oh, how ill deserved

---

* The Calcutta edition follows a different reading here in some passages.

This tenderness of all that either house
Yet boasts for one so pitiless as I!—
Yet let me haste to them.
Kuśa and *Lava.* This way—this way!

                                        [*Exeunt rapidly.*

END OF THE SIXTH ACT.

ACT VII.

AN AMPHITHEATRE ON THE BANKS OF THE GANGES.*

Enter LAKSHMAŃA.

I have obeyed the sage, and have arranged
A theatre to hold this vast assemblage
Of gods, and men, and spirits of earth, air, ocean,
The serpent deities, and all the forms
That move and breathe—called hither by Válmíki,
On Ganga's sacred banks, that they may hear
His inspirations, with dramatic art,
Recited by the nymphs of *Indra's* heaven.
All is prepared, and the assembly waits—
And lo! the prince, who in his palace bears
The hardships of the anchorite, approaches.

Enter RÁMA.

Now, Lakshmaña, is the assembly gathered
For this performance?
Lak. All is ready.
Ráma. Be the youths,
Lava and Kuśa, stationed with the prince,
Your son.
Lak. Your wishes are foreseen—they sit together.
This is the royal seat.

---

* A play in a play is a device familiar to our theatre; that in Hamlet need scarcely be mentioned. Beaumont and Fletcher go further, and combine four plays in one. They are not so essential to the plot, however, as this and the play in Hamlet, both which representations indicate the opinion entertained by the authors of the moral efficacy of such performances.

Ráma. (*Sitting.*) Let them begin.

Enter MANAGER.

The sage *Prachetas'* son, the oracle
Of truth, thus issues his commands: let all
Assembled here, attend to the high tales
Of wonder and of holiness, related
As by the eye of saintly prescience seen.

Ráma. Enough! we know the *Rishis* are all holy;
Their wisdom is exempted from the stain
Of passion, and with immortality
Impregnate; and their words can never fail
Our reverence and attention.

Sitá. (*Within.*) Alas, alas! where art thou, dearest lord!
Brave Lakshmaña, where thou? The beasts of prey
Press round me to devour me—me— alone,
Unsheltered, undefended, in the forest.
What dreadful pangs!—I can no more sustain
This agony—these fears.—I will devote
My life to *Bhágirathí.*

Lak. This is piteous!

The Manager. The daughter of the earth, the helpless queen,
Her lord abandons to the lonely woods—
Now, as the pains of travail agonise her,
Consigns herself to Ganga's sacred wave.   [*Exit.*

Ráma. (*Starting up.*) Dear love, forbear!
I fly to thy assistance.

Lak. Does my lord
Remember, what he views is but a fiction?

Ráma. Alas! that such a portion should have been
The gift of Ráma to his tender bride,
The dear companion of his forest dwelling!

Lak. Suppress these thoughts—let us attend the story.

Ráma. I am armed! pierceless as adamant.
                              [*Sits down.*

Enter SITÁ, *supported by* PRITHIVÍ (*the Earth*) *and* GANGÁ
(*the Ganges*), *each bearing a new-born Child.*

Ráma. Lakshmańa, I am lost; my senses stray
In sudden and bewildering gloom,—support me.

Gan. Revive, *Vaidehí!* Fate is now thy friend.
Amidst the waves, in safety hast thou given
Two hopes to *Raghu's* line.

Sítá. Can this be true?
Are these my infants? ah, my loved lord!
[*Fainting.*

Gan. Resume thy fortitude; my child, revive.

Sítá. Who art thou?

Pri. 'Tis *Bhágírathí*, the protecting goddess
Of your lord's line.

Sítá. (*Bowing to Gangá.*) Receive my adoration.

Gan. May the reward of virtue ever wait thee!
Behold thy mother, reverend goddess, earth.

Sítá. Am I so blest?

Pri. Let this embrace assure thee.   [*Fainting.*

Lak. The queen is fondly cherished by the deities.

Ráma. Their love for this, their child, o'ercomes their spirits.
This passion of the soul, the common attribute
Of sentient beings, is the knot that binds
The cord that holds the universe, and till
The end of all perpetuates the race.

Gan. (*To Sítá.*) Dear child, earth's progeny, console thy
parent.

Pri. What comfort can I know, being her parent,
Whose days, first blighted by the cruel fiend,
Are now by calumny unjust assailed?

Gan. 'Tis true; but subject to the will of fate,
What living thing may hope to bar its way?

Pri. But yet what plea can' be devised for Ráma,
Who would not trust to me, to Janaka,
To holy fire, nor past, nor future knowledge,

　　　　Nor credited this tender hand, the pledge
　　　　Of faith and love, in youth to him consigned!
Sítá. Ah! does my husband still remember me?
Pri. Thy husband! who is he?
Sítá. Even he whom now my mother spoke of.
Rámá. And spoke of as he merited.
Gan. Queen, reflect. (*To Prithiví.*)
　　　　Thou art the stay of all; and shalt thou share
　　　　The passions of the ignorant? Consider,
　　　　What he has done, the honour of his race
　　　　Imperatively willed; for wide and far
　　　　The stain upon his name was spread:—the test
　　　　In *Lanká* undergone, not elsewhere witnessed,
　　　　Was little credited, and it has been
　　　　The triumph of his high and royal race,
　　　　To claim the homage free and unreserved
　　　　Of all the world; what, then, remained for Ráma,
　　　　In this dilemma, else than to pursue
　　　　The course that he has trod?
Pri. Goddess, I hear
　　　　Your censures with delight; but strong affection
　　　　Controls my thoughts and language. Well I know
　　　　The love of Ráma, and the grief he feels
　　　　For loss of this dear child; yet, still he lives
　　　　For the sole benefit of his subject tribes,
　　　　For which, in other worlds, rewards await him.
Sítá. Oh, let my mother take
　　　　And hide me in her bosom!
Gan. Child, forbear.
　　　　Yet many years thy presence shall dispense
　　　　Delight upon mankind.
Pri. And for the present
　　　　These infants claim thy care.
Sítá. A widow I.
Pri. How should this be, whilst yet thy husband lives?

Sítá. I shall not live! how then have I a lord?
Pri. Think not so lightly of thyself, whose nature,
   Pure as it is, still purer from communion
   With us, shall shed new blessings on the world.
Lak. Heard you the queen?
Ráma. Let all the world receive
   This testimony. (*A noise without.*) Hark! what wonders
      more?
Sítá. The heavens are overcast.
Gan. 'Tis true; observe,
   The heavenly arms are visible, the ministers
   Of Ráma, from *Krishna* first descended,
   To *Visvámitra* next, and last to him.
(*Behind.*) Great queen, all hail!
   Behold the faithful servants of thy children—
   As *Raghupati* erst to thee announced,
   His servants we, the servants of thy sons.
Sítá. Oh, I am blest! the weapon gods appear
   In all their glory.
Gan. Hail! celestial ministers,
   Devoted to the race of *Raghu*—still to work
   The will of his descendants—hail! all hail!
   They disappear. Now, daughter, turn thine eye
   On these infantine pictures of thy lord.
Sítá. Ah! who shall minister the holy rites
   Their birth demands, that great *Vasishtha's* care
   Has ever solemnised for *Raghu's* race?
Gan. This, daughter, need not dwell upon thy thoughts.
   When they no more exact a mother's charge,
   We will convey them to Válmíki's bower.
   Prachetas' son, equal in power and knowledge
   To *Angiras* or to *Vasishtha*, shall
   Become their mighty master, and perform
   The ceremonial rites their years require.
Ráma. This was well thought.

Lak. Does not the prince perceive,
    In this, the birth of Kuśa and of Lava
    Is covertly apprised him? From their infancy
    Have they been masters of the heavenly arms;
    They have received each sacred ordinance
    From great Válmíki, and their vigorous youth
    Numbers the years that now have passed away
    Since the fair queen was sentenced to the woods.
Ráma. My heart beats high. I cannot speak my
    thoughts.
Pri. Come, daughter, with thy presence hallow earth.
Sítá. Most gladly; I am weary of the world.
Pri. Discharge thy dues maternal; when these boys
    No more require thee, thou shalt be contented.
Sítá. Let it be so.
        [*Exeunt Sítá, Gangá, and Prithiví.*
Ráma. Lo, earth receives her in its hollow caves!
    Dear queen, fond partner of my forest dwelling,
    Whose every thought is virtue, does, indeed,
    Another world divide us, and for ever?
                [*Faints.*
Lak. All-wise Válmíki, grant us thy protection—
    For, such the purpose of thy sacred poem.
(*Behind.*) Remove the instruments of harmony—and let
    All present mark the marvels that are wrought
    By great Válmíki's will.
Lak. The waters of the Ganges are upheaved
    With sudden agitation—all the sky
    Is crowded with divinities; behold,
    Where rising from the depth, the queen appears,
    By Gangá and by Prithiví supported:
    Hither she comes rejoicing.
(*Behind.*) Receive from us, Arundhatí, the pure
    And faithful Sítá.
Lak. Prince, behold these wonders:
    Alas! he still is senseless.

Enter ARUNDHATÍ *and* SÍTÁ.

Arun. Why thus bashful?
  Haste thee, my child, and let the consciousness
  Of that dear hand restore thy lord to life.
Sítá. (*Touching Ráma.*) He wakes.
Ráma. (*Reviving.*) My queen, my love!
  My honoured mother, pure Arundhatí,
  With Rishyasringa and the pious Sántá.—
  All here—all happy.
Arun. Prince, awhile attend;
  The goddess of thy race in favour speaks.
Gangá. (*Without.*) Lord of the world, remember thy
      appeal.*
  Thou hast invoked my cares for this thy queen,
  That as a mother I should guard her ever,
  Even as would Arundhatí. Behold,
  I have obeyed thy will; my debt is paid.
Arun. Again attend; thy mother earth addresses
      thee.
Prithiví. (*Without.*) Lord of the world, remember thy
      appeal;
  Thou hast committed Sítá to my charge,
  And called upon me to protect my child.
  I have obeyed thy will; my debt is paid.
Ráma. (*Prostrating himself.*)
  How have I, sinful as I am, deserved
  Such heavenly favour?
Arun. People of *Ayodhyá,*
  Receive your queen, whom the great goddesses,
  Gangá and Prithiví, thus highly honour,
  And now by me, Arundhatí, presented you.
  The gods themselves have testified her purity,
  And fire borne witness to her spotless virtue.

* See the First Act.

  From sacrifice she draws her birth,* and reigns
  Wife of the greatest of the Sun's descendants.
  Recall these things, and yield her veneration.
Lak. They feel the matron's censure : all the crowd
  Is bent in prostrate homage to the queen,
  Whilst from above, the guardians of the spheres,
  And rulers of the planets, shed delighted,
  A shower of heavenly flowers.
Arun. Lord of the world, imperial *Rámabhadra*,
  In place of her similitude, be *Sítá*
  Herself the partner of your sacred rite.
Ráma. Most joyfully.
Lak. (*To Sítá.*) Lady and queen, the shameless Lakshmańa
  Is bold enough to offer you his homage.
Sítá. May length of days reward such worth as thine.
Arun. Now may the sage lead forth the lovely twins,
  Kuśa and Lava, to embrace their parents.
Ráma. This is joy indeed!
Sítá. Where are my children?

   Enter VÁLMÍKI *with* KUŚA *and* LAVA.

Vál. Behold your parents, children ; the prince Lakshmańa,
  And there your grandsire—this your father's mother.
Sítá. My dear father, too !
Kuśa and Lava. Dear father ! dearest mother !
Ráma. (*Embracing them.*) This is a recompense for all our
  sorrows.
Sítá. Come hither, Kuśa—hither, Lava—come
  Embrace your mother, now indeed restored
  To life.
Kuśa and Lava. We are most blest.
Sítá. Lord, I salute thee (*to Válmíki*).
Vál. May thy days be many.
Sítá. My dear father! thus, with all I love encompassed,
  How can I bear so vast a weight of happiness.

  * Sítá was born of the earth at a sacrifice performed by Janaka.

(A noise behind.)

Vál. (Looking out.) The demon *Lavańa* is slain, and here
   The prince of *Mathurá* advances.

Lak. All
   Conspires to make our happiness complete.

Ráma. I scarce can credit what I see—yet thus
   Does fate oppress the prosperous.

Vál. Ráma,
   Is there ought else that may require our aid?

Ráma. Nought, holy sire, but this:
   May that inspired strain, whose lines impart
   This tale, delight and purify the heart;
   As with a mother's love, each grief allay,
   And wash, like Gangá's wave, our sins away.
   And may dramatic skill and taste profound
   Pourtray the story and the verse expound,
   So that due honour ever shall belong
   To the great master of poetic song,
   Alike familiar with a loftier theme,
   The sacred knowledge of the ONE SUPREME.*

                                           [Exeunt.

---

* The poet acquainted with the *Brahma-Sabda*, the inspired and uncreated *Vedas*, as identifiable with *Brahmaa* or the Supreme Being.

REMARKS ON THE UTTARA-RÁMA-CHARITRA.

This drama labours under the disadvantage of a subject drawn from national mythology; and although the more interesting on that account to those to whom it was originally addressed, it must lose much of its merit in the eyes of those to whom the mythos of the Hindus is unattractive or unknown.

Another defect, consequent upon the choice of its subject, is the want of action. The incidents are few, and although not unconnected with each other, nor independent of the *denouement*, they occur abruptly, and are separated by intervals of time and place, which trespass a little too strongly upon dramatic probabilities, and impair the interest of the story.

Apart from these defects, however, the drama has much to recommend it, and has more pretension to genuine pathos than perhaps any other specimen of the Hindu theatre. The mutual sorrows of Ráma and Sítá in their state of separation are pleasingly and tenderly expressed, and the meeting of the father and his sons may be compared advantageously with similar scenes with which the fictions of Europe, both poetical and dramatic, abound.

Besides the felicitous expression of softer feelings, this play has some curious pictures of the *beau idéal* of heroic bearing, and of the duties of a warrior and a prince. A higher elevation can scarcely be selected for either. The true spirit of chivalry pervades the encounter of the two young princes; and the quiet devotedness with which Ráma sacrifices his wife and domestic happiness to the prosperity of his subjects, is a worthy counterpart to the immolation of natural affections to public interest, which is so frequent in the early history of Greece.

The characters of the drama are individualised by the features just noticed as belonging to those of the heroic class, and by the sentiments of piety and the tone of authority which animate the religious personages introduced upon the scene; amongst whom, that females bear so important a part, may be regarded as another characteristic peculiarity. The incidents, as already noticed, are not numerous; but they are dramatic and interesting, and upon the feelings of a Hindu must have exercised a powerful influence. To a belief that vivifies all objects, and gives to mountains and rivers divine forms and sentient natures, the representations of this play must have been awful and sublime. The most inferior of the personages exhibited are the spirits of air, or of the forest, or the flood, who mingle familiarly and affectionately with demigods and deified sages. Earth, the mother of all beings, and Gangá, the river of the three worlds, are introduced in person; and the final reunion of Ráma with his family is witnessed, not only by the people of Ayodyhá and the elders of either race, but by the congregated deities of earth and heaven.

The language of the beings of fictitious existence is either narrative or descriptive, and in the former is simple, and in the latter picturesque. That of the human characters is, as usual with our author, rather passionate than poetical; but some brilliant thoughts occur, the justice and beauty of which are not surpassed in any literature. The comparison of Chandraketu to a lion's cub turning to brave the thunderbolt is one of these; and another is the illustration of the effects of education upon minds possessed or destitute of natural gifts. It is needless to specify other passages. The general tone of the piece is imaginative and elevated, and it is entitled at least to the designation of a dramatic poem.